THE FACES OF HUMAN RIGHTS

As human rights discourse increasingly focuses on analysing states and the institutions that promote and support the human rights machinery that states have created, this volume serves to recall that despite the growing size of the machinery and unwieldy nature of states, human rights began with real people. It samples a broad range of actors and localities where everyday people fought to ensure that the basic principles of human rights became a reality for all. This volume will give a face to the everyday people to whom credit is due for shaping human rights. It also responds to the perennial question of how to begin a career in human rights by highlighting that there is no single path into this dynamic field, a field built on the back of small initiatives by people across a broad spectrum of career paths.

The Faces of Human Rights

Edited by
Kasey McCall-Smith
Jan Wouters
and
Felipe Gómez Isa

·HART·
OXFORD · LONDON · NEW YORK · NEW DELHI · SYDNEY

HART PUBLISHING

Bloomsbury Publishing Plc

Kemp House, Chawley Park, Cumnor Hill, Oxford, OX2 9PH, UK

HART PUBLISHING, the Hart/Stag logo, BLOOMSBURY and the Diana logo are
trademarks of Bloomsbury Publishing Plc

First published in Great Britain 2019

A catalogue record for this book is available from the British Library.

Library of Congress Cataloging-in-Publication data

Names: McCall-Smith, Kasey, editor. | Wouters, Jan, 1964- editor. | Gâomez Isa, Felipe, editor.

Title: The faces of human rights / edited by Kasey McCall-Smith, Jan Wouters and Felipe Gâomez Isa.

Description: Oxford, UK ; Chicago, Illinois : Hart Publishing, 2019. |
Includes bibliographical references and index.

Identifiers: LCCN 2019002427 (print) | LCCN 2019005072 (ebook) |
ISBN 9781509926923 (EPub) | ISBN 9781509926916 (hardback : alk. paper) |
ISBN 9781509926930 (PDF)

Subjects: LCSH: Human rights workers—Biography. | Human rights—History.

Classification: LCC JC571 (ebook) | LCC JC571 .F229 2019 (print) | DDC 323.092/2—dc23

LC record available at https://lccn.loc.gov/2019002427

ISBN: HB: 978-1-50992-691-6
       ePDF: 978-1-50992-693-0
       ePub: 978-1-50992-692-3

Typeset by Compuscript Ltd, Shannon
Printed and bound in Great Britain by CPI Group (UK) Ltd, Croydon CR0 4YY

To find out more about our authors and books visit www.hartpublishing.co.uk.
Here you will find extracts, author information, details of forthcoming events
and the option to sign up for our newsletters.

Preface

I am often asked to speak at 'human rights' events. I have been interviewed by dozens of 8-year-old girls tasked with writing their first 'report on a person you admire'. In countries around the world, when I am introduced, women and men will spontaneously pull a well-thumbed copy of the Universal Declaration of Human Rights from a pocket or a pocketbook. I have been stopped on the street virtually all my adult life by people who say: 'don't I know you?' In each case, it is not ME they are looking for! It's Eleanor Roosevelt.

The global community – those who suffer and those who strive to bring about a just society – begs for the fulfilment of that declaration. That one human community that has acknowledged that our shared humanity bears the highest value of any creature on earth, has insisted that we bear, in our very being, an inherent dignity that should dictate our behaviours towards each other. Across cultures, across politics, across faith systems, across social orders and economic systems, the world still waits for the healing balm of justice and respect.

Yet, what we are talking about at conferences, in classrooms, at roundtables and kitchen tables is the many ways that we are failing our own standard. That standard started with my grandmother and the diverse team designated to write the Universal Declaration of Human Rights. A woman bent on living a quiet life in her home in the Hudson Valley stepped forward to wrangle a pledge to dignity that could live in any community in the world. Her calmness, her kindness, her graciousness, her thoughtfulness and her thoroughness, her firmness and her respect were required. Human rights is not about love and certainly not about affection. It is about radical and disciplined respect and it took all those attributes to shape a document about respect.

But a document is just a piece of paper unless it is used to shape our attitudes, our laws, and our public and private behaviours and it's not just the job of the United Nations or the scores of human rights professionals to get that done – and my grandmother knew it. Her seminal observation on this point is repeated often:

> Where, after all, do human rights begin but in the small places close to home…Unless these rights have meaning there, they have little meaning anywhere…Without concerted citizen action to uphold them close to home … we shall look in vain for progress in the larger world.

She knew that it was not someone else's responsibility to promote human rights. It is mine – it is everyone's.

So what words will tell the story of dignity and respect best? What stories will be indelibly convincing when we each have to choose one action over another? What are the terms that will trigger those convictions and how do we keep these terms vibrant and meaningful? Is the term 'human rights' becoming a cliché? Is the tension between 'freedom' and 'dignity' occurring because we have failed to communicate – to use the right words, to connect the dots and then cement them with language that is clearly understood?

In my grandfather's 1941 speech in which he outlined the four fundamental free-doms necessary for democracy to thrive EVERYWHERE in the world, there was no difference between 'freedom' and 'dignity'. In subsequent speeches throughout that year, FDR continued to explain these four freedoms as rights, emphasising their inter-dependency. He was teaching. He was giving just folks – the lay people, like me – the language to talk about human rights, to ourselves and to our neighbours.

Have we forgotten how to do that: how to talk about human rights in the small places close to home? How often do we use simple, clear words identified with human rights with our children, on the front porch with our neighbours, in our conversation with friends and relatives?

Scholars, diplomats and legislators, like those who gathered in Paris in 1948 to negotiate and write a global declaration, will continue to build the structures, the mechanisms, the law that societies need to function. The people featured in this book tried to talk to people in many different ways, to try to make a difference in the places closest to them and their homes. Some were known internationally and most were simply responding to the injustice around them – all ultimately contributing to the vision of a more just global community. They teach us – and we must listen, because all of us must remember to talk – in real ways – to our children, our children's children, our neighbours, our friends outside of the academic circle about **human rights** – that everyone, everywhere in the world, has the right to a dignified life. That is really the only way to honour them.

Anna Eleanor Roosevelt
Maine, United States
November 2018

Table of Contents

PART III
THE FIGHT AGAINST DISCRIMINATION
IN THE PLACES CLOSE TO HOME

PART IV
NAVIGATING THE POLITICS OF INTERNATIONAL ACTIVISM

List of Contributors

Joana Abrisketa has taught International Law, International Human Rights Law, and International Humanitarian Law since 2000, both at the University of Deusto and on the European Master Programme on International Humanitarian Action. She has been a guest speaker at several universities and institutions, both nationally (Carlos III de Madrid, Pompeu Fabra and Navarra) and internationally (Harvard University, Louvain in Belgium, Warsaw in Poland, and United Nations). Her recent publications include articles in prestigious journals such as *Revista Española de Derecho Internacional, Revista de Derecho Comunitario Europeo, Revista Electrónica de Estudios Internacionales* and the *Human Rights Yearbook*; and chapters of books published by Brill, Martinus Nijoff and Hart. In addition to Europe-wide projects, she was Vice-Dean for International Relations and Research at the Faculty of Law at Deusto for four years. Following this experience, she was designated her present position, that of Director of the Transnational Law Department in the same Faculty.

Wolfgang Benedek is the former Director of Institute of International Law and International Relations and of the European Training and Research Centre for Human Rights and Democracy of University of Graz, where he is a Professor of Law. He is also a Lecturer at the Diplomatic Academy Vienna and at the European Master Programmes on Human Rights and Democracy in Venice and Sarajevo. He publishes in the fields of international, regional and local human rights, is co-author of *Freedom of Expression and the Internet* (Council of Europe, 2014), co-editor of *Russia and the European Court of Human Rights, The Strasbourg Effect* (Cambridge University Press, 2018) and editor of *Manual on Human Rights Education, Understanding Human Rights*, which is available in 17 languages. He is also the executive editor of the *European Yearbook on Human Rights* 2009–2018.

Vivek Bhatt is a PhD candidate at the University of Edinburgh Law School. He holds a Master's in International Law from the University of Sydney and an MSc in Political Theory from the London School of Economics and Political Science. Vivek researches and teaches in international human rights law, humanitarian law, use of force, security studies and international political theory. His current research considers UN principal organs' construction of the role of human rights in counter-terrorism.

Narnia Bohler-Muller holds the degrees of BJuris LLB LLM LLD. She is the Executive Director of the Democracy Governance and Service Delivery research programme at the Human Sciences Research Council and an adjunct Professor of the Nelson R Mandela School of Law at the University of Fort Hare. Professor Bohler-Muller has represented South Africa in multilateral fora such as BRICS (Brazil, Russia, India, China, South Africa) and is the chairperson of the Indian Ocean Rim Association Academic Group after having led the Blue Economy Core Group of IORA. With over 100 academic publications, her research interests include constitutional law, democracy, governance, social justice, and gender equality. Her latest book, co-edited by M Cosser and G Pienaar, is entitled *Making the Road by Walking: the Evolution of the South African Constitution* (Pretoria University Law Press, 2018). In 2016 she was shortlisted by Parliament for the position of Public Protector of South Africa.

Anna Bruce is a Senior Researcher at the Raoul Wallenberg Institute of Human Rights and Humanitarian Law (RWI). Anna holds two LLMs and a PhD from the Faculty of Law, Lund University. Her main research focus is disability human rights, in particular UNCRPD and its connections to equality, intersectionality and disability theory. She lectures on the LLM in Human Rights at the Faculty of Law, and on the PhD in Human Rights at the Faculty of History. At RWI she designs and executes projects to implement UNCRPD, notably in Europe and Asia. She advises the Swedish government investigation on disability governance in light of UNCRPD and engages continuously with Funktionsrätt Sverige and Lika Unika, the two Swedish Umbrella Disabled Peoples Organisations.

Michelle Burgis-Kasthala is a Lecturer in Public International Law at the University of Edinburgh. Her research relates to the Arab world, where she has lived and worked. Her publications include the book *Boundaries of Discourse in the International Court of Justice: Mapping Arguments in Arab Territorial Disputes* (Brill, 2009) as well articles in the *Chinese Journal of International Law*, the *European Journal of International Law*, the *Leiden Journal of International Law* and the *London Review of International Law.*

Antoine Buyse is full Professor of Human Rights in a Multidisciplinary Perspective and Director of the Netherlands Institute of Human Rights (SIM) at Utrecht University. He is Editor-in-Chief of the *Netherlands Quarterly of Human Rights*. He is part of the Utrecht Centre for Global Challenges (UGLOBE), the Montaigne Centre for Judicial Administration and Conflict Resolution and the University's strategic theme 'Institutions'. Antoine has served on the boards of several Dutch and international NGOs, including the Association of Human Rights Institutes and the Dutch branch advisory board of the Scholars at Risk network. His current teaching and research focus on international and European human rights law, including the issue of shrinking civic space, and he hosts a weblog about the European Convention on Human Rights.

Ignacio de la Rasilla del Moral is the Han Depei Professor of International Law at Wuhan University Institute of International Law in China. He was educated in Spain (LLB (Hons), Universidad Complutense, Madrid), Switzerland (MA and PhD, The Graduate Institute, Geneva), the United States of America (LLM, Harvard) and Northern Italy (Max Weber Fellow, European University Institute, Florence). He has held visiting teaching or research appointments in various universities and research institutes in Germany, France, Italy, the United Kingdom, Luxembourg, Switzerland, China and Spain and taught as Lecturer and, then, as Senior Lecturer in Law at Brunel University London for some years. He is the author of around 60 journal articles and book chapters on international law and its history and the author or editor of five books including *In the Shadow of Vitoria – A History of International Law in Spain 1770–1953* (Brill-Nijhoff, 2017).

Cristina de la Cruz Ayuso holds a PhD in Philosophy and is presently researcher of the Pedro Arrupe Human Rights Institute and Professor in the Department of International Relations and Humanities at the University of Deusto, where she teaches graduate and undergraduate courses in Ancient Philosophy, Critical Thinking, Contemporary Critical Theories and Research Ethics. Her main research field is political philosophy with an emphasis on issues related to critical theories. She has participated in numerous investigations on the role of different social actors, mainly companies, universities and social organisations in context of social vulnerability, in particular in relation to the protection of the human rights. She has been a visiting scholar in numerous European and American universities. She has written and edited 15 books and more than a hundred articles and book chapters on political philosophy and applied ethics. She is currently working on methodology in human rights and she is the coordinator of the research ethics board at the University of Deusto.

Gamze Erdem Türkelli is a post-doctoral researcher at the University of Antwerp Law Faculty's Law and Development Research Group. She received her doctorate in law from the same university, where she focused on children's rights obligations and responsibility for businesses and financial institutions under international law. Gamze obtained her Bachelor's degree in Political Science and International Relations from Bogazici University (Istanbul, Turkey) summa cum laude and holds Master's degrees from the University of Paris 1, Pantheon Sorbonne (France) and from Yale University (US), where she was a Fulbright Fellow. Her research interests include transnational human rights obligations, children's rights and new economic actors in development financing and governance.

Felipe Goméz Isa is Professor of Public International Law and researcher at the Pedro Arrupe Institute of Human Rights of the University of Deusto (Bilbao). He is Vice-Dean for International Relations at the Deusto School of Law. He has published extensively on issues related to international human rights law, transitional justice, women's rights and indigenous peoples' rights. He is National Director of the European Master in Human Rights and Democratization, and Director of the UN Fellowship Programme for Human Rights Education for Indigenous Peoples developed at the Institute of Human Rights of the University of Deusto. He has worked as a consultant on the Colombian peace process.

Davinia Gómez Sánchez is a PhD candidate within the programme 'Human Rights: ethical, social and political challenges' at the Pedro Arrupe Human Rights Institute University of Deusto (Bilbao). Her research project is set within the framework of the DIRS-COFUND EU's Horizon 2020 Marie Skłodowska-Curie grant. Davinia's research focuses on indigenous peoples in Africa and examines the role of western development actors in reinforcing a specific human rights conception. She holds a degree in Law and in Philosophy (University of Deusto) as well as a Master's Degree in Human Rights and Democratization (EMA, EIUC). Previously she has worked as a human rights consultant, as well as for different NGDOs, UNESCO, think tanks and research centres in the human rights and development fields in various Latin American countries, MENA region, Southern Africa and Europe.

Dimitrios Kagiaros is a Lecturer in Law at the University of Exeter, where he teaches a variety of courses in the fields of human rights and constitutional law. His research and recent publications relate to whistleblowers and the austerity case law of the European Court of Human Rights. He is a member of the Edinburgh Centre for Constitutional Law and an active participant in the Association of Human Rights Institutes.

Eva Maria Lassen holds a PhD in history and is senior researcher at the Danish Institute for Human Rights. She is currently EMA Director (for Denmark) in the European and European Master Programme in Human Rights and Democratisation (EMA), and vice-president of the European Inter University Centre for Human Rights and Democratisation (EIUC) in Venice. In recent years, she took part, as WP leader, in 'Fostering Human Rights Policies among European Policies' (FRAME), a large-scale collaborative research project, funded under the EU's Seventh Framework Programme, FP7 (from 2013–17). She served as Executive Secretary of Association of Human Rights Institutes, AHRI, from 2012 to 2017. Her research interests include freedom of religion or belief in Europe; the history of human rights in different cultures; the balance between human rights and religious traditions; the universality of human rights.

Anna Lawson is a Professor at the School of Law in the University of Leeds. She directs the University's multidisciplinary Centre for Disability Studies and co-ordinates the Law School's Disability Law Hub. Her work on disability rights has been recognised through a number of lifetime achievement awards – including by the Equal Rights Trust and the Honourable Society of the Middle Temple.

Anya Luscombe is an Associate Professor of Media at University College Roosevelt, Utrecht University's Liberal Arts and Sciences Colleges in Middelburg. She is also an affiliated researcher with ICON, the Institute of Cultural Enquiry at the UU. Her research interests are focused on Eleanor Roosevelt's use of media, in particular radio. She has published in several journals on this subject and in 2017 edited a special issue of the *European Journal of American Studies* on Eleanor Roosevelt. Dr Luscombe is also the author of *Forty Years of BBC Radio News: From the Swinging Sixties to the Turbulent Noughties* (Peter Lang, 2013). In 2017 she was a Fulbright Scholar in Residence at Bard College in the USA where she taught and carried out research on Eleanor Roosevelt. She is member of the editorial board for the *Radio Journal: International Studies in Broadcast & Audio Media*.

Mikel Mancisidor is a law graduate and holds a doctorate in international relations. He is currently serving as a member of the UN Committee on Economic, Social and Cultural Rights (CESCR). He is Adjunt Professor at the Washington College of Law, American University, and lectures at the University of Deusto (Bilbao) and at the International Institute of Human Rights René Cassin, in Strasbourg. In addition he conducts training programs for diplomats, judges and magistrates, civil servants and students around the world. Professor Mancisidor was previously the Director of the UNESCO Centre for the Basque Country for 10 years (2004–2014) and also worked for several NGOs. His main areas of interest are international human rights law, civil diplomacy, human right to education, cultural rights, and science, technology and human rights. He was appointed as Rapporteur for a new CESCR General Observation on the Right to Science.

Kasey McCall-Smith is a Lecturer in Public International Law and the Programme Director of the LLM in Human Rights at the University of Edinburgh. She researches and publishes predominantly in the areas of treaty law, corporate social responsibility relating to modern slavery, treaty body jurisprudence and the domestic incorporation and implementation of human rights treaties. She works with local civil society organisations, including the Scottish Human Rights Commission and the Scottish Commissioner for Children and Young People. She is currently the Chair of the Association of Human Rights Institutes.

Dolores Morondo Taramundi is currently head of research at the Human Rights Institute of the University of Deusto. She studied law and obtained a PhD from the European University Institute with a thesis on the dilemma of difference in the reasoning of the European Court of Justice. Before joining Deusto in 2011, she taught legal philosophy, legal theory, history and philosophy of human rights and European law at the Law Faculty of the University of Urbino (Italy) and has worked as an independent expert in EC projects on human rights and institutional building. Her main research areas include antidiscrimination law, legal critical theories, especially feminist legal theory, human rights and legal methodology.

Manfred Nowak is Professor of International Human Rights at Vienna University, Co-Director of the Ludwig Boltzmann Institute of Human Rights (BIM) and Secretary General of the European Inter-University Centre for Human Rights and Democratisation (EIUC) in Venice. He was appointed in 2016 to lead the UN Global Study on Children Deprived of Liberty. In the past, he was Director of the Netherlands Institute of Human Rights (SIM) at Utrecht University and held human rights chairs at the University of Lund, the Graduate Centre in Geneva and at Stanford University. He was judge at the Human Rights Chamber for Bosnia and Herzegovina in Sarajevo, member of the UN Working Group on Enforced Disappearances, independent expert entrusted with the 'Special process on Missing Persons in the former Yugoslavia' and UN Special Rapporteur on Torture. He is author of more than 600 articles and books in the field of human rights.

Barbara Oomen holds a chair in the Sociology of Human Rights at Utrecht University, and teaches at University College Roosevelt, UU's Liberal Arts and Sciences College in Middelburg. She is the project leader of 'Cities of Refuge', an investigation into the relevance of human rights to how local authorities in Europe welcome and integrate refugees. In addition, she is part of the ETHOS project working on an empirically based theory of justice for Europe. Professor Oomen is the author of *Rights for Others: the Slow Home-coming of Human Rights in the Netherlands* (2013) and *Global Urban Justice, the Rise of Human Rights Cities* (2016), both with Cambridge University Press. She is a board member of the Roosevelt Foundation, which hands out the Four Freedoms Awards. Previous positions include chairmanship of the Netherlands Platform for Human Rights Education and membership of the Advisory Board of the Netherlands Institute of Human Rights.

Helena Pereira de Melo is a Professor and since 2009 she has been Vice-Director of Faculty of Law of Universidade Nova de Lisboa (FDUNL), where she also teaches Constitutional Law, Health Law and Bioethics and Social Equality Law. She graduated in law from the University of Coimbra, then completed a postgraduate degree in European Union Law and a Master's Degree in Law from the Faculty of Law of the University of Lisbon, and in 2005 she obtained the degree from the FDUNL. She is also president of Abio – an association dedicated to research, teaching and dissemination of biodiversity – and vice-president of the Portuguese Bioethics Association. In addition, she teaches subjects in the European Masters in Human Rights and Democratization, organised by the European Inter-University Centre for Human Rights and Democratization, and has published several books and articles on issues of women's rights.

Teresa Pizarro Beleza is full Professor at School of Law, NOVA University (Lisbon) where she served as Dean 2009–2018. Her main areas of research include criminal law and procedure, human rights, equality law and gender studies. She achieved her 'Habilitation' ('Agregação') in Public Law, NOVA University (Lisbon), 2008; a PhD in Law from the University of Lisbon, 1993; an MPhil in Criminology from Cambridge University, 1982; and a BA/Law, University of Coimbra, 1976. She was an elected member in reference to Portugal to the European Committee for the Prevention of Torture ('CPT', Council of Europe) 1999–2003 and acted as EU expert in Human Rights Dialogues with China and Iran (on torture, death penalty, women's rights) 1999–2002. Since 2001, she has been EMA Director (Lisbon, Portugal) as part of the European Inter-University Centre/ Global Campus in Human Rights, Venice, Lido.

Adam Redzik, is a lawyer and historian, Professor of the Warsaw University, author of hundreds of papers and more than a dozen books on civil, criminal, constitutional and international law, as well as about matters related to the bar and legal ethics, legal journals, history of humanities focusing on legal studies and criminology, and on the history of Lviv. He devoted much of his output to the law school of the University of Jan Kazimierz in Lwów, with its representatives including Juliusz Makarewicz, Ludwik Ehrlich, Rafał Lemkin and Hersch Lauterpacht.

Aimar Rubio Llona is a researcher, writer and feminist queer activist. He was awarded an International PhD in Development Studies in 2014, with a thesis covering the interplay between sexual orientation, homophobia and human rights in Africa: South Africa as a case study (Hegoa: Institute of Studies on Development and International Cooperation). A political scientist by training, he is a specialist in migration and holds a Master's in international studies (University of the Basque Country/Euskal Herriko Unibertsitatea). His academic and personal interests include African studies, human rights, feminist theory, gender studies, intersectionality, HIV/AIDS and the LGBTQI universe of which she is proudly a part. He works with academic publications that deal with these issues as well as through in-class training. His main goal is to identify those that are invisible and to reveal the fight of LGBTQI people in various corners of Africa. It is always worth looking at the South.

Elizabeth Salmón is Professor of International Law at the Faculty of Law of the Pontifical Catholic University of Peru. She holds a PhD in international law from the University of Seville, Spain. She is also Director of the Institute for Democracy and Human Rights of the same university (IDEHPUCP). Professor Salmón is currently a member of the UN Human Rights Council Advisory Committee and a Consulting

Expert of the Colombian Special Jurisdiction for Peace. She has acted as a consultant to the Ministry of Justice and Ministry of Defense of Peru, the Truth and Reconciliation Commission of Peru, the United Nations and the International Committee of the Red Cross. She also participates as a speaker in numerous seminars, conferences and events around the world, and is the author of several publications in public international law, human rights, international criminal law, international humanitarian law and transitional justice.

William A Schabas is Professor of International Law at Middlesex University in London. He is also Professor of International Human Law and Human Rights at Leiden University, distinguished visiting faculty at Sciences Po in Paris and honorary chairman of the Irish Centre for Human Rights. Professor Schabas holds BA and MA degrees in history from the University of Toronto and LLB, LLM and LLD degrees from the University of Montreal, as well as several honorary doctorates. He is the author of more than 20 books in the fields of human rights and international criminal law. Professor Schabas drafted the 2010 and 2015 United Nations quinquennial reports on the death penalty. He was a member of the Sierra Leone Truth and Reconciliation Commission. Professor Schabas is an Officer of the Order of Canada and a member of the Royal Irish Academy in 2007.

Stefaan Smis is Professor of International Law at the Faculty of Law and Criminology of the Vrije Universiteit Brussel. His research focuses on international law, international protection of human rights, states in transition, the prosecution of grave violations of human rights, and regional integration in Africa. At the University of Westminster (London) he has a part-time position as a reader in international law. He is editor-in-chief of the international peer reviewed journal *Human Rights & International Legal Discourse* and member of the editorial board of the *Revue de droit africain*. He is a former member of the ILA Committee on Indigenous Peoples, corresponding editor for Belgium of the International Legal Materials and member of the Law&Dev (law and development) inter-university network.

Rebecca Smyth is a PhD candidate at the University of Edinburgh Law School. Her project is concerned with feminist critiques of international human rights law, and the ways in which the language and mechanisms of international human rights law can be used to advance women's human rights, specifically in relation to abortion access. She holds an LLM in Human Rights Law from the same university, an MPhil in Gender and Women's Studies from Trinity College Dublin, and a first-class honours degree in European Studies, also from Trinity. A Trinity Scholar and the 2009 Thomas MacDonagh Easter Week Scholarship holder, she is committed to intersectional feminist research and activism.

Michael Stohl is a Professor of Communication, Political Science and Global Studies, and Director of the Orfalea Center for Global and International Studies, at the University of California, Santa Barbara. Michael's research focuses on organisational and political communication, with special reference to terrorism, human rights and global relations. He is the author, co-author, editor or co-editor of 19 books and more than a hundred scholarly journal articles and book chapters. He has been the recipient of numerous fellowships and awards, including three Fulbright Scholar Awards to New Zealand, Denmark, and Japan and Korea; the International Communication Association Applied/Public Policy Research Award for career work on State Terrorism and Human Rights in 2011 and the International Communication Association 2008 Outstanding Article Award for C Stohl and M Stohl, 'Networks of Terror: Theoretical Assumptions and Pragmatic Consequences' (2007) 47:2 *Communication Theory* 93.

George Ulrich is a full professor and is currently EIUC Academic Director and Programme Director of the European Master Degree in Human Rights and Democratisation (EMA). He held the position of Rector and Professor of Human Rights at the Riga Graduate School of Law from 2009-2016. Prior to this, he served as EIUC Secretary General from 2003–2009 and as Academic Coordinator/Programme Director of EMA from 2001–2004. From 1999–2001 he was Senior Researcher at the Danish Centre for Human Rights and from 1996–1998 Research Fellow at the Institute of Anthropology, University of Copenhagen, and visiting researcher at Makerere University, Kampala, Uganda.

Elaine Webster is a Senior Lecturer in Law and Director of the Centre for the Study of Human Rights Law at the University of Strathclyde Law School in Glasgow, Scotland. Elaine's research interests are in interpretation of human rights by judicial bodies and by civil society advocacy groups. Elaine has a particular interest in the right not to be subjected to torture, inhuman and degrading treatment and the concept of human dignity. Elaine studied Law and French Language (LLB) at the University of Glasgow, International Politics (MA) at the Université Libre de Bruxelles, Human Rights and Democratisation (MA) at the European Inter-University Centre for Human Rights, Venice, Italy/KU Leuven, and completed a PhD at the University of Edinburgh.

Ingrid Westendorp is Senior Lecturer and researcher in International Law and Women and Law with the International and European Law Department of Maastricht University, the Netherlands. She defended her PhD thesis on the right to housing from a woman's perspective in 2007. Since then, she has widely published on women's right to land, the link between domestic violence and adequate housing, the influence of culture on gender equality, and the right to adequate shelter for asylum seekers. She teaches bachelor's courses in International Law at the Faculty of Law and at the University College Maastricht, and a master's course on Human Rights of Women in the context of the master's programme Globalisation and Law of the Faculty of Law. She coordinates a subsidised capacity building International Law project at the Padjadaran University in Bandung in the framework of development cooperation between the Netherlands and Indonesia.

Roman Wieruszewski is Professor of Constitutional Law and Human Rights Law at the European High School of Law and Administration in Warsaw and retired Professor of the Institute of Law Studies of Polish Academy of Sciences. He is former Director of the Poznan Human Rights Centre and former member of Scientific Committee of the EU Fundamental Rights Agency. From 1996–1998 he was Chief of Mission of the UN High Commissioner for Human Rights Field Operation in the Former Yugoslavia in Sarajevo and is a former member of the UN Human Rights Committee (Vice-chairman from 2002–2004), was a member of the Polish Refugee Board from 1999–2014, and an ad hoc Judge of the European Court of Human Rights.

Jan Wouters is Full Professor of International Law and International Organizations, Jean Monnet Chair ad personam EU and Global Governance, and founding Director of the Institute for International Law and of the Leuven Centre for Global Governance Studies at KU Leuven. He is also President of KU Leuven's Council for International Policy. He studied law and philosophy at Antwerp University, obtained an LLM at Yale University and was Visiting Researcher at Harvard University. As Visiting Professor at Sciences Po (Paris), Luiss University (Rome) and the College of Europe (Bruges) he teaches EU external relations law. As Adjunct Professor at Columbia University he teaches comparative EU-US perspectives on international human rights law. He is a Member of the Royal Academy of Belgium for Sciences and Arts and practises law as Of Counsel at Linklaters, Brussels. He is Editor of the *International Encyclopedia of Intergovernmental Organizations*, Deputy Director of the Revue Belge de Droit International, and an editorial board member on ten other international journals.

1

The Faces of Human Rights – An Introduction

KASEY McCALL-SMITH, JAN WOUTERS AND FELIPE GÓMEZ ISA

I. 70 Years of the Universal Declaration: A Time for Reflection

In 2018, when the seventieth anniversary of the Universal Declaration of Human Rights (UDHR) was celebrated, many events and publications examined its relevance in the contemporary human rights agenda. *The Faces of Human Rights* was conceived both as a celebration of the UDHR and a tribute to those individuals who laid the groundwork for that document and, more generally, developed our current conceptions of human rights through their various distinguished contributions to the field: as academics, civil servants, civil society activists, judges, lawmakers, philosophers, politicians, and so on. The inspiration for the project was born in a meeting of the Association of Human Rights Institutes (AHRI) executive committee in Brussels in February 2018 and the contributors are drawn predominantly from the wealth of human rights academics across the AHRI network.

In the past 70 years, the human rights defined by the UDHR have been entrenched in the understanding of every state on the globe. They were reinforced and made legally tangible through the elaboration, adoption and ratification of the twin covenants, the International Covenant on Civil and Political Rights and the International Covenant on Economic, Social and Cultural Rights. The UDHR further served as the basis for a range of specialised international and regional human rights agreements. Each of these international agreements is underpinned by the core principle set out in Article 1 of the UDHR: 'All human beings are born free and equal in dignity and rights. They are endowed with reason and conscience and should act towards one another in a spirit of brotherhood'. Irrespective of gender, race, ethnicity, nationality or personal preferences, each and every individual on this earth is entitled to that most basic principle without distinction. Through its 30 articles, the UDHR sets out the protections to which all individuals are entitled, including: the right to life, liberty and security of person; freedom from slavery; freedom from torture and arbitrary arrest; the right to a nationality; the right to free movement and asylum from persecution; the right to thought, conscience and religion; the right to work in decent conditions without discrimination; to participate in public life, to name but a few. And while states' commitments to fulfilling these obligations have ebbed and flowed depending on the political and social landscape in and around their borders, the UDHR has been translated into over 500 languages and embedded in the promise of a better future for our children.

But that language and the fundamental value of human dignity are currently under major threat. The very states that rode the coat-tails of human rights toward democracy are increasingly ignoring or outright rejecting the fundamental precept that all human beings are born free and equal. Some leaders of the 'free world' eschew the idea of a collective international community based on the rule of law with the protection of individual citizens at the heart. In the aftermath of conflicts and mass migration, nationalist populist movements are once again in vogue and challenging even the most basic of human rights canons. The lack of moral leadership in formerly staunch human rights promoting states has given more space to oppression by various autocratic and non-democratic regimes. In some ways, this book responds to the threats to peace, the fear-mongering, the 'othering' that seem so trendy in political rhetoric as a means of degrading the basic dignity of humankind. Through these pages, we seek to recall the reasons why human rights are so essential to the post-Second World War peace and how the flame that is human dignity continues to burn and move individuals to act in its pursuit. It is through this reflection that we recall that behind the UDHR, the many additional human rights treaties, the bureaucracy, the struggle and the heartbreak are the people who have fought to maintain the inherent self-worth and freedoms of every human, and continue to do so, one cause, one speech, one article, one conversation, one kind word at a time.

Commencing a project that will freeze a list of individuals key to the development of international human rights at a single moment in time is daunting to say the least. Selecting the 'faces' is an exercise with many challenges, not the least of which includes the methodology for developing the list. Depending on one's education, career and field of travel in human rights, the spectrum of individuals who have impacted their development have done so in many ways and, much like beauty, human rights impact is often in the eye of the beholder. To pursue a complete compendium of human rights influences would be an impossible task, not least due to the fact that new voices are emerging daily and the thread of influence from the voices of the past are continually unearthed. Even among the editors we shared different priority lists. But as the terms of human rights were forged in a spirit of dialogue and consensus, so, too, were the individuals featured in this volume. In our view, the individuals celebrated here reflect a multidimensional perspective to understanding human rights at this point in time. These faces of human rights not only shed light on the birth of foundational human rights principles but speak also to the development of both measured and reactionary responses to inequality and oppression.

In developing our list of 'faces', we considered the chronology of human rights development, and took as our starting point the fifteenth century, when European nations were expanding across the globe. These great conquests reaped havoc across the local peoples and in the midst of this brutality, notions of formalised equality in law and policy came through. The notions were often shaped by religious theory and, in turn, the law of nature, which fuelled proponents of political, social and gender equality featured here through the Enlightenment and beyond. All of these primordial inklings of human dignity ultimately found their stronghold in a universal language developed through the UDHR. Thus those who shaped both the development of the UDHR and further international agreements were essential to the selection. Our criteria for selection also sought to reflect the many major struggles that played out in the lead up to or immediately following the adoption of the UDHR in addition to the two World Wars, such as the civil rights movement in the US, the anti-Apartheid movement in South Africa and the massive movements disenfranchising indigenous peoples across the globe. The selection also sought to present a regional balance as well as a broad range of different areas of advocacy in a volume that is necessarily limited. Thus women's rights, indigenous peoples' rights, LGBTQI rights and disabilities rights activists are featured and, where possible, we have drawn from as varied a pool of locations as research permitted.

Just as human rights do not exist in a vacuum and must be understood as ever-evolving, neither could a volume designed to pay tribute to human rights advocates be complete without a list of contributors that is equally diverse. The authors of these chapters are drawn from across several social science disciplines and are each pursuing their own intrepid hopes for human rights at different stages in careers, from PhD students to seasoned veterans of the UN system. Many of the authors could just have easily been one of the individuals written about in these pages, and will, no doubt, be featured in future projects such as this. Thus, in many ways, the selection of authors was a task on par with the selection of featured individuals.

The book is divided into five parts and, generally, each of the chapters presents a brief biographic history of the individual, their career and contribution to human rights and the author's personal conclusions on the individual's legacy in the field of human rights. In this vein, many of the more established contributors have included personal reflections or accounts of their relationships with the individuals they chose to celebrate. In particular, the final chapter written by *Manfred Nowak* about **Theo van Boven** is a testament to the way in which those who work in human rights are constantly grooming the next generation to carry the torch of human rights. In the development of these pages, what also became apparent was the mutuality of support, chance encounters, and unity of purpose across the pages. In many instances, the challenges faced by human rights defenders today are sobering in light of the struggles by those featured here, and in that way we must acknowledge the shortcomings of democracy and its failure to deliver well-rehearsed promises made on the back of these struggles.

II. Laying the Foundation for Human Rights through the Law of Nature and the Prism of Equality

The earliest portraits presented in this volume speak to the relationship between the law of nature and religion and how the principles derived therefrom shaped the philosophy and actions of the earliest proponents of human rights. *Ignacio de la Rasilla* recounts how **Bartolomé de las Casas** fought tirelessly as a humanitarian political adviser and religious figure to promote the livelihoods of the Amerindians throughout the Spanish conquest of the Americas. Through his defence of innate humanity, based upon natural law, he persisted in opposing evangelisation by gunpoint and sword and served as a precursor to Enlightenment philosophers. Over a century later, **John Locke** espoused individual freedoms and religious secularisation at the 'dawn of the modern world', as recounted by *Cristina de la Cruz-Ayuso*. His responses to specific situations, like his successors in the quest for protection of individual freedoms, shaped the man and the philosophy that led to him serving as a constant focal point in natural law discourse, and is reflected in the first article of the UDHR 'that all human beings are born free and equal'. His social contract theory was underpinned by the idea that individual freedom is an essential element of a civil society. He urged tolerance of religion and human knowledge, a message that echoes today, as explored later in the volume.

Close on the heels of Locke are two historic figures who set the stage for contemporary gender and social equality platforms. *Teresa Pizarro Beleza* and *Helena Pereira de Melo* introduce readers to **Olympe de Gouges**. Committed to her personal convictions and crusade for autonomy to her death, de Gouges' Declaration of the Rights of Women implores readers to recall that the contemporary challenges of hatred, bigotry and sexism of today are the same as those faced by de Gouges and her eighteenth century contemporaries. The contradictory life and writings of **Mary Wollstonecraft** are unpacked by *Dolores Morondo Taramundi.* Embattled by her own personal demons and the turbulent politics of the late eighteenth century Enlightenment, Wollstonecraft used the power of her pen to elucidate the case for universal justice comprised of gender equality and improved social conditions for the peasantry.

Henry Dunant, the father of humanitarian law, is brought to life by *Joana Abrisketa Uriarte*, who sets out how Dunant's personal experience of helping victims of war propelled him into a lifelong campaign for international consensus on rules enabling the aid and enduring dignity of civilians and wounded combatants, in what ultimately developed into the International Committee of the Red Cross and was codified in the 1899 and 1907 Hague Conventions. In the final chapter of part I, *George Ulrich* chronicles the principled, peaceful protest of a man emphatic that all human beings are born free and equal in dignity and rights; **Mahatma Gandhi** leveraged personal pleasure and comfort in the pursuit of social justice through the Satyagraha ideal of non-violent resistance. In the end, his non-Western values underpinned the ethos of the UDHR. As Ulrich observes:

> [i]n this respect his message to posterity can be seen as a baton – or perhaps better, an unpolished gem – handed over to the Commission on Human Rights, which at the very moment of his untimely death in January 1948 was engaged in drafting the UDHR.

III. In the Shadow of War: Developing Universal Human Rights

Part II shifts to the mid-twentieth century and the drafting of the UDHR. It begins with **Hersch Lauterpacht** and his vision of universal dignity and commitment to ensuring recognition of crimes against humanity. *Eva Maria Lassen* paints a portrait of his long-term contribution to human rights and the rule of international law in the face of personal tragedy. In tandem with Lauterpacht's work, **Raphael Lemkin** and his obsession with evidencing the horrors of the German extermination of millions of Jews, Roma and other minority groups is presented by *Adam Redzik*. In his quest, Lemkin pressed for recognition of genocide, a new term of his creation, in the Nuremburg prosecutions and its prohibition, concretised in the Genocide Convention.

The final chapters in part II deliver a rich insight into the people and process of developing the UDHR. An intimate portrait of the most well-known face in the drive to agree the Universal Declaration of Human Rights, **Eleanor Roosevelt**, is revealed by *Anya Luscombe* and *Barbara Oomen*. Her personal dignity, assiduity and respect for all humans ensured the realisation of this first universal human rights undertaking, which capped a life spent subtly pushing forward an agenda for equality across the globe, in the US and in 'the small places close to home'. Next, **René Cassin** is depicted by *Jan Wouters* as a man for all seasons: he saw himself as a foot soldier for human rights and contributed in the most diverse capacities to this cause. From his work on war victims and veterans after the first World War to his tireless efforts at the UN (including his role in the development of the UDHR), the European Court of Human Rights and in France for human rights and human dignity, Cassin remains a source of inspiration for generations to come. A reflection on the immense contribution made by **John Peter Humphrey** as the author of the first draft of the UDHR closes out part II. *William Schabas* presents how the Canadian life-long civil servant is often left out of the credit rounds when the drafting of the UDHR is celebrated. However, historical documents from his time with the UN Secretariat, as well as his own personal account, point to the crucial role he played in working with Roosevelt, Cassin and others to develop the text that serves as the bedrock document for all human rights.

IV. The Fight against Discrimination in the Places Close to Home

In the post-UDHR adoption era, the difficulty in ensuring human dignity and universal equality quickly became apparent. In particular, minority groups across the globe suffered a range of legal and social injustices, which cut to the core of what it means to be a member of the 'human' race. Across the United States, South Africa, Australia, South America and Asia, daily manifestations of discrimination and predatory suppression were the norm. Part III examines a number of the individuals who stood up to engrained, everyday discrimination and celebrates those who continue to do so.

Rosa Parks was not just a woman who was hassled on a bus at the dawn of the Civil Rights Movement in the 1950s southern US. *Kasey McCall-Smith* charts Parks' upbringing and life as a determined, considerate and well-trained activist who found herself cast as a leading face in a movement for equality that would occupy her until her last breath. But the alchemy behind the Civil Rights Movement was ultimately crafted by **Martin Luther King, Jr**, who found himself shoulder-to-shoulder with Rosa Parks following her arrest. *Vivek Bhatt* weaves the story of King and how he was catapulted into history through his natural, cosmopolitan leadership and dedication to a theology and philosophy of brotherly love that demanded – at all costs – peaceful protest against the habitual and often brutal racial discrimination in the US.

From the US part III then circles the globe surveying the many struggles against discrimination. *Narnia Bohler-Muller* recounts the parallel struggles of **Nelson Mandela** against Apartheid in South Africa. Against a long history of colonialism and white oppressions, Mandela never strayed from a message of love for his fellow man, regardless of skin colour. From the horn of Africa to Australia and another hotbed of discrimination, *Michelle Burgis-Kasthala* charts the gentle activism of **Faith Bandler** in the first of four chapters examining indigenous peoples' fight for equality and legal recognition. She describes Bandler's pursuit to construct a political and legal system acknowledging the dignity of the indigenous peoples of Australia and other minorities enslaved there because it was what 'we all should be doing'.

Moving to the southern Americas, the next chapter by *Elisabeth Salmón* details the heart-wrenching efforts of **Angélica Mendoza de Ascarza (Mamá Angélica)** in her campaign to discover the fate of her son, and the family members of many of her fellow Quechuan who suffered the programme of enforced disappearances by the Peruvian government during the tumultuous conflict that overshadowed the last quarter of the twentieth century. Her simple defiance of maintaining a curtain of ignorance for the victims of these atrocities made her a legend among the disenfranchised and oppressed of Peru. Another face of the Americas is the Guatemalan indigenous rights crusader **Rigoberta Menchú Tum**, revealed by *Felipe Gómez Isa*. As an indigenous Mayan, Menchú's family suffered brutal repression under the Guatemalan regime, with her family members kidnapped, tortured and killed. Following her exile to Mexico, she began denouncing the brutal regime on an international stage and was ultimately awarded the Nobel Peace Prize. To this day she continues her campaign for legal equality for her people.

Skipping back across the Pacific to Southeast Asia, *Davinia Gómez-Sánchez* details the work of **Victoria Tauli-Corpuz**, an indigenous Igorot Filippino who played a crucial role in the development of the UN Declaration on the Rights of Indigenous Peoples. So loudly has her voice resonated on the issues of injustice that the current Philippines government has declared her a 'terrorist' in an attempt to deflect the criticism she has tirelessly raised against its departures from the rule of law in countless international forums. We end in Pakistan, with a personal tribute to **Asma Jilani Jahangir** by *Mikel Mancisidor* following her untimely death in early 2018. In the same vein as those who struggled against oppression based on race or ethnicity, Jahangir dedicated her life to the ideals of democracy by taking a stand against the worst forms of injustice in her home country, including outlandish penalties for blasphemy and victims of rape, one case at a time, but also as a very vocal international activist figure as the Special Rapporteur on Extrajudicial, Summary or Arbitrary Executions.

V. Navigating the Politics of International Activism

Essential to developing the international framework of human rights protection on the back of many global struggles are the human rights activists and defenders who sought to shine a light and press for change through engaging in national or global politics and the international human rights system. Part IV opens with the coming of age account of **Sean MacBride**. *Dimitrios Kagiaros* navigates the transition of MacBride from an IRA gunman to peaceful lawyer to politician during the Irish Troubles. This turn in his life led him to represent Ireland in the founding conference of the Council of Europe where the European Convention on Human Rights was drafted, a document on the back of which he defended countless victims as a human rights barrister for the duration of his life, including the first case to reach the Strasbourg Court, *Lawless v Ireland*. From the politics of Ireland, the next chapter moves across the water to England to detail another lawyer's life spent dabbling in politics and taking up local then global human rights struggles. **Peter Benenson**'s urgent 'Appeal for Amnesty' for prisoners of conscience in undemocratic states and the concomitant creation of Amnesty International is the story of a pioneer in activism told by *Stefaan Smis*. By joining with other lawyers, writers and publishers, Benenson developed the model of collective individual action through networking with other activists, such as MacBride, that is the continuing hallmark of Amnesty to this day.

Antoine Buyse elaborates the indefatigable **Max van der Stoel**, a Dutch politician and diplomat during the Cold War. Rather than making bombastic speeches, van der Stoel took great care to quietly set out principled objections to threats to freedom from all sides as he travelled the globe in pursuit of reinforcing human dignity. Whether opposing the Greek military junta, communism in Czechoslovakia, Saddam Hussein's grave breaches of human rights as the UN Special Rapporteur on Human Rights in Iraq or High Commissioner on National Minorities at the OSCE, he maintained a consistent and commanding position that resonates still today: 'These enemies are almost invariably extreme nationalists ... not interested in promoting inter-ethnic harmony – they prefer to stir up inter-ethnic hatred'. Inter-ethnic strife, unfortunately, shaped much of European history. **Tadeusz Mazowiecki** and his unrelenting efforts to bring a humane approach to the politics surrounding the end of the Balkan conflict is recounted in a personal reflection by *Roman Wieruszewski*. As the Special Rapporteur on Human Rights in the Former Yugoslavia, Mazowiecki faced down the annihilation of civilians during the inter-ethnic civil strife following the breakup of Yugoslavia and maintained a commitment throughout his life that human rights 'indicate the direction to achieve a certain universal minimum, and determine the threshold for the realization of a sense of freedom, security and participation'.

The final chapters in Part IV chart the measured way in which academics and politicians lay a solid foundation for the continued construction of human rights architecture. In this way, *Michael Stohl* highlights **Jimmy Carter** and his 'signal achievement' in elevating human rights in American policymaking and international diplomacy. In his own words, Carter's legacy is an everyday reminder that '[b]ecause we are free, we can never be indifferent to the fate of freedom elsewhere'. In the next chapter, *Wolfgang Benedek* expounds the unwavering commitment to human dignity through the modest and principled life work of **Peter Leuprecht**, contributing to the understanding, prevention and protection of human rights not only in his role in the Council of Europe and as the UN Special Rapporteur for Human Rights in Cambodia, but also as a continuing prolific academic and voice for human rights. Much like van der Stoel, Leuprecht's staunch, yet generally low-profile, contestation against governments' human rights abuses in various international positions led to him being declared persona non grata (along with van der Stoel) by the governments deemed to violate those principles outlined by the UDHR and formalised in so many treaties.

As a figurehead in the fight against impunity for grave human rights violations, *Elaine Webster* details **Juan E Méndez**'s characteristic subtle, yet radical approach: a pragmatic perspective whilst nevertheless pushing the boundaries of current understandings. As an Argentinian torture survivor in exile, Méndez has dedicated his life to calling governments to account for breaching this fundamental prohibition as both the UN Special Rapporteur on Torture and as the director of the Anti-Torture Initiative at Washington University. **Mary Robinson** is the focus of the final chapter of Part IV. In this account of a strong academic, activist, politician and leader, *Rebecca Smyth* chronicles the fearless rebel with a cause. From her ambitious university days, as a member of the Irish Senate through to her service as the second UN High Commissioner for Human Rights, Robinson never wavered in her commitment to finding a way forward that ensured equal rights and dignity for all human beings and ensured that her public positions lent their full weight to that ideal.

VI. Human Rights and their Defenders: Moving Forward

The final part of the volume looks at the way in which contemporary activists have turned their personal and professional experiences into a message for the greater good of humanity. Born into an environment marked by ethnic strife, **Radhika Coomaraswamy** was exposed to the dire situation of different groups in Sri Lanka and the UN human rights mission at an early age when her father was appointed to the UN Development Programme. As *Ingrid Westendorp* explains, Coomaraswamy has devoted her career to standing up for the oppressed, regardless of the basis. As the Special Rapporteur on Violence against Women for almost a decade and the Special Representative on Children and Armed Conflict, to name but a few of the positions she has held, she directed the world's focus to rooting out the causes and dealing with the effects through a holistic approach to human rights. The next chapter introduces **Gerard Quinn**, the

Irish powerhouse behind human rights protections for persons with disabilities. *Anna Bruce* and *Anna Lawson* deliver the tale of how historic family heartbreak focused Quinn's mind on protecting all people in the places close to home. Dedicating his life to ensuring that individuals with disabilities are viewed as rights holders, not objects, Quinn's contribution to the development of the Convention on the Rights of Persons with Disabilities served to ensure that accessing rights under the convention was made real through a dedicated coordination mechanism that mandates disabled peoples' civil society organisations.

The two penultimate chapters examine how personal strife and tragedy can propel an individual into action. First, *Aimar Rubio Llona* chronicles the determined life of **David Kato** who brought hope and fought for change in the lives of LGBTQI people in Uganda. Kato's unifying power as 'the grandfather of the kuchus' mobilised the LGBTQI to stand against sexually repressive African regimes, a movement he led until his last breath and which continues to give purpose to those who continue to fight for equal protection regardless of their sexual identity. The youngest individual featured, **Malala Yousafzai**, is a widely recognised figure due to being shot in the head by the Taliban for the simple reason that she wanted an education in her home region, Swat, in Pakistan. *Gamze Erdem Türkelli* recounts that the daughter of an educator was unwilling to accept the Taliban regime's foreclosing of education for girls and the clamp-down on thoughts of any girl seeking to be something other than a child bride. Following her near-death experience, Malala has dedicated her young life to ensuring that the right to education and the right to be heard, detailed in the UN Convention on the Rights of the Child, along with the many other children's rights detailed in the Convention are recognised and protected in all places, but particularly in those regions where women and girl children are brutally repressed. As she has consistently implored: 'We cannot all succeed when half of us are held back'.

In the final chapter, *Manfred Nowak* gives a personal reflection on the life and work of **Theo van Boven**. His life-long pursuit of ensuring the right to individual petition as a way of ending impunity has led to his disagreement with other human rights activists, yet as a fixture of the UN human rights system for over three decades he has delivered countless reasons why the world cannot afford to let the human rights system fail. In that process he also educated, trained and mentored future generations of human rights activists, advocates and defenders, and continues to do so. It is fitting that the final face of human rights featured in this volume is one that has and will continue to endure as a life-long testament that every individual work to respect, protect and fulfil the basic principles necessary to ensuring human dignity for all people.

VII. Final Remarks

The 32 individual portraits contained in this volume were selected through a combination of mutual agreement between the editors and enthusiastic suggestions by many of the contributors. And though the selection process may have had some unavoidable shortcomings, it delivers our best efforts to recognise the brave work carried out in the name of human rights in a selection that is as inclusive as possible for a project of this nature. These chapters also serve as a witness to the many varied ways in which each person can contribute to the recognition of human dignity, from small actions close to home to grand interjections into the international framework. While everyone chooses to interpret the actions and contributions of the individuals we celebrate here, it is our utmost hope that the our underlying concept is conveyed: at the heart of human rights are humans, and we all have a role to play in fulfilling the promise of a future where dignity is at the core of all action.

Part I

Laying the Foundations for Human Rights through the Law of Nature and the Prism of Equality

2

Bartolomé de las Casas
A Radical Humanitarian in the Age of the Great Encounter

IGNACIO DE LA RASILLA

I had no choice but to unsheathe the sword of my pen.[1]

I. A Lifelong Defence of the Amerindian Cause

Few lives may be as propitious to an understanding of the biographical genre as a way of addressing a larger historical theme, than the life of the greatest advocate for justice and freedom for the Amerindian peoples in the sixteenth century. For generations, the life and works of Bartolomé de las Casas have served as lenses through which to examine events and processes unleashed by the 'great encounter' in regard to the treatment a sizable proportion of the native Amerindian population endured at the hands of the Spanish *conquistadores* and settlers. Interwoven with almost every stage, major episode, or controversy of the Spanish Conquest,[2] de las Casas' life and works remain an enduring manifestation of the complex intellectual, economic, spiritual and historical forces that were at play throughout the age of exploration, conquest and colonisation of the *Novus Orbis*. Throughout his fifty-year-long zealous dedication to the struggle for justice for indigenous peoples,[3] de las Casas demonstrated an extraordinary ability to influence the course of the *Derecho indiano* (Laws of the Indies) on

---

[1] B de las Casas, *Obras Completas*, P Castañeda (ed), Tomo IX: *Apología* (Madrid, Alianza Editorial, 1989) 73.

[2] A useful biographical introduction is LA Clayton, *Bartolomé de las Casas and the Conquest of the Americas* (Hoboken, John Wiley & Sons, 2011).

[3] The seminal work in English is L Hanke, *The Spanish Struggle for Justice in the Conquest of America* (Philadelphia, University of Pennsylvania Press, 1949).

their behalf. Furthermore, the reception of his large body of intellectual work went on to permanently shape the historical memory of an event that had turned upside down the medieval spatial order long after his death in 1566.

Born in Seville in 1485, Bartolomé de las Casas was the son of a small local merchant, who accompanied Columbus on his second voyage to the 'Indies' in 1493. In 1502, de las Casas embarked on the first of many transatlantic crossings to the 'New World' to live with his father on the island of Hispaniola where he would obtain natives to work for him under the institution of the *encomienda*. This Castilian legal institution subjected the Indians to a regime of semi-slavery in the tracts of land and mines awarded to the Spanish settlers in exchange for their duty to protect and instruct the indigenous population in both the Spanish language and the Catholic faith. In 1506, de las Casas returned to Spain. Having been ordained as a priest, in Rome, in 1507, he continued his studies in Salamanca until 1509. Following his return to Hispaniola, where he celebrated his first mass in 1510, de las Casas witnessed, and remained deeply impressed by the famous sermon of the Dominican friar, A Montesinos, during the Advent of 1511. This sermon, whereby Montesinos chastised the Spanish settlers for their abusive treatment of the Amerindian population, became the basis for the 'Laws of Burgos' (1512), an early legislative effort to regulate the working conditions of the native population. In 1513, de las Casas took part, in his role as a chaplain, in the Conquest of Cuba. Shocked by the abuse, exploitation and massacres he had witnessed the *Taino* and *Arawak* peoples suffer in both Hispaniola and Cuba, de las Casas decided to renounce his *encomienda* and return to Spain to plead before King Ferdinand for a reform of the early Spanish colonial system.

In 1516, shortly after King Ferdinand's death, the Spanish regent, Cardinal Cisneros, appointed de las Casas as a draftsman to an official commission charged with reviewing the application and effectiveness of the 'Laws of Burgos' (1512). Months later, de las Casas returned to Hispaniola as the newly appointed 'Universal Protector of all of the Indigenous in the Indies', to assist a commission of the order of Hieronymites in the practical implementation of his *Memorial de remedios para las Indias* (Memorial of Remedies for the Indies) in Hispaniola, Puerto Rico, Cuba and Jamaica. However, it was not long before de las Casas became disappointed with the mild application of his guidelines and recommendations and crossed the Atlantic once again, this time to plead with the new Spanish monarch, and soon-to-be Emperor of the Holy Roman Empire, Charles I of Spain, for alternative settlement arrangements. In the years that followed, de las Casas continued advocating for the formation of 'mixed communities of peaceful Castilian farmers and free indigenous peoples', whilst reportedly studying canon law in Valladolid and Salamanca.[4]

Meanwhile, conquest and colonisation continued to progress apace into both the southern and northern parts of the American mainland. The discovery of the Pacific Ocean in 1513, the first explorations of Florida, and, above all, the conquest of the

---

[4] K Pennington, 'Bartolomé de las Casas' in R Domingo and J Martínez-Torrón (eds), *Great Christian Jurists in Spanish History* (Cambridge, Cambridge University Press, 2018) 97–114.

Aztec Empire by H Cortes between 1519 and 1521, opened up hitherto unimaginable new horizons, ultimately confirmed by the completion of the first circumnavigation of the globe by JS el Cano in 1522. The Spanish expansion toward the American hinterland also presented de las Casas with an opportunity to obtain from the Crown the concession of a large settlement of 270 leagues in the Venezuelan coast and to work on the development of his project of 'mixed communities' in 1521. However, the avatars and the ultimate failure of what has been called 'the first American utopia',[5] eventually prompted de las Casas to enter the order of the Preachers in 1523. During the decade that followed his becoming a Dominican friar, de las Casas lived in Hispaniola, where he founded a convent, devoted himself to the study of law and theology, and began to compose his work as an historian of the early stages of the great encounter; all the while continuing to preach on behalf of the indigenous population and enter into copious amounts of correspondence on issues related to the protection and promotion of their wellbeing.

In 1534, following the conquest of the Incan Empire by F Pizarro (1532–34), de las Casas once again threw himself into action, this time to develop what proved to be a far more successful and peaceful evangelisation experiment in the territory of Guatemala. During the late 1530s, as the debate on the entitlement of Spain to exercise dominium over the territories of the new world continued to gather momentum in both intensity and political importance, de las Casas travelled once again to Spain, where, through incessant activity and written works, he continued to influence, as we shall see below, both legislative developments and religious doctrine. In 1543, at the pinnacle of his career and influence in court, he renounced the position offered to him to become the head of the rich bishopric of Cuzco, accepting instead the much poorer and peripheral bishopric of Chiapas. However, here, once again, his plans and polemical measures of implementation of the reformist 'New Laws' of 1542 were met with local uprisings and strong resistance by the colonial settlers and even by fellow clergymen.

After returning to Spain in 1547, de las Casas continued campaigning in court against the powerful lobby of the *encomenderos*, participating actively in debates concerning the early colonial institutional framework, most notably at the famous 'Controversy of Valladolid' (1550–51). From his residence in the quarters of the Dominican order in Valladolid, he also wrote memorials to the Council of the Indies and acted as the appointed *procurador de Indios*, responsible for communicating and acting on behalf of the Amerindians and supporting and drafting their *relaciones de agravios* (official accounts of harms) submitted to the Crown. Throughout this time, he continued to devote himself to his written works, which he began publishing in a systematic manner from 1552 onwards. In 1561, de las Casas moved to his final dwelling, the Dominican Monastery at Atocha in Madrid, where he continued writing and working incessantly for the Amerindian cause up until the very last days of his life in 1566.

[5] Clayton (n 2) 56–98.

II. Fuelling the *Duda Indiana* in Practice and Theory

Deeply intertwined with what came to be known as the *duda indiana* (the Indian Doubt) among Spanish intellectual and political elites, were three interwoven dimensions that help situate the praxis and theory of de las Casas' life and work within the larger historical context of the unprecedented intellectual tensions and practical problems triggered by the Spanish conquest and management of the *Novus Orbis*. First, the humanitarian dimension points to de las Casas' faith-driven efforts to temper the excesses of the early Spanish conquest and colonisation by targeting the institutional framework within which the abuses were committed. To translate his humanitarian impulse into a legal reformist project at a time when theological and legal arguments were deeply entangled in the minds of Spanish intellectual and political elites, de las Casas produced a defence of the innate humanity, and thus, according to natural law, the essential freedom of the natives. This postulate was a cornerstone of his strategy of peaceful evangelisation; one that furthermore, had to be freely embraced by the natives. This approach was in sharp contrast to the *requerimiento*,[6] a nine-point formula that was bureaucratically read as a warning to the natives, authorising the Spaniards, if faced with opposition to their becoming subjects of the Spanish King, to evangelise at gunpoint or by the sword, and force them into submission, and even slavery. Finally, the extent to which the conquest and colonisation was conducted in a manner congenial to evangelisation, which was the ultimate *ratio* or justification of the rights of conquest granted by the Pope to Spain, was essential for the legitimacy, or just cause of the titles of Spanish 'dominium' over the American territories and their populations. Questioning the manner in which the evangelisation was conducted thus opened up the possibility that the whole colonial enterprise might be considered illegitimate and thereby subjected to challenge.

De las Casas' humanitarian activism strategised as a legal-theological argument with geo-political implications, proved to be the bedrock of his semi-'prophetical' crusade made on behalf of the Amerindian cause; one that continued along the coordinate axis of the three-pronged theoretical framework just described, and lasted over five decades. His activism translated into numerous journeys made back and forth across the Atlantic, mainly to plead for the freedoms of the natives and often before the greatest monarchs and the highest ecclesiastical authorities of his time. These efforts became reflected in a series of alternative colonisation models, reform proposals of colonial institutions, and legislative initiatives addressed to ameliorate the plight of indigenous peoples. Although they were far from being whole-heartedly welcomed 'on the ground' by those settlers and colonial authorities living in faraway locations who seemed more inclined to adopt the formulaic approach of *obedezco pero no cumplo* (I obey but do not comply), de las Casas' initiatives had a notable influence on both the guidelines and new legislation of the Spanish Crown and the doctrine of the Church.

---

[6] L Nuzzo, 'Law, Religion and Power: Texts and Discourse of Conquest' in I de la Rasilla and A Shahid (eds), *International Law and Islam – Historical Explorations* (Leiden, Brill, 2018) 145.

Selected examples of de las Casas' activist endeavours include the 14 points of his *Memorial de Remedios* (1516), which contained plans to reform, and ultimately emancipate the Amerindians from the *encomienda* in the Greater Antilles. Emanating from this same early time period, in 1521, was his alternative plan of colonisation, based on having 'mixed communities' of indigenous and peaceful Castilian peasant immigrants at Cumaná on the Venezuelan coast. Despite its dramatic failure in practice, the thinking behind this initiative would go on to influence the institution of *corregimiento* (or new territorial divisions of free people under the Crown) many years later. Likewise, the inspiration for the anti-slavery law issued, and later partially rescinded, by Emperor Charles in 1530 has also been attributed to the impact of de las Casas' memorials in the late 1520s. Pope Paul III's encyclical *Sublimis Deus* (1537), often referred to as the 'Magna Carta of the Indians', insofar as it forbade their enslavement and the seizing of Amerindian property, is also traceable to a Mexican Episcopal conference which produced significant documents on the subjects of the Amerindian Church, the issue of slavery, and, in particular, the method of evangelisation promoted by de las Casas in his *De Unico Vocationis Modo* (c 1534), where he censured forcible Christianisation by military means. In 1537, de las Casas pioneered another noted experiment of peaceful evangelisation in Guatemalan territory, its success being acknowledged by a change of name from *Tierra de Guerra* (war land) to *Vera Paz* (true peace).[7]

The theological, moral and legal debates triggered by the Spanish Conquest have traditionally been considered as heralding the birth of international law,[8] with particular reference to the work of the Dominican Friar, Francisco de Vitoria, entitled *Relectio de indis recenter inventis* (1539) at the University of Salamanca. In defending Amerindian rights, whilst simultaneously justifying the Spanish evangelical mission, Francisco de Vitoria, the originator, along with Domingo de Soto of the School of Salamanca over which he presided, has exercised, like de las Casas, a significant influence on the history of international law, both in Spain and the world at large.[9] This broader debate on the 'just' titles of conquest provided the context for de las Casas' petition for a 'total remedy' in response to which the 'New Laws of the Indies' (1542) were promulgated. This prevented the continuation of the *encomiendas* and replaced the old formula of the *requerimiento* with a milder one that prohibited the enslavement of the native population.

However, the most renowned historical epitome of de las Casas' life-long activist engagement to shape both the Crown and Church's positions on the Amerindian question was his ability to persuade the Emperor Charles to suspend all conquests in the Indies and to instruct the Council of Indies to convene a committee of theologians and jurists to judge on the lawfulness of waging war on the Indians, who had not yet been subjected to any preaching of the gospel in order to facilitate their evangelisation.[10]

---

[7] Clayton (n 2) 103–106.

[8] M Koskenniemi, 'Empire and International Law: The Real Spanish Contribution' (2011) 61 *University of Toronto Law Journal* 1.

[9] I de la Rasilla, *In the Shadow of Vitoria. A History of International Law in Spain, 1770–1953* (Leiden, Brill-Nijhoff, 2017).

[10] L Hanke, *All Mankind is One: A Study of the Disputation Between Bartolomé de las Casas and Juan Ginés de Sepúlveda in 1550 on the Intellectual and Religious Capacity of the American Indians* (DeKalb, Northern Illinois University Press, 1974); A Pagden, *The Fall of Natural Man: The American Indian and the Origins of Comparative Ethnology* (Cambridge, Cambridge University Press, 1982).

Considered the greatest debate of the times, the so-called 'Controversy of Valladolid' addressed the key arguments put forward by two leading members of the Dominican order, over two sessions in 1550 and 1551. Confronting de las Casas' theological and juridical arguments promoting the innate freedom and humanity of the Indians and relying on the tradition of the *ius commune*,[11] was Juan Ginés de Sepúlveda, a leading member of the Spanish counter-reformation and the greatest expert on Aristotelian political philosophy of his times who, as the author of *Democrates alter, sive de justis belli causis apud Indos* (1550), had elaborated on the just causes of the war on the Indians. Favouring the cause of the *encomenderos*, Sepúlveda presented the natives as slaves by nature (in the sense described by Aristotle in his first book of Politics), whose conquest was justified because of their idolatry. Although no winner was pronounced, subsequent legislation arguably reflected the Lascasian positions and influence on the 'Laws of the Indies'. This new legislation included the *Instrucciones de 1556*, which advocated a peaceful and evangelical approach towards the peoples still to be conquered and, more specifically, the *Ordenanzas de descubrimientos, nueva población y pacificación de las Indias* ordered by Philip II to provide a methodical definitive solution to the colonisation of the 'Indies' in 1573.

De las Casas' practical activism was accompanied by extensive written work. His complete list of works, encompassing 14 weighty volumes,[12] include 'polemical tracts, histories, and political and legal works'.[13] Drawing on his own experience of living and working amongst the Indians, and his painstaking recollection of extensive materials, these works, based on the medieval juridical theory of the *ius commune*, reflect 'a broad way of thinking or a worldview that included economic, political, and anthropological understandings as well as theological teachings and his well-honed ability to take a juridical approach'.[14] It is widely understood that de las Casas drew inspiration from St Thomas Aquinas and his school of philosophy as this had been renewed in a humanist vein that brought to bear influences from *la via moderna* to the study of the new and important questions raised by those early days of the age of discovery. Compared to the abstract and methodical approach adopted by other noted scholars of the *seconda scholastica*, such as Francisco de Vitoria, the distinctive features of de las Casas' works are his empathetic account of the events that he witnessed first-hand and his intimate knowledge of the customs of indigenous peoples.

De las Casas' fundamental works include his *Historia de las Indias*, which he began writing as early as 1527, and which from 1552 onward benefited from his work in Seville at the archival library of the son of Columbus. This enabled him to copy the original diary of Columbus's first voyage, together with a monumental collection of historical documents and events covering the first three decades of colonisation. Part of his magnum opus was published as *Apologética historia sumaria* (1566). This ethnographic study, written with the aim of elevating the native Amerindian cultures and civilisations in the eyes of the Europeans, is considered to have inaugurated modern

---

[11] Pennington (n 4) 100.
[12] B de las Casas, *Obras Completas*, P Castañeda (ed), 14 vols (Madrid, Alianza Editorial, 1988–98). In English, see G Sanderlin (ed), *Bartolomé de las Casas: A Selection of His Writings* (New York, Knopf, 1971).
[13] Pennington (n 4) 101.
[14] DT Orique, 'The Life, Labor, and Legacy of Bartolomé de Las Casas' (2014) 26 *Peace Review* 325, 328.

cultural anthropology. However, de las Casas' most polemical work was his *Confesionario* (1547, revised in 1552). Written during his tenure in Chiapas, he strategically brought his commitment to the Indian cause into the delicate terrain of the sacrament of the confession. He did so by advocating 12 'rules' for confessors, instructing priests to deny confession and absolution to all Spanish settlers (even those who were dying) who did not commit to freeing their Indian slaves and to making legal restitution of all their unjustly acquired wealth in the New World.[15] In 1552, de las Casas would include as one of eight treatises known as 'the Sevillian Cycle', which contained the best of his juridical–philosophical–theological work, his most famous, and arguably most controversial pamphlet, *Brevísima relación de la destrucción de las Indias* (*Brief History of the Destruction of the Indies*). Originally written in 1542, the *Brevísima* famously became the basis for the 'Spanish black legend', according to which negative political propaganda about Spain and the Spanish Empire was 'absorbed and converted into broadly held stereotypes' that assumed that Spain was 'uniquely evil'.[16] Other notable works included his legal treatises *De thesauris qui reperiuntur in sepulchris Indorum* (1547), *De thesauris in Peru* (1561) and *De Regia Potestate*, published posthumously in 1571, and considered the definitive version of his natural law theory.[17]

III. The Three Renaissances of Bartolomé de las Casas

It is a defining feature of the nature of the 'classics' that their work had been the object of different interpretations and re-interpretations in the light of different historical circumstances over time. While the underlying preoccupations informing each of the three great themes which may serve to frame the legacy of de las Casas resurfaced at different historical times, each of them remains a testimony to the contemporaneous vitality of de las Casas' life and works. Chronologically speaking, the occasion for the first of these revivals of de las Casas' work and influence, was the 'Spanish black legend', whereas the questions of slavery and development of human rights, respectively, are representative of what one may term the second and third renaissances of Bartolomé de las Casas in the history of ideas.

De las Casas' most famous work, his *Brevísima*, owes its reputation to the fact that, since its early translation into Flemish (1578) and through its subsequent editions in many European languages, it became a central element of the 'black legend'. This was part and parcel of a Hispanophobic propaganda war encompassing the military, political, religious and cultural struggle and competition both in Europe and, in the wake of their extra-European imperial enterprises, between the Catholic and Protestant camps over the next centuries. Fuelled by its crude accounts of the atrocities imposed on the Amerindians, and of the cupidity and greed of the Spaniards, the contribution of de las Casas' work to the 'Spanish black legend' has been subjected to critical scrutiny in

---

[15] Clayton (n 2) 145.

[16] WB Maltby, 'The Black Legend' in *Encyclopedia of Latin American History and Culture* vol 1 (New York, Charles Scribner's Sons, 1996) 346–48.

[17] AE Pérez Luño, 'Estudio preliminar' in de las Casas, *Obras Completas* (n 12) vol XII, 5.

modern times on account of the stylish distortion and exaggeration of his descriptions of the virtuous nature of the Indians alongside the evils of the Spaniards and their actual effects on the Amerindian depopulation. Whether the Spaniards, inheritors of a martial Catholic culture that brooded over the centuries-long 'reconquest' of the Peninsula against Islam, were uniquely cruel in their conquest and subjection of the Amerindians, or whether they were merely acting within the practices and mind-set of their times in Europe,[18] remains an open question among historians. Less doubtful, however, is that Spain was the 'only colonial power in which questions of just titles, ownership of human beings, and just sovereignty arose',[19] and that de las Casas' life and works are also, therefore, a testimony to the uniquely sophisticated political and intellectual milieu of the 'Spanish Golden Age'. The latter provided the historical background that enabled the son of a small local merchant to succeed in influencing and shaping Spanish legislation for half a century and to become an advocate of radical measures and reforms (including the across-the-board restitution of Indian sovereignty that de las Casas advocated in the last stages of his life) in the face of powerful economic interests before the mightiest monarchs of the world.

A second controversy surrounding de las Casas' lifelong crusade on behalf of the freedom and humanity of the Amerindians is linked to his 30 year-long parallel advocacy of a policy of substitution of imported black African slaves to alleviate the indigenous suffering in the Americas. His advocacy of the introduction of African slaves from Spain and Africa, where the African-to-African domestic slave system was already well developed by the fifteenth century, began in 1516 and continued up to the mid-sixteenth century. However, in his ulterior 'Treatise on Slavery' as well as in his 'History of the Indies', de las Casas subsequently recanted his position. Focusing on the innate freedom of all peoples based on the natural law tradition of the *omnium una libertas* (the common liberty of all), and publicly denouncing the greed of the Portuguese and Spaniards involved in the slave trade, arguably made de las Casas 'virtually the only European to speak out against black slavery in the sixteenth century',[20] thereby anticipating the origins of the abolitionist movement in the eighteenth century, which went on to crystallise into international law during the nineteenth and twentieth centuries.

The third, and chronologically speaking, most recent theme developed around de las Casas is his position as a milestone in the genealogy of human rights, the birth of which lies, according to some authors, at the foot of the 'encounter between sixteenth century Spanish Neo-Scholasticism and the New World'.[21] In this context, it has been argued that the 'essential achievement, on a theoretical level', of de las Casas 'was to graft, quite consciously, a juridical doctrine of natural rights onto Aquinas' teaching on natural law'.[22] Other authors have remarked that, quite literally, de las Casas 'may

---

[18] Clayton (n 2) 23.

[19] ibid, 112.

[20] R Adorno, *Intellectual Life of Bartolomé de las Casas* (New Orleans, Graduate School of Tulane University, 1992) 8.

[21] PG Carozza, 'From Conquest to Constitutions: Retrieving a Latin American Tradition of the Idea of Human Rights' (2003) 25 *Human Rights Quarterly* 281, 289.

[22] B Tierney, *The Idea of Natural Rights: Studies on Natural Rights, Natural Law and Church Law, 1150–1625* (Grand Rapids, Eerdmans, 1997) 275.

be the first writer to use the term "human rights" ('derechos humanos') and apply it to all human beings'.[23] Academic commentary in literature has also highlighted the Lascasian influence and his role as a precursor to a broad series of writers and intellectual movements. These range from the 'philosophers' of the Enlightenment such as Rousseau, Montaigne[24] and others, to revolutionary thinkers such as Simón Bolivar, who called de las Casas the 'Apostle of the Americas'. Other authors have traced a distinct form of rights discourse in Latin America leading up to the modern 'liberation theology' movement all the way back to the Lascasian influence.[25] In more recent times, one could argue that de las Casas' trendsetting, critical, and strategic activist practices resonate in their radical humanitarianism with those employed by contemporary international human rights' NGOs and activists who continue 'speaking truth to power' and 'naming and shaming' in the pursuit of their causes. Unsurprisingly, numerous institutions and centres for the defence and study of human rights now bear the name of de las Casas and the eponymous adjective 'Lascasian' has gained a life of its own as a common scholarly term attached to human rights advocacy.

Last but not least, the Lascasian legacy lies in its enduring interdisciplinary educational value. De las Casas' large body of writing, and the wide-ranging bibliographical materials his life and works have spawned in different languages over the last 500 years, are present in university syllabi covering a wide range of undergraduate and postgraduate courses across many different disciplines.[26] These include theology, history, imperialism, abolitionism, globalisation, indigenous peoples, law, human rights and others. Serving as a vehicle for knowledge and food for thought to successive generations of students and academics may well be the most lasting dwelling of the Lascasian radical humanitarian spirit.

---

[23] De las Casas, *Obras Completas* (n 12) vol X, 236.
[24] Orique (n 14) 331.
[25] Carozza (n 21) 228.
[26] Among the best online references are www.lascasas.org, and that of 'Biblioteca Virtual Miguel de Cervantes', at www.cervantesvirtual.com/portales/bartolome_de_las_casas/apunte_biobibliografico.

3

John Locke
The Natural Law Philosopher

CRISTINA DE LA CRUZ-AYUSO

> Men being ... by nature all free, equal, and independent, no one can be put out of this estate and subjected to the political power of another, without his own consent. The only way whereby any one divests himself of his natural liberty, and puts on the bonds of civil society, is by agreeing with other men to join and unite into a community for their comfortable, safe, and peaceable living amongst one another in a secure enjoyment of their properties, and a greater security against any that are not of it. ... When any number of men have so consented to make one community or government, they are thereby presently incorporated, and make one political body, wherein the majority have a right to act and conclude the rest.[1]

I. John Locke, a Practice-Oriented Philosopher

The ideas with the most influence on eighteenth century political thinkers were those of English philosopher John Locke (1632–1704). His work was the cornerstone of the early stages of liberal thought. He was also one of the great epistemologists, and the first to systematically consider the critical issue of knowledge. Locke is therefore deemed to be the founder of modern empiricism and the first major theorist of liberalism. His thinking indelibly marked Western culture in general and the culture of English-speaking countries in particular.

Locke was born in 1632, the same year as Spinoza, in Wrington, near Bristol in England. Brought up as part of the British gentry, he was educated in an environment akin to Puritanism, and at the age of 20 he entered Christ Church College, Oxford,

---

[1] J Locke, *Two Treatises on Government* Chapter VIII, section 95 [1689] (Peter Laslett (ed), Cambridge, Cambridge University Press, 1988).

one of the most prestigious academic institutions in England. He received a conventional philosophical, Aristotelian-Thomistic education, and was also interested in experimental sciences and medicine. In 1656 he received a *Baccalaureus Artiem* and two years later, a *Magister Artium*. In 1660, he was appointed tutor at Christ Church College, where he taught Greek and Rhetoric. His main interests were the natural sciences and the study of the philosophical bases of moral, social and political life. He read Descartes and challenged his thesis of innate ideas.

Despite his inclination for natural philosophy, Locke did not consider himself to be exclusively a philosopher, nor was he very enthusiastic about the university environment and the philosophical teachings he received, which he regarded as a peripatetic endeavour full of obscure words and useless searches. Locke therefore focused his interests on other areas and studied medicine, anatomy, physiology and physics. Robert Boyle, founder of modern chemistry, had a strong influence on him. He also studied with Sydenham, a prestigious doctor, and was a friend of Isaac Newton's towards the end of his life. In 1668, Locke gained membership of the prestigious Royal Society of London for the Improvement of Natural Knowledge, and throughout his life he was very close to the leading scholars in the experimental sciences.

In 1666 he met Lord Anthony Ashley Cooper, later 1st Earl of Shaftesbury, who was captivated by his personality. In addition to having Locke as his personal physician, Cooper also made him his secretary and right-hand man, and thus Locke joined Cooper's London family at Exeter House on the Strand. This friendship was a decisive factor in Locke's dedication to politics. The fundamental themes of the political conflicts of the time became his main object of study.

Shaftesbury was one of the most politically prominent people in seventeenth-century England. A defender of civil liberties, religious tolerance and the economic expansion of England, he supported the power of Parliament and was an important pillar of Whig ideology. Locke put himself at the intellectual service of these political interests. Under the auspices of Lord Shaftesbury, he wrote texts on religious and political tolerance in 1666 and 1667, probably intended to be used by Shaftsbury in his parliamentary speeches. These would be included in *Letter on Toleration* some years later.

In 1668, Locke was appointed as a secretary to the Lords proprietor of Carolina, the North American colony governed by Shaftesbury that became a destination for those fleeing from religious intransigence in Europe. This led Locke to assist in the drafting of *The Fundamental Constitution of Carolina* (1669), which guaranteed freedom of religion for all (except for atheists), among other provisions.

Shaftesbury's hostility to absolutism and Catholicism caused him to lose his position in 1673. In 1675 he became the leader of the opposition, which left him and Locke in a truly dangerous situation. This was the beginning of Locke's first period of exile in Paris and Montpellier (France), which lasted for four years, until 1679. On his return to London, he discreetly retired to Oxford, although he encountered strong hostilities towards the Whigs, an opposition group led by Shaftesbury, who defended the thesis that political power rested on a contract and that resistance to power is legitimate when that power is abused. They claimed that there was a plot to assassinate the King to replace him with his Catholic brother James, who would impose an absolutist government. Charles II dissolved Parliament in 1681 and Shaftesbury was accused of high treason. Locke followed Shaftesbury to Holland in 1683, where he remained for five years. In 1685 his name appeared on the list of traitors sought for extradition by the English government.

During the Glorious Revolution of 1688–89, Locke returned to England on the same ship as Queen Mary, wife of William of Orange. He witnessed the English revolution at first hand. This revolution abolished the King's divine rights and established the predominance of Parliament in the political system. Locke also became involved in the drafting of the English Bill of Rights, although the version finally adopted by Parliament did not go as far as he had intended in matters of religious tolerance. However, it contained the main political ideas for which Locke had fought so hard, since England became a constitutional monarchy controlled by Parliament.

Locke rejected a position as a diplomat and retired to the castle of Oates (Essex), where he spent the later years of his life dedicated to philosophical activity. There he wrote a series of letters that were finally collected in the essay *Some Thoughts Concerning Education* published in 1693. He died in 1704.

His three most important works were the product of many years of labour and saw the light of day in the same year: 1689. In addition to *Letter on Toleration*, his most important political work, *Two Treatises of Government*, was published, in which he laid the foundations of political liberalism, together with *An Essay Concerning Human Understanding*, his philosophical master work, which inaugurated the empiricist tradition of English philosophy. His two political works were published anonymously: the *Letter on Toleration* in Holland (in Latin); and *Two Treatises* in England. The political instability of the country and his own caution discouraged him from acknowledging authorship of these books. Only years later, when Locke had made his reputation as a philosopher, did he agree to have them published under his name.

Given the anonymous publication of his political works, Locke's contemporaries could not connect these works to him. Even so, his influence grew and survived him for more than a century. The heritage of Locke's political thought was part of the intellectual background of the American and French revolutions, and later, of the independence of Latin American countries. In addition to laying the foundations of liberal thought that has lasted for centuries, his own life has been recognised as an example of the freedom he always defended in his political writings.

II. The Traits of Modern Liberalism in Locke's Political Thought

Locke is one of the leading political thinkers in the theory of the social contract. His life circumstances led him to reflect on the philosophical and moral basis of political obligation, which he collected in *Two Treatises of Government*, his key political work. The first treatise was aimed at critically refuting the absolutist theory that Robert Filmer had expounded in *Patriarcha*, thus taking the first effective step towards theoretically justifying the idea of a representative bourgeois regime. The second treatise established the grounds for political constitutionalism, arguing for the rights of the bourgeoisie against the privileges of the monarchy, the nobility and the clergy. According to Locke, power comes from the voluntary consent of the governed.

A. The State of Nature and the Social Contract

Locke's proposal was to develop a theory that legitimised political authority, while at the same time setting its limits. This included a conception of human nature as a 'state of perfect freedom' and a 'state of nature' where freedom and equality reign. Like the other social contract philosophers, the state of nature was thought of as a hypothesis, an ideal, which recognised the basic rights of the person as a basis for the legitimacy of political life. By establishing individual freedom as an essential element of a civil society, Locke rejected the idea that no individual is born free and that every government is an absolute monarchy. For Locke, both claims were false, and were not substantiated by either the Bible or by reason. For Locke, political power was not justified by inheritance or privilege. In the natural order, all individuals are equally free.

His doctrine of natural rights was one of the most influential of the time. He considered that natural law was inscribed in the hearts of men. It consists in certain rules of nature that govern human behaviour and can be discovered by the use of reason. Natural law is an eternal law for all men, including legislators, whose positive laws have to be in accordance with natural laws, and were therefore endowed with a coercive power to enforce compliance on those who do not respect them.

Equality and freedom are the two essential features of Locke's state of nature and are a foundational aspect of modern political philosophy. The 'state of nature' is a state of freedom which does not entail that everyone can do whatever they want. Nor is it a state of war, as Hobbes claimed. However, it is evident that conflicts occur which prevent the development of natural law to preserve the freedom of each individual. Any arbitrary usurpation of power, not consented to by the governed, must be rejected in the name of the freedom and equality of all human beings. That is the moral foundation of political power. Therefore, a civil authority is necessary; a government that protects natural law, even if this involves legislating and setting limits to individual actions. According to Locke, this shift from the state of nature to a civil society takes place by consent, and it is only through this consent that individuals can be fundamentally free, equal and independent. Civil society is formed through a mutual agreement between all individuals to come together and live as a community.

That is the explanation and justification of the contract that Locke calls consent or agreement, which presupposes the tendency of individuals to live in society. In Locke, there is a continuity between the state of nature and civil society. It is the individual's own consent that leads them to accept the political order. The basis for that consent is trust, an essential assumption if the individual is to join in society. This is how Locke proposes to make individual freedom compatible with life in society and the constraints imposed by it.

The consent that accompanies the contract is taken for granted, as reason itself indicates that this must be so. The purpose of political power is to preserve society.

Nevertheless, it is a fact that political power can be perverted and that there is a constant danger of tyranny and despotism. That is why the logic of consent advocated by Locke, also incorporates the right to resistance or the right to sedition. If that tacitly agreed contract ceases to be fulfilled, the people must have the right to revolt and overthrow those in power. Locke sceptically addressed this right at the end of the *Second Treatise*, as he distrusted the willingness of individuals living in society to defend their own rights and interests. Locke established the theoretical basis for the recognition of individual rights and, at the same time, saw the difficulties of enforcing them in practice.

B. Freedom, Property and the Limitation of State Powers

Locke's political ideas defended the right to property as the natural right *par excellence*. Rousseau was one of the first philosophers to state that the origin of all inequalities lay in the concept of private property. Locke, perhaps due to optimism or ingenuity, differed from this view. He considered that property is a natural right, and justified it by resorting to the argument of the empirical observation of reality: ever since the world's earliest ages, individuals have appropriated the basic goods that they needed to survive. The right to preservation that human beings have since they are born justifies the right to possess what nature provides for their subsistence. The natural right to property is, for Locke, a moral principle, because it is the basis of individual freedom. Being free means being able to dispose of what one legitimately acquires. Property, in a broad sense, means for Locke 'life, liberty and property' and in a more restricted sense, goods, the right to inherit and the ability to accumulate wealth.

Locke hoped that political society would be a true commonwealth, a community of goods owned by those who produced them. He trusted the social and political organisation that was founded on individual freedom. In the state of nature, everything belongs to everyone until someone, by their own effort, appropriates something they need. That natural right to property must be governed by some rules: each individual must appropriate only what they need and use. Only then will the right to property be fair, because there will be a spontaneous distribution of the necessary goods.

To prevent the right to property from becoming a source of injustice, a civil society is needed that legislates and orders what is held to be indisputable under natural law. The objective of the state, therefore, will be to protect the individual's right to property. This idea is enthroned in Locke's work, and would be an essential idea throughout the history of economic and political liberalism, despite notable qualifications being introduced in the twentieth century with the appearance of the welfare state. Locke strongly argued that the main objective of individuals joining together and forming commonwealths and submitting to a government is the preservation of their property.

In this way, Locke's *Second Treatise* established the awkward coexistence within the liberal doctrine of two factually contradictory postulates that seemingly remain unresolved by liberal thought: Locke's incipient liberalism unreservedly proclaimed equal freedom for all and, at the same time, the universal right to property.

On the one hand, this represented an important advance, since it recognised all individuals as equally free beings. Freedom is an indisputable natural right. However, if freedom is essentially understood as being property, this justifies that any distribution of goods, however unequal, is a consequence of freedom and, therefore, is irrefutable. Therefore, if justice is defined as the duty to give each individual what is due to him or her, some form of political regulation must be put in place to ensure the practical implementation of this. This regulation must determine what and whom is referred to as 'what is due to each individual'. This was the first step taken on the path to the defence and recognition of social rights that would take place centuries later, which were a rare occurrence among the prevailing intellectual majority in Locke's time.

C. In Defence of Tolerance

The defence of individual freedoms made Locke one of the most notable founding fathers of tolerance. Locke argued that religious faith, understood as absolute truth, is not a good support for maintaining order and coexistence. Convinced that knowledge is limited and no one is in possession of absolute truths, he applied his ideas about tolerance both to religion and to his theory of human knowledge. Locke, along with his contemporary Spinoza, based his ideas on a process of religious secularisation that continues until this day. Both defended the idea that faith is a private matter and that it is necessary to separate the private from the public and, more specifically, religion from politics.

For Locke, religious persecution or coercion cannot be justified, since no one is in possession of absolute truth. Religious beliefs are convictions belonging to each individual that cannot be imposed. Being, as it should, a private matter, the state (whose main function is to guarantee peace and security) must recognise religious freedom and, at the same time, set its limits. He also believed that the state must persecute atheism.

Locke had a notable influence on the European intelligentsia and his ideas on political authority and natural law were widely disseminated by eighteenth century French encyclopaedists. The *Second Treatise* had a remarkable influence on the two declarations of the rights of man, the one proclaimed in the United States in 1787 and the one proclaimed in France in 1789. The separation of powers suggested by Locke was the backbone of Montesquieu's theory, and had a direct impact on the English parliamentary system and the governments emerging from bourgeois democracy to limit absolutism. Locke found that his much-desired limitation of state power was guaranteed by the doctrine of the separation of powers, which has been widely recognised and incorporated into the political constitutions of all modern liberal democracies. Despite the contradictions and limitations in his works, Locke joined his doctrine of the separation of powers with his principles on the political and economic rights of each individual and his ideas on religious and political tolerance. This created a theoretical system which contains all the essential features of modern liberalism.

III. Locke, a Key Background Source for the Creation and Definition of Human Rights

Locke's political legacy ushered in liberalism, defined its essential contours and introduced the main categories of the debate that has sustained it up to the present: individual and civil liberties, representative government, separation of powers, property, secularism and religious tolerance. His political thought remains one of the fundamental bases of the contemporary democratic liberal state.

In addition, Locke's legacy enables an understanding of the historical origin of human rights. They emerged in the dawn of the *modern* world in which Locke lived, of which he was one of the most prominent representatives. Human rights are not the result of an abstract reflection, but the response to specific situations in which human beings and their dignity were threatened or undermined for reasons such as intolerance, the concentration of power, legitimised by divine right, and the violence of an absolutist state. Therefore, the discourse of human rights cannot be separated from the experience of injustice. What they represent as a moral demand is an achievement resulting from the awareness of the experience of inhumanity. In this sense, Locke's contributions are important in explaining the origin and definition of human rights. Locke witnessed successive political crises and experienced the emergence of a progressive thought which was centred on individual freedom, and a breaking away from its religious ties.

The affirmation that human beings per se are holders of innate rights represents a Copernican turn in both political theory and praxis. This natural law-based conception advocated by Locke refuted the idea that power is superior to freedom, and that it is power that recognises and grants spheres of freedom. Only a hypothesis such as the one defended by Locke can sustain the initial wording of the Universal Declaration of Human Rights (Article 1) that all human beings are born free and equal.

Locke took a decisive step towards the modern theory of natural rights by questioning the legal basis of the obligation of sovereigns to respect natural law. His response was crucial: the governed simply have rights. The subjective natural right of the citizen is the basis of the government's duty to protect that citizen. It is the government's duty because it is also the citizen's right.

This individualist conception, which is present in the major declarations of human rights, affirms that the individual prevails over society, and the functionality of society for affirming the rights of individuals (Article 2 of Universal Declaration of Human Rights). Locke's expression of political authority has this voluntarist character. The importance of this conception is such that modern democracy, which equates the power of citizens, was born from it. Individual representation implies that all citizens are equal before the law. Without this individualistic conception of society, democracy cannot be justified.

Locke's political theory had a special impact in the United States. His ideas were strongly aligned with the objective reality of the US in the twentieth century.

He is, without doubt, the most representative thinker of the entire American political tradition. The ultimate purpose of guaranteeing rights in the American system lies in the recognition of the need to raise barriers against power in all forms and in all government compartments. This is why there were amendments to the 1787 Constitution, which came together in the 1791 Bill of Rights.

Locke's ideas also had an important repercussion on the French Declaration of the Rights of the Man and the Citizen of 26 August 1789, which represented the consolidation of the first major victory against the *ancien régime*, as well as the legal embodiment of the theoretical principles developed by natural law philosophers and by the founders of liberalism. John Locke led the way for all of them.

Locke was a moderate man. He was an empiricist who affirmed that sensorial perception provides the basis for everything that can be known. However, he was not a radical empiricist, insofar as he was also convinced of the pre-eminence of rational judgment over faith, beliefs and opinions. He opposed the principle of authority, both in the intellectual and political fields. He was one of the great defenders of tolerance and at the same time he was capable of identifying what the limits were for implementing tolerance on a practical basis. He was a religious spirit that was far removed from fanaticism. He was, above all, an independent man who was admired by his contemporaries and had great intellectual prestige. And his work was unquestionably a background source for the creation and definition of human rights.

4

Olympe de Gouges

Impressively Ahead of Her Time: A Visionary, Daring Activist and Martyr

TERESA PIZARRO BELEZA AND HELENA PEREIRA DE MELO

> La femme a le droit de monter sur l'échafaud ; elle doit avoir également celui de monter à la Tribune.[1]

I. An Improbable 'Femme de Lettres', a Feminist *Avant la Lettre* and a Committed, Democratic Revolutionary

Olympe de Gouges was born Marie Gouze, in Montauban, France, in 1748, officially the legitimate child of Anne-Olympe Mouisset, issued from a family of professional drapers, and Pierre Gouze, a butcher, the likely chosen husband for her mother. According to the habits of French society, a husband should be found for the mistress of a nobleman, a practice a century later masterfully caricatured by the composer Jacques Offenbach in the opera 'La Périchole', in 1868, using the example of the customs in the French court. She was most probably the natural daughter of her mother's publicly acknowledged lover, the Marquis Jean-Jacques Le Franc de Pompignan, intellectual and academician, who never legally recognised his love child. She seemed to have inherited his love of writing, if not his level of formal education, due to her inferior social status, wealth and gender. Married in 1765, at 17 years of age, to Louis-Yves Aubry, Marie soon became a widow (1766) with a son who grew up to become a military officer. He would serve for some time in the regiment of the Duke of Orléans and eventually become General Pierre Aubry.

---

[1] 'Women have the right to mount the scaffold, they should also be granted the right to step up to the tribune' (our translation), *Déclaration des Droits de la Femme et de la Citoyenne*, 1791, Article X.

She decided to leave her native province, and travel to Paris, and set her mind to self-improve her education by reading and studying the ideas of Rousseau, Beaumarchais, Choderlos de Laclos, Condorcet. She also managed to train herself to speak in a more fashionable, Parisian way and to learn about politics and public affairs in general. She left for Paris to remake herself as a *femme de lettres*, changing her appearance, her dress, her speech and her name. Transformed into Olympe de Gouges, she managed to become a welcome presence in the fashionable *salons* and lived to see and participate in the French Revolution (1789) that would change the political settings of Europe and inspire many revolutionary movements, ideas and writings for years to come. She soon noticed that many people, such as women and slaves, were not candidates for full citizenship and she did not hold back in voicing her criticism of this reality.

A gifted and prolific playwright, she also authored many incendiary political pamphlets, posters and letters to members of the French elite, such as Queen Marie Antoinette, to whom she actually dedicated her *Déclaration des droits de la femme et de la citoyenne*, the Duke of Orléans, and even Robespierre himself. She defied both the old and the new regimes, daring to insist on the possibility of popular choice of the system of government to come, when the Terror (1793–94) had already forbidden such liberties under the threat of death. Her preference was for a constitutional monarchy, but the public defence of such an opinion had by then become politically untenable. It would eventually flourish, many years later in many places, often at the cost of much resistance, bitter struggle and profuse bloodshed.

In 1792, King Louis XVI was deposed, his trial and conviction became unavoidable and his execution would take place in 1793. The sacrifice of the royal family had gained the support of the majority of the *Convention*. Other intellectuals opposed this fatal *derive* of the Revolution, like Madame de Staël, but de Gouges was particularly vocal and was publicly attacked for her 'moderate' political ideas.

She opposed the execution of the king and queen, as a matter of principle, actually offering her services to defend Louis XVI under trial. Not only was she defying the 'revolutionary authority', but also the idea that the proper place of women was at home caring for her family rather than in a court of law defending a king accused of treason. She believed he was a traitor, for his collusion with foreign powers, but she also believed that the royal family should be spared and that the political situation should evolve towards a constitutional monarchy.

She also incurred the anger of colonial plantation owners and slave traders by being a precocious outspoken advocate against the slave trade, producing essays like 'Réflexions sur les Hommes Nègres'[2] or writing and staging an abolitionist theatre play 'L'Esclavage de Nègres, ou l'Heureux Naufrage' (1792, a revised version of *Zamore et Mirza* in 1784). Even the actors at the Comédie Française were adamant about playing 'black' characters when the play was first staged; all 'white', they refused to paint their faces to look like black slaves.[3]

---

[2] '… En avançant en âge, je vis clairement que c'était la force et le préjugé qui les avaient condamnés à cet horrible esclavage, que la Nature n'y avait aucune part, et que l'injuste et puissant intérêt des Blancs avait tout fait': see slavery.uga.edu/texts/literary_works/reflexions.pdf.

[3] Many years later, somehow the reverse criticism would question the legitimacy of casting a disguised Laurence Olivier as the protagonist in Shakespeare's 'Othello' instead of finding a fine black actor.

II. A Holistic, Intelligent Sensitivity that Harboured an Almost Eerie Premonition of Claims to Come

Olympe de Gouges is mostly known to this day as the author of the *Déclaration des droits de la femme et de la citoyenne* (Declaration of the Rights of Woman and the Female Citizen) (1791). This Declaration echoes and somehow replicates the *Déclaration des droits de l'homme et du citoyen* (Declaration of the Rights of Man and the Citizen) (1789), and constitutes an enlightened, passionate claim for equality between men and women, after the Women's Petition to the French National Assembly[4] was ignored and the Marquis de Condorcet's efforts (amongst a few others) to extend civil and political rights to women in France was equally rejected.

But de Gouges' many writings and strongly-held convictions extended well beyond the question of gender equality. The most remarkable feature of her work and general life commitment is probably her surprising 'modernity': she anticipated claims and issues that would have to wait almost 200 years to emerge as obvious items on the women's or other rights agendas at the national, regional or international level. Political participation and an accepted, 'normalised' active public presence of women are two obvious *sine qua non* conditions of democracy. She insisted on both in her *Déclaration*, noting how the scaffold and the tribune should be equally accessible to women, a powerful if somewhat tragically foreboding image. She personally managed the former but not the latter, in her own lifetime. De Gouges' home country would wait until 1945 to recognise the right of women to vote;[5] other nations took longer.

However, de Gouges' daring statements and social and political proposals go much further than the question of voting rights. Alternative, better marriage contracts that would place women on an equal stance with men should replace religious marriage, which she considered a socially approved hypocrisy, a 'tomb for real love'. The need to ensure equal rights in case of separation or divorce, and the unfair unequal legal status of children born out of wedlock were also scrutinised under her proto-feminist gaze. She criticised the enforced claustration in convents of many young woman to preserve the family's wealth or avoid an unsuitable marriage.[6] But she also vituperated against the evils of slavery and the death penalty, much inspired by her friend Condorcet, and promoted the advantages of trial by jury, and the need to help and protect the poorest of the poor, somehow foreshadowing what would become the future social welfare state. Workhouses should be created for the unemployed; asylums for the homeless beggars. Such institutions were created in France, but much later. Slavery

---

[4] The 'Women's Petition to the National Assembly' was presented to the French National Assembly in November 1789, protesting against the leaving out of half the French people and demanding equality for women. It was never discussed.

[5] 'La conquête de la citoyenneté politique des femmes', a useful and clear timeline of women's suffrage in France, available at www2.assemblee-nationale.fr/decouvrir-l-assemblee/histoire/le-suffrage-universel/la-conquete-de-la-citoyennete-politique-des-femmes.

[6] One of her committed theatre plays deals with this issue: *Le Couvent ou les vœux forcés* (1790).

and the subjugation of black people were not based in nature and therefore should be abolished through law. Liberation of slaves would be progressive.[7] As in other fields, de Gouges' belief in progress through law is strong and coherent with her moderate political stance. Eventually, law should guarantee equality to everyone and that is why she stressed, in her *Déclaration*, that women should not be considered an exception in any way:

> VII. Nulle femme n'est exceptée; elle est accusée, arrêtée, & détenue dans les cas déterminés par la Loi. Les femmes obéissent comme les hommes à cette Loi rigoureuse.

She seems to have been blessed, inspired, moved by a holistic, intelligent sensitivity that was so very rare – and still is, to some extent, in some forums today – and impressively ahead of her time. René Viénet sums it up nicely: 'a prodigious power to anticipate future democratic demands'.[8] The death penalty would endure in French law until 1981, when it was finally abolished under President François Mitterrand. It still stands in many parts of the world, including in fully-fledged democracies like the United States of America. Slavery was legally abolished in France only in 1848.

When it comes to women's rights and gender equality, it is almost eerie the way she foretold much of what feminist movements and manifestoes would claim, in some cases much later: public and political participation of women; the right to identify the father of a child born out of wedlock; the right to divorce and a more equal contract of marriage; the practice of signing her own texts with her own name... She remained somewhat moderate in strict political issues, but she was amazingly radical in her vindication of the equality of the sexes, which was shocking and rare in her day. Few predecessors can be recalled, but François Poullain de la Barre (Paris, 1647 – Geneva, 1725) is most certainly one.

The simple fact that she was aware of interconnection – in terms of indivisibility of rights, multiple bases of discrimination, or the inevitable intersection between 'private' and 'public' life is noteworthy. Most legal systems today still have rules based on an imperfect understanding of such interconnections. She actually lived in accordance with her principles and beliefs, showing an amazing and rare self-confidence for a woman of her time and condition, refusing to marry the man who was probably the great love of her life, the rather important civil servant and her 'protector' in Paris, Jacques Bietrix de Rozière.[9] Her first and only, short-lived, marriage was most probably forced on her, according to social custom and practices.

In a very different context but with a somewhat similar inspiration, almost a century later, John Stuart Mill may be considered an (intellectual, sophisticated)

---

[7] R Tarin, 'L'Esclavage des noirs, ou la mauvaise conscience d'Olympe de Gouges' (1998) 30 *Dix-Huitième Siècle* 373–81.

[8] R Viénet (tr D Nicholson-Smith), '*Olympe de Gouges, a Daughter of Quercy on her Way to the Panthéon*' 2001, available at web.archive.org/web/20041019110242/http://www.quercy.net/hommes/ogenglish.html.

[9] French law forbade married women to publish without their husband's permission, a probable motive for de Gouges' refusal to remarry. About possible other reasons to refuse de Rozière's proposal of marriage and in general the relevance of de Gouges' life for her writings, and the connection between the two, see Olivier Blanc, 'Celle qui voulut politiquer', available online at www.monde-diplomatique.fr/2008/11/BLANC/16516.

activist relative, in terms of the recognition of the multifaceted, unnatural subjection of women – the actual title of one of his most famous essays (published in 1869).[10] The refusal of Olympe to remarry once she had been widowed reminds one of Mill's statement on marriage, in which he refused to exercise the rights the English laws on marriage bestow on husbands over their wives, when he was about to marry Harriet Taylor. Both Olympe and Mill are aware and quite vocal about the inherent injustice of the contract of marriage as per the legally binding, striking inferiority of women. Both in common law and in continental legal systems the subjugation of women was very much achieved by their domestication through family law, namely the regulation of marriage, together with customs and (tolerated) violence, jointly with practices and discourses in religion and sometimes perfunctory science.

Much closer to de Gouges in date, Mary Wollstonecraft published her *A Vindication of the Rights of Woman* in 1792. Her focus was on education and on the insistence on the rational character of women and the need to control emotions and excessive sensibilities ('passions'). Like de Gouges, she wrote as a reaction to contemporary events and ideas, strongly criticising Rousseau for his narrow views on women's education.

Olympe de Gouges' political views both inspired her writings and dictated her eventual downfall. She risked everything in what seems to have been a conscious decision, publicising her fiery pamphlet on choice of government by referendum under the title *Les Trois Urnes*. Her connection with the *Girondins* and her stated preference for a constitutional monarchy were just unacceptable in the political climate that prevailed. Guillotined under Robespierre, having been summarily accused, tried and convicted of treason, she seems to have been largely forgotten until recent years and was often considered a peculiar, hysterical virago that, according to some, got what she actually deserved, having interfered in public affairs instead of concentrating on family and home care work, as would have become a proper, normal, 'feminine' woman.[11]

III. A Buried Legacy Still Waiting to be Properly Celebrated

Olympe de Gouges' *Declaration of the Rights of Women* would be enough to justify the celebration of its author as a major character in the modern history of human rights. But her *oeuvre* goes well beyond that wonderful document. She was a humanist, a pacifist, a committed democrat; the bloodshed that marked the French Revolution was a disgrace that she abhorred and never hesitated to distance herself from. She significantly signs her letter to the Duke of Orléans (1789) as: 'A Friend to all my Fellow Citizens and to public calm'.[12]

---

[10] JS Mill, *The Subjection of Women* (London, Longmans, Green, Reader and Dyer, 1869).

[11] PG Chaumette, 'Speech at City Hall Denouncing Women's Political Activism' 17 November 1793, Liberté, Egalité, Fraternité, at chnm.gmu.edu/revolution/d/489/.

[12] Letter to his Lordship the Duke d'Orléans, First Prince of the Blood, July 1789, available at www.olympedegouges.eu/lettre_au_duc.php.

She lived – and tragically died – in accordance with her principles and convictions, both in her private and her public life. In fact this very distinction can be deconstructed taking Olympe's life as a brilliant example or case study. She anticipated 'The personal is political' feminist motto by almost two centuries. She vindicated her amorous and sexual autonomy and tried to educate her son along the lines of her strongly democratic and egalitarian beliefs. Unfortunately he turned against her at the end of her life, maybe out of fear for his post as an officer in the French Army or because he could not abide by her unusual, independent, strong convictions.

And yet her story is still very much left outside the gates of academia, and omitted from the textbooks that most history students read, from primary school to university, even in law schools, where human rights are often taught as compulsory or optional, specialised courses. Full public acknowledgement of her name and martyrdom has yet to come, even if she was somewhat recalled and publicly venerated during the bicentenary celebrations for the French Revolution (1789–1989).[13] Sometimes it takes a dedicated biographer to recover lost memories – in France it was to some extent the case with the book published in 1981 by Olivier Blanc.[14]

Still, de Gouges' Declaration inspired other human rights activists, and in particular one can say that the American Declaration of Sentiments (Seneca Falls, NY, 1848) echoes and replicates the American Declaration of Independence (Philadelphia, Pennsylvania, 1776) in a way that is reminiscent of the two French documents. The awareness of white American women of the similarity of their situation to black slaves that gave rise to the Seneca Falls Convention and its Declaration is curiously akin to the parallel that de Gouges denounced between colonial slavery and political oppression in France in some of her writings. But the differences in tone between the two Declarations are striking: almost a century later, American women present themselves in a much more sentimental, 'soft', ideal family mode, compared to which the passionate tone of the proud, autonomous, outspoken Olympe sounds wonderfully rational, precise, 'cold' and as sharp as steel. It is one of the greatest revolutionary manifestoes in the history of human rights and deserves to be celebrated, taught and read as an integral part of human rights education.

But her many other contributions to democracy, social justice and human rights remain rather overshadowed by the recent success and dissemination of her Declaration of the Rights of Women. After being declared insane by quite a few of her contemporaries and by some later intellectuals, for her 'reformatory paranoia' in favour of women, she was 'caricatured in reverse' by the reduction of her fights by some feminist

---

[13] Benoite Groult, one of the first authors to honour Olympe de Gouges in the feminist movement in the twentieth century, and the first to publish the full text of the *Déclaration*, sums up many reasons for the deliberate 'hiding' of the memory of de Gouges in modern times: live recorded lecture to the 'Colloque Olympe de Gouges' (n 9).

[14] 'Prior to Olivier Blanc's works, with their impeccable scholarship and infectious sympathy for their subject, Olympe was often condescendingly described as a political extremist, an author of little interest, or an illiterate suspected of libertinism': Viénet (n 8). Olivier Blanc is one of the contributors to the collection of essays on Olympe de Gouges published by Le Monde diplomatique, November 2008, under the general title 'Olympe de Gouges, une femme du XXIe siècle': 'Celle qui voulut politiquer'.

perspectives. Her legacy is greater than the fight for sex equality as such. She deserves to be celebrated for her true myriad commitments, challenges and proposals.[15]

In the age of internet and online social networks, the wide celebration of semi-forgotten heroes and heroines of human rights history, like Olympe de Gouges, should be much easier and matter-of-fact. Unfortunately, so is the diffusion of hatred, bigotry, sexism, racism, xenophobia, etc. It is a difficult but challenging task to redress the balance in favour of tolerance, diversity, peace and humanism.

Olympe is a great candidate for that struggle and the sheer number and quality of sites already devoted to her ideas, texts, life and work does seem quite promising.[16] Maybe a recreation of some sort of 'Wonder Woman' character in the shape of Olympe would be appropriate. After all, she dared to challenge all conventions, all powers, and all prejudices of her own lifetime. She could not avoid her final disgrace and execution, but not many heroes fought so bravely to the very end and faced the scaffold with such amazing courage and irony.

It is said that Olympe de Gouges, famous for her physical beauty and with a streak of 'coquetterie', asked for a mirror just before being lowered onto the guillotine platform and commented: '*Dieu merci, mon visage ne me jouera pas de mauvais tours!*'[17]

But she also remembered to address her son in a most moving letter, when aware of her impending execution, complaining about the refusal by the revolutionary court to let her have a defence lawyer and finally invoking her maternal love as a precious help to face her death with courage and bravery, producing this extraordinary statement: '*Mourir pour accomplir son devoir, c'est prolonger sa maternité au delà du tombeau*'.[18]

[15] The article published by Véronique Maurus in *Le Monde* in July 2003 is particularly convincing: 'Olympe l'imprécatrice' *Le Monde* (Paris, 25 July 2003), available at web.archive.org/web/20041020053041/http://www.quercy.net:80/hommes/lemondeolympe.html.

[16] A mere example, in English, can be found at www.olympedegouges.eu/index.php.

[17] Maurus (n 15): 'Thank God, my face will not let me down' (our translation).

[18] Blanc (n 4): 'To die for fulfilling one's duty is a way to prolong maternity beyond the grave' (our translation).

5

Mary Wollstonecraft

The Undutiful Daughter of the Enlightenment and Her Loud Demands for Justice

DOLORES MORONDO TARAMUNDI

> Virtuous equality will not rest firmly even when founded on a rock, if one half of mankind are chained to its bottom by fate.[1]

I. 'Those Who are Bold Enough to Advance Before the Age They Live in … Must Learn to Brave Censure'[2]

Mary Wollstonecraft is an *awkward* figure. Original and controversial in her lifetime, reviled immediately after her death, and rediscovered as a 'classic' in the twentieth century, 'she has shrugged off calumny and whitewash' and, although 'she was often bitter in her lifetime … she might have laughed … [at] the vagaries of her reputation after death'.[3]

She was born in 1759 in Spitalfields (London) to a middle-class family that saw a rapid economic decline during her youth due to her father's unwise financial management. The dire economic situation of the family affected Wollstonecraft's educational

[1] M Wollstonecraft, 'A Vindication of the Rights of Woman with Strictures on Political and Moral Subjects' in M Wollstonecraft, *A Vindication of the Rights of Woman*, edited by C Morgan (Köln, Könemann, 1998) 261.
[2] J Todd (ed), *The Collected Letters of Mary Wollstonecraft* (New York, Columbia University Press, 2003) 410.
[3] C Tomalin, *The Life and Death of Mary Wollstonecraft* (London, Penguin Books, 1985) 314.

opportunities and her share of the inheritance, both of which were settled on her eldest brother. Her lot in life was to care for her younger siblings. Yet neither her lack of formal education nor her situation can be said to have been uncommon at the time for a woman of her class. Her ideas on the injustice suffered by daughters and younger children within family arrangements under English law were thus founded on first-hand experience.

Unhappy at home, Wollstonecraft sought independence ('the grand blessing of life, the basis of every virtue'[4]) through the kind of employment available to educated women of no fortune at the time: from 1778 to 1787 she worked as a lady's companion, then she set up her own school with her sisters and a friend, and later she became a governess to a family in Ireland. During this time, she took up writing as a means of improving her income. In 1784 she met Richard Price, a moral and political thinker who was the head of a Dissenters' community in Newington (London) and, through that community, she met her future publisher and friend, Joseph Johnson. Her first writings were pedagogical: *Thoughts on the Education of Daughters: with Reflections on Female Conduct in the More Important Duties of Life* (1787), *Original Stories from Real Life; with Conversations, Calculated to Regulate the Affections, and Form the Mind to Truth and Goodness* (1788), and *The Female Reader* (1789).

In 1787, after less than a year as a governess, she returned to London and decided to live by her pen. Although she might not be the 'first of a new genus', as she wrote to her sister, women authors were rare, and those who could make a living from their writing were even rarer. Joseph Johnson, who was a successful publisher and bookseller, as well as a prominent figure in the radical British political and intellectual milieu, made that possible. Wollstonecraft embarked on a professional career as a translator, member of the editorial staff and reviewer for Johnson's *Analytical Review*, the first British literary and scientific monthly journal aimed at the general public, while she continued to work on her own writing. During her stay in Ireland she had completed her novel *Mary: A Fiction* (1788), which anticipated some of the themes developed in her later political writings.

In 1790 she wrote *A Vindication of the Rights of Man*,[5] the first reply to Edmund Burke's *Reflections on the Revolution in France, and on the Proceedings in Certain Societies in London Relative to that Event* (1790), where Burke had harshly attacked a speech by Richard Price in defence of the French Declaration of the Rights of Man. The publication of the second edition with Wollstonecraft's name on it in December 1790 made her a reputation as a political writer. She actively participated in the debate spawned by the French Revolution in Britain, and was an acknowledged figure among the radical and republican thinkers in Johnson's circle, such as Joseph Priestley, Anna Laetitia Barbauld, Thomas Paine, Henry Fuseli and William Godwin. In 1792 she published her most famous work, *A Vindication of the Rights of Woman: with Strictures on Political and Moral Subjects*.

At the end of 1792, Wollstonecraft travelled alone to Paris. She needed a change of scene and wanted to leave behind her turbulent affair with Henry Fuseli. She also

---

[4] Wollstonecraft (n 1) 81 (in the dedicatory letter to M Talleyrand-Périgord, late bishop of Autun).
[5] M Wollstonecraft, 'A Vindication of the Rights of Man' in Wollstonecraft (n 1).

wanted to gain a better understanding of, and write about, the French Revolution, which she and her radical fellows fervently hoped would stimulate reforms in Britain. In Paris she met Brissot de Warville, Madame Roland, and Madame Genlis, as well as her radical expat friends: Thomas Christie, John Stone, Helen Williams and Joel and Ruth Barlow. But the situation descended rapidly into the Terror, and most of her friends and acquaintances were associated with the Girondins. The war between England and France, declared in February 1793, made things even more dangerous for her. During that time, she met and fell in love with Gilbert Imlay, an American businessman. Although they never married, Imlay registered her as his wife so that US citizenship would protect her from detention. Their daughter (Fanny) was born in Le Havre in 1794, when Wollstonecraft had just finished her book *Historical and Moral View of the Origins and Progress of the French Revolution*. Imlay left Wollstonecraft in Paris with the baby and set off for London with promises that he would send for her. But Imlay's interest in their relationship had waned and when Wollstonecraft arrived in London in 1795 it was clear that he did not intend to set up a family life with her. After a first suicide attempt, Wollstonecraft tried to rekindle their relationship by travelling to Scandinavia to settle Imlay's financial affairs, taking with her their one-year-old daughter and a maid. She returned in September 1795 and, convinced as she was of his rejection, attempted suicide a second time. She wrote an account of her travel, *Letters Written during a Short Residence in Sweden, Norway and Denmark* (1796), which would influence many Romantic writers of the nineteenth century and was a pioneering work of travel literature.

In 1796 she was reacquainted with William Godwin, a political thinker in Johnson's circle, and they started a relationship. They married in March 1797, after Wollstonecraft got pregnant, and she died on 10 September 1797 of puerperal fever, 11 days after giving birth to their daughter Mary (later, Mary Shelley). At the time of her death, she left an incomplete manuscript of a second novel, *Maria: or, The Wrongs of Woman*, generally considered the fictionalised second part of *A Vindication of the Rights of Woman*. It was published posthumously in 1798 by Godwin.

II. 'Virtue can Only Flourish among Equals'[6]

Mary Wollstonecraft's name is now firmly associated with women's rights. She is aptly considered to be one of the first to claim equality, freedom and rights for her sex, and a forerunner of the feminist movement in Europe. From her early pedagogical work on the education of girls, Wollstonecraft argued for the moral equality of men and women, and for the equally rational nature of women. Following earlier female writers on education, such as Catherine Macaulay, she contended that the apparent weakness of women was due to their flawed education, and not to any natural weakness of their minds or bodies. Throughout the Enlightenment, education was considered a key element in social transformation, and it was no coincidence that some of the most

---

[6] Wollstonecraft (n 5) 74.

important theorists of the Liberal Revolutions also published works on education, such as John Locke (*Some thoughts Concerning Education*, 1693) and Jean-Jacques Rousseau (*Émile, ou De l'éducation*, 1762).

Yet, the promises of freedom and equality advocated by Enlightenment and Liberalism disregarded women. Rousseau's very influential ideas on female education were opposed by Wollstonecraft both in her early pedagogical writings, especially in *Original Stories*, and in the *Vindication of the Rights of Woman*. In Book V of *Émile*, Rousseau argued for the complementary nature of the sexes, sometimes appealing to the language of equality. However, this complementary nature turned out to be hierarchical and founded on no better argument than man's strength ('his merit is in his power; he pleases by the sole fact of his strength'[7]). From this physical difference, he extracted consequences for the 'moral relations' between men and women. If the man should be strong and active, the woman should be weak and passive: 'Woman is made specially to please man. (...) If woman is made to please and to be subjugated, she ought to make herself agreeable to man instead of arousing him'.[8] Female education should be directed to sustain this relationship:

> To please men, to be useful to them, to make herself loved and honoured by them, to raise them when young, to care for them when grown, to counsel them, to console them, to make their lives agreeable and sweet.[9]

According to him, a woman's so-called natural traits (chastity, modesty, decorum, vanity, coquetry, wit) should therefore be promoted so that she can learn to entertain her husband while guarding her reputation. He explicitly argued against the then flourishing literature on female education which advocated equality: 'The more women want to resemble [men], the less women will govern them, and then men will truly be the masters'.[10] It was only through the coy and sly arts of the weak that women could, and should, have power over men.

Wollstonecraft radically opposed this line of reasoning, including its depiction of the women's nature, of their abilities, of their role in society, and of their relationship to men: 'I do not want women to have power over men, I want them to have power over themselves'.[11] Frivolous, vain and sly women could not be proper companions for men, or reasonable and informed mothers for children; they would 'stop the progress of knowledge and virtue; for truth must be common to all'.[12] Wollstonecraft argued that education, both for men and women, had to be directed at self-discipline, honesty and skills by which they could make a decent living and a meaningful contribution to society.

Besides its transformative power in the realm of social relations, and the improvement of the individual's mind, education had very material consequences for women in Wollstonecraft's *Vindication*: it was the means to render women independent, together with the reform of the laws on marriage and property. In *A Vindication of the Rights*

[7] JJ Rousseau, *Émile or On Education* (ed A Bloom, New York, Basic Books, 1979) 358.
[8] ibid, 358.
[9] ibid, 365.
[10] ibid, 363.
[11] Wollstonecraft (n 1) 159.
[12] ibid, 82 (in the dedicatory letter to M Talleyrand-Périgord, late bishop of Autun).

of Woman, Wollstonecraft argued that employment should be open and extended to women (a claim that Rousseau had qualified as 'political promiscuity'). Women could be well-paid physicians as well as very poorly-paid nurses, study politics, run a farm, or pursue business of various kinds 'if they were educated in a more orderly manner'.[13]

Access to education and dignified employment were not merely economic rights for Wollstonecraft; she argued that these were the material conditions for autonomy and personal freedom (to '[stand] upright supported by their own industry, instead of hanging their heads'[14]). As such, they were closely connected to the much-needed reform of the institution of marriage. Without access to education and employment to be able to support themselves, women were expected to marry to secure a comfortable (or indeed any kind of) home; a situation that Wollstonecraft defined as 'legal prostitution'. Marriage further curtailed a woman's independence by giving her husband absolute control over her and their children (the 'absurd unit of a man and his wife', the coverture, which reduced women 'to a mere cipher, a nothing'[15]). Wollstonecraft thus called on men to 'generously snap our chains, and be content with rational fellowship instead of slavish obedience'.[16] The fact that she called on men's generosity to change the laws of the country, and that she made a fleeting reference to women's political representation has given rise to a debate on whether or not Wollstonecraft's *Vindication* included political rights for women.

It would be narrow-sighted to restrict Mary Wollstonecraft's contribution to human rights solely to the defence of women's rights: on the one hand, the vindication of the rights of women was, for Wollstonecraft, part and parcel of a wider-reaching social reform which was proposed at the time in the name of the rights of man and democracy; on the other, Wollstonecraft paid attention to many other kinds of hierarchies and forms of oppression and subordination. That Wollstonecraft intended her vindication of women's rights to be part of a wider project of social reform can be clearly concluded from the letter she wrote as a dedication of the second edition of her treatise on the rights of women to Talleyrand:

> It is then an affection for the whole human race that (...) leads me earnestly to wish to see woman placed in a station in which she would advance, instead of retarding, the progress of those glorious principles that give a substance to morality.[17]

The new relationship between the sexes that would result from respecting the rights of women and reforming their education, along the lines she was encouraging Talleyrand to consider (as an alternative to his proposal to the National Assembly[18]), was necessary for the progress of the whole human race. In her view, the oppressed condition of women corrupted not only women but the whole of the society, including men, who 'must, in some shape, act like a tyrant, and tyranny, in whatever part of society it rears its brazen front, will ever undermine morality'.[19]

---

[13] ibid, 270.
[14] ibid, 272.
[15] ibid, 267.
[16] ibid, 273.
[17] ibid, 81 (in the dedicatory letter to M Talleyrand-Périgord, late bishop of Autun).
[18] *Rapport sur l'instruction publique*, fait au nom du Comité de constitution (1791).
[19] Wollstonecraft (n 1) 84 (in the dedicatory letter to M Talleyrand-Périgord, late bishop of Autun).

Wollstonecraft's proposals for women's rights and improved education can be seen, then, as a necessary part of the Enlightenment's promise of emancipation. This was all too often neglected, downplayed or even denied by the Enlightenment's leading authorities. She placed that vindication in line with the Declaration of the Rights of Man; she had enthusiastically embraced the idea of natural rights that were not based on rank or tradition, but resulted from principles, from reason and from human nature. But she also paid attention to issues generally overlooked in writings on the rights of man: the material conditions of the poor and the working classes; the many forms in which rank and privilege infringed the liberty and property interests of those without power or representation; the suffering of children; and what today are called 'care and dependency issues'. Wollstonecraft also endorsed the theory of the social contract but wanted it to live up to its promises of emancipation from oppression ('the whole system of "representation" in this country is at present only a convenient label for despotism'[20]). Both of her *Vindications* described the material conditions in which most of the population lived as being a fundamental part of oppression. She argued that they could be clearly traced back to the legal and institutional arrangements which kept them in place, protecting rank, tradition and privilege at the expense of civic and political virtue:

> Security of property! Behold, in a few words, the definition of the English liberty ... But it is only the property of the rich that is secure; the man who lives by the sweat of his brow has no asylum from oppression ... when was the castle of the poor sacred?[21]

In her *Vindication of the Rights of Man* she criticised those who, like Burke, considered that poverty and social suffering were the result of men's vices, and accused the reform thinkers who attributed injustice to laws and institutions of unpatriotic folly. She went on to present a series of examples which showed the injustice resulting from laws that failed to protect those who had no political power: 'our penal laws punish with death the thief who steals a few pounds; but to take by violence, or trepan, a man, is no such heinous offence',[22] the game laws which 'are almost as oppressive to the peasantry as press-warrants to the mechanic',[23] 'the sweat of the laborious poor, squeezed out of them by unceasing taxation',[24] or the fact that 'a man of merit cannot rise in the church, the army, or navy, unless he has some interest in a borough'.[25] Poverty and unequal distribution of wealth and opportunities were not therefore dismissed as fate or as petty questions, irrelevant for the more elevated discussion on how a well-organised society should look. She strenuously opposed the idea that such problems could be addressed by the traditional resort to charity, as opposed to social transformation:

> ... true happiness arose from the friendship and intimacy which can only be enjoyed by equals; and that charity is not a condescending distribution of alms, but an intercourse of good offices and mutual benefits, founded on respect for justice and humanity.[26]

---

[20] ibid, 268.

[21] ibid, 20–21.

[22] She is referring here to 'impressments', colloquially known as the 'press gang', the practice of forcing men, generally sailors, to serve in the navy. Wollstonecraft (n 5) 21.

[23] ibid, 23.

[24] ibid, 28.

[25] ibid, 29.

[26] ibid, 15.

Wollstonecraft might be considered to have attempted a precarious balancing act between her sensitivity and her religion-inspired notion of virtue, on the one hand, and her rational demands for exposing and transforming the social institutions that resulted in social harm, on the other hand. She embraced the principle of universal benevolence preached by her admired Richard Price in *A Review of the Principal Questions in Morals* (1758), who thought that despite our deficiencies and weaknesses, the principle of benevolence should be 'cultivated to the outmost' to include the entire species. Wollstonecraft understood this to translate politically into a command to transcend the concern for one's own groups and communities, which she showed in various ways in the *Vindication of the Rights of Man*: through her work for the abolition of slavery; her defence of poor farmers against game laws; her support of the dissenters against civil and political disenfranchisement, of the victims of coerced enrolment in the Navy, and of the abused working classes. Furthermore, she espoused the ground-breaking notion of women's inter-class shared oppression in her last novel *Maria, or the Wrongs of Women*.

III. 'It is Justice, not Charity, that is Wanting in the World!'[27]

The scandal following the publication of *Memoirs of the Author of A Vindication of the Rights of Woman* (1798) by her grief-stricken widower, the philosopher William Godwin, shadowed Mary Wollstonecraft's ideas for over two centuries. For more than a century readers were shocked by her love affairs, illegitimate children and experimental union with Godwin, all of them taken as evidence of the depravation of women who explored revolutionary avenues. After the foundational nature of her work in modern feminism was acknowledged in the twentieth century, there has also been considerable uneasiness in talking about her life. Her suicide attempts, her despair and her submission to selfish and undeserving men seem at odds with the message of strength, independence and rationality conveyed in the *Vindication*.

Notwithstanding the difficulties in interpreting Wollstonecraft's legacy, it should be noted that her work and ideas were acknowledged and disseminated during her lifetime. She was part of the London-based radical groups and put forward some revolutionary reform proposals in a number of areas, including education, marriage, social relations, political representation, labour conditions and female employment. In February 1793 she wrote a plan of education for the Committee on Public Instruction in France, probably commissioned by Thomas Paine or Condorcet.[28] The restoration period that followed the French Revolution soon after her death swept aside almost all of these proposals and debates, and for a long time the role for women was again

---

[27] Wollstonecraft (n 1) 171.

[28] Todd suggests that it might have been Paine or Condorcet who commissioned the report to Wollstonecraft, since they were both members of the Constitution Committee of the failed Girondin Constitution: Todd (n 2) 221.

limited to domesticity and submission to fathers and husbands. Yet her ideas were packed into the debates on democracy and the unfulfilled promises of equality and freedom of the political Enlightenment, and when the time came for those ideas to rise again, Wollstonecraft's contribution re-emerged with them.

At first glance, Mary Wollstonecraft was an author of her time. Her work has been judged to fall short of current standards for women's autonomy, too tied to motherhood as their destiny (even though it was to be a new, politically meaning-ful and celebrated destiny); too ambiguous and thin on political participation and rights; and too grounded on her enduring Christian faith.[29] In her writings, the terms 'virtue', 'duty' and 'God' figure as prominently as 'equality' and 'freedom'. In her life and her novels there is also a disconcerting mixture of boldness and independence on the one hand, and emotional submission and self-pitied conformism on the other. Wollstonecraft had to pay for this first with her respectability and the white-washing attempts to present her more as a Romantic tragic figure than a pioneering revolution-ary, and later on with 'some strenuous efforts at feminist canonization',[30] which would hide away her private struggles and half of her literary production. And yet, these contradictions speak directly to the experiences of modern radical feminism:

> Feminism affirms women's point of view by revealing, criticizing, and explaining its impos-sibility. This is not a dialectical paradox. It is a methodological expression of women's situation, in which the struggle for consciousness is a struggle for world: for a sexuality, a history, a culture, a community, a form of power, an experience of the sacred.[31]

Her struggle for the world did yield a remarkable contribution to current ideas on human rights. Thanks to her, we have a more complex picture of the toils of the Enlightenment and the Liberal Revolutions. We have a glimpse of the dissenting and suppressed voices, which already at the time were warning against the incomplete-ness and the exclusions enshrined in the proposed arrangements, a real-time critique of what has become to be known as 'false universalism'. We have an antecedent of the idea of solidarity in her understanding of universal benevolence, which did not dissolve in abstract notions of Christian brotherhood or charity, but translated into the earnest fight against privilege of any kind as being incompatible with virtuous equality and social justice.

And remarkably, her 'disordered' claims for the rights of women can be interpreted as showing a pioneering understanding of rights as universal, indivisible, interdepend-ent and interrelated, as advocated by the Vienna Declaration in 1993, in an effort to dispel the many classifications and hierarchies among rights. In both *A Vindication of the Rights of Woman* and in her incomplete and fictionalised second part *The Wrongs of Woman*, Wollstonecraft makes demands for access to education, civil status, habeas corpus and political representation as the many faces of a single request for respect and dignity, for equality and public virtue.

---

[29] Although she spent all her adult life in the midst of groups of dissenters and non-believers, she did not change her religious affiliation.

[30] Tomalin (n 3) 314.

[31] C MacKinnon, 'Feminism, Marxism, Method, and the State: Toward Feminist Jurisprudence' (1983) 8:4 *Signs: Journal of Women in Culture and Society* 635, 637.

6

Henry Dunant

Paving the Way for Contemporary International Humanitarian Law

JOANA ABRISKETA URIARTE

Charity on the battlefield.[1]

I. Geneva, Algeria, Solferino: Compassion, Empathy, Indignation

Henry Dunant was born in Geneva on 8 May 1828. The date of his birth is celebrated as the World Red Cross and Red Crescent Day.[2] He came from a devout and charitable Calvinist family in which he acquired education and culture and a wide knowledge of the world. His household was not only religious, but also humanitarian and civic minded. His mother, Anne-Antoinette Colladon, whose brother was the celebrated physicist Daniel Colladon, was as a social activist who worked with sick and poor people and exerted a great influence over him. His ancestors were French, coming from Berry. His mother's family had abandoned Bourges after the Counter-Reformation. His father, Jean-Jacques Dunant, was a prosperous businessman as well as a magistrate in the Geneva Court of Wards.[3] Like his wife, he was a social activist who helped released prisoners and orphans. All the education he received was oriented to helping others.

[1] H Dunant, *L'Avenir Sanglant* (Geneva, Éditions Zoe, 1994) 7.
[2] ICRC, 'Henry Dunant (1828–1910)', available at www.icrc.org/eng/resources/documents/misc/57jnvq.htm.
[3] P Boissier, *Henry Dunant* (Geneva, Henry Dunant Institute, 1974) 5.

After leaving school, Dunant spent some time in a bank learning the business. When he was 27 years old, under the influence of a movement known as the 'Awakening', and moved by an intense personal faith, he became a member of the Young Men's Christian Association. This was founded in 1844 with the aim of promoting Christian ideals amongst the young. He received his friends in his family house, he created international projects and developed a network of contacts abroad.[4] He travelled and exchanged letters with similar groups in England, France, Germany, Holland and the United States. Five years later, Dunant entered the business world as the manager of the Compagnie Genevoise des Colonies de Sétif in North Africa and Sicily.[5]

In 1853, after his period of apprenticeship as a businessman, Dunant visited Algeria, Tunisia and Sicily. Fascinated and inspired, he wrote the book *Notice sur la Régence de Tunis*.[6] He began to study Islam, and, unlike most Christians of his time, approached this religion with the utmost respect. He took lessons in Arabic and practised the difficult art of Arabic calligraphy. He developed a great affection for the people of North Africa, and when he undertook to set up his business in Algeria not far from the large agricultural area of Mons-Djémila, he vowed to himself that on his property he would assure that Algerian workers were happy and well paid.[7]

In 1856, Dunant founded the financial and industrial company of the windmills of Mons-Djemila in Saint-Arganud (Algeria). His aim was to build a hydraulic windmill in order to grind cereals and trade them in the market of Sétif. This new company met all the conditions to become a successful business: the location, the capital and the equipment. However, the Algerian authorities denied the authorisation he needed for the land on which he would grow the wheat.[8] As the land concession was essential, he decided to approach the French Emperor Napoleon III in order to obtain the permission he needed to establish the windmills. At the time, the Emperor was taking up the cause of Italian independence and commanding the Franco-Sardinian troops fighting the Austrians who had occupied Northern Italy since the Congress of Vienna (1814–1815). It was a decisive battle in the struggle for Italian unity. The Franco-Sardinian armies were totally overwhelmed and Dunant, on his own initiative, organised humanitarian assistance and medical services for them. This was how he came to be present at the end of the battle of Solferino, in Lombardy (24 June 1859). Not only was he present and trying to alleviate the suffering of the wounded, he dedicated the following two years of his life to writing the book *Une mémoire de Solférino* (*A Memory of Solferino*)[9] Through this work, he inspired the codification of the contemporary international humanitarian principles and norms.

---

[4] O Goinard, 'Henry Dunant', at www.memoireafriquedunord.net/biog/biog06_dunant.htm.

[5] Boissier (n 3) 6.

[6] H Dunant, *Notice sur la Régence de Tunis* (Geneva, Imprimerie de Jules Gme Fick, 1858).

[7] Boissier (n 3) 6. In 1858 he published his first book, *Notice sur la Régence de Tunis* (*An Account of the Regency in Tunis*), made up for the most part of travel observations but containing a remarkable chapter, a long one, which he published separately in 1863, entitled *L'Esclavage chez les musulmans et aux États-Unis d'Amérique* (*Slavery among the Mohammedans and in the United States of America*).

[8] Boissier (n 3) 7.

[9] H Dunant, *Un Souvenir de Sólferino* (Geneva, Comité international de la Croix-Rouge, 2009 (reproduction textuelle de l'édition originale, Genève, 1862)).

Between 1874 and 1886 Dunant led a solitary existence in Stuttgart, Rome, Corfu, Basilea and Karlsruhe. He ended up in the Swiss village of Heiden, overlooking Lake Constance, where he fell ill. Financial difficulties led him into poverty. His inability to settle all his debts was something which weighed heavily on him. His health was deplorable, he faced critical privations and he suffered eczema on his right hand which inflicted such pain that he could not write. He lost his faith and never recovered it in later life. He found refuge in the local hospice. He was discovered in 1895 by a journalist, Georg Baumberger, who wrote an article about him which, within a few days, was reprinted in the press throughout Europe. In 1901, he received the Nobel Peace Prize along with the French peacemaker Frederic Passy.

Although Dunant was born into a wealthy home, he died in a hospice on 30 October 1910, in the year that saw the passing away of two great figures, Florence Nightingale and Leo Tolstoy, whom he admired.[10] Dunant's life was one of great extremes, moving from international fame to total obscurity, success in business to bankruptcy. In old age he was virtually exiled from the Genevan society in which he had once been lauded, and he died alone and mostly forgotten.[11] Dunant had not spent any of the prize monies he had received. He bequeathed some legacies to those who had cared for him in the village hospital, endowed a 'free bed' that was to be available to the sick among the poorest people in the village, and left the remainder to philanthropic enterprises in Norway and Switzerland.[12] Upon his death, there was no funeral ceremony, no mourners, no cortege. In accordance with his wishes he was carried to his grave 'like a dog'.[13] He was buried in the cemetery of Sihfeld, in Zurich.

II. The Founding of Contemporary International Humanitarian Law

Henry Dunant's experience at Solferino was critical in giving effect to the main principle of the International Committee of the Red Cross and international humanitarian law: to assist all those in need, whatever side they are on, simply because they are wounded and sick due to the consequences of war. This is the seed of international humanitarian law because it is from this that the principle is born of the distinction between combatants and non-combatants (civilian population and combatants who are no longer taking part in hostilities).

In 1859, the region of Lombardy was devastated by war. The Holy Alliance had come to an end.[14] Several battles had taken place in Italy (Montebello, Palestro and Magenta). The most decisive of these, the bloodiest in Europe since Waterloo, broke

---

[10] Boissier (n 3) 5.
[11] The Nobel Prize, 'Henry Dunant – Biographical', at www.nobelprize.org/prizes/peace/1901/dunant/biographical/.
[12] ibid.
[13] ibid.
[14] L Boissier, 'The Present Portent of Henry Dunant's Message' (1959) XII(1) *Revue Internationale de la Croix-Rouge* 4.

out on 24 June 1859 – the battle of Solferino. It took place in northern Italy between Austro-Hungarian armies on one side and the Franco-Sardinian Alliance on the other. Dunant was not far away and could hear the gunfire. He received the greatest shock of his life.[15] In 10–15 hours of fighting, approximately 5,000 soldiers were killed, more than 11,000 were captured or missing and over 22,000 were wounded.[16] When night fell, he entered the town of Castiglione, where he found a large number of wounded from the nearby battlefield. He went through the town and climbed the road leading to the main church, the Chiesa Maggiore. The church was filled with more than 500 wounded troops, some lying inert, some moaning, others screaming with pain.[17] Dunant asked the local women to help, but they were reluctant to take care of the French soldiers because they feared the Austrians would return in force and punish them for having assisted the enemy troops. He persuaded them by saying that suffering was the same for all people by claiming '*Tutti fratelli*'.[18] This would be the prelude of the principles of universality, neutrality and impartiality of the International Committee of the Red Cross.

For the thousands of wounded in Castiglione, Dunant found that there were only six French army doctors available. The disproportion between the number of troops and the medical services available was due to the fact that the latter were understaffed. Soldiers were supposed to be in a fit state exclusively to fight. As the medical services of the Franco-Sardinian armies were totally overwhelmed, Dunant decided to alleviate the suffering by organising different types of assistance. He offered water to the victims to assuage their thirst; he cleaned their wounds and changed their dressings; and he bought clothes, herbal infusions and fruit from the nearby city of Brescia.[19]

Therefore, the business aims of the trip to Solferino were put aside. He returned to Geneva on 11 July 1859, the day on which the Italian campaign ended. He neglected his own affairs, took a leave of his business interests for three years, and placed in jeopardy the commercial interests which had been entrusted to him.[20] He wrote *Un Souvenir de Solférino* (*A Memory of Solferino*), which, as detailed below, led to the creation of the International Committee for Relief to the Wounded, the future International Committee of the Red Cross.

A Memory of Solferino was published at the author's expense in Geneva, in October 1862. The book was an open letter to world leaders and opinion makers. A total of 1,600 copies were printed and on the title page was written: 'Not to be sold'. Dunant sent it to sovereigns and statesmen, renowned military commanders, doctors, writers and philanthropists. It had an immediate impact. Two further editions were printed in the months that followed and were sold to the public, with translations appearing in English, Dutch, Italian, Swedish, Russian, Spanish and German. What mattered, apart from the number of readers, was the status of the readership: messages of

---

[15] Boissier (n 3) 7.

[16] C Emmanuelli, *International Humanitarian Law* (Montréal, Éditions Yvon Blais, 2009) 143–68.

[17] Boissier (n 3) 7.

[18] ibid, 8.

[19] F Bugnion, *The International Committee of the Red Cross and the Protection of War Victims* (Geneva and Macmillan, ICRC and Oxford, 2003) 3.

[20] F Siordet, 'The Centenary of the Red Cross Idea: The Lesson of Solferino' (1959) XII(3) *Revue Internationale de la Croix-Rouge* 42.

support reached Dunant in their hundreds from influential people throughout Europe. Dunant had succeeded in creating a wave of enthusiasm in favour of the establishment of societies for the relief of the wounded in different countries of Europe. *A Memory of Solferino* was a book which shook contemporary society.[21]

The first part of the book recounted the horrors of war through a vivid description of scenes of pain and distress of the wounded and dead soldiers. The second part contained three proposals. The first one outlined the possibility, in time of peace, to form relief societies for the purpose of giving care to the wounded in wartime by zealous, devoted and thoroughly qualified volunteers.[22] The relief societies would rely on private support. So as to be able to act in good time, the societies would be set up on a permanent basis. When war broke out, the societies would send 'qualified volunteers' to follow the armies and place themselves at the disposal of the military commanders whenever they were needed. They would care for the wounded of all sides without distinction. Second, to be able to work safely and effectively, the volunteers had to be recognisable as such. They therefore had to be given a distinctive sign: '... a badge, uniform or armlet might usefully be adopted, so that the bearers of such distinctive and universally adopted insignia would be given due recognition'.[23] All of the voluntary personnel had to be shielded from the hostilities.[24] Finally, Dunant suggested the formulation of an international principle, sanctioned by a convention, which might constitute the basis for societies for the relief of the wounded in the different European countries.

Dunant sent the book to Gustave Moynier, a jurist by profession and the chairman of a local charity called the Geneva Public Welfare Society. Moynier invited him to a special meeting of the charity. Dunant told the 14 people who attended that he wanted to form an organisation that would send volunteer nurses to the battlefield. He also wanted to improve the methods of transporting the wounded and the care received in military hospitals. The meeting gave rise to the International Committee for the Relief of Wounded in the event of War. Guillaume Dufour became the president, while Henry Dunant and the two doctors Thomas Maunoir and Louis Appia agreed to serve as board members. This institution eventually became the International Committee of the Red Cross.[25]

In October 1863, the five men organised an international conference of 13 nations in Geneva to discuss the possibility of making warfare more 'humane'. It dealt with the 'gap between the peacetime complement of medical units and the needs in times of war that the Geneva Committee was seeking to fill'.[26] The conference laid the foundations for relief societies. Subsequently, several national committees were formed in numerous states, including Württemberg, Oldenburg, Belgium, Prussia, Denmark, France,

[21] Bugnion (n 19) 5–6.
[22] H Dunant, *Un Souvenir de Solferino* (Geneva, Imprimerie Jules-Guillaume Fick, 1862. English version by the American Red Cross, 1939 & 1959, reprinted by the ICRC in 1994) 115.
[23] ibid, 64.
[24] Bugnion (n 19) 13.
[25] It was at its meeting on 20 December 1875 that the Committee adopted the name 'International Committee of the Red Cross'.
[26] P Boissier, *History of the International Committee of the Red Cross: From Solferino to Tsushima*, (Geneva, Henry Dunant Institute, 1985) 74–75.

Italy and Spain. At the end of the conference, the representatives signed the Geneva Convention for the Amelioration of the Condition of the Wounded in Armies in the Field of 22 August 1864. The Convention, which was ratified by 12 states, became a landmark, first, because it was the first multilateral treaty concluded in time of peace to govern future armed conflicts between the contracting parties, and second, because it marked the beginning of international humanitarian law. The Geneva Convention of 1864 was revised in 1906, 1929 and 1949, when it became the Geneva Convention I for the Amelioration of the Condition of the Wounded and Sick in Armed Forces in the Field.

Moreover, the provisions of the Geneva Convention of 1864 were extended to the wounded, sick and shipwrecked at sea by the Hague Convention III of 1899. Subsequently, the provisions for that Hague Convention were revised in 1907. In 1949 both Hague Conventions were replaced by Geneva Convention II for the Amelioration of the Condition of the Wounded, Sick and Shipwrecked Members of Armed Forces at Sea. In the meantime, other Hague Conventions adopted in 1899 and 1907 identified the groups of combatants who would be entitled, when captured, to become prisoners of war. The relevant provisions of these Conventions were supplemented by a Geneva Convention of 1929, and complemented in 1949 by Geneva Convention III relative to the Treatment of Prisoners of War. Finally, the Geneva Convention IV relative to the Protection of Civilian Persons in Times of War was adopted to deal with the protection of civilians.[27]

With the signing of the Geneva Convention for the Amelioration of the Condition of the Wounded in Armies in the Field of 22 August 1864 a new branch of international law had come about. The Convention provided for the neutrality of ambulances and military hospitals, the non-belligerent status of persons who would aid the wounded and sick soldiers of any nationality, the return of prisoners to their country if they were incapable of serving and the adoption of a white flag with a red cross for use on hospitals, ambulances and evacuation centres.

Dunant acted as the secretary of the International Committee of the Red Cross. He was received by heads of state, kings and princes of the European courts. However, as a result of the scandal which his bankruptcy caused in Geneva, he resigned from his post. On 8 September 1867 the Committee decided to accept his resignation not only as secretary but also as a member of the organisation. Dunant went to Paris, where he was reduced to sleeping on public benches.

During the Franco-Prussian War of 1870, he visited and comforted the wounded brought to Paris and introduced the wearing of a badge so that the dead could be identified. When peace returned, Dunant travelled to London, where he endeavoured to organise a diplomatic conference on the problem of prisoners of war. While the Russian Czar encouraged him, England was hostile to the plan.[28] Almost 30 years later, in 1899 and again in 1907 this initiative would lead to the Hague Conventions,

---

[27] Emmanuelli (n 16).
[28] ICRC (n 2).

which identified the groups of combatants who were entitled when captured to the status of prisoners of war.

Although Dunant's major humanitarian concerns were centred on the treatment of victims of war, he was also sensitive to the horrors of slave trade. In 1875, an international congress for the 'complete and final abolition of the traffic in Negroes and the slave trade' opened in London on 1 February 1875, on Dunant's initiative.

For the next 20 years, from 1875 to 1895, Dunant disappeared into solitude. After brief stays in various places, he settled down in Heiden, a small Swiss village. A village teacher named Wilhelm Sonderegger found him in 1890 and informed the world that Dunant was alive, but the world took little note. As he was ill, he was moved in 1892 to the hospice at Heiden, where he spent the remaining 18 years of his life. Not, however, as an unknown. In 1895 when he was once more rediscovered, the world heaped prizes and awards upon him. In 1901 the Nobel Peace Prize was awarded by the Norwegian Parliament to him and to the pacifist Frédéric Passy. Despite the prizes and the honours, Dunant did not move from Room 12 in the Hospice of Heiden. He died on 30 October 1910.

III. A Humanitarian Response to the Suffering of the Soldiers

Henry Dunant is closely associated with the International Committee of the Red Cross. However, the texts he left show the modernity and the force of his thoughts beyond this specific institutional contribution. A *Memory of Solferino* planted the seed of one of the most generous ideas known in the recent history of humanity. He went to the heart of the matter: the suffering of a wounded soldier should be alleviated and this principle should be based on an international consensus. The three main contributions of the book illustrate his sensitivity to the suffering during war and his capacity to formulate ambitious solutions: (i) he proposed to establish relief societies in as many countries as possible in order to be prepared for times of war; (ii) he suggested that relief societies had to be given international protection by a distinctive and uniform flag – which became the red cross on a white field; and (iii) he advanced the idea that these proposals should be agreed as an international principle in a convention.

Dunant, without official support, succeeded in infusing his thoughts with a unique energy. The passage of time amplifies the modernity of his message. Now, 150 years later, the International Red Cross and Red Crescent Movement, comprising the International Committee of the Red Cross, the International Federation of Red Cross and Red Crescent Societies and national societies, boasts 100 million workers and volunteers in more than 186 countries and territories, offering assistance in times of peace, conflict and natural disasters and promoting the application of international humanitarian law.

Dunant's legacy has led to a classification in the humanitarian field: the term 'Dunantist' refers to the group of humanitarian organisations and practitioners who follow the traditional approach to humanitarianism, based on four fundamental principles: humanity, neutrality, impartiality and independence.[29] Whereas Dunantist organisations recognise the humanitarian principles and see themselves acting independently from politics, Wilsonian organisations accept that they work in the interest of their country and/or donors[30] At the root of this understanding, irreconcilable differences are evident, between, on the one hand, the core aims and principles of international humanitarian law, and the testimony of the violations of human rights on the other; the impartial delivery of aid of the former versus the strategic and conditional aid of the latter.[31]

Together with the humanitarian dimension, the ICRC has also become a unique and relevant actor for human rights during the past 130 years. It is in essence a private, non-governmental organisation, although it has received formal status and recognition in public international law.[32] Furthermore, although the ICRC has not been considered as a human rights actor – it is identified as a charitable and humanitarian organisation concerned about international humanitarian law – it has contributed to the promotion of international human rights law. These two branches of international law – international humanitarian law and international human rights law – mutually reinforce, and even overlap through the idea of the 'core' concepts of human rights. In fact, the blurring of humanitarian and human rights agendas, and the increasing attacks on the civilian population and on humanitarian personnel suggest a reading of Dunant's vision time and time again, inspired by the very clear and contemporary aim of helping the victims of war.

---

[29] A Stoddard, 'Humanitarian NGOs: Challenges and Trends' (2003) 12 *Humanitarian Policy Group*, July 2003, available at www.files.ethz.ch/isn/90825/hpgbrief_12.pdf.

[30] J Goodhand, 'Contested Boundaries: NGOs and Civil-Military Relations in Afghanistan' (2013) 32(3) *Central Asian Survey* 287.

[31] M Ferreiro, 'Blurring of Lines in Complex Emergencies: Consequences for the Humanitarian Community' (2012) *The Journal of Humanitarian Assistance*, sites.tufts.edu/jha/archives/1625.

[32] D Forsythe, 'Human Rights and the International Committee of the Red Cross' (1990) 12 *Human Rights Quarterly* 265.

7

Mahatma Gandhi

Advocate of Duty, Pioneer of Human Rights

GEORGE ULRICH

> I learned from my illiterate but wise mother that all rights to be deserved and preserved came from duty well done. Thus the very right to live accrues to us only when we do the duty of citizenship of the world. From this one fundamental statement, perhaps it is easy enough to define the duties of Man and Woman and correlate every right to some corresponding duty to be first performed. Every other right can be shown to be a usurpation hardly worth fighting for.[1]

Like many of my generation and generations before me, I was deeply inspired by Mahatma Gandhi while coming of age. At the time I did not associate his cause with human rights, but viewed in perspective, Gandhi's humble, fervent commitment to social justice and the dignity of the human person played an important role in preparing the ground for the global human rights movement in the second half of the twentieth century. From his time as a campaigner against racial discrimination in South Africa to his emergence as leader of the Indian national independence movement and mobiliser of the masses of underprivileged poor, Gandhi's work resonates strongly with human rights. Yet he always framed his endeavours principally as a moral commitment and thus first and foremost as a commitment to serving others.

While one of the great human rights champions of our time, Gandhi was sceptical of, or at least hesitant about, the very concept of human rights. This is reflected in the quotation selected as caption for this short article, which is his response to

---

[1] M Gandhi, 'Letter to the Director General of UNESCO' in UNESCO (ed), *Human Rights Comments and Interpretations* (New York, Columbia University Press, 1949) 18. See also *The UNESCO Courier* vol II, no 9, October 1949, 5.

a UNESCO inquiry in 1947 about the relevance and utility of drafting a universal declaration of human rights. Seventy years later, as we celebrate another anniversary of the Universal Declaration of Human Rights (UDHR), and at a historical juncture when the value system associated with human rights has once again come under stress, there are important contemporary lessons to be learned from this voice from another era.

I. Life and Times

Mohandas Gandhi was born on 2 October 1869 to a high-ranking civil servant father and a deeply religious mother in Porbandar, the capital of a small principality in western India in what is now Gujarat State. Aiming to follow in his father's footsteps as a civil servant, Mohandas pursued legal studies and at the age of 19 was given the opportunity to study law at University College London in England. For him, the experience of living abroad marked the beginning of rediscovering and embracing his Hindu identity. Upon completing his studies, he encountered difficulty in finding employment in India and instead accepted a position in South Africa, which became his adopted home for more than two decades. This was a deeply formative period in which the initially shy and withdrawn young lawyer emerged as a prominent public figure and campaigner for social justice.

When returning to India in 1915, at the height of First World War, Gandhi was greeted with great expectations. He soon rose to prominence as leader of the Indian national independence movement, alongside leaders of the Indian National Congress and representatives of India's other main religious and ethnic communities. Travelling extensively throughout the subcontinent, Gandhi fostered a deep affinity with the Indian people, the impoverished masses, who in turn viewed him as a source of natural authority. The designation Mahatma (Great Soul) reflects this esteem in which he was (almost) universally held.

Over the course of the following three decades, Gandhi led repeated campaigns against the British rulers and at the same time took action to curb trends towards division and violence within the ranks of his own people. His name became inextricably linked to a strategy of non-violent civil disobedience. This proved remarkably effective as it resonated strongly not only with the local population but also with the people of Great Britain and with a global audience, who through the meek resistance and moral supremacy of a loincloth-clad sage were confronted with the intrinsic violence of colonial rule.

Gandhi put his own life at stake on several occasions by embarking on protracted fasts as penance for violence perpetrated by his followers or to force a détente, if not genuine reconciliation, between the conflicting populations of the subcontinent. This endeavour was ultimately unsuccessful, as witnessed most glaringly by the partition of India at independence. In January 1948, less than half a year after independence, Gandhi's life ended poignantly at the hands of a Hindu nationalist seeking a more aggressive approach to the assertion of narrowly-defined communal interests.

II. Human Rights Achievements

The theme that runs as a red thread through Gandhi's lifelong social and political engagements, linking them closely to human rights, is his spontaneous sense of indignation at the violation of human dignity. He encountered this in the context of colonialism, which rendered seemingly perennial patterns of human degradation all the more pernicious. Gandhi's quest for social justice was thus always linked with a struggle against colonial rule, and a reconstruction of the most salient human rights dimensions of this struggle will help us recognise how much the contemporary human rights movement owes to the historical shifts set in motion during the first half of the twentieth century with 'third world' leaders like Gandhi as the primary catalysts. The following focuses on five main aspects of Gandhi's life endeavours, which in different ways are foundational to contemporary human rights – or ought to be recognised as such.

A. The Fight against Racial Discrimination

Gandhi's first cause with a strong human rights resonance was his fight against racial discrimination. According to legend, this began with a visceral reaction to being personally exposed to discriminatory and degrading treatment. On a journey from Durban to Pretoria he was forcibly removed from a first class train compartment on account of his racial identity, physically assaulted by a white stagecoach driver for refusing to yield his space, and barred access to hotels reserved 'for Europeans only'.[2] These were formative experiences which led Gandhi, in his capacity as lawyer, to assume the role as rights advocate and political leader of the South Asian community in the province of Natal. He was instrumental in establishing the Natal Indian Congress in 1894 and the British Indian Association in 1903. A pivotal cause was the mobilisation of a decade-long opposition to legislation adopted in Transvaal in 1907, which required people of Asian descent to carry a registration certificate with them at all times. Gandhi openly encouraged his fellow Indians to refuse to register and led those who had done so to make a public display of burning their identity cards.

This was the context in which Gandhi first developed his signature strategy of non-violent civil disobedience that has since become a source of inspiration for civil rights movements worldwide. In order to avoid associations with the misleading notion of 'passive resistance', Gandhi coined the phrase *Satyagraha* to underscore the dynamic, and indeed extremely demanding nature of his approach to social

---

[2] See BR Nanda, 'Encyclopædia Britannica entry on Mahatma Gandhi', available at www.britannica.com/biography/Mahatma-Gandhi. See also South Africa History Online, 'Mohandas Karamchand Gandhi' www.sahistory.org.za/people/mohandas-karamchand-gandhi. Much of the present summary of Gandhi's life and engagements is based on these sources. See also O Lacombe, 'Mahatma Gandhi: Landmarks in an Extraordinary Life' in UNESCO, *Commemorating 125th Anniversary of the Birth of Mahatma Gandhi* (Paris, UNESCO, 1995).

activism. Directly translated, *Satyagraha* means 'truth force' and connotes an aspect of '"natural right", a right granted by nature and the universe that should not be impeded on by man. In practice, Satyagraha was a focused and forceful nonviolent resistance to a particular injustice'.[3] The essential premise of Satyagraha is that a just end never justifies unjust means. The just demand to be treated with dignity, in Gandhi's view, required a rigorous display of moral integrity and consideration of the interests and wellbeing of the opponent. It was on this account that he more than once called off mass movements, even when in a position of strength vis-à-vis the adversary, and undertook personal penance in the form of protracted fasts when violence erupted among his followers.

Satyagraha is a spontaneous assertion of human dignity in the face of injustice and in this sense the antithesis to discriminatory conduct. In the contemporary human rights framework, the principle of non-discrimination is foundational, as it conditions the application of all other rights. This is notably reflected in the non-discrimination provisions in Article 2 of both the International Covenant on Economic, Social and Cultural Rights (ICESCR) and the International Covenant on Civil and Political Rights (ICCPR), which together with the UDHR constitute the Universal Bill of Rights. Standards against discrimination are further elaborated in the Convention for the Elimination of All Forms of Racial Discrimination (ICERD) and the Convention for the Elimination of All Forms of Discrimination against Women (CEDAW) as well as in numerous regional human rights instruments (eg the European Convention on Human Rights (ECHR) Article 14, the African Charter on Human and Peoples' Rights (ACHPR) Article 2 and the American Convention on Human Rights (ACHR) Article 1).

Reaching far beyond its legal ramifications, the principle of non-discrimination has in recent decades emerged as an (almost) incontrovertible global policy standard that is applied to multiple identity parameters – from race and gender to language, religion, political or other opinion, national or social origin, sexual orientation, age, disability, and others. It is, however, relevant to recall that the societal discourse of the late nineteenth and early twentieth century was replete with pseudo-scientific notions of racial supremacy, eugenics, fear of racial contamination, etc. In Gandhi's lifetime, such beliefs had not yet been effectively discredited, and while he pioneered opposition to discrimination, it appears by recent accounts that he did not fully extend his claim to equal treatment to black South Africans.[4] However, he set a standard for subsequent anti-apartheid campaigns and for the African American civil rights movement in the second half of the twentieth century, and it is telling that he was remembered and honoured by the Republic of South Africa in 1994, immediately following the end of the Apartheid regime.

---

[3] South Africa History Online, 'Mohandas Karamchand Gandhi'.

[4] Questions about Gandhi's legacy in this regard have been raised notably by A Desai and G Vahed, *The South African Gandhi: Stretcher-Bearer of Empire* (Stanford, Stanford University Press, 2015). See also S Biswas, 'Was Mahatma Gandhi a Racist?' BBC News (Delhi, 17 September 2015), available at www.bbc.com/news/world-asia-india-34265882.

B. The Struggle for National Independence

The second, and undoubtedly most important human rights campaign of Gandhi's career was the struggle for independence from colonial rule. This motivated his return to India in 1915 and remained a guiding objective for the remainder of his life. Over the course of the following three decades, Gandhi spearheaded numerous non-violent mass campaigns against British rule. He was repeatedly imprisoned, but this only reinforced his moral authority as he came to be seen as father (Bapu) of the nation. Alongside his intimate relation with the repressed masses, throughout his political career Gandhi was continually engaged in complex negotiations with more conventional political leaders representing India's many religious constituencies and political factions. He played a central role in reviving the Indian National Congress in the early 1920s and maintained close relations with leaders of the Muslim and Sikh communities, among others.

Three major campaigns were organised, respectively, from 1920–22, 1930–34, and 1940–42. All were conducted in conformity with the Satyagraha concept of non-violent civil disobedience. The immediate trigger of each campaign was a particular, and particularly degrading, aspect of colonial rule, including: sedition laws which empowered the British authorities to imprison dissidents without trial; police brutality in reaction to peaceful demonstrations; and salt taxes which targeted an essential commodity and disproportionately burdened the poor. Beyond the immediate object of protest, however, the campaigns always also involved an emphasis on asserting a right to self-determination, which for Gandhi was fundamentally a matter of asserting human dignity. National independence was symbolically proclaimed by the Indian National Congress in December 1929 and was finally attained in 1947, shortly after the end of the Second World War, however at the price of partition of the subcontinent. This marked the beginning of a new epoch in world history, the epoch of decolonisation. Within the human rights framework, the legacy of anti-colonial struggles crystallised in the form of a right to self-determination, which is recognised in Article 1 of both the ICESCR and ICCPR, thus figuring as a precondition for the realisation and protection of all other human rights.

C. Communal Outreach

A hugely important corollary of the pursuit of national independence had to do with negotiating inter-faith, communal relations in the diverse and multifaceted South Asian subcontinent. As witnessed in other multi-ethnic societies being released from the pressure of an externally imposed central authority, India was confronted with deep and acrimonious ethnic and religious divisions both in the protracted struggle against colonial rule and in the immediate aftermath of independence. Gandhi was highly sensitive to such latent and increasingly overt hostilities and repeatedly made a public display of reaching out to other communities. To win trust and appease fears of unequal treatment, he advocated a disproportionate political representation for Muslim community leaders, at one point established his political base in a Muslim dominated district, and towards the end of his life, on the eve of independence, embarked on a fast to the death in order to halt inter-ethnic conflict. Such gestures were fully in line with his lifelong passion for inter-faith dialogue premised on mutual respect, but they were also strategically opportune, as the rising tensions between ethnic and religious communities posed the greatest threat to effective Indian self-rule and provided the colonialists with an excuse to delay the transfer of authority.

In the end, Gandhi came to view the partition of India as the greatest failure of his life endeavours. The breakup of the empire immediately led to a vast displacement of entire communities and was accompanied by intense suffering and continued hostility. This cast an ominous shadow over the achievement of national independence. Yet, precisely because of the tragic consequences of failing to reconcile the divided subcontinent, it is clear in retrospect that Gandhi's emphasis on outreach, reciprocal perspective taking, and mutual understanding and respect was prescient and stands out for posterity as a quintessential expression of an ethos of universal human rights.

D. Stance against Caste Discrimination

A fourth dominant theme of Gandhi's life which emphatically reflects his affirmation of universal human dignity, was his solidarity with the lowest strata of society, notably the 'untouchable' Dalit. This placed him in stark opposition to a deeply rooted aspect of Hindu culture, the caste system. In characteristic fashion, Gandhi manifested his protest against this ideology of unequal human worth by personally cleaning toilets and undertaking other forms of menial labour deemed unfitting for a person of his caste and social stature. This was in turn leveraged into a political cause. At one point as he started to fast Gandhi passionately confessed before members of the press:

> My ambition is to represent and identify myself with, as far as possible, the lowest strata of untouchables, ... for they have indeed drunk deep of the poisoned cup ... if they are ever to rise, it will not be by reservation of seats but will be by the strenuous work of Hindu reformers. ... What I want, and what I should delight in dying for, is the eradication of untouchability root and branch.[5]

Gandhi's principled stance in this regard reads as an emphatic affirmation of Article 1 of the UDHR, which states that 'All human beings are born free and equal in dignity and rights'. Viewed in a historical perspective, this foundational tenet of the universal human rights system is by no means to be taken for granted, as many traditional cosmologies assign differential worth to different categories of human persons. The concept of dignity, accordingly, is often understood not as an absolute quality pertaining to all human persons but rather as a relative quality that comes in degrees and underpins hierarchical social relations. The caste system is an extreme expression of this manner of thinking. It has been a point of contention in recent discourse whether caste should be understood as a form of racism or something entirely different, but be this as it may, the very concept of caste, and in particular the notion of untouchability,

---

[5] S Wolpert, *Gandhi's Passion: The Life and Legacy of Mahatma Gandhi* (Oxford, Oxford University Press, 2001) 167.

is in blatant contradiction of Article 1 UDHR. Gandhi placed himself firmly on the side of human rights and in so doing projected a brave vision for modern independent India.

E. The Campaign against Poverty

A fifth main theme of Gandhi's career, which is intrinsically linked with human rights but not always recognised as such, was his devotion to the impoverished masses. Gandhi viewed poverty in all its manifestations and consequences as a violation of human dignity and undertook both in his personal life and through sustained political actions to defy this. His somewhat idiosyncratic campaign to revive traditional crafts was motivated by economic considerations, based on the idea that a greater degree of economic self-sufficiency would contribute to securing the autonomy and functionality of independent India while alleviating the poverty of the masses. But his relentless insistence on devoting hours each day to the practice of spinning, and his reduction of garment to a simple loincloth, was also a way of demonstrating solidarity with and respect for the poor. By actively and visibly sharing their plight, he modelled the very sense of universal dignity that he aimed to boost.

This aspect of Gandhi's life and being is readily understood as the expression of a religious calling – which undoubtedly it was. But for Gandhi, the voluntary embrace of poverty, abstinence from sensual pleasure and various forms of self-mortification, while familiar religious idioms, were leveraged in pursuit of social justice. Like other human rights themes examined in the present context, large-scale poverty was and still remains a systemic feature of modern development and a by-product of colonial subjugation and exploitation. The resolve to address this within a framework of internationally recognised economic, social and cultural rights is a human rights agenda that was not clearly defined in Gandhi's day and age, but it was prefigured by his actions and personal demeanour.

III. Heritage: Contemporary Lessons

Gandhi's legacy is as complex as it is profound and is claimed by countless factions representing widely divergent visions for the development of modern society. The aim of the present brief exposition has been to highlight the human rights dimension of his lifelong quest for social justice. This, as we have seen, was remarkable, even if during Gandhi's lifetime the idiom of human rights had not yet attained prominence in international relations and his own interpretation of the issues at stake tended to be articulated in different terms. Normative guideposts for Gandhi were the anti-colonial political struggle, the Satyagraha ideal of non-violent resistance, and his inexorable emphasis on duty and moral perfection. Each of these idioms is distinct from the present-day concept of human rights yet arguably compatible with it. In taking stock of what Gandhi's legacy means to *us*, the inhabitants of a different era, my intuition is that there are important lessons to be learned from Gandhi's own normative bearings and from the inherent friction that from time to time surfaces between his thinking and the emerging framework of international human rights.

A. Historical Underpinnings

An interesting initial observation emerging from this review of Gandhi's legacy in relation to human rights is that the primary themes tend to cluster consistently around issues addressed in the Preface and opening articles of contemporary human rights instruments, such as Article 1 of the UDHR and Articles 1 and 2 of the ICESCR and ICCPR. This, one might argue, reflects his influential role in laying a foundation for the post-Second World War normative order. In this respect his message to posterity can be seen as a baton – or perhaps better, an unpolished gem – handed over to the Commission on Human Rights, which at the very moment of his untimely death in January 1948 was engaged in drafting the UDHR.

Viewed at a distance of some 70 years, it is tremendously important that this legacy was forged by a pioneer of the anti-colonial movement. In an era when the very idea of universal human rights is often (mistakenly) associated with distinctly European values and geopolitical interests, it is instructive to be reminded that principal drivers of the nascent human rights regime were not only non-Western but in fact ardent advocates of the values and interests of the Global South. Coming at the same point from a different angle, the UDHR and subsequent human rights treaties are commonly understood to manifest a resounding 'never again' in response to the atrocities of Second World War, which to a large extent were perpetrated on European territory. What is less commonly recognised, is that they project an equally emphatic repudiation of the subjugation of a large proportion of the world's population in the colonial era. This complementary historical perspective speaks to the question of whose experience counts and whose experience is reflected in the international normative framework. It urgently needs to be recaptured in a contemporary context whenever doubts are being raised about the geopolitical relevance of human rights. Elements of such a perspective are reflected in Christof Heyns' 'struggle approach to human rights', if only in embryonic form.[6] It similarly informs the seminal research undertaken by a new generation of human rights historians who have been focusing on the 1960s as the otherwise widely overlooked decade most notably shaped by the post-colonial reality of newly liberated nations beginning to assert a voice in the international arena and in fact exercising considerable influence on the emerging normative architecture.[7] A reconstruction of Gandhi's deep influence on and affinity with the emerging human rights regime helps to cement such historical links and thereby reinforce the contemporary resonance of the international human rights framework.

---

[6] C Heyns, 'The Struggle Approach to Human Rights' in C Heyns and K Stefiszyn (eds), *Human Rights, Peace and Justice in Africa: A Reader* (Pretoria, Pretoria University Law Press, 2006).

[7] See for example R Burke, *Decolonization and the Evolution of International Human Rights* (Philadelphia, University of Pennsylvania Press, 2010) and SLB Jensen, *The Making of International Human Rights: The 1960s, Decolonization, and the Reconstruction of Global Values* (Cambridge, Cambridge University Press, 2016).

B. Exposing Institutionally Embedded Violence

Posterity remembers Gandhi first and foremost for his strategy of non-violent civil disobedience. While not expressly linked with human rights, this unique approach to contesting injustice is eminently compatible with the underlying values and objectives of human rights and contains important lessons for the current era. I shall concentrate on two considerations.

The practice of Satyagraha, first, places exceptionally high demands on its adherents, who are required to willingly subject themselves to physical abuse and, moreover, to not express resentment in the face of degrading treatment. As a vehicle of political change, the aim is to expose structural and institutionally embedded violence – not merely random acts of violence perpetrated by particular individuals – and thereby to expose the illegitimacy of repressive rule. In so doing, Satyagraha appeals to the conscience of the protagonists involved in the given conflict, but also at the same time to the opinion of the general public and eventually of a global audience. In this sense, Gandhi's method of civil disobedience was entirely dependent on mass media coverage. Despite its seemingly simplistic character, it was firmly embedded in and calibrated to the emerging context of globalisation. This, indeed, may have been key to its efficacy. In a contemporary context, the need to expose systemic injustices is as pressing as ever. A perennial possible pitfall of openly contesting injustice through acts of hostility is that this risks creating a perception of moral equivalency between the conflicting positions, thereby lending legitimacy to further acts of suppression and to the very structural injustices that from the outset were a target of resistance. By staking claim to a moral high ground, Satyagraha pre-empts such a development and human rights advocacy may be well advised to devise analogous strategies.[8]

A corollary to Gandhi's insistence on unassailable moral conduct among his followers, second, is the unwavering faith that there are morally attainable solutions even to the most complex problems confronting society. Expressed with reference to human rights, the implication would be that it is not permissible to contribute to further human rights violations in order to redress existing ones. And conversely, we must maintain confidence that it is possible to find human rights compliant solutions to complex societal challenges. This is a profoundly optimistic message which once again, with reference to the example of a visionary 'third world' leader intent on challenging an unjust global order, affirms the contemporary relevance of the international human rights framework.

C. Rediscovering the Ethos of Human Rights

Continuing along the same line of reflection, it may by way of conclusion be opportune to revisit the significance of Gandhi's response to UNESCO when he was asked in 1947 to provide a comment on the idea of a universal declaration of human rights. As stated in the quote prefacing the present article, Gandhi's spontaneous response

---

[8] This general theme is interestingly explored in 'Gandhi: The Heritage of Non-Violence', *The UNESCO Courier*, October 1968.

was to recall his 'illiterate but wise' mother's emphasis on 'duty well done' rather than rights. The sentiment that rights without corresponding duties are unwholesome is a recurrent theme is Gandhi's writings, such as in the assertion that 'The true source of rights is duty. If we all discharge our duties, rights will not be far to seek. If leaving duties unperformed we run after rights, they will escape us like a will-o'-the-wisp'.[9]

How to make sense of the apparent paradox that one of the preeminent human rights champions of our era appeared sceptical, at best, of the very idea of human rights? The key to resolving the dilemma, I submit, is to avoid positing a mutually exclusive relationship between rights and duties. It is not a question of either one or the other. Gandhi's essential message is that the realisation of a culture respectful of human dignity places ethical requirements on all inhabitants of society. While explicitly focused on vertical government obligations towards individual members of society, the human rights paradigm also contains an implicit *ethos of human rights*, which defines horizontal obligations that we as members of a just society hold vis-à-vis one another. It defines, in other words, a manner of living which fundamentally respects the inherent dignity of the human person.

Gandhi made this a central tenet of his social philosophy and political action. Through his rigorous focus on self-cultivation and lived solidarity with the poor and disenfranchised, he modelled it in an eminent fashion in his personal life, more so than any other human rights advocate of our time, with the possible exception of Nelson Mandela, who drew profound personal inspiration from Gandhi's example. At a time when human rights advocacy is increasingly being subsumed by impersonal bureaucratic dynamics, and where the fundamental values underpinning universal human rights are being called into question on a hitherto unprecedented scale, or simply disregarded, it is of crucial importance to rediscover, rearticulate, and revive the underlying ethos of human rights. If Gandhi's legacy for posterity in relation to human rights should be boiled down to one essential point, this undoubtedly is it.[10]

---

[9] M Gandhi, *India of My Dreams* (Gujarat, Navajivan Publishing House, 1959) 57.
[10] Analogous observations can be found in S Moyn, 'Rights vs. Duties: Reclaiming Civic Balance', *Boston Review* (16 May 2016), available at bostonreview.net/books-ideas/samuel-moyn-rights-duties.

Part II

In the Shadow of War: Developing Universal Human Rights

8

Hersch Lauterpacht

The Visionary: Preparing the World for Human Rights

EVA MARIA LASSEN

[The] State, however widely its object may be construed, has no justification and no valid right to exact obedience except as an instrument for securing the welfare of the individual human being.[1]

I. A Witness to Xenophobia and Catastrophe: The Life of Hersch Lauterpacht

A quick glance at the curriculum vitae of Hersch Lauterpacht would allow the reader to assume that his life was one of a rather straightforward rise of a privileged young man to the academic stardom of international law. In less than two decades, the young student who started his studies at the Jan Kazimierz University and the University of Vienna grew into a renowned international lawyer, to be elected to the prestigious Whewell Chair of International Law at the University of Cambridge in 1937 at the age of only 40. One of the greatest international lawyers of the twentieth century, he was a key figure in developing both international human rights law, and international criminal law through the Nuremberg Trials. Appropriately, the British Queen knighted him in 1956, and around the same time his illustrious career culminated when he was elected to the International Court of Justice.

However, this picture of a linear and glorious career has to be qualified, as it disguises the fact that the poison contaminating Europe for much of his lifetime

---

[1] H Lauterpacht, *International Bill of the Rights of Man* (New York, Columbia University Press, 1945) 16.

marked his personal life and also had a profound effect on his career: xenophobia, anti-Semitism, state-induced persecution, and eventually the killing of six million of Europe's Jews.[2]

Lauterpacht was born on 16 August 1897 in Zolkiew, a small village close to Lwów, in Galicia, then part of Austria-Hungary; after the First World War, the region was included in Poland. Central Europe at the time had a large Jewish population and a flourishing Yiddish culture, and Lauterpacht himself grew up in a middle-class orthodox Jewish family. However, fierce waves of anti-Semitism, including pogroms, marred the region, and also the young Lauterpacht's life. He began his legal studies at the Jan Kazimierz University in Lwów. Soon after the end of the First World War, however, the university initiated anti-Jewish measures, notably in the form of limiting the number of Jewish students. In order for him to continue his studies, the family moved to Vienna. He obtained his doctorate of law at the University of Vienna in 1921 for his thesis on domestic sources as a means of ensuring the realisation of international law, and, in addition, a doctorate of political science. In Vienna, also a seat of strong streaks of anti-Semitism, he became leader of the Zionist student union. In 1923, Lauterpacht married Rachel Steinberg, a Palestinian Jew, and later that year moved to England, probably in part motivated by the assessment that there he and his wife would be able to live a life – and he to pursue a career – free from anti-Semitism. From then on England was his home. He became a British national in 1931.

Although Lauterpacht, his wife and son did not lead an orthodox life in England, he maintained his Jewish identity. In his son's words, he never demonstratively displayed his Jewishness, nor did he try to hide it. In fact, his life, both personal and professional, was to a large extent determined by his identity as a Jew, which from early childhood opened his eyes for the plight of the Jewish minorities. At a young age, at the universities in Lwów and Vienna, his experience of anti-Semitism steered his studies in the direction of human rights.

From his place of safety in England, Lauterpacht observed the rise of the Nazi regime in the 1920s and 30s and its devastating effect on democracy and the rule of law. He witnessed how the persecution of Jews committed at state level steadily increased, eventually leading to the Holocaust and his own personal tragedy. His parents, his siblings, and his entire extended family, apart from one niece, were murdered in the Holocaust. The inter-connectedness of his personal life and the fate of continental Europe gave him an acute sense of the need to protect the individual against the abuse

---

[2] Quite a lot has been written about Hersch Lauterpacht's work in recent years. Further reading includes M Koskenniemi, *The Gentle Civilizer of Nations. The Rise and Fall of International Law 1870–1960* (Hersch Lauterpacht Memorial Lectures, Cambridge, Cambridge University Press, 2002); AF Vrdoljak, 'Human Rights and Genocide: The Work of Lauterpacht and Lemkin in Modern International Law' (2009) 20(4) *EJIL* 1163. For the particular conflict between Lauterpacht and John Humphrey over the Universal Declaration of Human Rights, see EM Lassen, 'When peers are pressing for progress. The clash between Hersch Lauterpacht and John Humphrey over the Universal Declaration for Human Rights' in EA Andersen and EM Lassen (eds), *Europe and the Americas: Transatlantic Approaches to Human Rights* (Leiden, Martinus Niijhofer Publishers, 2015) 16. The biography of Hersch Lauterpacht, written by his son, contains a wealth of documentation covering both his professional and personal life: E Lauterpacht, *The Life of Hersch Lauterpacht* (Cambridge, Cambridge University Press, 2012).

of the state, and strengthened his efforts to develop a legal response to the political disarray of his time. The result was an outstanding contribution to the creation and promotion of modern international human rights.

II. International Law as a Catalyst for Human Rights: A Visionary's Career

A. A Life in Academia

In 1923, the young Lauterpacht became a research student and then a teacher at London School of Economics. He was called to the Bar by Gray's Inn in 1935, but it was academia that became his main occupation, and in 1937 he was appointed Professor of International Law at the University of Cambridge. With his life-long teaching, editing and writing, he contributed significantly to the developing scholarship on international law in the English-speaking world. As for international human rights law in particular, he wrote numerous articles and a number of ground-breaking monographs on the subject. At the centre of this work was his intellectual effort to provide a legal basis for an international law system, at the heart of which was the protection of individual human rights and the preservation of peace. In this endeavour, he dismissed the legal positivists' defence of supreme state sovereignty. Lauterpacht was particularly inspired by natural law and Grotius, commonly known as 'the founding father of international law', from whose writings he formulated the principle of humanitarian intervention, namely 'the principle that the exclusiveness of domestic jurisdiction stops where outrage upon humanity begins'.[3]

His work on human rights led him to innovative discussions in areas of legal philosophy, theory and history. Thus, for instance, he wrote extensively about the history of human rights, and this history appears exceptionally modern, alluding as it does to a multifaceted history of international law and offering insight into both Western and non-Western legal and cultural traditions. Although a considerable proportion of his work concerned the role of international law in furthering the rights of the individual, what characterises Lauterpacht's scholarship is its astounding diversity, covering a large number of areas of international law. Lauterpacht would put this diversity to good use in his venture into scholarly activism in the 1930s and 40s.

B. Bridging Academia and the Challenges of the Times: The Years of Nazism

In 1933 Lauterpacht wrote the memorandum entitled 'Persecution of Jews in Germany'. It was intended as a supplement to Professor Bentwich's Memorandum addressing the League of Nations on the issue of the persecution of Jews in Germany.

[3] Lauterpacht (n 1) 41.

In the memorandum, Lauterpacht argues in favour of holding Germany accountable according to public international law:

> No specific rule of conventional international law binds Germany not to persecute her Jewish minority, ... But the principle that in the modern State individuals must not be persecuted or discriminated against because of their race or religion does enjoy general recognition as part of the public law of the world.[4]

This attempt to use international law to curb state abuse was obviously futile.

More successfully, he put his expertise to the use of the Allied powers during the Second World War. He assisted the UK Ministry of Foreign Affairs in the support of Anglo-American relations, for instance by means of lecturing in the United States in 1940 and 1941 on the transatlantic relations from the point of view of international law. He also prepared opinions on various issues linked to the war, for instance on the US-UK lend-lease scheme, which was fundamental to the British warfare. In this period he formed a professional friendship with the US Attorney, Robert Jackson, a relationship which was to prove significant at the Nuremberg Trials. He then set off to write a proposal for an international bill of the rights of man.

C. Ahead of Time: Proposing a Post-war International Bill of the Rights of Man

In the middle of the war, the American Jewish Committee invited Lauterpacht to write a book on international law. By the autumn of 1943 he had completed the work, which he entitled 'International Bill of the Rights of Man'. Published by Columbia University Press in June 1945, the proposed bill was a product of many years of scholarship. The bill was to be legally binding, it underlines the obligations of the state, and it includes suggestions for instruments of enforcement. In the introduction to the bill, Lauterpacht stated that the main problem of law and politics has always been the relationship between the individual and the state:

> That problem has consisted in the reconciliation of two apparently conflicting factors. The first is that the State, however widely its object may be construed, has no justification and no valid right to exact obedience except as an instrument for securing the welfare of the individual human being. The second is that the State as a political institution has come to be recognized as the absolute condition of the civilized existence of man and of his progression towards the full realization of his faculties. It is a matter of absorbing interest to note that in the history of political and legal thought and action the conflict between those two factors has been bridged by the notion, appearing under various disguises, of the fundamental right of the individual, of the natural, or inherent, or inalienable rights of man.[5]

Parts One and Two of the bill cover political and civil rights and social and economic rights (including the rights of ethnic, linguistic, and religious minorities) respectively. Part Three concerns the implementation, supervision and enforcement of the bill by means of both national and international instruments. In his commentary to this part,

---

[4] H Lauterpacht, 'The persecution of Jews in Germany' in E Lauterpacht (ed), *International Law, being the collected papers of Hersch Lauterpacht* vol 5 (Cambridge, Cambridge University Press, 2004) 728, 732.
[5] Lauterpacht (n 1) 16.

Lauterpacht argues that enforcement mechanisms must be in place to uphold international peace. He suggests a combination of national and international instruments of supervision and enforcement. The State 'must be the normal agency for implementing the Bill of Rights, which must, for that purpose, contain provisions enabling and obliging the States to act in that capacity'. As for the international instruments:

> The international guarantee of the Bill of Rights must be of a general character. This means that it must be concerned not only with persistent and grave violation of its clauses but also with the normal supervision of its observance. It follows that that there must exist a permanent international authority, neither judicial nor political in nature, charged with a task of general supervision, of investigation of complaints, and of initiation by the political international authority in case of disregard of the safeguards of the Bill of Rights on a scale warranting international action for their enforcement.[6]

Lauterpacht's proposal of an international bill of rights was exceptionally well prepared, forward-looking, and in part radical, keeping in check state sovereignty and placing human rights at the centre of international law. The book attracted international lawyers' attention on both sides of the Atlantic. A scholarly review accurately describes Lauterpacht's work, his method – and probably also his personality:

> Professor Lauterpacht's great contribution lies in the fact that he has brought the idea [of an international bill of rights] into focus and has elaborated his plan… with a quiet and moderate assurance which, in the light of developments, makes the book particularly persuasive.[7]

D. The Nuremberg Trials and Crimes against Humanity

Lauterpacht's long advocacy of human rights as part of international law fell on fertile soil at the time of the Nuremberg Trials (1945–49), and he went on to shape the preparations for and the actual legal proceedings of these trials to a considerable degree. After the war, the Allied victors had to decide on how to deal with the Nazi leaders and worst war criminals. Lauterpacht propagated the view that the war criminals must have a fair trial as defendants under international law. For many years, he had been reflecting and publishing on the legal basis for war crimes trials and the subject of individual criminal responsibility in international law; from 1941 onwards he advised both the British and the Americans on these issues.

Lauterpacht successfully suggested that the case against the war criminals should be presented under three headings: crimes against the peace; war crimes; and crimes against humanity.[8] Accordingly, crimes against humanity came to occupy Article 6(c) of the London Charter of 1945:

> Crimes against humanity: namely, murder, extermination, enslavement, deportation, and other inhumane acts committed against any civilian population, before or during the war; or persecutions on political, racial or religious grounds in execution of or in connection with

---

[6] ibid, 177.
[7] Quoted from Lauterpacht (n 2) 255.
[8] ibid, 272.

any crime within the jurisdiction of the Tribunal, whether or not in violation of the domestic law of the country where perpetrated. Leaders, organisers, instigators and accomplices participating in the formulation or execution of a common plan or conspiracy to commit any of the foregoing crimes are responsible for all acts performed by any persons in execution of such plan.

In Lauterpacht's own words, the inclusion of crimes against humanity in Article 6 affirmed that 'international law is not only the law between States but also the law of mankind and that those who transgress against it cannot shield themselves behind the law of their State or the procedural limitations of international law'.[9]

As member of the British War Crimes Executive and part of the British team at the Nuremberg Trials, Lauterpacht counselled British officials and drafted key parts of the British Chief Prosecutor's opening and closing speeches. The British prosecution, using Lauterpacht's life-long argumentation, placed violation of the rights of the individual as a matter of international law, and emphasised both state and individual responsibility. Thus, individual responsibility for crimes must be upheld even if the individual commits the crimes on behalf of the state and those acts are sanctioned by the law of the state.

E. Confronting the Universal Declaration of Human Rights

Lauterpacht was able to pursue his career in England mostly unhindered by sentiments adverse to his personal background. However, at one of the most important moments in the history of international human rights, namely the time of the creation of the Universal Declaration of Human Rights, such sentiments prevented him from taking centre stage. In 1946, a British representative to the UN Human Rights Commission was to be elected, and not surprisingly, Lauterpacht was on the short list of potential members. More surprisingly, he was not actually invited to become part of the delegation. Much later, the reason for this decision came to light: the legal adviser of the Foreign Office was of the opinion that as he was 'a Jew recently come from Vienna' (although he had, in fact, been a British national for 15 years), he was not suitable for the task.[10] Because of this decision, Lauterpacht did not directly take part in the UN debates linked to the future Universal Declaration of Human Rights.

When in 1946 John Humphrey, the UN Director of Human Rights, set out to formulate a first draft of a universal bill of human rights, he read Lauterpacht's 1945 International Bill of the Rights of Man and incorporated the articles on nationality and aliens into his first draft. Similar to Lauterpacht's proposal, Humphrey's draft contained legally binding provisions and principles on enforcement mechanisms. However, as there was no political will to move forward with this far-reaching draft, Humphrey went on to facilitate a process that led to the less ambitious and non-binding declaration.

---

[9] Quoted from Lauterpacht (n 2) 274.
[10] Lauterpacht (n 2) 258.

As an outsider to the UN process, Lauterpacht, for his part, was free to hold on to the core principles of his own proposal of 1945. In the period between 1946 and 1948, when the work on what was to become the Universal Declaration of Human Rights evolved, he became increasingly critical towards both the content of the declaration – because, in his words, such a declaration did not have 'binding force as an instrument of international law' – and the process leading to its adoption.

He was not quiet in his objections, neither in scholarly settings nor wider circles. In July 1947, for instance, *The Times* published a letter to the editor, in which he argued that the work on an international human rights bill was too hasty and that experts of international law and human rights should be given the opportunity to get involved in legal scrutiny and discussion.[11] This was a reference to the fact that only few experts of international law and human rights were involved in creating the Universal Declaration of Human Rights.

Lauterpacht's reservations were largely supported by the International Law Association (ILA), a network of international lawyers. Lauterpacht had the advantage that his own proposal for an international human rights bill was made public before a draft for a Universal Declaration of Human Rights was circulated. At the ILA's annual conference in September 1947, therefore, it was Lauterpacht's proposed bill and not the UN draft that served as a basis for discussions. Both at this conference and at the annual conference held in August 1948, the ILA, echoing substantial parts of Lauterpacht's criticism, expressed its reservations about the Universal Declaration of Human Rights.

John Humphrey was extremely concerned about the opposition of the ILA and in particular of Lauterpacht, a scholar he held in great esteem. In an entry to his diary August 1948, for instance, he noted with alarm Lauterpacht's talk on the Universal Declaration at the ILA conference:

> Lauterpacht delivered a brilliant but devastating talk to the International Law Association on human rights. But he fails to appreciate the political difficulties in our work and hence does not understand that the Commission has already achieved important results. I am afraid that in spite of his good intentions he is colouring the thinking of many people against us.[12]

Although he may have coloured the thinking of many of his colleagues, Lauterpacht did not win the battle over the Universal Declaration of Human Rights, which was adopted on 10 December 1948.

F. Moving on: Lauterpacht in the 1950s

In the first decade of the post-war years, Lauterpacht proceeded with his prolific writings, including the monographs *Recognition in International Law* (1947) and *International Law and Human Rights* (1950). The latter book included a slightly revised

---

[11] Quoted from Lauterpacht (n 2) 259–61.

[12] JP Humphrey, *On the Edge of Greatness: the Diaries of John Humphrey, First Director of the United Nations Division of Human Rights* 4 volumes (AJ Hobbins (ed), Fontanus Monograph Series 4, 9, 12 and 13, Montreal, McGill-Queen's University Libraries, 1994–2001) 36.

version of his 1945 proposal of an International Bill of the Rights of Man, as well as a critical analysis of the newly adopted Universal Declaration of Human Rights. The book also scrutinised the legal possibilities and challenges linked to the preparation of the establishment of a binding European Convention of Human Rights and a European Court of Human Rights, a project in which he was engaged in various ways. He was elected to the International Law Commission (1953 and 1954), where he became Special Rapporteur on the Law of Treaties. In 1955, he was elected a judge of the International Court of Justice, where he served until his death on 8 May 1960 at the age of 63.

III. Conclusion: Lauterpacht's War

Winston Churchill famously proclaimed: 'history will be kind to me for I intend to write it'.

Lauterpacht was not so fortunate. He never wrote a history of international human rights, in which he played a central part. John Humphrey, on the other hand, both intended and indeed did write a history of the Universal Declaration of Human Rights, of which *he* played such an important and successful role. Thus from his retirement in Canada, 35 years after the Universal Declaration of Human Rights was adopted and 25 years after the death of Lauterpacht, he wrote about the creation of the Declaration and his experience as UN Human Rights Director. His portrayal of Lauterpacht reflects the unease that Humphrey still felt about his fundamental disagreement with Lauterpacht. Thus whilst depicting himself as the pragmatic realist, Lauterpacht, on the other hand, was painted as a man of unrealistic impatience: '[H]e was an impatient man who wanted to move faster than political realities would permit. He could be satisfied with nothing less than an immediately binding commitment to respect human rights'.[13] This portrayal of Lauterpacht has lived on in some modern, often very positive, assessments of the creation of the Universal Declaration.

On the other side of the Atlantic, at the University of Cambridge, another and very different legacy was taking form. At the core of this legacy was a Hersch Lauterpacht who was portrayed, not as a man of impatience but as an eminent scholar of courage who did not give in and did not give up. In the decades after Lauterpacht's death, the University of Cambridge continued as an intellectual seat for the progressive development of international law, and many of Lauterpacht's students subsequently became prominent international lawyers. In 1983, the University's Research Centre for International Law was established on the initiative of his son Eli Lauterpacht, himself a distinguished international lawyer. The centre eventually came to be housed in the old family home of Hersch Lauterpacht. In 1996, the University renamed the centre, which today is called the Lauterpacht Research Centre for International Law

---

[13] JP Humphrey, 'The Memoirs of John P Humphrey, the First Director of the United Nations Division of Human Rights' (1983) 5(4) *Human Rights Quarterly* 387, 436.

in honour of both father and son. Hersch Lauterpacht is honoured annually in the Sir Hersch Lauterpacht Memorial Lectures. In the period between the 1970s and 2002, Cambridge University Press published four large volumes containing the major writings of Hersch Lauterpacht, excluding his monographs. In 2012, Eli Lauterpacht published the first substantial biography on Hersch Lauterpacht, offering a wealth of documents illuminating his father's life and work.

Although it is difficult, in the particular context of the Universal Declaration of Human Rights, completely to discard John Humphrey's portrayal of Lauterpacht, it is probably fair to say that as a general characteristic, Lauterpacht's impatience was tempered by the thoroughness and exceptional quality of his work. His academic excellence and his personal qualities of resilience and sincerity combined to make his struggle for human rights remarkably powerful, authoritative and compelling.

It seems appropriate to end this chapter with another quotation by Winston Churchill, namely a quotation used by Hersch Lauterpacht himself in his International Bill of the Rights of Man. The Preamble begins with a reference to the British Prime Minister, who in a message to the World Jewish Congress in London in 1942 expressed the hope that the war would end with 'the enthronement of human rights'. Lauterpacht's 'war effort', and his greatest legacy, was that he prepared the post-war world for the enthronement of human rights by means of a scholarly expansion of international law, which placed human rights at the heart of the international community. For today's human rights researchers, experts and practitioners, the immense richness of his scholarship stimulates modern discussions of international human rights. In addition, Lauterpacht the visionary may serve as inspiration because of his insistence, regardless of political currents, on the urgency of human rights.

9

Raphael Lemkin
Father of the Genocide Convention

ADAM REDZIK

> Genocide is the crime of destroying national, racial or religious groups. The problem now arises as to whether it is a crime of only national importance, or a crime in which international society as such should be vitally interested. Many reasons speak for the second alternative. It would be impractical to treat genocide as a national crime, since by its very nature it is committed by the state or by powerful groups which have the backing of the state. A state would never prosecute a crime instigated or backed by itself.[1]

I. The 'Eminent Polish Scholar'

Raphael Lemkin was descended from a moderately wealthy Jewish family that lived in the District of Wołkowysk (now Vawkavysk, Belarus), east of the town of Białystok. The population of the region was rather poor, irrespective of nationality. The district was inhabited predominantly by Roman Catholics, who constituted around 45 per cent of the population followed by members of the Orthodox Church (circa 40 per cent), while followers of Judaism composed about 12 per cent of the population. In 1921, 70 per cent of the inhabitants declared their nationality as Polish; 20 per cent claimed they were Byelorussians, and only 0.3 per cent admitted they were Jews. However, the religious and ethnic composition looked rather different in the town of Wołkowysk, which was inhabited by about 8,000 people towards the end of the nineteenth century. Here, followers of the Judaic faith constituted the most numerous denominational group (circa 40 per cent), while Roman Catholics composed about 35 per cent, and

---

[1] R Lemkin, 'Genocide' (1946) 15(2) *American Scholar* 227–30.

members of the Orthodox Church around 20 per cent.[2] There were also somewhere between 10 and 20 Protestants and Muslims (ie Tartars) each in the town.[3]

The administrative district of Wołkowysk was somehow spared by the successive waves of anti-Jewish violence which had swept across the Russian Empire, particularly in 1903–1906, when an anti-Semitic campaign resulted in pogroms, in which the military often took part as well, in about 700 towns and villages (including Białystok in 1906). This campaign was fuelled by *The Protocols of the Elders of Zion*, a text fabricated to the order of the Russian Tsar and his secret police (the *Okhrana*) and then widely publicised.

Our understanding of Lemkin's family comes mostly from his own accounts. There is no doubt that his father, Joseph, was an enterprising man hired to manage land estates, including one situated at quite a distance from the town of Wołkowysk. Languages spoken at Lemkin's home certainly included Yiddish, Polish (the local nobility and much of the district's population spoke Polish) and Russian. Referring to his mother, Bella, née Pomeranc, Lemkin wrote that she was an enlightened woman of wide reading. It was Bella who kept a collection of Jewish, Russian and Polish literature at home.[4]

Raphael (actually Rafał) Lemkin was most probably born during his father's stewardship at the Bezwodne/Bezwodna estate (currently Bezvodna in Belarus), on 24 June 1900. The estate was located to the south of Wołkowysk, in the Międzyrzecz commune. Lemkin himself does not even refer to Bezwodne in his autobiography (*Totally Unofficial*). Instead, he mentions a different place, namely, the grange of Ozierzysko (now Ozerisko in Belarus), located in the Izabelin commune, about 20 kilometres west of Bezwodne as the crow flies. It was there that Raphael spent his childhood. He declared Bezwodne as his birth-place, however, in all enrolment documents for Jagiellonian University and the Jan Kazimierz University of Lwów (now Lviv, Ukraine). Most probably in Lemkin's early childhood his family moved to the Ozierzysko grange, which is mentioned in his autobiography. In the 1910s, however, the Lemkins gave up country life and settled in Wołkowysk. Lemkin had two brothers, Elias (d 1983) and Samuel, who died during a dysentery epidemic in 1917.[5]

His parents were certainly very particular about their sons' education. The young Lemkin probably attended the *cheder* (traditional Jewish school) in Wołkowysk and

[2] See W Karpyza, Ziemia Wołkowyska vols 1–4 (Lębork, 2005–2007); Historia społeczności, see sztetl.org.pl/pl/miejscowosci/w/1579-wolkowysk/99-historia-spolecznosci/138270-historia-spolecznosci; *Skorowidz miejscowości Rzeczypospolitej Polskiej: opracowany na podstawie wyników pierwszego powszechnego spisu ludności z dn. 30 września 1921 r..., T. 5 – Województwo białostockie* (Warsaw, Główny Urząd Statystyczny, 1924).

[3] Historia miejscowości, see sztetl.org.pl/pl/miejscowosci/w/1579-wolkowysk/96-historia-miejscowosci/70426-historia-miejscowosci.

[4] DL Frieze (ed), *Totally Unofficial. The Autobiography of Raphael Lemkin* (New Haven & London, Yale University Press, 2013); JF Cooper, *Raphael Lemkin and the Struggle for the Genocide Convention* (Palgrave Macmillan 2008); D Irvin-Erickson, *Raphaël Lemkin and the Concept of Genocide* (Philadelphia, University of Pennsylvania Press, 2017); P Sands, *East West Street: On the Origins of Genocide and Crimes against Humanity* (New York, AA Knopf, 2016); A Redzik, *Rafał Lemkin (1900–1959) – Co-creator of International Criminal Law. Short Biography* (Warsaw, Oficyna Allerhand, 2017); R Szawłowski, *Rafał Lemkin, warszawski adwokat (1934–1939), twórca pojęcia „genocyd" i główny architekt konwencji z 9 grudnia 1948 r. ('Konwencji Lemkina'). W 55-lecie śmierci* (Warsaw, Redakcja Palestry, 2015).

[5] Cooper (n 4); Irvin-Erickson (n 4); Sands (n 4); Redzik (n 4).

the local *Realschule* (a secondary school).[6] At the latter institution, the language of instruction was Russian until 1915; afterwards it was Polish for the most part. In his autobiography, Lemkin mentions a gymnasium in Wilno (now Vilnius, Lithuania), but in university enrolment documents he declared that he had passed the examination for a secondary-school certificate in Białystok on 30 June 1919.[7] In the same year he migrated to the city of Kraków, where he entered the Faculty of Law and Administration at Jagiellonian University. In October 1919, he commenced his four-year legal studies in law. During the first year, he attended lectures by Stanisław Estreicher, Stanisław Kutrzeba, Rafał Taubenschlag, Michał Rostworowski, and by Edmund Krzymuski, the legal philosopher and expert in criminal law.[8]

At that time, Poland – still in the process of reconstructing its statehood – was waging war against Soviet Russia. Everyone was called to arms to combat the enormous forces of the Bolshevik Empire. Academic institutions throughout the country adopted a principle, which said that every student who enrolled for the 1920–21 academic year had to show that he had served in the Polish Army or in the allied forces, including in auxiliary formations. Therefore, Lemkin volunteered for service in auxiliary troops of the second Polish Army, whose third Legion Infantry Division under General Leon Berbecki had liberated Wołkowysk and the surrounding area. At first, Lemkin worked in so-called sanitary units. Then, surely yielding to the persuasion of his friends, he thought it was insufficient to satisfy the university. Using his contacts at the Field Court Martial of the second Polish Army, he managed to obtain a false certificate, which said he had been employed by that court. Someone then informed the University authorities about the forgery. Given the circumstances, disciplinary action was inevitable. When Lemkin's guilt was proved, the proceedings could end in no other way than in his expulsion from the University. However, the Dean of the Faculty of Law, Professor Kutrzeba, released Lemkin's documents without any reference to the relegation. This enabled Raphael to go to Lwów and enrol for a second year of legal studies at Jan Kazimierz University in October 1921. He could not have done any better. At that time, the Lwów Faculty of Law was the leading centre of legal education in Poland. He had the opportunity to listen to the lectures of the most eminent scholars of the era, including Oswald Balzer (history of law), Stanisław Starzyński (constitutional law), Ludwik Ehrlich (international law), Ernest Till (civil law), Maurycy Allerhand (civil procedure), Piotr Stebelski (criminal procedure), and Juliusz Makarewicz (criminal policy).[9] Makarewicz made the strongest impression on Lemkin, who attended Makarewicz's seminar on criminal law for several years.

Juliusz Makarewicz was one of the most distinguished Polish jurists of the twentieth century. He was a representative of the sociological current in the positivist theory of criminal law, and the author of a fundamental work on the philosophy of criminal law,[10] as well as an excellent codifier who was the chief writer of the project

---

[6] Przemysław Mikusiński, *Ziemia Wołkowyska* vol V (Lębork) 84–85.

[7] I was unable to confirm this in the municipal archives of Białystok.

[8] PM Żukowski, 'Krakowskie czasy studiów Rafała Lemkina' (2011) 1 *Dzieje Najnowsze* 139.

[9] For more details, see Redzik (n 4) 13–18.

[10] J Makarewicz, *Einführung in die Philosophie des Strafrechts auf entwicklungsgeschichtlicher Grundlage*, (Stuttgart, F Enke, 1906).

of the Polish Penal Code of 1932, considered an excellent example of codification and model for other similar law projects in Europe.[11] It was at Makarewicz's seminar that Lemkin developed his scholarly apparatus.[12] Makarewicz also prefaced Lemkin's first publication in the field of law (*Kodeks Karny Republik Sowieckich*).

Lemkin completed his university studies in 1924, becoming a Doctor of Laws two years later, on 9 July 1926, not on the basis of a doctoral dissertation, though, but following three exams – the *Rigorosum*.[13] From 1924 onwards, he prepared for the profession of public prosecutor. Having completed his apprenticeship, he became a prosecutor in the town of Brzeżany (now Berezhany, Ukraine), east of Lwów.

In Lwów, Lemkin met Makarewicz's colleague, Judge Emil Stanisław Rappaport, who, in the capacity of Secretary General, directed the work of the Codification Commission of the Second Polish Republic, a body composed of more than 40 eminent lawyers tasked with the unification of civil and criminal law in newly independent Poland.[14] It was Rappaport who invited Lemkin to cooperate with the Commission in Warsaw. Lemkin kept the minutes of the sessions of one of the Commission's sections. In this manner he learned about the procedural aspects of the Commission's work, and how to draft legislation. He also attended Wacław Makowski's seminar at the Faculty of Law of the University of Warsaw. Makowski was an eminent expert in criminal and constitutional law and, at the same time, a close associate of the Marshal (and ruler) of Poland, Józef Piłsudski. Under Makowski's supervision, Lemkin prepared his successive legal works, including the translations of the penal codes of fascist Italy and the Soviet Union. Towards the end of the 1920s, he was already a prosecutor working in Warsaw. Thanks to Rappaport, he began to lecture at the Free Polish University in Warsaw, where he co-founded the Institute of Criminology, the first of its kind in Poland, in the 1930s. The two jurists also published their works together. In 1933, Lemkin issued a treatise on the judge in the context of the latest criminal law and criminology.[15] From 1930, thanks to Rappaport's support, Lemkin was able to participate in numerous legal conferences and congresses throughout Europe as a delegate of the Polish government. This, in turn, enabled him to establish many contacts. He often delivered lectures, too. In 1933, he prepared a paper for a congress in Madrid in which he stipulated the regulation of new types of crime – barbarity and vandalism (see section II below).

In 1934, Lemkin gave up his job at the public prosecutor's office and launched his own law firm as an advocate in downtown Warsaw, which markedly improved his financial standing. After the outbreak of war in 1939, he fled Warsaw, as did many of the intelligentsia and the Polish government, thus avoiding the repressive and

[11] R Lemkin (M McDermott (trans)), *The Polish Penal Code of 1932, and the Law of Minor Offenses* (Durham, Duke University Press, 1939).
[12] Recent claims made by Sands (n 4) 155 and by Irvin-Erickson (n 4) 37, that Makarewicz was a 'Polish Nationalist and anti-Semite', as well as a converted Jew, are based on an entirely unreliable report and thus are false. Indeed, Makarewicz was a scion of a Polish noble family from the eastern borderlands of Poland, while his political leanings linked him with Christian Democracy rather than with either the Nationalists or Galician Conservatives. He also surrounded himself with Jewish students and associates.
[13] Redzik (n 4) 18.
[14] The former lands of Poland belonged to different occupying powers before 1918, hence different legal systems were operative in different regions of the newly reconstituted country.
[15] Redzik (n 4) 22–24.

murderous conduct of the Nazi Germans that soon followed. Through Wołkowysk, Vilnius, and Riga he reached Stockholm, where he worked for a year and even gave lectures at the local university. At an unusually rapid pace, Lemkin also mastered the Swedish language (he had already spoken many, including Yiddish, Russian, Polish, French, German, and English). In the meantime, he collected legal acts issued by the government of Nazi Germany and those of its European allies.

In 1941, through Russia and Japan, Lemkin made his way to the United States and began to work at Duke University in Durham, North Carolina. In the middle of the following year, he left for Washington, DC, where he assumed the post of chief consultant to the Board of Economic Warfare. Having published his *chef-d'œuvre* in 1944 – the book in which he defined 'genocide' – he began to make efforts to have the crime introduced into the international forum.[16] Eventually, his persistent efforts helped in the adoption of the Convention on Genocide (see section II below) by the newly-established United Nations. He then devoted himself to establishing an international court that would implement the Convention in practice. Such a court did not emerge until after the end of his life.

Afflicted with illness, he died in obscurity in New York City on 28 June 1959, and was consigned to his last resting-place at the Mount Hebron Cemetery in the borough of Queens.

II. Totally Unofficial – 'Lemkin's Convention'

Raphael Lemkin's most important contribution to human rights was defining a brand-new category of crime – a crime which constitutes a threat to the most fundamental human rights, as it relies on exterminating a group of people on grounds of racial, national, or religious hatred – and persuading the UN General Assembly to adopt an appropriate legal convention.

Lemkin wrote that in his childhood, while reading *Quo Vadis*, the work of Polish Nobel Prize winner, Henryk Sienkiewicz, he wondered why the Romans, who murdered Christians just because of their religious beliefs, had never been punished for their hideous crimes. This thought remained in his mind into his adult life. During Lemkin's legal studies, the case of Soghomon Tehlirian went to court: the case of the Armenian who had assassinated the former Turkish Minister of Internal Affairs, Talaat Pasha, in Berlin on 15 March 1921. Pasha was responsible for the genocide of Armenians in 1915–1917. After an open trial, well-known and publicised throughout Europe, Tehlirian was exculpated by the jury. In his autobiography, Lemkin writes that he asked his professors from the Lwów University[17] why the international community had not reacted when several hundred thousand Armenians were murdered in Turkey. The professors allegedly told him that only the sovereign authority of the state was

---

[16] For more details, see Sands (n 4) 183–90; Irvin-Erickson (n 4); Cooper (n 4) 56–75; A Dirk Moses, *Raphael Lemkin, Culture, and the Concept of Genocide* (Oxford, Oxford University Press, 2010) 20–41; Szawłowski (n 4) 33–37.
[17] Lemkin (n 4) 20.

capable of punishing the guilty parties. That authority, however, could have no inter-est in punishing the perpetrators of the crime, since they were the same people who had taken part in establishing and wielding the power of the guilty parties. Lemkin's interlocutors must have been experts in criminal and international law and prob-ably included his mentor, Juliusz Makarewicz. Lemkin may also have asked other professors such as Stanisław Starzyński or Ludwik Ehrlich. The answer offered by the scholars from Lwów University reflected contemporary thought in positive legal theory, which invoked the principle of non-interference in the internal affairs of sovereign states.

Still, this case kept haunting Lemkin. In the meantime, he expanded his knowledge of the law and, thanks to the assistance of prominent lawyers and professors such as Makarewicz, Makowski, and Rappaport, he began actively to participate in inter-national congresses in his late twenties. In 1931, with Rappaport's support, Lemkin became a member-secretary of the Polish Society of Criminal Legislation, which was the Polish branch of the *Association Internationale de Droit Pénal* (AIDP, the International Association of Criminal Law); several years later he became its Secre-tary General and held that post until 1939. In 1927, Rappaport, under the auspices of the AIDP, organised a congress of the representatives of European codification commissions in Warsaw. During its proceedings it was agreed that such meetings should go on with the object of unifying criminal law, including its international regulations. Thus seven congresses were held before 1939. Lemkin, as a delegate of the Polish government, took part in most of them; for instance, in the third Inter-national Conference for the Unification of Criminal Law in Brussels in June 1930, and in the fourth International Conference for the Unification of Criminal Law in Paris in December 1931, where he presented a paper on the purposeful use of chemi-cal and biological agents that can cause widespread damage to human life. Lemkin also participated in the First International Congress on Comparative Law, which was held in The Hague in August 1932. The following year, Lemkin was due to attend the fifth International Conference for the Unification of Criminal Law in Madrid. For that conference, he prepared a paper in which he postulated the regulation, by the international community, of five crimes committed against international law, namely barbarity, vandalism, causing a shipwreck, plane crash, or other civil disaster, caus-ing a telecommunications breakdown, and intentional spreading of human disease. Four of the above crimes are connected to human rights; two of them, in turn, fore-shadow the idea of 'genocide.' In his draft of the convention – which he attached to the paper – Lemkin defined barbarity as follows:

> Whoever, out of hatred towards a given racial, religious or social collectivity or with the goal of its extermination, undertakes a punishable action against the life, bodily integrity, liberty, dignity or economic existence of a person belonging to such a collectivity, is liable for the offence of barbarity, to a penalty of … unless punishment for the action falls under a more severe provision of the given Code. The perpetrator will be liable for the same penalty, if an act is directed against a person who has declared solidarity with such a collectivity or has intervened in favour of one (Article 1).[18]

---

[18] R Lemkin, *Acts Constituting a General (Transnational) Danger Considered as Offences Against the Law of Nations*, available at www.preventgenocide.org/lemkin/madrid1933-english.htm.

Vandalism, meanwhile, is considered a crime when the perpetrator, acting on the same motives as in Article 1, 'destroys works of cultural or artistic heritage'. Lemkin issued his paper, in French[19] in Paris and Madrid, then in Polish in Lwów[20] and, in an abbreviated version, also in German in Vienna.[21]

The composition of the Polish delegation to Madrid was, however, changed at the last minute and Lemkin did not go to the conference. He was dissuaded from attending by the Minister of Justice Czesław Michałowski and by his own mentor, Rappaport. This may have been caused by anticipated misgivings regarding the response of some delegates, and states, to the propositions included in Lemkin's paper, and to the fact that Poland had started to negotiate a non-aggression pact with Germany;[22] the latter was the reason suggested by Lemkin himself. Another important fact – then unknown to Lemkin – is underrated, namely, that Poland, at Piłsudski's suggestion, held secret talks with France, trying to induce her to launch an armed intervention in Germany in 1933.[23]

The fact remains, though, that Lemkin did not go to Madrid. However, he sent his paper to the participants of the conference; perhaps at the instigation of Rappaport, whom he explicitly mentions in its content. However, the conference papers published afterwards include no information whatsoever that might suggest that Lemkin's arguments were considered. The only certainty is that many conference participants received this paper. The matter, however, made no further progress, though Lemkin continued to attend numerous congresses.

Lemkin went, for instance, to the sixth Conference of the International Bureau for the Unification of Criminal Law, held in Copenhagen in 1935, where he presented a paper on terrorism, comprising his own definition of that term and a proposal of a relevant international convention. In July 1937, he participated in the fourth International Congress of Criminal Law, organised by the AIDP, where he delivered a presentation on the preservation of peace *through internal criminal law*, in which he referred to the innovative solutions embodied in the Polish Penal Code of 1932. In 1939, together with Malcolm McDermott, whom he had met in Poland four years earlier, Lemkin published the English translation of the Polish Penal Code and Law of Minor Offences in the United States.[24] This particular acquaintance also resulted in an invitation to the United States, which Lemkin received in 1940 (see section I above).

Just before leaving Poland, in September 1939, Lemkin met an eminent penologist and professor from the Stephen Báthory University in Wilno (now Vilnius),

---

[19] R Lemkin, 'Les actes constituant un danger général (interétatique) considérés comme délits de droit des gens' Rapport spécial présenté à la V-me Conférence pour l'Unification du Droit Pénal à Madrid (14–20 octobre 1933), available at www.preventgenocide.org/fr/lemkin/madrid1933.htm.

[20] *Przestępstwa polegające na wywołaniu niebezpieczeństwa międzynarodowego jako delicta sui generis (Wnioski na V Konferencję Międzynarodowego Biura do spraw Unifikacji Prawa Karnego w Madrycie)* (1933) 10 'Głos Prawa'.

[21] *Akte der Barbarei und des Vandalismus als delicta iuris gentium* (1933) 1 Internationales Anwaltsblatt.

[22] Sands (n 4); Cooper (n 4); Irvin-Erickson (n 4).

[23] In 1933, Marshal Piłsudski sent General Bolesław Wieniawa-Długoszowski and Senator Jerzy Potocki on a mission to France. Their task was to probe the potential French standpoint in case of a Polish invasion of Germany as part of a preventive war.

[24] See n 11.

Bronisław Wróblewski, with whom he talked about the war and discussed his plans. At one point, the scholar turned to him with the following words: 'Were you not stopped in 1933 when you tried to establish your new definitions for the international crimes of barbarity and vandalism?' Lemkin's answer was: 'I will try again. I might be stopped again, and then I will do it again'.[25] So he promised he would return to the matter of the criminalisation of barbarity at the international level and would not yield. From that moment on, he prepared himself to do just that. In November 1944 he published his most important book, *Axis Rule in Occupied Europe*, in which he defined a new kind of crime against international law, namely genocide, which was a slightly modified version of his conception of genocide from 1933. He immediately took up a 'single-handed struggle' for the introduction of his conception into international law. He sent scores of copies of his book to leading jurists around the world, including Judge Robert H Jackson, who was preparing the trial of Nazi war criminals in Nuremberg on behalf of the United States and other allied powers. Jackson invited Lemkin to join his team. The legal assumptions of the Nuremberg Tribunal were prepared by, among others, a person who was unenthusiastic about Lemkin's book, namely, a former student of law from the University of Lwów, and now professor of international law at the University of Cambridge, Hersch Lauterpacht. In his opinion, Lemkin's book was merely a useful collection of regulations, which were valid in countries occupied by the Third Reich. Article 6 of the Charter of the International Military Tribunal enumerated the crimes for which the leaders of the German State were to be brought to trial. They were: crimes against peace, war crimes, and 'crimes against humanity' as defined by Lauterpacht, who was of the opinion that the concept of genocide was detrimental. Lemkin only managed to induce Jackson to use the term 'genocide' in referring to the crimes perpetrated by the Germans in the indictment of 6 October 1945, which read as follows: 'They conducted deliberate and systematic genocide, ie the extermination of racial and national groups, against the civilian populations of certain occupied territories', and then added: 'particularly Jews, Poles and Gypsies and others'. The term, however, did not appear at all in the subsequent proceedings, since it was unknown in the law at the time.

Both during and after the Nuremberg Trials, Lemkin spared no effort to persuade the international community to adopt the genocide convention. He published frequently, and wrote scores of letters, which he supplemented with off-prints of his articles. He was lobbying, explaining, and appealing to various institutions. In 1946, he wrote in *American Scholar*:

In the case of Germany, it would be ridiculous to speak of the Germanization of Jews or Poles in western Poland, since the Germans wanted these groups eradicated entirely. Hitler stated many times that Germanization [p. 228] could only be carried out with the soil, never with men.

These considerations led the author of this article to the necessity of coining a new term for this particular new concept: genocide. This word is constructed from the ancient Greek word

[25] Lemkin (n 4) 64.

genos (race, clan) and the Latin suffix *cide* (killing). Thus, genocide linguistically corresponds to such words as tyrannicide, homicide, and patricide.[26]

This paper is just one example of Lemkin's activity in that period. Lemkin was introduced and described as a 'noted Polish scholar and attorney';[27] it was also pointed out that 'he served on the staff of the US Chief of Counsel for Prosecution of Criminality'.[28] Both statements were highly exaggerated at that time; nonetheless, they consolidated his standing. In collaboration with the UN Legal Committee, Lemkin finally managed to bring about the unanimous adoption of the Resolution on Genocide on 11 December 1946. Thus the way was cleared for the subsequent establishment of the Genocide Convention. On 9 December 1948, Lemkin's determination in persuading many people, including the representatives of individual states, resulted in the adoption of the Convention on the Prevention and Punishment of the Crime of *Genocide*.[29] Although many people who had contributed to the creation of this document in different ways then claimed its co-authorship, it may safely be called 'Lemkin's Convention'. If it had not been for Lemkin's idea, the draft of the Convention and, above all, his stubbornness – verging on importunity – the document would never have come into being.

The Convention's Article 2 states that 'genocide' is:

> any of the following acts committed with intent to destroy, in whole or in part, a national, ethnical, racial or religious group, as such: (a) killing members of the group; (b) causing serious bodily or mental harm to members of the group; (c) deliberately inflicting on the group conditions of life calculated to bring about its physical destruction in whole or in part; (d) imposing measures intended to prevent births within the group; (e) forcibly transferring children of the group to another group.

According to one of the accounts, late in the evening on 9 December 1948, Lemkin confessed, among sobs and tears, that the Convention was an epitaph for the tomb of his mother, who was murdered in Poland by the Germans, and a proof that many millions of people had not died in vain. The next day, when asked by a journalist about the moment when the idea of genocide first came to his mind, Lemkin answered: 'When I was reading my compatriot Henryk Sienkiewicz's *Quo Vadis* in my childhood'.

III. An Epitaph for Humanity

Lemkin's tomb bears the following inscription: 'Dr Raphael Lemkin (1900–1959). Father of the Genocide Convention'. It is thus indicated that his life's work was the Convention on the Prevention and Punishment of the Crime of Genocide.

---

[26] Lemkin (n 1) 227–30.
[27] R Lemkin, *Axis Rule in Occupied Europe: Laws of Occupation, Analysis of Government, Proposals for Redress* (Washington, 1944) 7.
[28] Lemkin (n 1) 230.
[29] See M Lewis, *The Birth of the New Justice: The Internationalization of Crime and Punishment, 1919–1950* (Oxford, Oxford University Press, 2014) 187–228.

The Convention came into force on 12 January 1951 but remained suspended in a legal vacuum due to the lack of an international judicial body that could try those accused of the crime of genocide. For the last ten years of his life, Raphael Lemkin made efforts to put the Genocide Convention into operation and to establish a relevant tribunal. He also kept pointing out the omission of political and social groups as targets of the crime of genocide, eliminated from the Convention under the influence of the Soviet Union and others. Indeed, Lemkin collaborated with the diasporas of various European nations, including the Assembly of Captive European Nations (ACEN), at whose first congress he explicitly used the term 'genocide' to describe crimes committed by the Soviets, such as the Great Famine in Ukraine (*Holodomor*). He investigated and publicised cases of genocide from all corners of the world. Lemkin was increasingly afflicted by poor health and financial problems, all the more so because he did not manage to secure a permanent job either at Yale University or at any other university. Although his candidacy for the Nobel Peace Prize was recommended to the Norwegian Nobel Committee several times, he never actually received that distinction. The few honours he did receive were unable to make up for his problems or for the bitterness he felt because his 'single-handed struggle' was not fully understood. Just before his death he started writing his memoirs, which he did not finish.[30]

Not before half a century had passed since the adoption of the Genocide Convention – and almost 40 years after Lemkin's death – was a permanent international tribunal called into being. It was the International Criminal Court (ICC), with the seat in The Hague, in whose statute (Rome Statute of 1998[31]) the crime of genocide was defined in the same way as in 'Lemkin's Convention'. Genocide has also been given the definition of one of the gravest crimes in many national penal codes or laws. This ushered in the recognition of Lemkin's important contribution. In February 1991 the first conference in commemoration of Lemkin was held at Yale University, the Raphael Lemkin Symposium on Genocide, and in October 2000 the Raphael Lemkin Centenary Conference was organised in London. In the same year, the Institute for the Study of Genocide in New York began to grant its biennial Lemkin Award.

In recent years, the achievements of Lemkin have entered the popular consciousness, with numerous publications in the field of research science and popular science; in many countries there are Raphael Lemkin foundations, associations, institutes, and university departments, and many studies are conducted on genocide. There have been films and theatre plays devoted to Lemkin and his life's work on the concept of genocide in the field of law. Several commemorative plaques have also been unveiled, including one on the house in which he lived in Warsaw (2008) and in Lviv (2017). It is difficult to overestimate Philippe Sands' book entitled *East West Street. On the Origins of Genocide and Crimes Against Humanity*, in which Lemkin, carrying on his 'single-handed struggle' for the criminalisation of genocide, is one of the main protagonists.

---

[30] The portion he actually wrote was published and edited by Frieze (n 4).
[31] Rome Statute of the International Criminal Court (ICC), adopted in Rome on 17 July 1998.

The book was an immense success and has already been translated into more than ten languages.

Genocide is the gravest crime that man can perpetrate; essentially, it constitutes a qualified form of a 'crime against humanity'. Thanks to Raphael Lemkin, it has been defined, criminalised, and penalised by the international community. Today, perpetrators of genocide no longer go unpunished, since the international community possesses a legal instrument that enables it to judge and punish them for this hideous crime.

10

Eleanor Roosevelt

Driver of the Universal Declaration of Human Rights

ANYA LUSCOMBE AND BARBARA OOMEN

Where, after all, do universal human rights begin? In small places, close to home – so close and so small that they cannot be seen on any map of the world. Yet they are the world of the individual person: the neighbourhood he lives in; the school or college she attends; the factory, farm or office where he works. Such are the places where every man, woman, and child seeks equal justice, equal opportunity, equal dignity without discrimination. Unless these rights have meaning there, they have little meaning anywhere. Without concerted citizen action to uphold them close to home, we shall look in vain for progress in the larger world.[1]

I. From Shy Child to Important Influencer

With the benefit of hindsight, Eleanor Roosevelt's whole life prepared her for what she considered the most important task: chairing the Human Rights Commission in its foundational years. Her youth, in which she lived the effects of exclusion, her role as an activist for social justice in the United States, and the diplomatic, political and rhetorical acumen that she accrued in her position as the First Lady of the United States all contributed to her key role in laying the foundations for human rights as we know them today and in carving out pathways towards their realisation.

As the granddaughter of philanthropist Theodore Roosevelt Sr, who helped found the Metropolitan Museum of Art and the New York Children's Orthopedic Hospital,

---

[1] Eleanor Roosevelt at the presentation of *In Your Hands: A Guide for Community Action for the Tenth Anniversary of the Universal Declaration of Human Rights*, 27 March 1958, New York, FDR Library Holdings.

and the niece of President Theodore Roosevelt (1901–1909), Eleanor Roosevelt was accustomed to the idea of 'noblesse oblige' and the importance of political influence. She was born on 11 October 1884, the daughter of Elliott Roosevelt (brother of Theodore Jr) and Anna Hall Roosevelt. Her childhood was miserable: her parents' marriage was an unhappy one and Eleanor never felt very close to her mother. She recounts in her autobiography *This Is My Story* how she quickly learned that one could make oneself appreciated by being useful: she would sit for hours stroking her mother's head when Anna suffered from very bad headaches. Her mother died in 1892, followed less than two years later by the alcohol-related death of her father.

Following the deaths of their parents, Eleanor and her younger brother went to live with their grandmother. At the age of 15 Eleanor was sent to Allenswood School in London. There she met Mlle Marie Souvestre, the school principal, a woman deeply committed to liberal causes and to encouraging her young students to make the most of themselves. During the three years at Allenswood, Eleanor studied literature and history and learned to argue on controversial subjects. During the summers on travels through Europe with her headmistress, Souvestre insisted that the young Eleanor see the deprivation and squalor in the cities they visited and not just the tourist sites. 'Mlle. Souvestre shocked one into thinking, and that on the whole was very beneficial', Eleanor reminisced in her autobiography. Allenswood not only increased Eleanor Roosevelt's confidence in her abilities but also fostered in her a keen interest in helping the less fortunate, and being civically engaged.

On her return to the United States, Eleanor joined the Junior League for the promotion of settlement movements and volunteered to work at a settlement home in New York City. She also became a member of the National Consumers League. She married her fifth cousin, Franklin Delano Roosevelt (FDR) on 17 March 1905. Within 11 years Eleanor had six children, one of whom died in infancy. In 1913 when FDR became Assistant Secretary of the Navy, the family moved to Washington, DC. Soon, the threat of world war relieved ER (as she was known by then) from the much detested compulsory social commitments required of a cabinet wife and she was able instead to dedicate herself to working for Navy relief in the Red Cross. Such activities made her realise that not only could she direct her energy to something other than her husband's political career, but that such other activities for the good of society gave her great joy.

In the 1920s ER joined a host of organisations that engaged in 'concerted citizen action' and through which she felt she could make a difference, including the bi-partisan Women's City Club (dedicated to social reform in New York City), the Women's Division of the New York Democratic State Committee, and the New York chapters of the League of Women Voters and the Women's Trade Union League (WTUL). The women she met in these organisations, including Carrie Chapman Catt, Agnes Brown Leach, Molly Dewson, Lillian Wald, Frances Perkins and Belle Moskowitz, formed part of a support network who helped and inspired ER. Many became close friends, such as educator and consumer activist Esther Lape and her partner Elizabeth Reid, ER's personal lawyer and financial adviser in the 1920s. Both encouraged ER to represent the League of Women Voters on the women's joint legislative committee. They got ER to study the Congressional Record and interview members of Congress and the state assembly. In 1923 Lape was asked by the publisher

Edward Bok to administer a competition offering $100,000 for the best practical peace plan by a member of the public. At Lape's invitation, ER joined the contest's Policy Committee. Of the more than 20,000 entries, a plan proposing American membership in the World Court and cooperation with the League of Nations was selected. Isolationists were outraged and lambasted both the proposal and the Policy Committee members.[2] The personal criticism may have surprised ER, but it did not make her waver in her support for internationalist and pacifist endeavours. She supported the National Conference on the Cause and Cure of War and the Women's International League for Peace and Freedom and in October 1927 hosted the launch of a woman's peace movement in support of the Kellogg-Briand Treaty to outlaw war.[3]

In addition to international matters, ER took a keen interest in local issues. In 1922, a year after her husband FDR contracted polio and Eleanor had decided to keep the Roosevelt name active in Democratic circles, she travelled through New York State with her friends Nancy Cook, Marion Dickerman, Elinor Morgenthau and Caroline O'Day to encourage the formation of democratic women's clubs. ER also became the editor of the *Democratic News* publication. In addition, she joined the board of the Women's City Club.

> During her four-year tenure... ER chaired its City Planning Department, coordinated its responses on housing and transportation issues, chaired its Legislation committee, pushed through a reorganization plan, arbitrated disputes over child labor laws, promoted workmen's compensation and, in a move that made banner headlines across New York State, strongly urged the adoption of an amendment to the Penal Law legalizing the distribution of birth control information among married couples.[4]

In 1927 ER together with Dickerman and Cook bought a girl's school, Todhunter, in New York City and she taught American history and literature. ER, Dickerman and Cook also set up a non-profit furniture factory, Val-Kill industries, aimed at providing additional income for poor farming families.

Another lifelong friend who influenced ER greatly was Rose Schneiderman, President of the New York and national WTUL. Polish-born Schneiderman, who started work at 13 and became the organiser of the Jewish Socialist United Cloth Hat and Cap Makers Union at age 21, taught ER about the difficulties facing women workers and the problems of worker-management relations. ER responded by 'donating the proceeds from her 1932–1933 radio broadcasts to the WTUL, and promoting WTUL in her columns and speeches. As Schneiderman recalled in her autobiography, ER overcame the trappings of privilege to become "a born trade unionist"'.[5] ER introduced Schneiderman to FDR and in 1933 he appointed Schneiderman to the advisory board of the National Recovery Administration.

By learning from the many activists with whom she worked and from talking to the many ordinary people she met during her travels throughout the country, ER gained

[2] L Scharf, *Eleanor Roosevelt, First Lady of American Liberalism* (Boston, Twayne Publishers, 1987).

[3] B Wiesen Cook, *Eleanor Roosevelt Vol 1, 1884–1933* (New York, Penguin, 1992) 364.

[4] A Black, 'Anna Eleanor Roosevelt', *Eleanor Roosevelt Papers Project*, George Washington University, available at erpapers.columbian.gwu.edu/anna-eleanor-roosevelt.

[5] 'Rose Schneiderman', Eleanor Roosevelt Papers Project, available at erpapers.columbian.gwu.edu/rose-schneiderman-1882-1972.

important insights into political and social issues which she would use to influence her husband's thinking.

II. Career and Contribution to Human Rights

When FDR was elected to the Presidency in 1933, ER was concerned that she would have to give up her own career. Rather than falling into the role performed by First Ladies that had gone before her, she decided to carve out a whole new role for herself. She held press conferences for women reporters (348 during her time in the White House), travelled thousands of miles to see conditions in communities affected by the Depression, wrote numerous articles, books and columns (including the long running syndicated column *My Day*, read by millions), gave speeches and presented her own radio programmes.[6] The criticism from some quarters that her behaviour was unbecoming to a woman, let alone a First Lady, made her more determined to chart her own course and to use her influence to help those causes that needed her support: 'I'll just have to go on being myself, as much as I can … I'm just not the sort of person who would be any good at any job. I dare say I shall be criticized, whatever I do'.[7] She laid herself open to particular criticism when she, albeit very reluctantly, assumed the role as co-director of the Office of Civilian Defense (OCD), created by FDR in 1941 to counter cuts in social service programmes. The OCD was accused by its opponents of spending money on frivolous activities and ER resigned after being ridiculed for unwisely appointing a friend to help with a physical fitness project. The whole episode was a useful lesson in management skills.

ER encountered similarly useful lessons on the difficulties of effecting change when trying to make progress of the rights of minorities. While she successfully lobbied her husband to appoint women to key posts in the administration, to open up Federal New Deal programmes to others besides healthy young white men and to meet with Civil Rights leaders, ER failed to make headway with him on anti-lynching legislation and was ignored on the internment of Japanese Americans during the Second World War. Nor could she overcome State Department obstruction to the efforts to give refuge to more German Jews who were being persecuted in Hitler's Germany.

A few months after her husband's death, President Truman asked Eleanor Roosevelt to be a member of the first US delegation to the opening United Nations General Assembly in London. Supporters of ER were delighted. The Berkeley Women's Forum wrote to the President applauding his decision because ER would be able to voice the concerns of 'the many millions of plain people both at home and abroad, whose interests are pleading for understanding and who fervently desire a wise solution of the

---

[6] All the My Day columns have been digitised and are available at erpapers.columbian.gwu.edu/my-day.
[7] Cited in A Black, *Casting Her Own Shadow: Eleanor Roosevelt and the Shaping of Postwar Liberalism* (New York, Columbia University Press, 1996) 21.

problems that lead to war'.[8] But others, including her fellow US delegates, were more wary of her progressive ideals. They assigned her to the Third Committee, working on humanitarian, educational and cultural questions because, in her own words, 'she could not do much harm there'. The committee decided to take forward the objective of the UN, defined in the Charter as promoting 'respect for human rights and fundamental freedoms for all' by formulating an International Bill of Rights. When the UN's Economic and Social Council subsequently decided to put in place a Human Rights Commission, Eleanor Roosevelt, was elected its Chair.

This marked the beginning of a two-year process in which the Commission relentlessly worked to formulate an International Bill of Rights. Such a document, ER's Commission decided, would consist of three parts: a Declaration focused on the principles, one or more binding Conventions for states to ratify and to which they would be legally bound, and provisions on enforcement. In deciding which rights should be included in the Bill, the Commission drew upon a list of worldwide rights developed by its secretary, John Humphrey, and a UNESCO survey of rights. Out of the 18 Member States in the Commission, ER opted to work with a core team of eight: René Cassin, a French Jewish scholar who had lost many family members during the war; the funny and philosophical Peng-Chun Chang of China; Hernán Santa Cruz of Chile, with his staunch dedication to social and economic rights; Colonel William Roy Hodgson of Australia; Vladimir Koretsky and later Alexei Pavlov of the USSR who put sovereignty above all; and the cosmopolitan philosopher Charles Malik of Lebanon.

In taking up her role as a chairperson, Eleanor Roosevelt had promised to be 'not only an impartial Chairman, but perhaps at times a harsh driver'. Even if she, in her autobiography, describes her role as the person to pour tea whilst members like Chang, Malik and Humphrey engaged in lofty conversations over Confucianism and pluralism, it is clear that she did much more than that. Glendon, for instance, is one of the many scholars to state that the Declaration would probably not have come about without the chairperson who 'provided the leadership that kept the project moving along, the political influence that held the State Department on board, and the personal attentions that made each member of the Commission feel respected'.[9] This leadership included listening to long litanies of the Russian representatives, who felt the project was defective from the start, but did not boycott it altogether either. It also entailed enabling all parties to have their say on each article. It took six days of discussions, for instance, before Article 1 was agreed upon in its final version: 'All human beings are born free and equal in dignity and rights. They are endowed with reason and conscience and should act towards one another in a spirit of brotherhood'. With regard to other articles, issues like the role of the place of social and economic rights, State enforcement of rights, the place of duties, religious freedom and the right to equal treatment were all deeply contentious.

---

[8] Eva Lane of Berkeley Women's Forum to Truman, cited in F Fasce, M Vaudagna and R Baritono (eds), *Beyond the Nation: Pushing the Boundaries of U.S. History from a Transatlantic Perspective* (Turin, OTTO, 2013) 68.

[9] MA Glendon, *A World Made New: Eleanor Roosevelt and the Universal Declaration of Human Rights* (New York, Random House, 2002) 206.

The fact that she spoke several languages and her ability to draw upon experiences from her childhood, such as the intense loneliness she had felt back then, contributed both to the diplomatic skills she needed as Chair of the Declaration's drafting group and gave her the sensitivity to identify with those in the world whose human rights were trampled upon. In addition to the debates within the Commission, a large part of Eleanor Roosevelt's diplomatic skills were needed to navigate the relationship with the US State Department. Even with the support of President Truman, her outspoken position on race relations, equality and Palestine led to numerous tensions between the two. Often, she would combine diplomacy, her high-level contacts and sheer stubbornness to make the most out of the leeway she had as the chairperson. In other cases, she took into account the fact that the Declaration, and later on the Covenants, would have to pass through the US Senate. For this reason, she took seriously the need for a federal state amendment, to ensure the Covenant would not put powers that previously belonged to states under federal control, and was far less vocal on equal treatment issues and social and economic rights than would have been expected on the basis of her background.

On 10 December 1948, after 3,000 hours of meetings and debates, Eleanor Roosevelt introduced the Universal Declaration of Human Rights to the UN General Assembly. Taking as its point of departure that 'recognition of the inherent dignity and of the equal and inalienable rights of all members of the human family is the foundation of freedom, justice and peace in the world' and how 'disregard and contempt for human rights have resulted in barbarous acts which have outraged the conscience of mankind' the Declaration, for the first time in history, set out 30 civil, political, social and economic rights for every human being, everywhere in the world. Asserting that the document could well become the 'international Magna Carta of all men everywhere', she also emphasised that it was not a statement of law, but rather a 'common standard of achievement for all peoples of all nations'.

Boutros Boutros Ghali, in his introduction to the Eleanor Roosevelt papers, remarks how

> Few people realize that Eleanor Roosevelt did not spend most of her tenure as a United Nations delegate working towards passage of the Universal Declaration of Human Rights, but instead worked towards the more arduous endeavour of making it an enforceable directive of international law.[10]

Indeed, as soon as the Declaration was passed, the Commission continued its work on the Covenants and the mechanisms of enforcement. As the Covenants would be legally binding documents, Eleanor Roosevelt was well aware of the need to formulate them in such a manner that it would be necessary to get the support of as many governments as possible. The advent of the Cold War between East and West also had an impact in this pursuit. The Commission decided to first proceed with a Covenant stating civil and political rights, in line with Western preferences and ideologies, and to then develop a separate Covenant on Social, Economic and Cultural rights. In addition, the Commission working on enforcement mechanisms,

---

[10] A Black (ed), *The Eleanor Roosevelt Papers Volume 2* (Charlottesville, University of Virginia Press, 2012) xxix.

under the leadership of Hansah Mehta, proposed a Committee to enforce the rights concerned.

Eleanor Roosevelt, however, would not live to see the materialisation of all this. She resigned from the Human Rights Commission when Eisenhower took office in 1953, to immediately offer her volunteer services as an 'educational volunteer' to the American Association of the UN. Here, she spent the last nine years of her life tirelessly advocating for the UN and the Declaration in a country, and a world, which had increasingly turned against the idea of human rights. President John F Kennedy re-appointed her as a UN delegate in March 1961. It was only four years after her 1962 death that the twin Covenants were passed, thus completing the International Bill of Rights; it would take another ten years before they had enough signatures to enter into force.

III. The Hope for the Universal Declaration

The International Bill of Rights was merely the foundation for today's UN human rights architecture, with its nine core treaties, wide range of monitoring and enforcement mechanisms and an ever-strengthening influence of regional human rights treaties. Within all this, however, the UDHR retains a special place as a source of inspiration. It has been translated into over 500 languages, causing the former High Commissioner for Human Rights, Navi Pillay, to state 'that it has probably had more impact on mankind than any other document in history'.[11] Its universal acceptance was underscored by the 1993 World Conference on Human Rights in Vienna, when all UN Member States of the time reaffirmed that all human rights are 'universal, indivisible and interdependent and interrelated'. Even if today's world is still fraught with human rights violations, scholars have pointed out the tangible impact of ratification of human rights treaties, and activists worldwide have drawn inspiration and courage from the Declaration. At the same time, its mobilisation and translation differed over place and time – in line with Eleanor Roosevelt's permanent emphasis on the fact that the Declaration would not 'be understood in the same way in every area', and that it was not an American Bill, but a universal minimum standard of achievement.

The flaws in the architecture that resulted from the politics and the power relations of the time can nevertheless be felt, in many ways, today. The division of civil and political and social and economic rights between the two Covenants led to different mechanisms of implementation, and to different degrees of enforcement of the rights concerned even if civil and political rights alone, in Roosevelt's words, 'will not mean a great deal to people, not even in our own country, because these rights have proved of little value when not accompanied by some measure of economic and social

---

[11] N Pillay, Statement by the UN High Commissioner for Human Rights Navi Pillay on the occasion of the 60th Anniversary of the Universal Declaration of Human Rights, 10 December 2008, available at www.ohchr.org/EN/NewsEvents/HRDay2007-2008/Pages/60UDHRHCStatement2008.aspx.

rights'. The lack of an explicit provision on equal treatment – again, a result of US politics – necessitated specific Conventions to clarify that the rights in the Declaration did apply to women, children and persons living with disabilities. The fact that the right to self-determination was explicitly left out of the Declaration, to keep colonial powers on board, resulted in an ongoing discussion on human rights as a product of western imperialism – precisely the discussion that Eleanor herself, with her search for common moral ground and consensus, had sought to avoid.

The most enduring heritage, possibly, lies in Eleanor Roosevelt's vision of human rights and of pathways to their realisation. In spite of all her work in getting states to commit, she also emphasised 'concerted citizen action', to be partially directed towards politicians; 'Our trouble is that we do not demand enough of the people who represent us', she wrote in her last book *Tomorrow is Now*. At the same time, her tireless work in promoting the Declaration worldwide was based on her vision that 'people must accept and respect these rights and freedoms in their own communities and own lives, and by doing so, create countries, and in time, a world where such freedoms are a reality'. Here, the legal character of the Declaration comes second to its ability to inspire action, as it has in many ways. As she put it in her *My Day* column of 22 December 1948:

> In the present case it is a great variety of peoples that have accepted these principles and have agreed to begin the long trek toward making a reality the rights and freedoms of the individual human being. One should never belittle the value of words, however, for they have a way of getting translated into facts, and therein lies the hope for our universal declaration.

11

René Cassin
The Foot Soldier of Human Rights[1]

JAN WOUTERS

Ténacité, intransigeance, modestie, ses vertus furent celles d'un homme libre fidèle à une certaine idée de la France et de la fraternité humaine. Ce 'Fantassin des Droits de l'Homme' comme il aimait à s'appeler, a creusé dans son siècle un sillon que nul ne pourra sans péril laisser se refermer. Parce que cet homme n'appartient à personne, il mérite, exige l'hommage de tous.[2]

I. A Man for All Seasons

The roots of the Frenchman René Samuel Cassin trace back to three border areas: Italian, German and Spanish. He was born on 5 October 1887 in Bayonne, in the Basque Country in the southwest of France, close to the Pyrennées, where the prosperous family of his mother, Gabrielle Dreyfus, lived. The roots of her family go to the frontier zone with Germany, however: his great-grandfather was an Askenazi Jew born in Alsace. René's father, Azaria (or Henri) Cassin, was a French-Jewish wine merchant whose family came to Nice after living for centuries in the southwest of France. During periods of persecution, they had sought refuge cross-border in Cuneo, in nearby Piedmont. His mother and father had an unhappy marriage: unlike his mother, his father kept his distance from the Jewish religion, an agnosticism René would share. They would divorce in 1910. As a teenager Cassin was deeply moved by

---

[1] After the expression 'le fantassin des droits de l'homme' coined by M Agi, *René Cassin: fantassin des droits de l'homme* (Paris, Plon, 1979).
[2] François Mitterrand, President of the French Republic, Speech at the occasion of the transfer of the ashes of René Cassin to the Panthéon (*Discours du transfer des cendres de René Cassin au Panthéon*) 15 October 1987.

the Dreyfus affair, which had shown the full depth of antisemitism in France. Later in his life, he would deeply engage with the Jewish cause: from 1943 to 1969 he was president of the *Alliance Israélite Universelle* and would have close ties with Israel, in particular its Prime Minister Golda Meir.

After attending the Lycée Masséna in Nice, Cassin accomplished brilliant studies in both law and history at Aix-en-Provence. There he met a young artist and actress, Pauline (stage name: Simone) Yzombard, with whom he fell in love and married years later. In July 1908 he became *licéncié en droit* and *licencié ès lettres*. He continued his legal education in Paris, where he became *docteur ès sciences juridiques, politiques et économiques* in 1914. At the same time he was called to the bar, earning the title of *Avocat à la Cour de Paris*. His doctoral thesis was seemingly about a technical subject of private law: the exception of non-performance in reciprocal contracts (known in Latin as the *exception non adimpleti contractus*).[3] But in essence, it had already a moral dimension: the mutual respect for the word given and good faith as foundations for every human society.[4] Winter and Prost observe that Cassin's thesis 'showed all the strengths that would serve him well in later years: clarity of prose; logical exposition; balanced judgment. It was a formidable achievement, and the thesis is still referred to today'.[5]

On 2 August 1914, Cassin was called up and participated as master corporal in the early battles of the First World War in the north-east of France. He would later recall the hallucinatory experience of seeing entire villages in flames and of the many comrades who fell, including a brother-in-law who left four orphans.[6] In the night of 12–13 October 1914 he was heavily wounded at Saint-Mihiel by German machine gun fire. Trying to get the attention of stretcher-bearers by rapping his drinking cup on a stone, he had the good fortune to be heard, and was taken behind the front lines. Cassin had to undergo surgery, which was only partly successful, and retained a traumatic hernia due to an explosive bullet lodged in his hip. He would wear an orthopedic belt for the rest of his life. His stay in hospital lasted six months. Simone Yzombard was by his side, as she had been assigned as a nurse to the hospital where Cassin was treated. In March 1916 Cassin was dismissed from the army – he was declared incapacitated – and was awarded the Military Medal and Croix de Guerre. On 27 March 1917 he married Simone.

Cassin then pursued an academic career: apart from his many roles as a legal adviser, lawmaker, judge, diplomat, civil servant and civil society advocate, he had always been in the first place a teacher and a scholar. From 1916 to 1919 he taught as lecturer in civil and criminal law at the Faculty of Law of Aix-en-Provence. After successfully passing the state competition for university posts, he took up a professorship at the Faculty of Law of Lille in 1920, in the region of France that had

---

[3] R Cassin, *De l'exception tirée de l'inexécution dans les rapports synallagmatiques et de ses relations avec le droit de la relation, la compensation et la résolution* (Paris, Sirey, 1914).

[4] G Israel, *René Cassin, la guerre hors la loi, avec De Gaulle, les droits de l'homme* (Paris, De Brouwer, 1990).

[5] J Winter and A Prost, *René Cassin and Human Rights. From the Great War to the Universal Declaration* (Cambridge, Cambridge University Press, 2013) 13.

[6] See the remarkable testimony Cassin gave of this during a talk broadcast by the BBC on 8 September 1940, quoted by Winter and Prost (n 5) 21.

been most devastated by the war. It would imply a difficult weekly commute, with teaching Monday to Wednesday in Lille, and living in Paris for the rest of the week. In 1929 Cassin took up the post of professor of civil law at the Faculty of Law of the University of Paris. He taught there until his retirement in 1960 but continued to work until his death in 1976, only interrupted by the Second World War. Cassin taught around the world: by the 1920s and 1930s he was visiting professor at various universities in Europe, the Middle East, the Far East and French Africa. He was deeply convinced that the cause of human rights had to be pursued, to a great extent, through education.

Cassin was a prolific legal scholar who initially wrote mainly books and articles on contract and inheritance law, the concept of domicile and the inequality of men and women in civil law. Traces of his thinking on human rights and sovereignty gradually emerged throughout his pre-Second World War writings. For instance, when he taught about the new concept of domicile in the settlement of private international law disputes at the Hague Academy of International Law in 1930,[7] he refused to recognise the pre-eminence of nationality over domicile, seeing it as an indication of an undesirable omnipotence of the state over the individual.

Apart from his academic career, Cassin displayed a tireless civic engagement. One could call it his 'civil society' dimension, and it shows the emerging role of non-governmental organisations for humanitarian causes at the national and international levels long before the UN human rights machinery came about. The deep tragedies of the First World War had given him a strong sense of solidarity, especially for those mutilated by the war, and for widows and orphans. Around the time of assuming his chair in Lille, he founded, and became secretary-general and subsequently president for many years of, the *Union fédérale des associations françaises d'anciens combattants et victimes de guerre*, a large association of wounded veterans and former soldiers. His work for this association brought him also to Geneva and triggered, in a sense, his international career.

The International Labour Organization (ILO) had helped to launch the International Conference of Associations of Wounded Soldiers and War Veterans (the *Conférence internationale des associations des mutilés et d'anciens combattants* or CIAMAC), which Cassin co-founded in 1925–26 and brought together former soldiers of the two sides from the First World War. CIAMAC advocated inter alia for the right of reparation of war victims and contributed significantly to international reconciliation and pacification in the turbulent years between the First and Second World Wars, operating especially in Germany in an increasingly hostile climate after the rise of Nazism. Cassin acted as its representative and *rapporteur permanent* until the outbreak of the Second World War. From 1924 onwards, Cassin was also a member of the French delegation to the League of Nations, acting as a delegate for the veterans. Every year he spent a month in Geneva working at the League of Nations, notably

---

[7] R Cassin, 'La nouvelle conception du domicile dans le règlement des conflits de lois' (1930) 34 *Collected Courses of the Academy of International Law* 655. Cassin would also teach a course at the Academy in 1951 and in 1974: 'La Déclaration Universelle et la mise en œuvre des droits de l'homme' (1951) 79 *Collected Courses of the Academy of International Law* 241; 'Les droits de l'homme' (1974) 140 *Collected Courses of the Academy of International Law* 321

on matters of disarmament. His period at the League enabled him to forge friend-ships with important players such as the Czech foreign minister Edvard Beneš and the Greek foreign minister Nikolas Politis. The dynamics at the League convinced him of the need to revise the theory of absolute state sovereignty. For a brief while, there was the hope – inter alia expressed in the Briand-Kellogg Pact of 1928, which prohibited war as an instrument of foreign policy and was strongly advocated by CIAMAC – that states would opt for peaceful instruments to settle their disputes. However, in the 1930s the League was confronted with many successive crises, from the Japanese invasion of Manchuria in 1931 to the Munich accords of 1938, and it began fading gradually away into irrelevance. Cassin resigned after the Munich accords.

While Cassin operated outside the limelight in most of his functions, it may be noted that he also briefly tried in vain to start a political career: in 1928 he was a candidate at the departmental elections in Antibes, in the Maritime Alps, but did not get elected; in 1932 his candidacy for Albertville was refused.

When the Second World War broke out and France capitulated in June 1940, Cassin was among the first to join General Charles de Gaulle in London. He embarked on a British vessel, the Ettrick, at Saint-Jean-de-Luz on 24 June 1940. The Vichy regime prosecuted him for treachery before the military tribunal at Clermont-Ferrand, which condemned him to death and deprived him of his French nationality. In London, Cassin proved invaluable as chief legal adviser to de Gaulle. He drafted the legal texts of de Gaulle's free French government-in-exile and assisted in the negotiations with Prime Minister Winston Churchill, who recognised the free French government as the only legitimate one and provided financial assistance to it. Cassin occupied various high-level positions in London, such as permanent secretary of the Council of Defense of the French Empire, National Commissioner of Justice and Public Instruction, President of the Legal Committee of the Provisional Government and President of the Legislative Committee at the Consultative Assembly set up by the government-in-exile in Algiers. Still in London, he was the delegate to the United Nations War Crimes Commission from 1943 onwards. After the liberation of France, he became Vice-President of the Council of State (*Conseil d'État*) and President of the National School of Administration (the famous 'ENA', *École Nationale d'Administration*).

While Cassin's contributions to the human rights machinery of the United Nations (UN) and Council of Europe are discussed below, one should point to his judicial career after the Second World War and to the important missions he fulfilled to serve his country in the UN. From 1944 to 1960 he was Vice-President of the *Conseil d'État*, the highest judicial body in France in administrative law cases. It is well-known that he left a deep trace of reform on that institution. From 1960 to 1970, Cassin served on the Constitutional Council (*Conseil Constitutionnel*), the body ruling on the constitutionality of French legislation. Moreover, from 1959 onwards Cassin served as one of the founding Judges at the European Court of Human Rights, of which he was Vice-President from 1959 to 1965 and President from 1965 to 1969.

Last but not least, René Cassin represented France in the UN and at international conferences on multiple occasions. In 1946, 1948, 1950, 1951 and 1968 he was a French delegate to the UN General Assembly. Between 1945 and 1960 he also repeatedly served as delegate to the General Conference of UNESCO and lobbied for it to have its headquarters in Paris. But the most important contribution was his work on human rights as French representative in the UN Commission on Human Rights, where he served as Vice-President at the side of Eleanor Roosevelt (who was president from 1946 to 1953) from the Commission's very creation in 1946 to 1955, as President from 1955 to 1957, and again as Vice-President in 1959. Initially, Cassin had to lobby hard to become the French representative in the Commission, as he had in fact been assigned to represent his country in ECOSOC's nuclear commission.[8] His role in the genesis of the 1948 Universal Declaration of Human Rights is described below.

The coronation of Cassin's long and extremely distinguished professional life came with the award of the Nobel Peace Prize on 10 December 1968 in Oslo, at the occasion of the twentieth anniversary of the Universal Declaration. The same year, he was awarded – together with Eleanor Roosevelt (posthumously) – the UN's Prize for Human Rights.

Cassin died in Paris on 20 February 1976. His fondest wish would be fulfilled 11 years later, when his ashes were transferred to the Panthéon on 15 October 1987.

II. The 'Père Fondateur' of the Universal Declaration

Public opinion, especially in France, sees René Cassin as the 'father of the Universal Declaration'. There has been a lot of myth-building in this respect, and some biographers and former disciples may well have contributed to it.[9] Cassin himself always expressed himself cautiously about his own role in the drafting of the Declaration.[10] In 1984, a controversy arose in this respect because of the publication of the memoirs of John Humphrey, head of the Human Rights Division of the UN Secretariat from 1946 to 1966, whose portrait is also included in this volume.[11] In his book *Human Rights and the United Nations: a Great Adventure*,[12] Humphrey took issue with a statement of Cassin from 1968 according to which he had been entrusted to prepare, in his personal capacity, a first draft of the Universal Declaration.[13] Humphrey found this 'patently wrong' as it 'leaves the impression that Cassin prepared an original draft based on a more or less undigested mass of material collected by the Secretariat'.[14]

---

[8] E Decaux, 'L'élaboration de la Déclaration universelle des droits de l'homme' in Commission nationale consultative des droits de l'homme (ed), *De la France libre aux droits de l'homme. L'héritage de René Cassin* (Paris, La documentation française, 2009) 123, 124.

[9] This is also observed by MA Glendon, *A World Made New. Eleanor Roosevelt and the Universal Declaration of Human Rights* (New York, Random House, 1999) 65 and notes on 252–53.

[10] P Alston, 'Book review of John P Humphrey, Human Rights and the United Nations: A Great Adventure' (1984) 6 *Human Rights Quarterly* 224, 227.

[11] See the contribution by William Schabas, ch 12 in this volume.

[12] JP Humphrey, *Human Rights and the United Nations: A Great Adventure* (Dobbs Ferry, New York, Transnational Publishers, 1984).

[13] R Cassin, 'Quelques souvenirs sur la Déclaration universelle de 1948' (1968) 15 *Revue de droit contemporain* 11, 16.

[14] Humphrey (n 12) 43. Humphrey goes on by indicating that 'Cassin's next text reproduced my own in most of its essentials and style' and that many of Cassin's proposed changes (in terms of order and substance of articles) were rejected.

However, as highlighted by Philip Alston in his review of Humphrey's book, Cassin himself repeatedly acknowledged that both Humphrey and his French colleague Emile Giraud had prepared an excellent working document with concrete texts, accompanied by the corresponding texts from national constitutions or declarations.[15] It may have been the tradition of invisibility of the work of an international secretariat, combined with certain hagiographic excesses by biographers and disciples of Cassin, that caused the hiccup with Humphrey 25 years after the facts and eight years after the death of Cassin.[16] In her 1999 book *A World Made New. Eleanor Roosevelt and the Universal Declaration of Human Rights*, Mary Ann Glendon demonstrated how Cassin had indeed revised Humphrey's draft and that 'under his hand the document acquired an internal logic and achieved greater unity', adding notably a preamble and six introductory principles to guide the interpretation of each specific provision, thereby valorising his unique experience in drafting legislation according to the (French) civil law tradition.[17] Moreover, Cassin continued to play a key role by being rapporteur of the Commission's Working Group on the Declaration, as one of the most active members of the Commission, and as a French delegate to the Third Committee of the General Assembly when the Declaration was adopted later in 1948.[18] In any event, Humphrey was right to observe that:

> The Universal Declaration of Human Rights has no father in the sense that Jefferson was the father of the American Declaration of Independence. Very many people in the Commission on Human Rights, in its drafting committee, in the Commission on the Status of Women, in the two sub-commissions, in the General Assembly, in the specialized agencies, in departments of national governments and in non-governmental organizations contributed to the final result. It is indeed this anonymity which gives the Declaration some of its great prestige and authority.[19]

In their book *René Cassin and Human Rights*, Jay Winter and Antoine Prost describe how, throughout his later work at the UN, René Cassin became increasingly frustrated by the slow progress and resistance in the area of human rights. The Cold War had made the US wary of human rights, while the Soviet Union systematically used blocking procedures to delay things. The drafting of the two covenants (the International Covenant on Civil and Political Rights and the International Covenant on Economic, Social and Cultural Rights, respectively) became a painstaking process: it took until 16 December 1966 before the UN General Assembly could formally adopt the two treaties (and another 12 years for their international entry into force on 3 January 1976, just before Cassin's death). Cassin struggled also, as a French representative, with the challenge of reconciling his government's official positions on human rights with his personal convictions. When he proposed, in June 1948, that the Human Rights Commission be given the power to investigate individual complaints and eventually that the office of UN Attorney General be created, the *Quai d'Orsai*

[15] Alston (n 10) 227, referring to various writings of Cassin, notably R Cassin, 'La Déclaration universelle des droits de l'homme' (1951) II *Recueil des Cours* 237, 273.
[16] Alston (n 10) 227–28; Decaux (n 8) 129.
[17] Glendon (n 9) 63.
[18] Alston (n 10) 228.
[19] Humphrey (n 12) 43.

(French Foreign Ministry) was not amused: it feared masses of complaints from the French colonies.

Looking for other ways to serve the cause of human rights, Cassin was nominated by France to become one of the founding judges on the European Court of Human Rights. Cassin was Vice-President of the new Strasbourg Court from 1959 to 1965 and President from 1965 to 1969. It was a delicate task, especially as France itself had not yet ratified the European Convention on Human Rights: it only did so in 1974. Still, Cassin presided over a number of landmark cases which helped to establish the authority of the European Court. The most important of these was the *Lawless* case, the first judgment of the Court.[20] The Irish government had detained without charge or trial Gerard Lawless, a member of the Irish Republican Army (IRA). Lawless argued that Ireland had violated his rights under the European Convention, by detaining him and denying him a fair trial. The Irish government argued that under Article 15(1) of the European Convention, it had the right to derogate from its obligations under the Convention:

> [i]n time of war of other public emergency threatening the life of the nation [...] to the extent strictly required by the exigencies of the situation, provided that such measures are not inconsistent with its other obligations under international law.

The Court threaded a careful balance. On the one hand, it held that there had been a long-term armed campaign of the IRA to subvert the Irish government, and that the Irish government had the right to suspend its obligations under the European Convention during the IRA campaign, in order to secure the safety and well-being of the Irish population. On the other hand, the Court made clear that the decision whether such an emergency existed rested with the Court – again a rejection of the theory of absolute sovereignty, which rejection Cassin had defended for so long.[21]

III. The Lasting Heritage of Cassin

When the ashes of Cassin were transferred to his last resting place in the Panthéon on 15 October 1987, French President Mitterrand gave a memorable speech in which he described Cassin's legacy:

> Il est des hommes illustres pour avoir incarné la douleur ou la gloire d'une époque. Il en est d'autres dont la grandeur est d'avoir su anticiper sur leur temps, en y semant les germes du futur. René Cassin est de ceux là. L'hommage rendu aux premiers nous confronte à l'histoire, le message des seconds annonce l'avenir.[22]

---

[20] *Lawless v Ireland* App No 332/57 (ECtHR, 1 July 1961).

[21] See the discussion of the *Lawless* case in Winter and Prost (n 5) 255–57. These authors discuss also the *de Becker* case and the *Belgian Language* case at 257–58. For another interesting analysis of these cases see WJ Ganshof van der Meersch, 'René Cassin, judge international' in *René Cassin Amicorum Disciplinorumque Liber* I (Paris, Pedone, 1969) xxxv–xlxi.

[22] (n 2).

When looking back at the life of René Cassin, one can hardly escape the impression that he has had, in fact, many lives: as a teacher and scholar, as legal adviser, lawmaker, judge, diplomat, civil servant, and as a tireless civil society advocate. He was truly a man for all seasons. He also epitomises through his life the history of France and, more broadly, international relations in the twentieth century. He belonged to the generation of those who, to paraphrase the preamble of the UN Charter, had 'twice in their lifetime' been brought 'untold sorrow' by 'the scourge of war'. Both World Wars left indelible traces on Cassin and triggered his unrivaled determination to make a stunning contribution, through his unique talents and his various high-level roles, to the national, international and European recognition of human rights and the limitation of unhampered state sovereignty.

Cassin's heritage continues to be with us through a number of lasting initiatives: the French *Commission consultative des droits de l'homme* (the French National Human Rights Commission), which was founded by a ministerial decree in 1947 upon the insistence of Cassin, in order to follow the work of the UN with legal experts and civil society representatives, and for which he served as the first president;[23] the *Institut International des Droits de l'Homme* (now replaced by the *Institut International des Droits de l'Homme – Fondation René Cassin*) in Strasbourg, which Cassin founded in 1969 with the funds from his Nobel Prize and over which he presided until his death; the *Association pour la fidélité à la pensée du Président René Cassin* created in 1977; the international student moot court *Concours européen des droits de l'homme René Cassin*, the oldest and most prestigious French-speaking moot court on European human rights law; and prizes for theses and for primary schools which bear his name.

---

[23] E Decaux, 'René Cassin: entre mémoire et histoire' *Droits fondamentaux* (2010) para 33.

12

John Peters Humphrey

The Man Behind the First Draft of the Universal Declaration of Human Rights

WILLIAM SCHABAS

Human rights without social and economic rights have little meaning for most people.[1]

I. Present at the Creation

John Humphrey was born in Hampton, New Brunswick, in eastern Canada, on 30 April 1905. Both of his parents died when he was quite young. He also lost his left arm in an accident. As an adult, Humphrey often sported a bow-tie, like many international lawyers of the time. How he managed to tie it with only one hand remains a mystery, as most men can't tie one with two hands. Humphrey studied at Mount Allison University, in New Brunswick, from the age of 15. Later, he transferred to McGill University in Montreal, living there with his sister Ruth, who was a teacher. McGill remained his academic home throughout his entire life. He graduated from McGill at the age of 20, with a Bachelor of Commerce degree. By 1929, he had also obtained Bachelor of Arts and Bachelor of Law degrees.

Humphrey received a fellowship to study in Paris. He sailed from Montreal on the RMS Aurania. Onboard, he met Jeanne Godreau. The two were married shortly after arriving in Paris. The couple returned to Canada, where Humphrey practised law for five years as a member of the Quebec Bar. In 1936, he took up a teaching post at McGill. During the Second World War, Humphrey became good friends with Henri Laugier, a refugee from Nazi-occupied France. Humphrey was both francophone and

---

[1] JP Humphrey, *Human Rights and the United Nations: A Great Adventure* (Dobbs Ferry, NY, Transnational Publishers, 1984).

francophile, and he thought Laugier welcomed the relationship at a time when many French residents of Montreal were 'Vichyards or fence-sitters'. Laugier left Montreal in 1944 for Algeria, where he served the Free French and held the position of rector of the University of Algiers. A year later, that University awarded Humphrey a doctorate *honoris causa.*

When the United Nations was established, Laugier was named Assistant Secretary General for Social Affairs. Laugier appointed Humphrey as the first Director of the United Nations Division of Human Rights. Humphrey served as Secretary to the Commission on Human Rights, the body then charged by the General Assembly with preparing what was initially called the 'International Bill of Rights'. Humphrey's responsibilities included preparation of background documents on international human rights for the Commission. On his own initiative, but with the involvement of Laugier and of Eleanor Roosevelt, the chairman of the Commission, Humphrey prepared a 48-article draft that served as a starting point for the negotiations. For this reason, he can claim to be the author of the first version of the Universal Declaration of Human Rights.

The General Assembly eventually agreed that the International Bill of Rights would comprise four instruments: a manifesto or declaration; two substantive treaties dealing with various categories of human rights; and an instrument for implementation. Although the first text, the Universal Declaration of Human Rights, was completed in less than two years, drafting of the others took almost two decades. Humphrey was intimately involved in the process. He stepped down from his position after serving the UN for 20 years, in 1966. The same year, the General Assembly completed the International Bill of Rights by adoption of the International Covenant on Civil and Political Rights, its first Optional Protocol, and the International Covenant on Economic, Social and Cultural Rights. Humphrey had also contributed to the preparation of several other human rights treaties, including the International Convention on the Elimination of All Forms of Racial Discrimination and the early treaties on women's equality. He is also credited with proposing that the post of UN High Commissioner for Human Rights be established.

After leaving the UN, Humphrey returned to McGill University. Even after retiring, he continued to teach courses on human rights subjects, including one on minority rights. He was also very active in civil society both within Canada and at an international level. In 1968 he was appointed a member of the Royal Commission on the Status of Women. He helped found the Canadian chapter of Amnesty International as well as the Canadian Human Rights Foundation, now known as Equitas. Humphrey also served on a number of international commissions of inquiry. After he passed away in 1995 a commemorative Canadian postage stamp was issued in his honour.

II. Drafting the International Bill of Rights

John Humphrey's claim to be the author of the first draft of the Universal Declaration of Human Rights is not without some controversy, because credit for this achievement is also attributed to René Cassin. In 1968, on the twentieth anniversary of the adoption of the Declaration, Cassin received the Nobel Peace Prize. From 1946 to 1948, Cassin served on various UN bodies including the Commission on Human Rights and to that extent he was unquestionably one of the authors of the Declaration. He also wrote an early text prepared on the instructions of the Drafting Committee. Humphrey, on the other hand, was an international civil servant whose job it was to assist the Commission, not to take its place. The role of such individuals is always more discreet and subdued. Inevitably, they work in the background, taking instructions rather than giving them, and modestly letting others receive the kudos for ideas of which they were in fact the originators.

Some of the founding members of the UN hoped that the Charter itself would contain a declaration of fundamental rights. But after initially proclaiming the centrality of human rights in the Atlantic Charter, when victory seemed more certain the most powerful countries lost their enthusiasm. The Charter of the United Nations confines itself to seven rather summary references to human rights, including recognition of the equality of men and women and of the prohibition of discrimination based on race, sex, language, or religion. Humphrey credited these references to non-governmental organisations. Without their efforts, he said, the Charter would have had nothing more than 'a passing reference' to human rights.[2] When the Charter was adopted, in June 1945, United States President Harry S Truman declared 'we have good reason to expect an international bill of rights, acceptable to all the nations involved' would soon be adopted.[3]

Although several UN bodies were involved in drafting the Universal Declaration of Human Rights, most of the work was conducted in the Commission on Human Rights, from early 1947 until mid-1948, and then in the Third Committee of the General Assembly, from October to December 1948. A preliminary series of meetings of what was known as the Nuclear Commission on Human Rights took place early in 1946. When Humphrey took up his position at UN headquarters, in August 1946, the Commission on Human Rights had been created but had not yet begun its activities. Later that year the General Assembly, with Humphrey in attendance, confirmed that the Commission on Human Rights was responsible for preparing a draft international bill of rights.[4]

The Commission on Human Rights held its first session in January and February of 1947. It devoted considerable attention to preparation of the international bill of rights. However, nothing resembling a draft emerged from these initial meetings. Nor did the Commission make any real headway on the subject of the form that the bill of rights was to take. Later, it would recommend that the international bill of rights consist of a number of distinct instruments. The Commission was reluctant to assign

[2] JP Humphrey, 'The UN Charter and the Universal Declaration of Human Rights' in E Luard (ed), *The International Protection of Human Rights* (London, Thames & Hudson, 1967) 30, 39–40.

[3] Verbatim Minutes of the Closing Plenary Sessions, Opera House (26 June 1945) UN Doc 1209 P/19, 26 in *Documents of the United Nations Conference on International Organisation, San Francisco* vol I (London, United Nations Information Organisations, 1945) 683.

[4] UNGA, Draft Declaration on Fundamental Rights and Freedoms (11 December 1946) UNGA Resolution 43(I).

the preparation of an initial draft to the Secretariat. With some reluctance, it mandated this task to its three officers, Eleanor Roosevelt, who was the chairman, Peng Chun Chang, the vice-chairman, and Charles Malik, the rapporteur. The committee was to work 'with the assistance of the Secretariat'.[5]

After the Commission had finished its first session, Roosevelt convened a meeting with Chang, Malik, and Humphrey at her apartment in Washington Square. Humphrey said it became obvious that this committee could not draft a bill because 'Chang and Malik were too far apart in their philosophical approaches to be able to work together on a text'.[6] Chang suggested that Humphrey ought to put his other duties aside for six months and study Chinese philosophy before attempting to prepare a draft. According to Humphrey, this was 'his way of saying that Western influences might be too great, and he was looking at Malik as he spoke'.[7] Malik, a Lebanese Arab and a devout Greek Orthodox Christian, retorted with a lengthy exposition on the philosophy of Thomas Aquinas.[8] Before the tea party had finished, it was decided that Humphrey would prepare a preliminary draft. 'I didn't go to China nor did I study the writings of Confucius!', Humphrey recalled.[9]

Humphrey began work on the project almost immediately. The Humphrey papers in the McGill University Archives contain an untitled typewritten version of the 'outline' with the handwritten annotation '3rd Draft. Shown to Mrs. Roosevelt, Feb. 28, 1947. Certain changes made March 3, including addition of art. 43a'. The document has a three-paragraph preamble with a fourth paragraph added by hand: 'that there can be no human freedom or dignity unless war is abolished'. Alongside this are the following words, also handwritten: 'Mrs. R. suggested that the preamble might also say that there can be no human rights without peace'.[10] In his memoirs, Humphrey wrote that he could not get started on the draft bill of rights until after the meetings of the Economic and Social Council, which concluded at the end of March 1947.[11] But that is hard to reconcile with the drafts in the McGill archives that prove he was working on this from mid-February 1947. Moreover, the documents also confirm that he was collaborating closely with the chairman of the Commission, Eleanor Roosevelt.

The Secretariat of the Commission had already prepared a number of important documents for the Commission. These were distributed to the Commission during its January-February 1947 session. Humphrey had a small staff in the Division of Human Rights. It is not possible to attribute to him personally the authorship of all of the materials. Some of the names of others within the Division appear on the official records: Émile Giraud, Edward Lawson and AH Hekimi. Yet, as the person responsible he is obviously entitled to much of the credit. Humphrey's superior, Henri Laugier, seems to have had great trust in him and essentially gave him

---

[5] Commission on Human Rights, Summary Record of the 2nd Meeting held at Lake Success, New York (27 January 1947) UN Doc E/CN.4/SR.12, p 5.
[6] Humphrey (n 1) 29.
[7] ibid.
[8] E Roosevelt, *On My Own* (New York, Harper, 1958) 77.
[9] Humphrey (n 1).
[10] McGill University Archives, 1988-0102.01.4.T1.
[11] Humphrey (n 1) 29.

a free hand. Unquestionably, decisions taken by Humphrey in late 1946 and early 1947 impacted decisively upon the form and content of the Universal Declaration of Human Rights. His claim to be the author of the first draft of the Declaration is based upon the 'outline' he circulated in June 1947. Nevertheless, the various memoranda and analyses that were circulated by the Division at that time are also part of his contribution.

Humphrey's methodology can be discerned from the bundle of documents assembled for the first session of the Commission on Human Rights. At this point, no official guidance had been provided by any of the organs of the UN, including the rather informal 'Nuclear Commission', as to how to go about generating a draft international bill of rights. A 'Working Paper on an International Bill of Rights' was issued by the Secretariat in January 1947. It reviewed the existing materials on human rights at the international level, including the references in the Charter of the United Nations, post-war peace treaties, trusteeship agreements, and the instruments of the International Labour Organization, UNESCO, the World Health Organization, and the International Refugee Organization.[12] The Secretariat also prepared a tabular analysis of four draft declarations that had already been formally submitted to the United Nations[13] by Panama,[14] Cuba,[15] Chile,[16] and the American Federation of Labor.[17] More substantial was a detailed analysis of these preliminary materials, as well as of several unofficial proposals from scholars and public intellectuals like Hersch Lauterpacht and HG Wells.[18]

Finally, during the first session of the Commission, Humphrey circulated a concise document entitled 'List of Types of Rights Contained in Drafts of Proposed International Bills of Rights'. The outlines of the future instruments, including the Declaration, can be discerned. The List of Types of Rights grouped human rights into three broad categories of which the first was 'status of equality without distinction' and 'prohibition of discrimination'. An enumeration of grounds was provided: race, sex, language, religion, professed belief, colour, class, citizenship, civil status, wealth, birth, culture, and 'other reasons'. This went well beyond what was in the Charter of the United Nations. The expansive approach proposed by Humphrey was retained in Article 2 of the Declaration. The second, 'status of liberty', included 'life', 'personal liberty', 'prohibition of slavery and compulsory labour', 'sanctity of home', 'secrecy of correspondence', 'fair trial', 'non-retroactivity of penal laws', 'right of property', 'freedom of movement (migration)', and 'freedom to resist oppression'. It is perhaps noteworthy that this preliminary list did not include the prohibition of torture, a right that would later take on monumental importance and that is today the only fundamental right to be declared to be part of customary international law by the International

---

[12] Working Paper on an International Bill of Rights, UN Doc E/CN.4/W.4 and Add.1.

[13] Textual Comparison of the Proposed Drafts of an International Bill of Rights, UN Doc E/CN.4/W.8.

[14] Draft Declaration on Fundamental Human Rights and Freedoms and on the Rights and Duties of States, UN Doc A/148, E/HR/3.

[15] Draft Declaration on Human Rights and Letter of Transmittal, Cuban Delegation, UN Doc E/HR/1.

[16] Draft Declaration of the International Rights and Duties of Man, UN Doc A/C.1/38, E/CN.4/2.

[17] International Bill of Rights, Proposal Submitted by American Federation of Labor, UN Doc E/CT.2/2.

[18] Analysis of Various Draft International Bills of Rights, UN Doc E/CN.4/W.16.

Court of Justice.[19] Humphrey added a reference to torture in the draft declaration. The final category, 'status of social security', encompassed food, housing, 'work under suitable conditions', 'security against unemployment disease and old age', medical care, education, 'recreation and rest' and the 'right to share in the benefits of science'. In an approximate sense, this preliminary list prepared by Humphrey resembles the final text of the Universal Declaration of Human Rights.

During February 1947, the Economic and Social Council intervened to countermand the approach taken by the Commission, mainly at the behest of the Soviet Union. The Council determined that preparation of the international bill of rights be undertaken by a larger and more representative 'Drafting Committee' of the Commission on Human Rights. Eleanor Roosevelt agreed to constitute an eight-member Drafting Committee that included representatives of Australia, Chile, France, the Soviet Union, and the United Kingdom. The Economic and Social Council also charged the Secretariat with preparing a 'documented outline' of the international bill of rights in order to assist the Drafting Committee in it work.[20] Humphrey said that he might well have interpreted the term 'outline' as meaning 'merely a list of rights'. But, he wrote, 'I chose not to, and prepared a draft declaration which was however always known as the Secretariat Outline'.[21] In a letter Humphrey boasted to his sister that he had been asked to 'play the role of a Jefferson',[22] referring to the author of the American Declaration of Independence. In his memoirs he wrote more modestly: 'I was no Thomas Jefferson'.[23]

Humphrey and his team in the Secretariat prepared three related documents in response to the mandate from the Economic and Social Council for a 'documented outline'. The first, dated 4 June 1947, is a 48-article 'Draft Outline of International Bill of Rights'.[24] This is truly the first draft of the Declaration. Humphrey said that Laugier agreed he should take a week away from the office and devote his full attention to preparing the text. He had 'some help from Émile Giraud', a French legal academic who worked with him in the Division.[25] Humphrey said that the 'best of the texts from which I worked' was the one submitted to the UN by Panama, which was originally attributed to the American Law Institute.[26] A second document, issued 9 June 1947, is entitled 'Plan of the Draft Outline of an International Bill of Rights'.[27] It divides the 48 articles into chapters: Liberties, Social Rights, Equality, and General Dispositions. Under these four headings, the individual articles are organised. Finally, the third document, a massive piece of research running to hundreds of pages, labelled

[19] *Questions relating to the Obligation to Prosecute or Extradite (Belgium v Senegal), Judgment* [2012] ICJ Reports 422, para 99.
[20] Draft Declaration on Fundamental Human Rights and Freedoms, UN Doc E/325.
[21] Humphrey (n 1) 30.
[22] MA Glendon, *A World Made New, Eleanor Roosevelt and the Universal Declaration of Human Rights* (New York, Random House, 2001) 47.
[23] Humphrey (n 1) 31.
[24] Draft Outline of International Bill of Rights (prepared by the Division of Human Rights), UN Doc E/CN.4/AC.1/3.
[25] Humphrey (n 1) 31.
[26] ibid, 32.
[27] Plan of the Draft Outline of an International Bill of Rights (Prepared by the Secretariat), UN Doc E/CN.4/AC.1/3/Add.2.

'documented outline',[28] was issued on 11 June 1947. This was a compilation of fundamental rights drawn from national constitutions and the drafts that had already been submitted to the UN. It used the 48 articles as headings.

Consequently, when the Drafting Committee convened on 9 June 1947, its members had a very substantial volume of background materials that had been prepared by the Human Rights Division, under Humphrey, over the previous six or seven months. The centrepiece of these documents was the 'draft outline' attributed to Humphrey. When she introduced the 'outline' to the Drafting Committee, Eleanor Roosevelt explained that it was 'not a proposed Bill of Human Rights, but simply a working document on the basis of which the Drafting Committee hoped to prepare a preliminary draft bill for the consideration of the Commission on Human Rights'.[29] No doubt this was prudent language on her part, because some members might have bristled at the suggestion that they were being spoon-fed a text. Indeed, it may also be quite reasonable to view the Humphrey draft as somewhat of a menu, in the sense that he was setting out a series of options from which the Drafting Committee could make choices. But in reality, it cast the die. Everything that was to follow amounted to an amendment of the draft that Humphrey had written.

After several days, the Drafting Committee decided to establish a 'Temporary Working Group' consisting of René Cassin, Charles Malik, and Geoffrey Wilson. Its task included preparing a 'logical rearrangement' of the Humphrey draft outline in light of the discussions that had taken place.[30] The Working Group decided, in turn, to ask René Cassin to formulate a 'rough-draft Declaration'. Cassin's text, prepared over the course of a weekend, consisted of a preamble and 44 articles.[31] It has sometimes been described as the original version of the Universal Declaration. In an article in the *UNESCO Courier* published on the twentieth anniversary of the adoption of the Universal Declaration, Cassin was identified in the headline as 'the author of the first draft of the Universal Declaration'.[32] Cassin himself explained: 'An eight-member drafting committee then called on me to prepare a preliminary draft Declaration, on the basis of material assembled by Professors John P. Humphrey and Emile Giraud, and proposals submitted by certain governments (Panama and Cuba).'[33]

Cassin's description of the Humphrey draft as 'material assembled' understates its significance. Mary Ann Glendon cites the verbatim transcript, where on 17 June 1947, Eleanor Roosevelt, who was chairing the Drafting Committee, is quoted as stating: 'Now we come to Mr. Cassin's draft, which has based itself on the Secretariat's comparative draft'.[34] Glendon says the Cassin draft 'preserved most of the substantive

---

[28] International Bill of Rights Documented Outline, UN Doc E/CN.4/AC.1/3/Add.1.

[29] Commission on Human Rights Drafting Committee, 1st Meeting, 9 June 1947, UN Doc E/CN.4/AC.1/SR.1, 5.

[30] Commission on Human Rights Drafting Committee, First Session, Sixth Meeting, 16 June 1947, UN Doc E/CN.4/AC.1/SR.6, 8.

[31] Suggestions Submitted by the Representative of France for Articles 7–32 of the International Declaration of Rights, UN Doc E/CN.4/AC.1/W.2/Rev.1

[32] The impression lingers in the literature. See, for example, F Benoît-Rohmer, 'France: The Origins, with the Prospect of Increasing Effect' in V Jaichand and M Suksi (eds), *60 Years of the Universal Declaration of Human Rights in Europe* (Antwerp, Oxford, Portland, Intersentia, 2009) 19, 19–20.

[33] R Cassin, 'How the Charter of Human Rights Was Born' *UNESCO Courier* (January 1968) 4.

[34] Glendon (n 22) 65.

content of Humphrey's draft, but under his hand the document acquired an internal logic and achieved greater unity'.[35] Cassin's biographer, Marc Agi, acknowledges that he was not 'le père exclusif de la Déclaration', but contends that 'en comparaison de ce que d'autres personalités ont apporté au projet à titre individuel, il en est le principal inspirateur'.[36] Agi cites Cassin's remarks at a press conference, held in early July 1949, where he recognised that the United Nations Secretariat had prepared 'une documentation préparatoire remarquable' but then insisted that 'une Déclaration internationale ne saurait être la photographie, même agrandie, des nombreuses déclarations des droits de l'homme ...'[37]

Drafting of the Universal Declaration continued for another eighteen months. Many small changes were made to the texts proposed by Humphrey and Cassin. Nevertheless, the general approach that was set out in Humphrey's 'draft outline' was not significantly altered. In particular, the Declaration retained the emphasis that Humphrey had placed on economic, social and cultural rights. 'It is by no means certain that economic and social rights would have been included in the final text if I had not included them in mine', he wrote in his memoir. 'There was considerable opposition in the drafting committee to their inclusion'.[38]

III. Conceiving the Last Utopia

Humphrey was one of several extraordinary individuals whose personal involvement was so important during the drafting of the Universal Declaration of Human Rights. What is astonishing is that few of them appear to have given much thought or attention to the codification of international human rights until the task was thrust upon them. They were all gifted, intelligent, and capable people with great careers in both past and future. What was it that attracted them to the human rights project, rather than to the many other opportunities provided by the dynamic post-Second World War environment? Humphrey was a legal academic specialised in public international law, a man of progressive political views but with no demonstrated expertise in the area of human rights. Serendipity brought him to New York, the fact that a good friend happened to be in charge of the section of the UN with responsibility for human rights. Humphrey excelled at the job as if he had been training for the role his entire lifetime. 'Some are born great, some achieve greatness, and some have greatness thrust upon them', wrote Shakespeare in Twelfth Night. Humphrey answers to both the second and third of these descriptions.

John Humphrey had 'always thought that the Declaration would be the most important part of the international bill of rights'. Although 'not technically binding', it would apply to all states and would have the great authority of the United Nations behind it', he wrote. 'It would also be a catalyst of national and international

---

[35] ibid, 63.
[36] M Agi, *René Cassin, Prix Nobel de la Paix (1887–1976)* (Paris, Perrin, 1998) 229.
[37] ibid.
[38] Humphrey (n 1) 32.

legislation'.[39] On this issue, his views and those of Cassin were completely aligned. In the General Assembly, several speakers discussed the legal nature of the declaration. René Cassin linked it to the binding provisions of the Charter of the United Nations, explaining that although it was 'less powerful and binding than a convention':

> it had no less legal value, for it was contained in a resolution of the Assembly which was empowered to make recommendations; it was a development of the Charter which had brought human rights within the scope of positive international law.[40]

But other contemporary observers were less enthusiastic. Hersch Lauterpacht responded very harshly to the Declaration's adoption, dismissing entirely its claim to any legal status:

> Not being a legal instrument, the Declaration would appear to be outside international law. Its provisions cannot properly be the subject-matter of legal interpretation. There is little meaning in attempting to elucidate, by reference to accepted canons of construction and to preparatory work, the extent of an obligation which is binding only in the sphere of conscience.[41]

Humphrey was so angry at Lauterpacht's pessimistic report on the Declaration to the International Law Association that he allowed his own membership in the organisation to lapse. But he wrote much later that it was 'only fair' to note that Lauterpacht's comments were made 'shortly after the adoption of the Declaration, before it began to have any real impact and before the subtle processes began to work which would make it part of the customary law of nations'.[42] Whatever the view taken from the perspective of 1948, however, the legal significance of the Declaration cannot today be reduced to an analysis of the understanding of those who drafted it. The conservative forecasts of scholars like Lauterpacht have not come to pass. The 70 years following its adoption have established and confirmed its role as a source of 'legal value', in Cassin's words; as 'a catalyst of national and international legislation', in Humphrey's, and indeed of legal obligation taken in a broad sense.

---

[39] ibid, 64.
[40] ibid, 866.
[41] H Lauterpacht, 'The Universal Declaration of Human Rights' (1948) 25 *BYBIL* 369. Along similar lines, JL Kunz, 'The United Nations Declaration of Human Rights' (1949) 43 *AJIL* 321: 'it is not law'.
[42] Humphrey (n 1) 74.

Part III

The Fight Against Discrimination
in the Places Close to Home

13

Rosa Parks
Tired of Giving In

KASEY McCALL-SMITH

> I would like to be remembered as a person who wanted to be free ... so other people would also be free.[1]

I. Surviving in 'Jim Crow' South

When Rosa Parks refused to give up her seat to a white passenger in the 'coloured' section on a public bus in Montgomery, Alabama, on 1 December 1955, her refusal was because she 'was tired of giving in'.[2] She simply did not think that she should have to continue to suffer the casual, daily discrimination that pervaded the 'Jim Crow' South.[3] The police were called, she was arrested and released on bail later in the evening. Her simple act of defiance was driven by her exhaustion with years of being treated as a second-class citizen in the highly segregated southern United States.

Rosa Louise McCauley entered this world on 4 February 1913, born to Leona (née Edwards) and James McCauley in the rural town of Tuskegee, Alabama, at a time when black men, despite their emancipation in the previous century, were not supposed to use anything other than first names when identifying themselves and black children were treated very differently from their white peers. Most men, women and children of colour in 1913 spent their days working in the cotton fields 'from can to can't',[4] but change was on the horizon with the impending First World War and resurgence

---

[1] Rosa Parks, from a 1992 interview with PBS Radio.
[2] R Parks with J Haskins, *Rosa Parks: My Story* (New York, Puffin Books, 1992) 116.
[3] 'Jim Crow' was the term used for the legal system of racial segregation following the US Civil War. See CR Wilson, 'Jim Crow' in CR Wilson and W Ferris (eds), *Encyclopedia of Southern Culture* (Chapel Hill, University of North Carolina Press, 1989) 213–14.
[4] Parks (n 2) 35.

of the Ku Klux Klan with its unchecked, indiscriminate violence against the black population. Rosa's mother, a teacher with an insatiable thirst for knowledge, shaped her ideas about the struggles that black Americans faced in their pursuit of the basic components of a dignified life. Education of minority children was not a core concern of Alabama nor of other southern states at the time. As a result, Leona was forced to leave Rosa and her younger brother Sylvester in the safekeeping of their maternal grandparents during the week so that she could pursue her passion as a teacher in Pine Level, the nearest school for black children, and earn a wage to support her family as James McCauley was often away working as a carpenter.

From an early age, Rosa navigated the complexities of race. A major irony of that period was that her grandparents, like so many of their generation, were the products of forced sexual relations by white 'masters' upon their 'coloured' help. This history of injustice resonated loudly in Rosa's early life in the company of her grandfather, a former slave, who was so fair he could 'pass for white', a point of which he took full advantage. Rosa's first glimpse into civil disobedience was the actions of her grandfather, such as shaking hands with white men and introducing himself by his last name 'Edwards', a direct affront to the 'Jim Crow etiquette that black men introduce themselves only by their first names and always address whites as "Mister" or "Miss"'.[5]

Rosa's mother and grandparents subscribed to Booker T Washington's belief that 'high moral character and absolute cleanliness were "civilizing agents" that would help blacks excel in America'.[6] Even in his mischievous moments and in the face of racist abuse, her grandfather maintained a decorum that impressed Rosa. This commitment to unimpeachable morals would come to be a defining feature for the future heroine of the civil rights movement. Maintaining this level of civility must have proved particularly difficult as a child watching her grandfather's light skin also work against him when he tried to join black activist groups, highlighting the exclusionary obsession with race at the time. In response, Rosa turned to the African Methodist Episcopal (AME) Church, also known as the 'Freedom Church', as a source of strength to 'stand up for rights' and a constant reminder that 'a heart filled with love could conquer anything, even bigotry'.[7]

By her own admission and no doubt driven by her devotion to religion, Rosa had a strong sense of fairness and independence that was not always well received in the South of her youth. These qualities were developed through the guidance of her mother, the example of her grandfather and her education from the age of 11 at Miss White's Industrial School for Girls in Montgomery, Alabama. Led by Alice White from Massachusetts, the school also followed Booker T Washington's example that 'cleanliness was next to godliness' and opened up the world to the young Rosa.[8] The school, however, was burned to the ground before she could finish her high school education, but this did not dampen Rosa's drive for self-improvement and knowledge. Her strength of purpose and unwillingness to accept the status quo

[5] Douglas Brinkley, *Rosa Parks: A Life* (New York, Penguin, 2000) 22.
[6] Brinkley (n 5) 18.
[7] ibid, 15–16.
[8] ibid.

race inequalities led her grandmother to forecast that she 'would probably be lynched before the age of 20'.[9]

After Rosa met Raymond Parks in her late teens, she grew to love his rebellious attitude during a time when the South was generally divided between 'Uncle Tom' – a name generally used to refer to meek or submissive blacks – and 'Mr Charles' – the counterpart referring to oppressive white landholders. In her view, 'Parks', as she called him, was intelligent and interesting despite his lack of formal education. He was also the first real social and political activist she had ever met. In 1931, as Rosa's relationship with her future husband quickly developed, it marked not only the beginning of her own family, but also her introduction to a number of activist groups in Alabama, including the National Association for the Advancement of Colored People (NAACP). Raymond Parks had been a long time member of the NAACP and was part of a secret group of its members trying to assist the 'Scottsboro Boys' – nine young black men aged 14–19 years of age that had been arrested and charged with raping two white women in 1931. His dedication to helping these strangers endeared him to Rosa and she grew to greatly admire him. It was not simply his commitment to saving the nine boys from what were largely viewed as fabricated charges that would lead them to death row, but his understanding that the black community was fast approaching a breaking point. Later in life she recalled of her husband, 'I came to understand that he was always interested in and willing to work for things that would improve life for his race, his family and himself'.[10]

Rosa McCauley became Mrs Raymond Parks in December 1932 at her mother's home in Pine Level. After her marriage, she finished her high school degree in 1933 at the age of 20. At the end of that decade only seven in a hundred black Americans had a high school education. Rosa's empathy, consummate attention to detail and dignity in all her actions, including her trademark hat and bag, overshadowed her meagre education and became the enduring trademarks of a selfless rights activist. Following the lead of the biographer Jeanne Theoharis, the remainder of this chapter refers to Rosa as 'Mrs Parks', a title form of respect that was denied to black women during the Jim Crow years but used by most of her colleagues and comrades through the turbulent times of the civil rights movement.[11]

II. Dismantling 'Separate but Equal', One Law at a Time

In the early twentieth century, black people in the United States, as in many other nations across the globe, had no civil rights and no one to listen to their complaints. Though President Roosevelt has ordered the desegregation of public places, transportation and military bases in 1941, the southern American states continued to maintain

[9] Parks (n 2) 23.
[10] ibid, 64.
[11] J Theoharis, *The Rebellious Life of Mrs Rosa Parks* (Boston, Beacon Press, 2013) xvi.

discriminatory practices in all aspects of life, from segregated drinking fountains to separate, and by no means equal, schools.[12]

From the beginning of her marriage, Mrs Parks' eyes were increasingly opened to the daily bullying and disrespect of a segregated society and she often suffered these indignities. The change at this point in her life was that she became determined to fight the system while maintaining dignity and self-respect. In addition to supporting the activist work of her husband in his campaign to free the Scottsboro Boys, Mrs Parks found herself naturally drawn to the fight against general racial injustice that was rampant across Montgomery and the rest of Alabama. Following Raymond's lead, her first foray into activism was directed toward prevailing over segregationists as they blocked black people from voting. In the pursuit of black voter registration, the Parkses joined forces with Edgar Daniel (ED) Nixon, a prominent desegregation activist in Alabama.

ED Nixon was not only a key figure in galvanising black voter registration, he was also instrumental in bringing Mrs Parks formally into the fight for racial equality. Nixon was president of the local branch of the Brotherhood of Sleeping Car Porters and in the early 1940s was also active in the NAACP. In December 1943, Mrs Parks attended her first NAACP meeting – at the time few women were actively involved. As it happened, it was the annual officer election meeting and she was the only woman in attendance; thus, when the handful of men in the room asked for a secretary, Mrs Parks recalled that she was too timid to decline. Later in life she noted that the fight for racial equality left her little room to consider the simultaneous struggle for gender equality, yet she maintained a clear figure of female strength to the very end of her life. Being active in the NAACP came with a constant risk to life. After a meeting about the Scottsboro Boys, Mrs Parks recalled 'I was very, very depressed about the fact that black men could not hold a meeting without fear of bodily injury or death'.[13] But it was not just the men that were in potential danger; public association with the NAACP in Alabama in the 1940s and 1950s was viewed as an act of bravery in light of the growing aggression of the Ku Klux Klan and McCarthyism in the 1950s.

Nixon was elected president of the Montgomery branch in that same December 1943 meeting and though he thought women belonged 'in the kitchen', he admired Mrs Parks' secretarial skills and levelheadedness and encouraged her in her role with the NAACP. In her early years with the organisation this meant training young people to be activists and recording by hand countless accounts of injustice against black people at the hands of the local authorities, or abuse and assault by white segregationists. 'Sometimes it was very difficult to keep going when all our work seemed to be in vain'.[14] The way in which the law oppressed African Americans, either through its application or disapplication, was the focal point of Mrs Parks' career.

---

[12] The 'separate, but equal' doctrine permitting discrimination was laid down in the case of *Plessy v Ferguson* in 1896. For a history of the case and the foundation it laid for the civil rights movement see WH Hoffer, *Plessy v. Ferguson: Race and Inequality in Jim Crow America* (Topeka, University of Kansas Press, 2012).

[13] Parks (n 2) 67.

[14] ibid, 71.

Alongside Nixon, voter registration in Alabama was the first major campaign in which Mrs Parks was personally, closely involved. In 1940s America, very few black people voted. To register, a black adult had to find a white voter to vouch for them and pay backdated poll taxes to the date when they first became eligible to register. Many members of the black community, including Raymond Parks (after several failed attempts), ultimately refused to take part in this humiliating subservient process. Even though many voter registration activists of the time understood that the only way to effect enduring change was through the ballot box, many blacks viewed the vouching system as another means of oppressing their race and, by extension, a further incarnation of the 'Uncle Tom' characterisation they were trying to overcome. But along with Nixon, Mrs Parks maintained that exercising the legal right to vote was key to equality and unlocking the future of black people in America. She exhorted, 'The right to vote is so important for Americans. We vote for people to represent us in government. If we do not like the way they represent us, we can vote for someone else'.[15] It took Mrs Parks multiple attempts over three years to register in the face of adversity and certain danger. By creating a hand-copy of the 21 voter registration test questions and her answers – a basis upon which a lawsuit against the voter registration board could be brought if she was denied again – Mrs Parks began her life-long common sense approach to using the law to fight oppression and, in 1945, after they payment of $16.50 in back-dated poll taxes, she finally was registered to vote.[16]

In the years that followed, she continued to register African Americans to vote, but the NAACP was exploring other ways to make positive changes in the daily lives of the local black community. The May 1954 Supreme Court decision in *Brown v Board of Education* overturned the longstanding 'separate, but equal' principle set out in the 1896 case of *Plessy v Ferguson*.[17] Mrs Parks reminisced that the Court had ruled 'Separate education could not be equal, and many of us saw had the same idea applied to other things, like public transportation'.[18] The insidiousness of public bus segregation had grown more acute over the first half of the twentieth century. Though blacks in Montgomery made up a greater percentage of the daily passengers, they were subjected to countless daily degradations, such as the bus company's refusal to extend bus lines into predominantly black neighbourhoods. This forced black customers to walk half a mile to the nearest bus stop while their white counterparts enjoyed stops at every block in their neighbourhoods. With so many perpetual indignities suffered by the black population of Montgomery, the idea of a bus boycott germinated.

Before her personal stand on the bus, Mrs Parks had already been testing whether there was fertile ground for a bus boycott as a means of forcing the city to move away from segregationist policies. At the same time, the Montgomery NAACP was also angling to sue the city of Montgomery over bus segregation. It had been considering the cases of various women who had been arrested for refusing to give up their seats, but they had yet to find the perfect victim for their claim – a woman who was 'above reproach'.

---

[15] ibid, 71.
[16] ibid, 75–76.
[17] *Brown v Board of Education of Topeka* 247 US 483 (1954).
[18] Parks (n 2) 108.

On 1 December 1955 when Mrs Parks was asked to give up her seat at the front of the coloured section of the bus, she refused while others obeyed. The law of segregation was one that she refused to accept. Though her day had started just as the previous day, her simple act of refusal began a watershed movement across black American society. Even with the silent urging of the other black passengers and the more vocal admonition of the white passengers, driver and police officer, Mrs Rosa Parks had finally had enough.

> People always say that I didn't give up my seat because I was tired, but that isn't true. I was not tired physically, or no more tired than I usually was at the end of a working day. I was not old, although some people have an image of me as being old then. I was forty-two. No, the only tired I was, was tired of giving in.[19]

She was promptly arrested, booked, given a trial date and released on bail. How often in our lives do we hear the old adage, 'the rules are the rules' or 'the law is the law'? The latter was the response that Mrs Parks received from one of the two police officers dispatched to arrest her for breaching the bus seating policy when she asked 'why do you all push us around?'[20]

On 5 December 1955, the day of her trial, all African Americans in Montgomery were urged to 'not ride the buses to work, to town, to school, or anywhere' and to Mrs Parks' surprise, they did not; they 'had finally had enough of segregation on the buses.'[21] On the same day, local black ministers met and quickly established the Montgomery Improvement Association (MIA), electing the Reverend Martin Luther King, Jr, as its leader. He had moved to Montgomery in October 1954 as the Dexter Avenue Baptist Church pastor with his wife, Coretta Scott King, an Alabama native. Mrs Parks was convicted, given a suspended sentence, fined $10 and $4.00 in court costs. But her commitment to the fight for equality was only further entrenched and she proceeded from the courthouse to a citywide meeting of the MIA. Her conviction for breach of the Montgomery public ordinance segregating bus seating signalled a tide change and the local black community prepared for action. No longer would the minority community permit their continual, unchecked discrimination. King, who was a casual acquaintance of Mrs Parks before her stand on the bus, said of her arrest and conviction:

> Since it had to happen, I'm happy it happened to a person like Rosa Parks, for nobody can doubt the boundless outreach of her integrity. Nobody can doubt the height of her character, nobody can doubt the depth of her Christian commitment.[22]

In the meeting the MIA launched a boycott of public buses in Montgomery that would ultimately last 381 days. In Mrs Parks' words, 'The direct-action civil rights movement had begun'.[23] The income lost through loss of the custom of the roughly 40,000 African Americans in Montgomery all but crippled the public transit authority.

---

[19] ibid, 116.
[20] ibid, 117.
[21] ibid, 130.
[22] ibid, 139.
[23] ibid, 160.

At the same time, a federal suit challenging the legality of bus segregation was filed in US federal court. In response, white lawyers revived a 1903 law that criminalised boycotts and Mrs Parks, along with Dr King and 87 others were indicted in February 1956 but the ploy did not break the boycott. Eventually, on 13 November 1956, the Supreme Court ruled that bus segregation in Montgomery was unconstitutional.[24] Over a year after the Montgomery bus boycott began, on 20 December 1956, the City of Montgomery received its order from the US Supreme Court to integrate its transportation system. Though many factors ultimately contributed to the success of the 1955–56 Montgomery bus boycott, many viewed the 'spiritual presence' of Mrs Parks, a good Christian woman who was above reproach, as the '"heaven-sent" messenger', the mention of whose name would relieve even the weariest of black workers having thoughts of riding the bus during that year.[25]

It was only when the official order arrived that black people began riding the buses in the face of continuing adversity and sporadic violence, including instances of sniper fire. However, the boycott had delivered an incontrovertible message that the African American community would no longer accept the Jim Crow status quo. 'Never before had black people demonstrated so clearly how much those city buses depended on their business. More important, never before had the black community of Montgomery united in protest against segregation on the buses'.[26] Following her arrest, Mrs Parks had gained immediate notoriety for her stand on the bus, and received constant invitations to speak to civic organisations across the south and further afield. In the wake of the Montgomery bus boycott, other cities followed suit. Their African American communities, too, were tired of giving in.

Even after the Supreme Court decision and the end of the boycott, Montgomery was a bed of white supremacist activity. The White Citizen's Council disseminated continuing messages of hate and repression, with specific venom for Mrs Parks or any white person deemed sympathetic to the black community.[27] In 1957, Mrs Parks, her husband and her mother moved to Detroit, where her brother had been based following his return from the Second World War and it remained her home and base for activism for the remainder of her life.

III. A Touchstone for Dignity

Rosa Parks' refusal to submit to segregation laws on the Montgomery bus was one of many small, individual acts of defiance that culminated in the Civil Rights Movement in the United States. In the late 1950s and into the 1960s, all over the south and, eventually, in the capital, African Americans and others who understood that equality

[24] *Browder v Gayle* 352 US 903 (1956).
[25] Brinkley (n 5) 142.
[26] Parks (n 2) 132.
[27] Theoharis (n 11) 107.

was the only path forward marched, protested and boycotted as a means of effecting change of segregationist laws that prevented them from voting, from drinking water in particular fountains and from equal access to transportation. Progress was made, but it was a slow-moving reward. Twenty years after the start of the Montgomery bus boycott, more than 1.5 million African Americans had registered to vote.[28] But many were also killed in unadulterated violence fuelled by the sole factor of skin colour. The Montgomery bus boycott, described as 'impeccably lawful, orderly, dignified – and effective'[29] set the stage for what would prove to be a tide change for segregation. Mrs Parks continued to appear and speak about desegregation and progressing civil rights after she left Alabama.

> Her authentic self-deprecation was just Parks being herself as always. Never the prima donna, her genuine dignity made her shine even in the erudite, college-educated company of King, Nixon, Gray and Abernathy ... She may have lacked her cohorts' vocabulary and worldliness, but part of her lasting appeal is that nobody ever had a bad word to say about her.[30]

The well-known male leaders of the Montgomery bus boycott and subsequent civil rights movement viewed Mrs Parks as a natural maternal figure. She was about 20 years their senior, and they continued to consult her as their crusade for civil rights gained traction. She was in Birmingham on the stage with Martin Luther King, Jr, when he was attacked by a white member of the American Nazi Party at the Southern Christian Leadership Conference, which fought against segregation in many areas of southern life. After the ordeal, she gave King two aspirin and a coke for the headache that followed the attack.[31] Along with King, she supported peaceful protest through love of other human beings, though she acknowledged on occasion that perhaps a not entirely peaceful approach may have produced change more quickly.

By her own admission, Mrs Park's life was 'a life history of being rebellious'.[32] She peacefully protested as part of the civil rights march on Washington, DC, in 1963. The following year, President Lyndon B Johnson succeeded in getting the monumental 1964 Civil Rights Act through Congress, which made some headway in securing legal protections for African American Americans in their battle for equality. In the 1970s and 1980s she organised further boycotts in Detroit and other places when ordinances that harkened back to Jim Crow were put in place. She continued to 'fight the good fight' throughout her life. She shared company with many other civil rights heroes, including Septima Clark, Eleanor Roosevelt, Thurgood Marshall and Malcolm X. She comforted Coretta Scott King before Dr King's funeral in April 1968 and later dipped in and out of the Black Power movement that followed King's death.

In 1987, Mrs Parks founded the Rosa and Raymond Parks Institute for Self-Development offering programmes for youth to give them hope for the future. For much of the end of her life she worked to ensure the enduring nature of the foundation while simultaneously struggling to keep her own finances in order following the

[28] Brinkley (n 5) 208.
[29] Quoted from *The Washington Post* editorial in Theoharis (n 11) 112.
[30] Brinkley (n 5) 127.
[31] Parks (n 2) 164.
[32] Theoharis (n 11) 1.

deaths of her husband, brother and mother within three years of one another. Rosa Parks died on 24 October 2005 in Detroit. She became the first black woman to lie in state in the US Capitol building rotunda. Shortly after her death, a permanent memorial to Mrs Parks was ordered for the US Capitol's Statuary Hall, the first full statuary of an African American. At the unveiling of the statue, President Obama paid tribute saying:

> She defied the odds, and she defied injustice. She lived a life of activism but also a life of dignity and grace. And in a single moment, with the simplest of gestures, she helped change America – and change the world.[33]

And while many acknowledge that 'Rosa Parks helped her fellow African-Americans claim their God-given freedoms and made America a better place',[34] the United States of today does not seem to have kept her message safe. African Americans and other minority groups continue to be habitually brutalised by police and imprisoned at a much higher rate than whites. Minorities still suffer every day indignities that go unnoticed and unpunished. It is fitting that at the unveiling of her memorial statute it was noted, 'Here in the hall, she casts an unlikely silhouette – unassuming in a lineup of proud stares, challenging all of us once more to look up and to draw strength from stillness'.[35] And while '[she] moved the world when she refused to move her seat', her legacy is one of concerted action in the everyday pursuit of dignity.[36]

---

[33] E Goodin, 'Rosa Parks Statue Unveiled', *The Hill*, 27 February 2013, available at thehill.com/capital-living/cover-stories/285385-rosa-parks-statue-unveiled.

[34] Office of the Press Secretary, 'President Signs H.R. 4145 to Place Statue of Rosa Parks in U.S. Capitol', 1 December 2005, available at georgewbush-whitehouse.archives.gov/news/releases/2005/12/20051201-1.html.

[35] Representative John Boehner, quoted in S Gamboa, 'Rosa Parks Statue Unveiled at Capitol', *Real Clear Politics*, 27 February 2013, available at www.realclearpolitics.com/articles/2013/02/27/rosa_parks_statue_unveiled_at_capitol_117189.html.

[36] Senator Harry Reid, quoted in Gamboa, ibid.

14

Dr Martin Luther King, Jr

A Visionary Citizen of the American South and the World

VIVEK BHATT

Injustice anywhere is a threat to justice everywhere. We are caught in an inescapable network of mutuality, tied in a single garment of destiny.[1]

I. From Mike to Dr King

Michael Luther King, Jr, was born in Atlanta, Georgia, on 15 January 1929. He spent his formative years in Sweet Auburn, a 'Negro' ghetto on the outskirts of downtown Atlanta. Here, 'Mike' witnessed the roles of the state, racial prejudice and God in the lives of African American residents of the segregated south. The Kings led a 'relatively comfortable middle-class existence' in Sweet Auburn.[2] Atlanta was divided into 'white' and 'Negro' neighbourhoods in 1906, when the outbreak of race riots led to the adoption of segregation laws. By the time of Mike's birth, Sweet Auburn had become the 'most important residential and business centre in black Atlanta'.[3] It was an entrepreneurial and eclectic neighbourhood, where youths such as Mike experienced firsthand African Americans' abilities to prosper despite the constraints of segregation.[4]

King looked back on his childhood with great fondness. 'It is quite easy for me to lean more toward optimism than pessimism about human nature', he wrote, 'Mainly

---

[1] ML King Jr, 'Letter from Birmingham Jail' (first published 1963, Carson Newman University, November 2007) 1, available at web.cn.edu/kwheeler/documents/Letter_Birmingham_Jail.pdf.
[2] R Bruns, *Martin Luther King, Jr: A Biography* (Westport, Greenwood Press, 2006) 6.
[3] R Lischer, *The Preacher King: Martin Luther King Jr and the Word that Moved America* (Oxford, Oxford University Press, 1997) 19.
[4] ibid; Bruns (n 2) 5.

because of my childhood experiences'.[5] This was not only because of the 'environmental circumstances' of his childhood,[6] but also because of his family relationships. Mike's upbringing and family life were centred upon the church. His maternal grandfather, Reverend Alfred Daniel Williams, was the founder of Ebenezer Baptist Church on Auburn Avenue. Michael, Sr later assumed leadership of the church, transforming it into 'one of the largest and most prestigious Baptist churches in Atlanta'.[7] Mike's mother was, meanwhile, the church organist and the conductor of its choir.[8] She nurtured young Mike's musical talent, taking him to sing in various smaller congregations around Atlanta.[9] In 1934, Michael, Sr changed both his and his son's names to Martin Luther, a transformation that signified the family's increased affluence and social standing.[10]

As a founding member of the Atlanta chapter of the National Association for the Advancement of Coloured People (NAACP), King's maternal grandfather was extensively involved in race relations. As his grandson would many years later, Reverend Williams advocated for nonviolence, coordinating a successful boycott of the newspaper *The Georgian* when its editor made derogatory comments about Atlanta's black community.[11] Martin, Sr also played an active role in race relations, sponsoring programmes in aid of Atlanta's youth and becoming a charter member of the Atlanta Voters' League. Nevertheless, King grew up 'insulated against the most brutal aspects of Southern bigotry';[12] Sweet Auburn was both a symptom of and a shield against the cruelty of race relations at the time.

Racism was, however, an unavoidable aspect of life in the south, and witnessing it evoked great anger in King as he approached adolescence. As a high school student, King had a number of experiences of segregation on transportation. On a bus home from a speaking competition in Dublin, Georgia, he was scolded by the driver for occupying a seat reserved for white passengers, and subsequently was advised by his speaking coach to vacate the seat so as to appease those on board. Reflecting upon the incident in a 1965 interview, King said it made him angrier than he had ever been.[13] Looking back on his youth, King admitted that he came close to following a different path to that of nonviolence:

> I had passed spots where Negroes had been savagely lynched, and had watched the Ku Klux Klan on its rides at night. I had seen police brutality with my own eyes and watched Negroes receive the most tragic injustice in the courts. All of these things had done something to my growing personality. I had come perilously close to resenting all white people.[14]

[5] Quoted by Lischer (n 3) 19.
[6] ibid, 19.
[7] DL Lewis, *King: A Biography* (Champagne, University of Illinois Press, 2013) 4.
[8] Bruns (n 2) 5.
[9] Lewis (n 7) 4.
[10] ML King Jr, *The Papers of Martin Luther King, Jr. Volume I* (C Carson ed, Berkeley, University of California Press, 1992) 31.
[11] R Burrow Jr, *Martin Luther King, Jr, and the Theology of Resistance* (Jefferson, NC, McFarland & Company, 2015) 80.
[12] Lewis (n 7) 11.
[13] Bruns (n 2) 8.
[14] ML King Jr, *Stride Toward Freedom: The Montgomery Story* (Harper & Bow, 1958) 90.

One might expect that King's upbringing and childhood experiences naturally led him to assume positions of leadership within both the church and the American Civil Rights Movement. Indeed, Martin, Sr continually spoke about race relations around the dinner table, at church and in public. 'He played a great part in shaping my conscience', King wrote. 'I still remember walking down the street beside him as he muttered, "I don't care how long I have to live with this system, I will never accept it"'.[15] Yet as he entered into college, King was unwilling to fulfil the community's expectation that he, like his forebears, would be a pastor and activist. As a teenager, King developed reflexivity and an appetite for intellectual rigour, struggling to subscribe to religious teachings. 'I guess I accepted biblical studies uncritically until I was about twelve years old', he wrote. 'But this uncritical attitude could not last long, for it was contrary to the very nature of my being'.[16] Having skipped two grades in high school and aged only 15, King enrolled in Morehouse College with the hope of studying medicine.[17]

As with religion, King struggled to unquestioningly accept scientific laws and principles. Having performed poorly in philosophy, he enrolled as a sociology major. It was during his time as a sociology student at Morehouse that King was inspired by the 'old biblical literalism and almost carnival pulpit dramaturgy' of Professor George Kelsey and Benjamin Mays, president of Morehouse.[18] By the end of his first year in college, King had decided that he intended to enter the ministry, but he did not do so as a full-time pursuit until he had acquired a higher education. Having completed his bachelor's degree, King relocated to Chester, Pennsylvania, to undertake further study at Crozer Theological Seminary. Here, King began 'a serious intellectual quest for a method to eliminate social evil'.[19] Reading Rauschenbusch's *Christianity and the Social Crisis* enabled King to make an intellectual connection between religion and social justice.[20] 'Any religion which professes to be concerned about the souls of men and is not concerned about the social and economic conditions that scar the soul', King wrote, 'is a moribund religion'.[21]

King proceeded to examine the works of Plato, Aristotle, Rousseau, Hobbes, Bentham, Mill, Locke, Hegel, and Marx, among others.[22] As part of this 'intellectual quest', he also audited a number of classes at the University of Pennsylvania. One afternoon, King attended a lecture given by Dr Mordecai Johnson about a recent trip to India. In this presentation, 'Gandhi's spiritual leadership and pacifist techniques attained an immediate and luminescent dimension'.[23] King purchased a number of books on Gandhi's life and works, reflecting on pacifism's value as a form of resistance. Inspired by the writings of Gandhi, King developed his philosophy that love and

[15] Quoted by Bruns (n 2) 9.
[16] King (n 10) 361.
[17] Lewis (n 7) 20.
[18] ibid, 24.
[19] King (n 14) 91.
[20] ibid; W Rauschenbusch, *Christianity and the Social Crisis* (first published 1907, Louisville, KY, John Knox Press, 1991).
[21] King (n 14) 91.
[22] ibid, 92.
[23] Lewis (n 7) 34.

nonviolence are potent forms of political activism.[24] 'True pacifism', he wrote many years later, is a 'courageous confrontation of evil by the power of love, in the faith that it is better to be the recipient of violence than the inflicter of it'.[25] King graduated from Crozer in June 1951 with the highest grades in his class. And, in September 1951, he commenced his PhD at Boston University. Recognising his promise, members of faculty kept the doctoral candidate engaged in the 'practical applications of nonviolent philosophies'.[26] Thus, Mike became Dr Martin Luther King, Jr: a scholar, preacher, pacifist and activist.

II. Making his Dream a Reality through Pacifism, Reform and Internationalism

A. King the Pacifist

Many remember King as the leader of the 1963 March on Washington and the 1965 Selma to Montgomery March for Voting Rights, which led to Congress's passage of the Civil Rights Act and Voting Rights Act respectively. But long before affecting legal change, King worked to spread the ideas of pacifism and nonviolence within discontented African American communities in the south. King was a skilled orator with a commanding presence, evoking emotional responses from behind both the pulpit and the podium. By invoking religious imagery, he convinced those around him of the value of expressing their anger and discontent through peaceful protest. 'I am grateful to God', he wrote, 'That ... the dimension of nonviolence has entered our struggle. If this philosophy had not emerged, I am convinced that by now the streets of the South would be flowing with floods of blood'.[27]

King and his philosophical views rose to prominence during the Montgomery bus boycott. The boycott began on 5 December 1955 as a one-day demonstration to mark the trial of Rosa Parks, who was removed from a bus and arrested when she did not acquiesce to a white passenger's demand that she vacate her seat. Parks' story quickly turned into the centrepiece of a wider struggle relating to segregation of the city's transportation. King was appointed as president and spokesperson of the newly founded Montgomery Improvement Association,[28] and led a 381-day boycott with participation by nearly all of Montgomery's African American residents. The boycott ended after the US Supreme Court's decision in *Browder v Gayle*, in which the Court held that the segregation of buses was unconstitutional. It was during the boycott that King 'adopted a philosophical as well as tactical commitment' to Gandhian

---

[24] King (n 14) 97.
[25] ibid, 98.
[26] Lewis (n 7) 39.
[27] King (n 1) 4.
[28] T Jackson, *Becoming a King: Martin Luther King Jr and the Making of a National Leader* (Lexington, University Press of Kentucky, 2008) 96.

philosophy.[29] He later reflected that 'Montgomery contributed a new weapon to the Negro revolution. This was the social tool of nonviolent resistance'.[30]

From then on, King consistently called upon members of his community to resist oppression using nonviolent means. In 1957, he was elected the leader of the Southern Christian Leadership Conference (SCLC), an appointment that formalised his position at the helm of the American Civil Rights Movement. Several years later, King led a wide coalition of civil rights groups in a campaign of civil disobedience aimed at Birmingham, Alabama, which he described as 'the most thoroughly segregated city in the United States'.[31] Imprisoned for his involvement in this campaign, King penned *Letter from Birmingham Jail*, a manifesto that is now studied in schools of politics and philosophy around the world. In the open letter, King outlines his version of radical nonviolence, the creation of a crisis and 'creative tension' that forces an actor or community vehemently opposed to negotiation to enter into a dialogue with the dissenting party.[32] 'Nonviolence', he concluded, 'demands that the means we use must be as pure as the ends we seek'.[33]

Thus, King's earliest – and arguably most significant – contribution was not to civil rights as law but rather as a social movement. King's strategy for the American Civil Rights Movement was the culmination of many years of religious and philosophical study. He fashioned himself – and was seen by media and supporters – as the 'American Gandhi',[34] demonstrating that the strategy of *satyagraha* adopted against British colonial powers in India was in fact an effective form of activism in a range of political contexts. King remained steadfastly committed to this strategy even when other members of the African American community employed different methods. While the Black Panthers became involved in a series of violent encounters with the police, for example, King continued to call for a peaceful 'revolution' of human rights at home and abroad.

B. King the Reformer

Later in 1963, King was one of the principal organisers of the March for Jobs and Freedom, more commonly known as the March on Washington. Over a quarter of a million people gathered on the National Mall in Washington, DC, for the march and to hear King deliver his 'I Have a Dream' address. The speech 'became shorthand not only for King's life but for the whole civil rights movement and even the 1960s itself'.[35] King was named *Time* magazine's 1963 Man of the Year, and in 1964, he became the youngest person to have won the Nobel Peace Prize. Even if it was not a direct result

---

[29] TF Jackson, *From Civil Rights to Human Rights: Martin Luther King, Jr, and the Struggle for Economic Justice* (Philadelphia, University of Pennsylvania Press, 2013) 10.
[30] C Carson (ed), *The Autobiography of Martin Luther King, Jr* (New York, Hachette, 2001).
[31] King (n 1) 1.
[32] ibid, 2.
[33] ibid, 6.
[34] Jackson (n 28) 7.
[35] EJ Sundquist, *King's Dream* (New Haven, Yale University Press, 2009) 2.

of the 1963 march, Congress's adoption of the Civil Rights Act in 1964 was definitely an acknowledgment of the impetus that the civil rights movement had gained the previous year. The Act eliminated institutionalised segregation and made it illegal to discriminate against African Americans or other racial minorities in the workplace, employment decisions, schools, universities and on public transportation.

Despite the adoption of the Civil Rights Act, the everyday struggles of African Americans continued. Chief among the injustices suffered by African American communities were the discriminatory voter registration practices of states in the Jim Crow south and the brutal, arbitrary police responses to black registration rallies.[36] In response, the SCLC organised the March for Voting Rights from Selma to Montgomery, Alabama. The first day of the marches, 7 March 1965, became known as 'Bloody Sunday', after protesters were attacked with clubs and tear gas as they made their way across Edmund Pettus Bridge in Selma. On 15 March 1965, and following consultations with King, President Johnson addressed a joint session of Congress, imploring members to vote in favour of the voting rights bill he was to introduce. Johnson signed the Voting Rights Act into law in August 1965. The Act prohibited the 'denial or abridgement of the right of any citizen of the United States to vote on account of race or color'.[37]

As a leader, orator and advocate of nonviolence, King played a pivotal role in the development of civil rights laws in America. King and the SCLC not only led thousands in a peaceful campaign of direct action in the face of violent, arbitrary conduct on the part of state authorities; they also set forth a vision for reform that gained recognition in the legal developments of the time. Yet many have observed that scholars and journalists fixate upon King's dream, the Selma to Montgomery March, the Civil Rights Act and the Voting Rights Act, overlooking King's 'more radical' political vision.[38] King was also a democratic socialist, a critic of the Vietnam War, an internationalist and, ultimately, an exponent of the international human rights movement.

C. King the Internationalist

'For most Americans', writes Jackson, 'King's freedom dreams have become a sound bite recorded in August 1963 on the steps of the Lincoln memorial'.[39] He is remembered as the leader of the American Civil Rights Movement and a relentless campaigner for domestic legal reforms. Yet in the 1960s, King became increasingly vocal about international human rights issues.[40] He openly condemned the 1960 Sharpeville Massacre,

---

[36] DJ Garrow, *Protest at Selma: Martin Luther King, Jr, and the Voting Rights Act of 1965* (New Haven, Yale University Press 1978) 31.

[37] Quoted in T Conroy, 'The Voting Rights Act of 1965: A Selected Annotated Bibliography' (2006) 98 *L Libr J* 663, 665.

[38] Sundquist (n 35) 3.

[39] Jackson (n 28) 1.

[40] DJ Garrow, 'Martin Luther King, Jr, and the Spirit of Leadership' in PJ Albert and R Hoffman (eds), *We Shall Overcome: Martin Luther King, Jr, and the Black Freedom Struggle* (New York, Pantheon Books, 1990); HJ Richardson III, 'Dr Martin Luther King, Jr as an International Human Rights Leader' (2007) 52 *Vill L Rev* 471.

in which the apartheid government murdered over 160 black South Africans.[41] And, in the mid-1960s, King vehemently called for an end to the Vietnam War, arguing that the US government could not militarily oppress peoples abroad whilst ostensibly pursuing social equality and justice at home.[42]

King linked the civil rights campaign he had led with both the international human rights movement and the broader quest for economic equality and social justice within America. He spoke out against British colonialism and US economic imperialism, arguing that the 'southern black freedom struggle and anticolonial movements were both expressions of a global human rights revolution against "political domination and economic exploitation"'.[43] King spoke of the United States' moral obligations as a superpower and its legal obligations as a signatory of the UN Charter; both gave rise to a responsibility to respect others' human rights in its foreign policy, and a responsibility to fulfil American citizens' rights.[44] At home, therefore, King moved from campaigning purely for African American civil rights to coordinating a multiracial effort for both civil and economic rights. King's final campaigns aimed to demonstrate the 'juridical equality of the two primary categories of international human rights: political and civil rights, and economic, social and cultural rights'.[45] They reflected his long-held view that racial inequality is in fact reinforced by economic injustice;[46] 'What good is a hamburger in a desegregated restaurant', he asked, 'if you cannot afford to pay the check?'[47]

Although King the philosopher is mainly known as a pacifist, his writings and speeches resonate with both the Gandhian internationalism and Kantian cosmopolitanism that he encountered as a university student. In *Letter from Birmingham Jail*, King argued that 'we are caught in an inescapable network of mutuality'.[48] He said of the African American, 'With his black brothers of Africa and his brown and yellow brothers of Asia, South America, and the Caribbean, he is moving with a sense of cosmic urgency toward the promised land of racial justice'.[49] Here, King invoked not only the religious image of the promised land, but also the Kantian notion that – through the exercise of rationality – human beings will inevitably uncover nature's intention for them to be free.[50]

Perhaps it was inevitable that, when he received the Nobel Peace Prize in 1964, King associated the civil rights movement with the broader international human rights movement. 'I have the audacity to believe', he said in his acceptance speech, 'That peoples everywhere can have three meals a day for their bodies, education and

---

[41] Richardson (n 40) 471.

[42] ibid, 475; ML King Jr, 'Beyond Vietnam: A Time to Break Silence' (Riverside Church, NYC, 4 April 1967), available at www.crmvet.org/info/mlk_viet.pdf.

[43] Quoted by Jackson (n 28) 12.

[44] Richardson (n 40) 472.

[45] ibid, 473.

[46] Lewis (n 7) 21.

[47] Quoted by Jackson (n 28) 18.

[48] King (n 1) 1.

[49] ibid, 4.

[50] I Kant, *Essays and Treatises on Moral, Political, and Various Philosophical Subjects* vol 1 (W Richardson (trans), William Richardson Publishing, 1798) 414.

culture for their minds, and dignity, equality and freedom for their spirits'.[51] Yet as the Vietnam War continued, King's dream of an international human rights revolution was replaced by frustration with America's irresponsible foreign policy. King's commentary on Vietnam suggested that he, like Gandhi, understood himself as a *vishvamanav*, a citizen of the world.[52] He said in his 1967 Riverside Church address in New York City:

> Every nation must now develop an overriding loyalty to mankind as a whole in order to preserve the best in their individual societies. This call for a world-wide fellowship that lifts neighbourly concern beyond one's tribe is in reality an all-embracing and unconditional love for all men.[53]

King's philosophy of love and nonviolence, therefore, transcended national boundaries. His campaigns relating to African Americans' civil rights might be understood as manifestations of his desire for a world free of oppression upon the bases of class, race and nationality.

III. King the Martyr

Martin Luther King, Jr, was assassinated on 4 April 1968 in Memphis, Tennessee, where he had arrived to support a strike of African American sanitation workers. King is remembered as a fiercely determined advocate for justice and equality who died fighting for the cause of African Americans. Yet he contributed far more than legal change. King contributed the narrative of a man who, in the face of brutality at the hands of Klansmen and police, refused to depart from his ideology of radically nonviolent resistance. King's story continues to inspire generations of nonviolent protesters; the 2003 anti-Iraq War marches across America were, for example, coordinated with his birthday.[54] Yet King's story and the ongoing struggle he inspired also demonstrate that quests for the realisation of human rights are always gradual, often frustrating, and ultimately driven by individuals or communities seeking to free themselves of oppression. As he drew connections between the American Civil Rights Movement and the international human rights movement, King also 'projected an African American alternative to international relations and international law'.[55] He presented the principles of love and nonviolence as an alternative basis for the conduct of international affairs, giving his Gandhian philosophy import beyond both national borders and the time he spent as leader of the civil rights movement.

Of course, King's achievements and contributions are not his alone. They were enabled by a family that loved and nurtured him; a wife – Coretta Scott King – who made great personal sacrifice to support his work; university professors who fostered

---

[51] ML King Jr, 'Acceptance Speech' (Oslo, 10 December 1964), available at www.nobelprize.org/prizes/peace/1964/king/26142-martin-luther-king-jr-acceptance-speech-1964.
[52] B Parekh, 'Cosmopolitanism and Global Citizenship' (2003) 29 *Rev Int'l Stud* 3, 8; Jackson (n 28) 22.
[53] King (n 42).
[54] Richardson (n 40) 473.
[55] ibid, 473.

his talent; and the individuals who recognised his capacity to lead the Montgomery Improvement Association and SCLC with dignity and courage. Yet while King was indeed a 'single wave in the vast ocean of the movement',[56] he was an irreplaceable leader. As a student and later as a leader, King seized every opportunity to question and problematise the power structures, human decisions, and political processes that led to any particular set of circumstances, particularly those of African American communities. Through his powerful words and his mobilisation of thousands of others, King effectively held a mirror to the intersecting injustices rife within America and around the world.

Today, King's contributions are studied in schools, discussed in history books, and celebrated in the many streets and town squares around the world that have been named after him. Yet his vision for America remains a dream. While films about King's work win critical acclaim and visitors to Washington, DC, marvel at his towering memorial statue in West Potomac Park, African American communities continue to struggle for fair treatment and equal opportunity. At times, their voices are heard internationally, as with the 'take a knee' protests against police brutality initiated by NFL players in 2016, and the protests that erupted after the 2014 grand jury decision not to indict Darren Wilson, a police officer who shot and killed Michael Brown in Ferguson, Missouri. Most of King's struggle, however, continues outside the spotlight: in the workplace, on waiting lists for medical treatment and on busy city streets. 'No social advance rolls in on the wheels of inevitability', King wrote. 'Every step towards the goal of justice requires sacrifice, suffering, and struggle'.[57]

---

[56] RP Moses, quoted by Jackson (n 28) 6.
[57] Quoted in JJ Ansbro, *Martin Luther King, Jr: The Making of a Mind* (Ossining, Orbis Books, 1984) 225.

15

Nelson Rolihlahla Mandela
Free at Last

NARNIA BOHLER-MULLER[1]

I have fought against white domination, and I have fought against black domination. I have cherished the ideal of a democratic and free society in which all persons will live together in harmony with equal opportunities. It is an ideal which I hope to live for, and to see realised. But my Lord, if needs be, it is an ideal for which I am prepared to die.[2]

I. The Path that Led to a Long Walk: A Brief Biography

In defending an ethics of plurality and relation and placing 'the embodied singularity of a unique being' as central to action and politics, Cavarero presents to us the possibility of imagining 'another story for the community of lovers who neither want to be separated nor to die'.[3] This is a glimpse of the embodied story of a freedom fighter who told 'another story' about human rights and humanity.

A. The Early Life of Madiba: A Young Troublemaker

Born on 18 July 1918 in Mvezo, a small village outside Umtata, under the name Rolihlahla, meaning 'one who pulls the branch of a tree' in isiXhosa or, more

---

[1] My gratitude goes to Ruehl Muller, Thobekile Zikhali and Marie Wentzel for their invaluable research support and insights.

[2] N Mandela, Defence statement during the Rivonia Trial, 20 April 1964, available at www.sahistory.org.za/archive/i-am-prepared-die-nelson-mandelas-statement-dock-opening-defence-case-rivonia-trial-pretoria.

[3] A Cavarero (A Kottman (trans)), *For More Than One Voice: Towards a Philosophy of Vocal Expression* (Stanford, Stanford University Press, 2005) 241.

colloquially, 'troublemaker',[4] few expected Nelson Mandela to become the first President of the democratic Republic of South Africa or the 'most venerated, iconic political figure of the late twentieth and early twenty-first century'.[5]

Mandela, of the Madiba clan, was born to Nonqaphi Nosekeni and Gadla Henry Mphakanyiswa Mandela, both a chief and main counsellor of Chief Jongintaba Dalindyebo, acting regent of the Thembu people. In keeping with his (nick)name, Mandela and his friends would use the dregs of beer to lure pigs away from the village, out of earshot of their owners, where they would be slaughtered and cooked.[6] In later years Mandela became known affectionately as 'Madiba' in reference to his clan. In African culture a clan or family (ancestral) name is used as a sign of respect and affection and considered more important than a surname.[7]

He attended school in Qunu, where he was given the English name 'Nelson' by his teacher, as Africans during the colonial period were obliged to have both a Western and an African name. After the death of his father in 1930, Chief Dalindyebo became Mandela's guardian and he lived in the royal household in Mqhekezweni, the provincial capital of the erstwhile Thembuland.[8]

Mandela matriculated at Healdtown, after which he enrolled for a BA degree at the University College of Fort Hare, but did not complete his studies as he was expelled from the university for joining a student protest. However, Mandela eventually did graduate from Fort Hare in 1943 after completing the course through correspondence. He subsequently enrolled for a law degree at the University of the Witwatersrand (Wits) which he did not complete due to his continued involvement in political activities. He reminisced about his time there: 'Wits opened a new world to me, a world of ideas and political beliefs and debates, a world where people were passionate about politics'.[9]

In the early 1940s Mandela moved to Johannesburg, where he briefly worked as a mine policeman before joining Witkin, Eidelman and Sidelsky, a white law firm, as an articled clerk. After qualifying as an attorney in 1952, he and Oliver Tambo opened the first black legal practice in the country, offering affordable and frequently free advice to poor black clients.[10]

Having journeyed through some of Nelson Mandela's earlier years, the next section focuses more on his activist years within the African National Congress (ANC) and how influential he was in the demise of the National Party (NP) and its oppressive apartheid regime.

---

[4] RN Mandela, *A Long Walk to Freedom* (Randburg, MacDonald Purnell, 1994) 3.

[5] P Maylam, 'Archetypal Hero or Living Saint? The Veneration of Nelson Mandela' (2009) 54(2) *Historia* 21.

[6] BBC News, 'Mandela the Teenage Pig Stealer' 17 March 2006, available at news.bbc.co.uk/1/hi/world/africa/4816266.stm.

[7] Collins English Dictionary 'a title of respect for Nelson Mandela, deriving from his Xhosa clan name', available at www.collinsdictionary.com/dictionary/english/madiba.

[8] Mandela (n 4).

[9] ibid, 85.

[10] N Manyathi-Jele, 'Late President Mandela's Academic Life and Legal Career' (2014) *De Rebus* 4.

II. The Political Life of Madiba: Along the Road to Freedom

Mandela, an amateur boxer in his early adulthood, ascribed much of his political philosophy to the pre-colonial stories of his elders, where tribes self-governed and owned land.[11] Mandela visualised a South African society with equal treatment for all irrespective of status, age and race similar to the situation in a boxing ring. For Mandela, 'Boxing is egalitarian. When you're probing your opponent's strengths and weaknesses, you're not thinking about his colour or his social status. In the ring, rank, age, colour and wealth are irrelevant'.[12]

By 1944 Mandela had joined the ANC and assisted with the establishment of the ANC Youth League whilst becoming increasingly involved in political activities, to such an extent that through most of the 1950s he was periodically arrested, imprisoned and banned as an important political actor in the ANC. Mandela's increased political activities were spurred by the racial segregation policy of the National Party that came into power in 1948, resulting in large scale discrimination and violation of human rights of the majority of the population under a system known as apartheid or 'separateness'. Towards the end of 1961 the ANC realised that peaceful resistance would not result in freedom for the oppressed in South Africa; this realisation resulted in a decision to attack symbols of apartheid by forming Umkhonto we Sizwe (known as MK), the armed wing of the ANC.[13]

As a lawyer, Mandela utilised the courts to further vocalise his condemnation of the growing racial oppression and the deteriorating standard of living of Africans in South Africa. Most notable in this regard are his 1962 'black man in a white court' statement, made during his trial on charges of mobilising persons to strike and encouraging 'illegal' travel outside the country, and his 1964 'I am prepared to die' statement, made during the Rivonia trial on charges of sabotage.[14] Maylam described the speech as being 'extraordinarily powerful' and 'principled, defiant, uncompromising, lofty and dignified, revealing Mandela's own great integrity and spirit of self-sacrifice',[15] echoing Tom Lodge's description of it as 'one of the most effective rhetorical texts delivered by a South African politician'.[16] Ultimately, Mandela was implicated in

---

[11] N Mandela, *The Struggle is My Life* (London, International Defence and Aid Fund for Southern Africa, 1978).

[12] P Martin, 'Nelson Mandela: How the Former South African Leader was Inspired by Sport in the Freedom Struggle' *The Independent* (London, 7 December 2013), available at www.independent.co.uk/sport/general/others/nelson-mandela-how-the-former-south-african-leader-was-inspired-by-sport-in-freedom-struggle-8989792.html.

[13] G Bizos, 'Nelson Mandela's Contribution to the Rule of Law' *SABC News* (Johannesburg, 18 June 2014), available at www.sabcnews.com/sabcnews/nelson-mandelas-contribution-to-the-rule-of-law.

[14] Mandela (n 11) 4, 8, 125, 155.

[15] Maylam (n 5) 26.

[16] T Lodge, *Mandela: A Critical Life* (Oxford, Oxford University Press, 2006) 113.

MKs activities and found guilty on charges of sabotage at the Rivonia trial (1963–64) and sentenced to life imprisonment, served mainly at the Robben Island prison off the coast of Cape Town.[17]

Towards the middle of the 1980s the ANC, supported by the international anti-apartheid movement, introduced the 'Release Mandela Campaign' as a 'medium of South Africa's liberation'.[18] Winnie Madikizela Mandela, his wife at the time, indicated that 'a deliberate decision was taken by the ANC to use him as a symbol of resistance ... so that the people struggled with a symbol of resistance and he remained that'.[19] As a result the National Party banned his image.

Due to political unrest in South Africa and international pressure, former State President PW Botha announced in late January 1985 that Mandela and the other Rivonia prisoners could be released on condition that he would reject violence and abandon the armed struggle. Mandela refused this offer and issued a statement, read by his daughter, Zindzi, at a rally in Soweto in February 1985:

> I cherish my own freedom dearly, but I care even more for your freedom. Too many have died since I went to prison. Too many have suffered for the love of freedom. I owe it to their widows, to their orphans, to their mothers, and to their fathers who have grieved and wept for them. Not only I have suffered during these long, lonely, wasted years. I am not less life-loving than you are. But I cannot sell my birthright, nor am I prepared to sell the birthright of the people to be free ... Only free men can negotiate. Prisoners cannot enter into contracts ... I cannot and will not give any undertaking at a time when I and you, the people, are not free.[20]

It was clear at that stage that no agreement could be reached for his release and he remained a prisoner as 'prisoners cannot enter into contracts ...'.[21] However, negotiations continued behind closed doors and eventually on 2 February 1990 de Klerk announced in Parliament that Mandela would be released from prison. He was released on 11 February 1990 and addressed a large crowd in Cape Town.[22] Following his release, Mandela said:

> Friends, comrades, and fellow South Africans, I greet you all in the name of peace, democracy, and freedom for all. I stand here before you not as a prophet but as a humble servant of you, the people. Your tireless and heroic sacrifices have made it possible for me to be here today. I, therefore, place the remaining years of my life in your hands.[23]

The fact that so much political energy was expended on his release was a clear indication that he was considered to be a key figure in the period of transition to democracy.

---

[17] Mandela (n 11).
[18] A Sitas, 'Madiba Magic: The Mandela Decade' (2012) 18(1) *Indicator SA* 21.
[19] ibid, 23.
[20] Mandela (n 4) 510.
[21] ibid.
[22] N Mandela, *Nelson Mandela Speeches 1990* (New York, Pathfinder Press, 1990).
[23] ibid.

III. 'To Deny People Their Human Rights is to Challenge Their very Humanity'

Mandela, portraying a sense of deep humanity accepted that all people, even his oppressors, possessed inherent goodness.[24] Whilst in prison, Mandela maintained good relationships with many of the wardens and perceived them as 'human beings with hopes and aspirations' and equally victims of apartheid. He even assisted poorly educated Afrikaners with filing lawsuits and writing letters during his imprisonment.[25] Mandela seemingly received a 'special kind of treatment' from prison wardens which George Bizos, a close friend, explained as follows: 'his superiority as a human being had its effect even on the most inhuman of the people that he had to deal with'.[26]

During a 2000 interview with Larry King, Mandela highlighted that upon release from prison, revenge against his oppressors was not an issue and that the liberation of his people was of utmost importance.[27] In this sense, Mandela has been regarded as a 'paradoxical figure' by some analysts. Maylam, for example, emphasised that 'he can display deep humility, but also an aristocratic air, derived perhaps from his chiefly family background'.[28] Throughout his career as a political leader and as President, he emphasised the need for consensus in decision-making, but, inspired by the works of Marx and Lenin, could also be authoritarian and a disciplinarian.

Mandela arguably existed within an intricate and often indiscernible realm of humility, stoicism, and authority. He believed that Africa 'needed discipline and self-control, and he wanted to be a guiding light for Africa in his own self-conduct'.[29] Richard Stengel recalls from a *Time* magazine interview with Mandela that

> ... he was extremely punctual. There's an expression in Africa, 'African time', which means very late [or] casual about appointments. In some ways, [Mandela] was trying to rebut that racial stereotype. He would look at his watch and sigh 'African time' if someone was late for an appointment.[30]

While some contestations to the extent of Mandela's contribution towards the realisation of human rights may exist (as it is with any other person), he remains with

---

[24] Maylam (n 5).

[25] CNN.com transcripts, 'Larry King Live: President Nelson Mandela One-on-One' 16 May 2000, available at transcripts.cnn.com/TRANSCRIPTS/0005/16/lkl.00.html.

[26] J Carlin, 'George Bizos: Interview by John Carlin on the Long Walk of Freedom of Nelson Mandela' Frontline, available at www.pbs.org/wgbh/pages/frontline/shows/mandela/prison/bizos.html.

[27] See n 25.

[28] Maylam (n 5) 35.

[29] J Evans, 'Mandela's Stoicism' (Philosophy for Life and Other Dangerous Situations, 14 April 2010), available at www.philosophyforlife.org/mandelas-stoicism/.

[30] ibid.

little doubt one of the most influential world leaders and an icon of human rights.[31] When his presidential term ended, Mandela was involved in advocacy work and is also remembered for his involvement in contemporary issues such as LGBT+ rights, HIV/AIDS, women's empowerment, child protection rights, and education, amongst others. He continued to vocalise tolerance of others and saw the need to create a free space where every South African had room to become whatever they desired to be – as long as it 'respects and enhances the freedom of others'.[32]

In 1995, South Africa hosted and won the Rugby World Cup. At that time he was criticised for embracing the white-dominated team by wearing a Springbok rugby jersey.[33] This, however, was in line with Mandela's goal of prioritising 'reconciliation, development, peace, freedom and culture'.[34] In that light, Pietersen quotes Mandela: '[i]f you talk to a man in a language he understands, that goes to his head. If you talk to him in his language, that goes to his heart'.[35]

Mandela was actively involved in HIV/AIDS activism and worked closely with the Treatment Action Campaign (TAC). Despite being a retired president and not getting support from the then President Thabo Mbeki – an AIDS denialist – and other senior members of the ANC, Mandela worked hand in hand with the TAC to ensure that there was awareness and access to antiretroviral treatment.[36] His tireless work to save lives at a time when HIV/AIDS was claiming hundreds of thousands of lives[37] was testament not only to his empathy but also to his willingness to disagree with ANC and government policy on the matter at that time. Today, the Nelson Mandela Foundation continues to work on HIV/AIDS-related issues to the benefit of many people.

Through the Nelson Mandela Children's Fund, Mandela generously raised money to cater for child-related projects, particularly for those living in informal settlements. One of the many ways to raise funds was to invite business leaders and encourage them to pledge or contribute to the building of schools in those areas.[38] The products of his work and the differences witnessed because of his influence are now referred to as 'Madiba magic'.[39] It is evident from his charity work that he did not only believe in freedom for the sake of it, but freedom with a focus on the socio-economic upliftment and empowerment of the poor and vulnerable.

---

[31] J Daniel, 'Soldiering On: The Post-Presidential Years of Nelson Mandela 1999–2005' in R Southall and H Melber (eds), *Legacies of Power: Leadership Change and Former Presidents in African Politics* (Cape Town, HSRC Press, 2006).

[32] Mandela (n 22).

[33] Daniel (n 31).

[34] K Asmal, D Chidester and WG James, *Nelson Mandela: In His Own Words: From Freedom to the Future* (Johannesburg, Little, Brown and Co, 2003).

[35] W Pietersen, 'What Nelson Mandela Taught the World About Leadership' (2015) 76 *Leader to Leader* 60.

[36] Daniel (n 31). South Africa now has the highest numbers of people on antiretroviral treatment in the world.

[37] In 2007 South Africa had the highest incidence of HIV/AIDS in the world, and in that year alone, AIDS killed 350,000 South Africans: South African History Online, 'A History of HIV/AIDS in South Africa' (last updated 9 February 2018), available at www.sahistory.org.za/article/hivaids-south-africa.

[38] South African History Online 'The Nelson Mandela Presidency: 1994 to 1999' (last updated June 2016), available at www.sahistory.org.za/article/nelson-mandela-presidency-1994-1999.

[39] ibid.

From Mandela we learnt (and continue to learn) forgiveness and the spirit of *ubuntu*: the overarching ideology of the South African Constitution. During Mandela's 2013 memorial, President Barack Obama reiterated the spirit of *ubuntu*:

> [Mandela] not only embodied *ubuntu*, he taught millions to find that truth within themselves. It took a man like Madiba to free not just the prisoner, but the jailer as well; to show that you must trust others so that they may trust you; to teach that reconciliation is not a matter of ignoring a cruel past, but a means of confronting it with inclusion, generosity and truth. He changed laws, but also hearts.[40]

Describing Mandela as a system leader, Senge, Hamilton and Kania applaud him for being able to bring together a divided society under a common ideal.[41] For example, in 1991, the Convention for Democratic South Africa (CODESA) saw the coming together of different political parties to discuss the future political trajectories of the country. In 1993, these sometimes contested negotiations managed to set a date for the first free elections in South Africa, held on 27 April 1994. Another example of the collective engagement that Mandela encouraged was the Truth and Reconciliation Commission (TRC). Through the TRC Mandela worked with former President FW de Klerk and Archbishop Emeritus Desmond Tutu in an attempt to bring national healing to all societal groups.[42] Though many disagreed with the concept of forgiving their former oppressors, there was a general acknowledgment that the work of the TRC was a necessary step towards peace and stability.[43]

Ultimately Mandela fought the system rather than the individuals: 'I wanted South Africa to see that I love even my enemies while I hated the system that turned us against one another'.[44] As a result, he and FW de Klerk shared the 1993 Nobel Peace Prize for their role in liberating South Africa from apartheid.

Mandela also emphasised the need for international relations to be informed by human rights principles.[45] His involvement in the 2000 Burundi Crisis earned him the 'African Peace Maker' title,[46] and he is credited for bringing an end to the bloody civil war in a single year where others had struggled for years to find a solution.[47] In all his dealings, on the national, regional and international stages, he used human rights as

[40] CNN Politics, 'Nelson Mandela Memorial: Barack Obama's Speech in Full' (Atlanta, 10 December 2013), available at edition.cnn.com/2013/12/10/politics/mandela-obama-remarks/index.html.
[41] P Senge, H Hamilton and J Kania, 'The Dawn of System Leadership' (2015) Stanford Social Innovation Review, available at ssir.org/articles/entry/the_dawn_of_system_leadership.
[42] ibid.
[43] Pietersen (n 35).
[44] Mandela (n 22) 680.
[45] N Mandela, 'South Africa's Future Foreign Policy' (1993) 72(5) *Foreign Affairs* 86; G Bizos, 'Mandela's Trials and Tribulations' *The Mail & Guardian* (Johannesburg, 6 December 2013), available at mg.co.za/article/2013-12-06-00-george-bizos-mandelas-trial-and-tribulations; P de Rezende Saturnino Braga, 'Human Rights and the Origins Myths of Post-Apartheid South African Foreign Policy' (2017) 39(2) *Strategic Review for Southern Africa* 25.
[46] Daniel (n 31).
[47] KA Bentley and R Southall, 'An African Peace Process: Mandela, South Africa and Burundi' (2006) 3 *Journal of Modern African Studies* 481; Daniel (n 31); de Rezende Saturnino Braga (n 45).

tools for transformation and the building of relationships and he used his 'image' as a respected and loved defender of human rights to influence others.

During the 21 March 2018 Human Rights Day celebrations at the Apartheid Museum in Soweto, Johannesburg, participants reflected on the role played by Mandela in the realisation of human rights. According to Sizwe Mpofu-Walsh, the worshipping of Mandela led to three inaccurate assumptions: (1) that South Africa was an exceptional country; (2) that there was hope for a desirable life; and (3) that the country was progressively turning this hope to reality.[48] Such a narrative enabled the postponement of reparative justice. While for many South Africans the ideals of a democratic and free society are yet to be realised, the contribution that Nelson Mandela added to human rights realisation remains remarkable.[49] In his address on the death of Nelson Mandela, Obama echoed the sentiment that Mandela 'lived for [an] ideal, and he made it real'.[50]

Critics of Mandela often base their arguments on his failure to *completely* transform the socio-economic situation of Black Africans who were severely disenfranchised by the apartheid regime. According to Torchia, Mandela's role as a freedom-fighter and activist is celebrated, whereas there is limited analysis of the shortcomings during his presidential term.[51] However, Torchia also notes that Mandela's short term as President could not, realistically, have facilitated the significant changes needed to address poverty, inequality and dispossession.[52] Mandela did not eliminate racism, and Afrikaner groups continue to maintain a system of privilege.[53]

A study of Mandela's speeches and writings show that he was aware of many of the shortcomings of the negotiated settlement. For example, in his acceptance speech for an honorary degree awarded by the Taiwanese Soochow University, Mandela echoed that '[t]he end of apartheid will not guarantee the beginning of democracy. But until apartheid is totally destroyed, there can be no democracy'.[54] Such sentiments reflect an understanding by Mandela that he was not claiming to have achieved true democracy, but rather a long walk towards it. In *A Long Walk to Freedom*, he admits that he, too, was a flawed human.[55]

In his 2018 State of the Nation address, South African President Cyril Ramaphosa reminded people of the significant role that Mandela played in realising the rights of

---

[48] Khulumani Support Group, 'A Human Rights Day 2018 Reflection on Mandela's Legacy to South Africa' (23 March 2018), available at www.khulumani.net/truth-memory/item/1339-a-human-rights-day-2018-reflection-on-mandela-s-legacy-to-south-africa.html.

[49] The Washington Post, 'Transcript: President Obama's Remarks on the Death of Nelson Mandela' (Washington DC, 5 December 2013), available at www.washingtonpost.com/politics/transcript-president-obamas-remarks-on-the-death-of-nelson-mandela/2013/12/05/7ee29e14-5df9-11e3-bc56-c6ca94801fac_story.html?noredirect=on&utm_term=.da56179cc780; Senge, Hamilton, Kania (n 41).

[50] CNN Politics (n 40); The Washington Post (n 49).

[51] C Torchia, 'Nelson Mandela: Remembering an Icon, His Flaws Remain a Footnote' CTV News (Toronto, 7 December 2013), available at www.ctvnews.ca/world/nelson-mandela-remembering-an-icon-his-flaws-remain-a-footnote-1.1579248.

[52] ibid.

[53] de Rezende Saturnino Braga (n 45).

[54] N Mandela, 'Address at Investiture as Doctor of Laws, Soochow University, Taiwan', Nelson Mandela Foundation, available at www.mandela.gov.za/mandela_speeches/1993/930801_taiwan.html.

[55] Mandela (n 22).

all South Africans. He urged all South Africans to recall that the Nelson Mandela centenary birthday celebrations were not dedicated to celebrating the past but meant to instil the spirit of integrity, forgiveness and oneness that Mandela had; the spirit that South Africans should carry in bringing about a non-racial, equitable and democratic society.[56]

IV. Continuing to Tell the Story of a Long Walk

Mandela was arguably at his most powerful when he reflected on justice and the law. His court speeches – some quoted above – were illustrative of his yearning to have just laws that protected the human rights of all.

On 18 July 2018 Nelson Rohlihahla Mandela would have turned 100. In paying homage to her late husband at the 16th Annual Mandela Lecture, Graca Machel reminisced about his firm belief that we are 'inextricably connected to one another as human beings' and called for the youth to keep the legacy of Mandela alive. In his keynote speech at this celebration held at the Wanderers Stadium in Johannesburg, Barack Obama paid tribute to 'the troublemaker'. Obama focused on Mandela's influence, which extended across the globe, long before he became the first democratically elected President of South Africa. Obama acknowledged that Mandela's struggle was focused on ending apartheid and ensuring political and socio-economic equality for all, but his message went further by emphasising that Mandela's sacrifice, leadership and moral example came 'to signify something larger'. Mandela 'came to embody the universal aspirations of dispossessed people all around the world, their hopes for a better life, the possibility of a moral transformation in the conduct of human affairs'. In describing Mandela's impact on his own life, Obama described that his 'light shone so brightly, even from that narrow Robben Island cell' that 'a wave of hope washed through hearts all around the world'.[57]

Writing through the lens of Derrida, Barnard-Naude argues that it is Mandela's words that serve as the universal appeal to human conscience[58] and to the light of justice, 'a light that will not go out'.[59] This is a light that all South Africans need to carry with them, and as Obama reminded us in his 2018 keynote address, a light to be carried in an increasingly darkening world. Carrying the 'light of justice', however, is by no means a *light task* – it is often heavy and arduous, and, in some instances,

---

[56] C Ramaphosa, 'State of the Nation Address' 16 February 2018, available at www.into-sa.com/uploads/download/file/583/State-of-the-nation-address__2018_.pdf.

[57] NPR, 'Transcript: Obama's Speech at the 2018 Nelson Mandela Annual Lecture 2018' NPR (17 July 2018), available at www.npr.org/2018/07/17/629862434/transcript-obamas-speech-at-the-2018-nelson-mandela-annual-lecture.

[58] J Barnard-Naude, 'Mandela in Reflection: The Laws of Admiration' *Thought Leader, The Mail & Guardian* (Johannesburg, 6 December 2013), available at thoughtleader.co.za/jacobarnardnaude/2013/12/06/nelson-mandela-in-reflection-the-laws-of-admiration/.

[59] ibid.

perhaps impossible without the embodiment of Mandela's stoic persistence and ability to 'stand at peace with pain'. This line is echoed in Dennias Mashegwane's 2016 poem:

> At the tone of silence
> From the mist of sorrow
> To rivers of Bantu songs
> You stood at peace with pain
> For Africa and her soul at pulse
> When Dawn saw flames of anger
> As we shouted slogans of man in chains
> To free mother and son at noon
> As the smoke of blood found freedom
> From the sky that gave birth to our rainbow nation
> We salute men of bold at arms
> Waving in chant as we bow ... *Mayibuye iAfrica*
> For in your heart we found melodies at Birth
> Dancing unity to Mother earth.[60]

When looking back and looking forward, as this contribution has tried to do, the balance between remembering and forgetting and passing on memories of struggle to a new generation is a subtle one. Former Constitutional Court Justice Albie Sachs has pondered this often as someone who stood at Mandela's side and, having done so, lost the an arm and the sight in one eye as a result of a car bomb targeting him as a 'terrorist' outside his home in Mozambique in 1968.[61] As Sachs expressed it, there is so much we take for granted and 'it's wonderful we take it for granted and it's terrible we take it for granted'.[62] Sachs reminds us that the democracy South Africa is now did not come into being without much sacrifice and pain, and planning. The process of the creation of the new South Africa has

> ... the sense of surprise, amazement, of a miracle ... but every single detail was planned and worked for. I used to think that when we got freedom we'd have no more meetings. And then we had more meetings. Freedom isn't miracles ... It was just persistence.[63]

The importance of this message is that the work of freedom is never fully done: to quote Mandela, 'after climbing a great hill, one only finds that there are many more hills to climb'. The work of democracy and the protection of human rights did not end in 1994 when Nelson Rolihlahla Mandela became South Africa's first Black President; the persistent work continues and the light of justice must not be allowed to be extinguished.

---

[60] D Mashegwane, 'On the occasion of Nelson Mandela's Death' (2016) unpublished.

[61] JD Battersby, 'White Foe of Pretoria Injured by a Car Bomb in Mozambique' The New York Times (New York, 8 April 1988), available at www.nytimes.com/1988/04/08/world/white-foe-of-pretoria-injured-by-a-car-bomb-in-mozambique.html.

[62] P Barkham, 'Albie Sachs: I Can't Tell My Son Everything' *The Mail & Guardian* (Johannesburg, 8 October 2011), available at mg.co.za/article/2011-10-08-albie-sachs-i-cant-tell-my-son-everything.

[63] ibid.

16

Faith Bandler

Striving to Make Rights a Reality for All Human Beings

MICHELLE BURGIS-KASTHALA*

All rights must now be recognised, and it's our job to make sure that they are. It is rare that a government will deliver out of the goodness of its heart, but history has shown that a genuine people's movement can move more than governments. It can move mountains ... [M]uch pain has been endured in the past, and that pain is no longer designated to hopelessness. It's time to move the process of reconciliation forward with a little more speed. That is the task. If not now, when? If not us, who?[1]

I. The Personal is the Political: A Life of Activism

Over the course of her 96 years, Faith Bandler not only witnessed, but was also intimately involved in defining moments of Australia's modern history. As it was only during her parents' lifetime that Australia became independent from British rule with Federation in 1901, Faith's biography tracks the evolution of her own maturing country. Ida Lessing Faith Bandler was born in 1918 on a banana farm in a small town in northern New South Wales. She was the second youngest of eight children. Her mother, Ida Venno, was of Indian-Scottish descent and her father, Wackvie Mussingkou, a former slave for Queensland sugar cane production, was abducted at the age of 13 from the island of Ambryn, Vanuatu, in 1883. Her father died when Faith was five,

* Many thanks to Sophia Collins for excellent research assistance. This research was funded by the Australian Research Council.

[1] F Bandler, 'It's time for us to remember that rights are not handed on a platter by governments, they have to be won' (Hope and Reconciliation Speech, Wollongong, 1999), available at www.speakola.com/ideas/faith-bandler-faith-hope-reconciliation-1999.

leaving her to learn about the details of his capture and enslavement later in her life as one central aspect of her activist activities. Her mother instilled in her a deep love of music, and Faith's lifelong passion for classical music and dance provided a number of serendipitous encounters, both personal and political. Faith was in secondary school when the Great Depression hit her fatherless family, and it took the unwavering support of her mother to sustain her studies until she was 16. Faith later continued to study at night school in Sydney, where she also worked in a shirt factory.

It was during the Second World War that Faith witnessed the appalling conditions experienced by Indigenous Australians. She had volunteered for the Australian Women's Land Army (November 1942–October 1945) and this took her to a variety of rural country towns in New South Wales. While always segregated and closely controlled, Faith still glimpsed Indigenous men and women at work for a fraction of her already meagre wage. Her own work in a variety of farms was backbreaking and paid around half that of men at the time. It was during this period that Faith lost one of her brothers serving in the Australian army on the Burma Railway. After the war and unlike the experience of returning soldiers, there was little recognition of these efforts by women, but for Faith it resulted in enduring female friendships and a sense of resilience and independence. Once the war was over, Faith seized on the chance to visit Europe with the Margaret Walker Dance Group as well as a trip to the International Youth Congress in Berlin in 1951. There she performed in the 'Dance of the Aboriginal Girl'. Although officially forbidden from visiting Eastern bloc countries due to Australia's communist fears, she went anyway. Witnessing the devastation wrought by the war and Nazi concentration camps would inspire her long-term commitment to the peace movement on her return to Australia. She also developed a very personal connection with these wartime atrocities through her husband Hans Bandler, an Austrian Jew who had managed to escape Dachau concentration camp in 1938. They met through a mutual love of classical music. They married in 1952 and had their daughter, Lilon, in 1954. Together they also fostered an Aboriginal boy called Peter for a decade. An engineer by training, Hans was himself deeply committed to a variety of social justice issues and was seminal in supporting Faith throughout the course of her activist career. The home they built together in the northern suburbs of Sydney was for a long time a buzzing haven for friends and colleagues in their shared political and cultural commitments. Life was so busy for Faith as a mother and an activist that she installed a separate telephone line in her house to cope with the constant flurry of planning, particularly around the 1967 Referendum (discussed below).

Although not Aboriginal herself, Faith experienced discrimination personally and so the 'colour of her skin was a major factor in radicalising her'.[2] She saw it as her lifelong struggle for all people to be treated equally, not only along racial lines, but also in terms of gender. The civil rights struggles in America resonated particularly for her during this period. As a result of her Eastern bloc travel, the Australian secret service (ASIO) kept a file on Faith and prevented her from travelling for ten years.

---

[2] A Summers, 'Faith and Feminism' (Memorial Service for Faith Bandler, University of Sydney, 24 February 2015), available at www.annesummers.com.au/speeches/faith-and-feminism/.

According to one ASIO officer, 'it is considered that the colour of her skin caused her to swing towards the peace movement',[3] which with its leftist leanings was cause for alarm at the height of McCarthyist hysteria. In raising her child, she was conscious of her husband's progressive stance in taking an active role in Lilon's raising. This provided Faith with a great degree of latitude for her dogged commitment to a variety of causes, most prominently Indigenous Australians, especially during the 1950s and 1960s, and later on in her work on the particular rights of South Sea Islander descendants of former slaves like her father. Faith's passion for general rights struggles as lived out through her family experiences informed her writings. She was the author of a non-fiction, personal account of the 1967 Referendum, *Turning the Tide: A Personal History of the Federal Council for the Advancement of Aborigines and Torres Strait Islanders*[4] along with two novels about her father, *Wacvie*[5] and sibling, *Welou, My Brother*.[6] She also co-wrote *Marani in Australia*[7] and co-edited *The Time Was Ripe: A History of the Aboriginal-Australian Fellowship*.[8]

Her indefatigable commitment was recognised during her lifetime through a number of high-profile awards. Faith declined to accept the award of an Officer of the Most Excellent Order of the British Empire (OBE) in 1976, but was the recipient of 'Australia's highest honour',[9] the Companion of the Order of Australia (AC) in 2009. She also received the Human Rights Medal from the Australian Human Rights and Equal Opportunity Commission in 1997, along with a 'Meritorious Award in Honour and Gratitude for a life of Courageous Advocacy for Justice and for Indigenous People, for Love and Reconciliation' awarded by Nelson Mandela at the Sydney Peace Foundation in 2000. Faith received an honorary doctorate from Macquarie University in 1994. Upon her death in 2015 she was honoured with a state funeral.

II. Faith's Key Public Contributions: Aboriginal, South Sea Islander and Women's Rights

Throughout her life, Faith nurtured a fervent commitment to realising the fair and equal treatment of all people. Her own personal history had already instilled in her a keen awareness about racial prejudice and mistreatment, particularly the experience of her father. Her key contributions centred on securing Aboriginal rights, through the

---

[3] ibid.

[4] F Bandler, *Turning the Tide: A Personal History of the Federal Council for the Advancement of Aborigines and Torres Strait Islanders* (Canberra, Aboriginal Studies Press, 1989).

[5] F Bandler, *Wacvie* (Adelaide, Rigby, 1977).

[6] F Bandler, *Welou, My Brother* (Glebe, Wild & Woolley, 1984).

[7] F Bandler and L Fox, *Marani in Australia* (Adelaide, Rigby, 1980).

[8] F Bandler and L Fox, *The Time Was Ripe: A History of the Aboriginal-Australian Fellowship* (Chippendale, Alternative Publishing Co-operative, 1983).

[9] M Lake, 'Faith Bandler, 1918–2015' (2015) 14:1 *Evatt Journal*, available at evatt.org.au/news/faith-bandler-1918-2015.html.

1967 Referendum, recognition of South Sea Islander 'blackbirding' and acting as an inspiring feminist icon across the political spectrum.

Faith's astute awareness of the racial discrimination she experienced translated easily into a tireless dedication to Aboriginal rights. After the Second World War, the situation of Australia's Indigenous peoples was woeful and the government of the time resisted any significant change through a United Nations 'national minorities' framework.[10] As a settler colony, Australia had been built on the myth of white Britons settling and improving an 'empty' land – *terra nullius*.[11] The persisting presence of the land's original peoples undermined this narrative and so a variety of repressive assimilationist policies were pursued in the belief that eventually indigenous people would simply vanish. Many Aboriginal people had been forced from their ancestral lands and lived on reservations. They were denied financial autonomy over any pitiful wages received and had to apply for permission to travel. Being served alcohol at a pub was even forbidden, as Faith herself also experienced first-hand. Beginning first with the Victorian Aboriginal Protection Act of 1869, a series of legislative and broad policy changes at the state and federal levels facilitated the removal of Indigenous children from their families to the care of white families, church missions or other state-sponsored facilities. This has come to be known as the 'Stolen Generations' Policy. In its 1997 report, *Bringing Them Home*, the national commission of inquiry stated that 'we can conclude with confidence that between one in three and one in ten Indigenous children were forcibly removed from their families and communities in the period from approximately 1910 until 1970'.[12] The effects of this practice decimated the cultural, social, economic and political resilience of Indigenous Australians.

In this climate of pronounced racism, Faith realised that something had to be done and her close connections with left-wing activists in Sydney facilitated her burgeoning activism during the 1950s, 1960s and 1970s. In the 1950s, it was clear already that Faith possessed a magnetic charisma and a talent for public speaking. After meeting the older, veteran Aboriginal activist Pearly Gibbs, the two of them established the Aboriginal-Australian Fellowship (AAF) in 1956. Although initially the AAF supported 'assimilation' policies in New South Wales,[13] it then shifted to support 'integration' with a four-pronged focus in 1962 on: (i) raising public awareness about Aboriginal rights; (ii) improving living conditions; (iii) having Aborigines on the executive committee; and (iv) operating in a non-partisan manner.[14]

Another veteran leftist activist, Jessie Street, appreciated Faith's qualities too and from 1957 worked with her through the AAF to launch a petition campaign to the Commonwealth government for a constitutional referendum on the status of

---

[10] M Lake, *Faith Bandler: Gentle Activist* (Sydney, Allen & Unwin, 2002) 65.

[11] Especially see P White, 'Settler Colonialism and the Elimination of the Native' (2006) 8 *Journal of Genocide Research* 387.

[12] *Bringing Them Home*, Report of the National Inquiry into the Separation of Aboriginal and Torres Strait Islander Children from Their Families, 1997, available at www.humanrights.gov.au/sites/default/files/content/pdf/social_justice/bringing_them_home_report.pdf.

[13] Bandler (n 4) 63.

[14] ibid, 64.

Aborigines, held in 1967.[15] In 1958, the Federal Council for the Advancement of Aborigines and Torres Strait Islanders (FCAATSI) was established. Increasingly for Faith and other activists, it was through FCAATSI that the referendum campaign was coordinated, along with other key concerns about land rights and equal wages.[16] Faith was the New South Wales FCAATSI secretary from 1962 and then a member of its executive committee in the lead up to the referendum. According to Faith,

[we] were bowled over by the power of a social movement which had taken on a life of its own. Totally unprepared for its impact on our lives, we lived, breathed, slept and dreamed its progress, our existence caught up by its existence.[17]

Either planning and discussing by telephone or speaking at countless public events, Faith devoted herself to the cause of political activism and constant fundraising. As a middle class married woman supported financially and personally by her husband, she was able to throw herself into events of her day and forge alliances with a number of trade union, church and women's organisations. According to her official biographer, Marilyn Lake,

Faith shone as a communicator. She talked, she persuaded, she lobbied, she cajoled and she trounced her opponents with great panache. In all these modes of public speaking, and through more personal conversations, Faith made a crucial contribution to turning Australian hearts and minds against racism.[18]

Over this ten-year period, Faith was central to persuading the vast majority of Australians to vote 'yes' to constitutional change by the time the referendum took place in May 1967. According to Faith, we 'faced the almost impossible task of turning the tide against years of a flow towards segregation of Aboriginal people'.[19] Voters were asked to vote yes or no to the following question,

DO YOU APPROVE the proposed law for the alteration of the Constitution entitled – 'An Act to alter the Constitution so as to omit certain words relating to the People of the Aboriginal Race in any State and so that Aboriginals are to be counted in reckoning the Population'?

Over 90 per cent of voters supported the change to two parts of the Constitution. First, Section 51 (xxvi) had outlined that the federal government could enact laws in relation to 'people of any race, other than the Aboriginal race in any state, for whom it is deemed necessary to make special laws'. This provision was changed with the deletion of 'other than the Aboriginal race in any state'. Second, Section 127 had read 'reckoning the numbers of the people of the Commonwealth, or of a state or other part of the Commonwealth, Aboriginal natives shall not be counted'. This was

[15] Jessie Street (1889–1970) was Australia's only female delegate to the 1945 San Francisco Conference. She worked with other feminists there to that ensure equal treatment irrespective of sex was included in the United Nations Charter (see especially Art 1). See also Summers (n 2).
[16] See Bandler (n 4) for treatment of the Referendum, equal wages and land rights.
[17] ibid, 87.
[18] Lake (n 10) 88.
[19] Bandler (n 4) 94.

changed so that Aborigines were included in the census. What was surprising about the referendum was the absence of a 'no' campaign altogether. For Faith, as New South Wales' 'yes' campaign director, '[w]hen you write Yes in the lower square of your ballot paper you are holding out the hand of friendship and wiping out nearly 200 years of injustice and inhumanity'.[20] For her, the referendum was very much more than a superficial legal change; it signalled the inclusion of Australia's first peoples as members of the modern nation.

The referendum marked a turning point in Australia's history and it enabled the federal government to pass legislation relating to Aboriginal people – either to their benefit or their detriment.[21] Such a resounding vote for change vindicated the efforts of Faith and her fellow campaigners and, she reminisced that '[they] went *mad* with excitement' over the result.[22] Though Australia's Indigenous people did not witness as much positive change as had been hoped, the referendum was still a momentous turning point for the nation's history.

Faith continued to work for Aboriginal rights after the referendum, but divisions within the movement over the nature of 'black power' and her own identity as a non-Aboriginal black woman saw her turn to other projects in the 1970s. It was the story of her father whom she barely knew that drew Faith to work for recognition and special benefits of the descendants of the South Sea Islander community. She recounts how her father would tell his children stories in the evening:

There were certain stories which happened to be, if not my favourite, maybe the favourite of one of my sisters or one of my brothers, and as soon as we would all gather round the fire, we'd all put in for our favourite story and I had one and if he told it once he told it a thousand times, and I would say to him, 'Tell it again' and 'Tell it again' and 'Tell it again' … how when he was kidnapped and taken in to the boat by the slavers, and what it was like in the boat coming over from his island Ambrym in the New Hebrides, and how rough it was and how they were all held in the hull and how sick there and those who died would be thrown overboard and how it was when the boat would arrive in Australia and how strange everything seemed to him.[23]

This history of slavery that had supported a variety of white economic interests on the east coast of Australia during the second half of the nineteenth century was little known in Australia. People from a variety of South Pacific Islands were taken by boat especially to work on Queensland's sugar cane farms. This practice of 'blackbirding' of around 60,000 people ranged from violent seizure, to trickery, to willing participation. Once bound for Queensland, many died en route or worked in appalling conditions.

---

[20] Quoted in R McGregor, '"Right wrongs, write Yes": what was the 1967 referendum all about?' (*The Conversation,* 25 May 2017), available at www.theconversation.com/right-wrongs-write-yes-what-was-the-1967-referendum-all-about-76512.

[21] At the time, Aboriginal rights activists had assumed that this constitutional change would lead to the government enacting beneficial legislation. The High Court, however, confirmed in 1997 that legislation can be to the detriment of any race, such as in the case of the construction of the Hindmarsh Bridge against the wishes of the Ngarrindjeri community in 1996: *Kartinyeri v Commonwealth* (1998) 195 CLR 337.

[22] Quoted in B Atwood and A Markus, *The 1967 Referendum: Race, Power and the Australian Constitution* (Canberra, Aboriginal Studies Press, 2007) 57.

[23] F Bandler, quoted in M Lake, '2001 Eldershaw Memorial Lecture: Founding Fathers, Dutiful Wives and Rebellious Daughters' (2001) 48:4 *THRA Papers and Proceedings* 268.

The practice ended around the time that the colony of Queensland was incorporated into the Federation of Australia in 1901. Many people were forcibly repatriated in this period as a result of the Pacific Island Labourers Act 1901. Faith's own father ran away from his Queensland sugar cane farm, hiding his identity until he reached New South Wales and later married her mother in 1906.

Perhaps the hardest part of this second struggle for Faith was simply raising awareness about the issue at all. A prevailing consensus suggested that these South Sea Islanders, far from being enslaved, had willingly come to Australia as indentured workers. In seeking to understand her father's story as part of this broader practice, Faith visited his island and gained a valuable sense of identity and connection to the people there. Although this is a struggle that requires more work in the wake of Faith's death in 2015, as a first step, the Queensland government conducted a 'recognition ceremony' at Parliament House in 2000.[24] While activists claim that most Australians still do not learn about this home-grown practice of slavery, consciousness is slowly growing.[25] In August 2018, the South Sea Islander flag was raised at the inner west Sydney council, the first government building ever to do so.[26] Faye's own work helped propel this momentum, but far greater awareness is still needed so that the particular challenges of around 70,000 descendants can be better addressed.

Alongside her dedication to ending racial discrimination, Faith personally lived the life of a feminist and was an active member of various women's organisations later in life, including the Women's Electoral Lobby and a board member of Sisters, a feminist publishing house in Melbourne.[27] At a time when few women of colour entered public life, Faith insisted on dedicating herself to political change as well as her family. Her husband, Hans was supportive of Faith in her various endeavours. Faith's long life was one filled with personal and political commitment to social change.

III. Living Legacies

Faith left a lasting contribution to progressive change in Australia, particularly in relation to Indigenous recognition and South Sea Islanders. Yet the hopes imbued in the referendum were perhaps too high and in spite of some improvements since 1967, the socio-economic, cultural and political situation of Australia's first people remains dire. In light of this, what can we make of Faith and her struggle for racial equality through

---

[24] L Ryan, 'Review of Marilyn Lake's biography of Faith Bandler, "Faith Bander, Gentle Activist"' (2003) 29 *Australian Humanities Review*, available at www.australianhumanitiesreview.org/2003/05/01/review-of-marilyn-lakes-biography-of-faith-bandler-faith-bandler-gentle-activist/.

[25] N Haxton, '"Australia's slave trade": the growing drive to uncover secret history of Australian South Sea Islanders' *ABC News* (Sydney, 22 December 2017), available at www.abc.net.au/news/2017-12-22/australian-south-sea-islanders-blackbirding/9270734.

[26] B Bryce, 'Raising of South Sea Islander flag a step towards recognition for Australia's "forgotten people"' *ABC News* (Sydney, 29 August 2018), available at www.abc.net.au/news/2018-08-29/south-sea-islander-flag-raising-a-step-towards-recognition/10177124.

[27] Summers (n 2).

constitutional reform? For Faith, the referendum constituted the 'greatest victory the Aborigines have had or ever will have.'[28] To this day, its symbolism is powerful in light of the scant resources available to the 'yes' campaign over the decade leading up to the vote. For Atwood et al, what is undeniable is that the Referendum's

> symbolic recognition of citizenship rights for Aboriginal people created a context in which campaigners for Aboriginal rights, especially those who were Aboriginal, were more able to conceive or articulate a claim for a different kind of rights and even a different kind of relationship between Aboriginal people and the Australian nation, than they had been for a very long time; and it gave momentum to a campaign for these [claims].[29]

As a result of the referendum, Australia's Indigenous people had a vocabulary and a sense of empowerment that increasingly moved from a minority rights and citizenship framework to self-determination, Indigenous sovereignty and land rights. None of these more recent struggles would have been possible without the referendum, even if we accept its limited impact. Faith laid the groundwork for these later developments, but as a non-Indigenous Australian, increasingly she relinquished her own role to that of a younger generation of Indigenous activists. She also grounded her sense of social justice in her own personal identification of a woman fathered by a South Sea Islander slave. These parts of her identity instilled in her a keen awareness of discrimination and it was to the benefit of all Australians that she could marshal so much of her energy in working on Australia's greatest historical and contemporary struggle for justice, the struggle of its first and sovereign peoples for their lands and their culture. Faith always understood this struggle as both specific and general:

> I don't look at the Aboriginal people today and expect them to say to me, well, thanks Faith, you know. Not at all. This is what we all should be doing. Everyone should be getting up and everyone should be involved in preventing what is going on in different countries that has to do with putting one group down against another on the grounds of race. And whether it's in South Africa or whether it's in what was Yugoslavia or in any other part of the world, we should be doing just that, and I see it just as a human being's duty to get involved in raising people to be equals in society.[30]

Irrespective of one's reading of the role of legal reform in social change,[31] Faith typifies the passionate and committed activist as both insider and outsider,[32] who was galvanised by her own personal experiences to work tirelessly for improving the lives of others.

[28] F Bandler quoted in Atwood and Markus (n 22) 67.
[29] ibid, 71.
[30] 'Faith Bandler (1918)' (National Museum of Australia), available at www.indigenousrights.net.au/people/pagination/faith_bandler.
[31] For advocacy on further constitutional change for Indigenous rights, see F Brennan, *No Small Change: The Road to Recognition for Indigenous Australia* (Brisbane, University of Queensland Press, 2015).
[32] On this point, see Ryan (n 24).

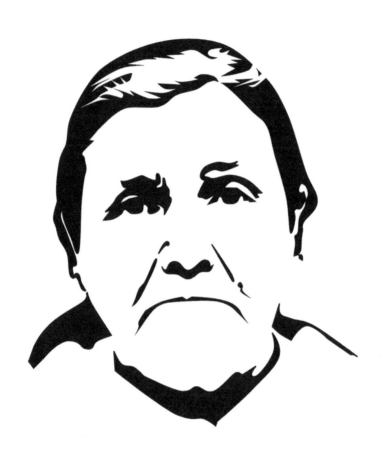

17

Angélica Mendoza Almeida de Ascarza

The Struggle of Mamá Angélica for the Victims of Enforced Disappearance in Peru

ELIZABETH SALMÓN[1]

> It is not possible to forget this; we will never forget. We will continue walking until we find justice. I am not afraid of life or death, as long as I do not know the truth. If I die, or if I disappear, the young people who follow me will continue walking until finding justice.[2]

I. Woman, Mother, and Peasant of the Peruvian Andes

Angélica Mendoza de Ascarza was born on 1 October 1929, in Huambalpa, in the district of Vilcashuamán, province of Ayacucho. This region is one of the most affected by the armed conflict that took place in Peru, from 1980 to approximately the year 2000. The conflict was a consequence of the armed action initiated by *Sendero Luminoso* (Shining Path) and the Tupac Amaru Revolutionary Movement and the response to it by the armed forces of Peru. Angélica Mendoza's parents were originally from Ayacucho and were people who worked the land, so from a very young age, she had a particular affection for the countryside, trees and animals. Like her parents and grandparents before her, she was a Quechua native speaker. At a young age she married Estanislao Ascarza, who was an educator. They went on to have three sons and five daughters.

---

[1] With my gratitude to Lucero Ibarra for her research assistance.
[2] COMISEDH (producer) and C Del Prado (director), 'Mamá Angélica: memoria para los ausentes [Documental]' (Perú, COMISEDH, 2012) 24m 4 s.

At dawn on 2 July 1983, an army squad broke into Angélica's house and arrested her son Archimedes Ascarza Mendoza. Archimedes was a 19-year-old student; he liked to play the guitar and, according to his mother, he wanted to be part of the Civil Guard.[3] That morning, they dragged him barefoot to a military truck with other armed men. Angélica did not hesitate to go after the car and watched it as it headed towards the Barracks *Los Cabitos*. The next day, Angélica went to the barracks, where the military denied having taken her son. Following that first denial she went on to seek information on her son from multiple government bodies in charge of security, including the Civil Guard, the Republican Guard and the Army. All systematically claimed to be unaware of her son's whereabouts.

Fifteen days after her son's disappearance, Angélica received a document from an Army sub-official which contained a note written by her son. In the letter, Archimedes told her that he was at the *Los Cabitos* Barracks in a difficult situation and asked her to get money and a lawyer to recover his freedom.[4] Despite this, the police and military authorities continued denying knowledge of his whereabouts, but Angelica did not give up and started a long and tireless search for her son.

Angélica then went to the district of Quinua, in the province of Huamanga, where, according to some neighbours, corpses were scattered on the heights. With the determined impetus that would later come to characterise her, she went there alone and found the bodies of old and young men with bullets in their heads and backs; without hesitation, she turned each body over as she looked for her son. She did not find him.

The Truth and Reconciliation Commission (TRC) established that the members of the Army that belonged to Barracks No 51, referred to as *Los Cabitos*, located in Huamanga, Ayacucho, committed severe violations of human rights. Between 1983 and 1984, these soldiers perpetrated arbitrary detentions, torture, disappearances, and extrajudicial executions of approximately 136 citizens from the local population.[5] After decades of violence that produced massive human rights violations and affected mainly the Andean rural population, the transition government created the TRC on 4 June 2001. Angélica Mendoza, whose quest for truth and justice was an inspiration for this commission, gave her testimony in a public hearing and in this way she gave face and voice to the victims of the conflict and to the members of ANFASEP.

In a continued effort to determine the fate of her son Angélica Mendoza never stopped visiting the caves and ravines where corpses of (mostly young) people were piled up. As a result of her efforts she faced death more than once, but she was never intimidated. The pain and grief over the disappearance of her son were stronger than fear. During one of her searches, in the Puracuti ravine, she was shot at by a group of soldiers while she was shouting her son's name. She was not hit. When the soldiers threatened to kill her, she told them: 'Sir, I am not afraid of dying, I will die, I will give you the five *solcitos* (Peruvian currency) that I have, for the loss of your bullet; but first tell me where my son is, when I know where my son is, I will die in peace'.[6]

---

[3] Asociación Nacional de Familiares de Secuestrados, Detenidos y Desaparecidos del Perú (ANFASEP), *¿Hasta cuándo tu silencio? Testimonios de dolor y coraje* (Ayacucho, ANFASEP, 2007) 153.

[4] Comisión de la Verdad y Reconciliación (CVR), 'Desapariciones, torturas y ejecuciones extrajudiciales en la base militar Los Cabitos (1983–1985)', *Final Report*, vol VII, ch II (Lima, CVR, 2003) 74–77.

[5] ibid.

[6] ANFASEP (n 3).

The story of Angélica Mendoza was not the only one of grief over the unknown fate of a family member during that period of time in Ayacucho. There were many other women in the region whose children and husbands were kidnapped and disappeared. It was precisely these women, brave and determined, who joined her in the search for information about their relatives, walking day after day through the gorges of Casaorcco, Infiernillo, of the Huatatas River, even reaching Pampa Cangallo – places where they would find mutilated bodies with signs of torture. Unfortunately, Angélica Mendoza, like so many other of her compatriots, never found her son.

II. Leadership and Legitimacy in the Search for Missing Persons

Between 1980 and 2000, Peru lived its most violent, extensive internal armed conflict. This conflict had the most significant impact and caused the highest number of fatal victims and economic costs in Peru's entire Republican history. According to the Final Report of the TRC, the total number of victims of this conflict was 69,280.[7] According to the leading actors of the conflict, the proportions[8] of accountability were attributed as follows: Shining Path caused 46 per cent of the victims; agents of the state caused 30 per cent; and other agents or circumstances, 24 per cent. These actors carried out the most serious violations of human rights through assassinations and extrajudicial executions, enforced disappearances, torture, cruel, inhuman or degrading treatment, among other serious human rights violations. The same report found that the number of missing persons was 8,555. However, this number officially increased ten years later when the Public Ministry announced that the number of missing persons was 15,700. In April 2018, the Ministry of Justice presented a new list of missing persons during the armed conflict. The number of disappeared persons from the conflict period now stands at 20,329.[9]

Facing this context of impunity, corruption and systematic violations of human rights, Angélica Mendoza represented the strength, struggle, and courage of a peasant woman who did not remain silent and who sought, in the name of her son, justice for all victims of enforced disappearance. Along with Teodosia Layme and Antonia Zaga, whom she met during her daily visits to the barracks and the prosecutor's office, she formed a movement composed of Andean and Quechua-speaking women whose objective was to find their taken children, husbands and family members. In 1983, they initially established the Committee of Relatives of the Disappeared, under the leadership of Angélica, who organised walks through different towns in pursuit of justice.

---

[7] CVR, 'Los datos centrales del Conflicto Armado Interno', *Final Report*, vol II, ch I (Lima, CVR, 2003) 1–7.
[8] ibid.
[9] The authority provides qualified support for the proposition. Base list of the National Register of Missing Persons and Burial Sites (RENADE) of the Directorate General of Search for Missing Persons of the Ministry of Justice and Human Rights, 23 April 2018.

As time went on, more people joined in, denouncing the enforced disappearance, detentions, torture and executions of their relatives. Because the committee overflowed its capacity by increasing the number of people who supported the cause and with the objective of institutionalising it to give legitimacy to their claims, they decided to found ANFASEP. In this way, Angélica Mendoza, with the help of the young lawyer Zósimo Roca, founded the National Association of Relatives of the Kidnapped, Detained and Disappeared of Peru (ANFASEP) on 2 September 1983. This association consisted mainly of Quechua-speaking women, who, like Angélica, came from rural areas and had not completed a school education; however, their lack of education was no obstacle to their tireless struggle for truth, justice and reparation. The other women in the campaign for the disappeared saw in Angélica the woman who organised and led them in the search for their loved ones in the face of an exclusionary, sexist and discriminatory society. She was the woman they loved as a mother, and therefore they called her *Mamá Angélica*. Angélica Mendoza served as president of ANFASEP from its foundation until 2006 when, at the age of 78, she became Honorary President. She is the image and inspiration of this association.

In February 1985, during his visit to Peru, Pope John Paul II travelled to Ayacucho to pledge for peace and to give support to the victims of armed violence. During his visit, at the airport in Ayacucho, he gave a speech condemning terrorism and the practices of violence perpetrated by Peruvians. Also, he presented the members of ANFASEP with a wooden cross bearing the phrase 'Do not kill'. During this visit, the mothers of ANFASEP presented their claims to the Supreme Pontiff through a document delivered by a priest. The cross given by John Paul II became one of the symbols of ANFASEP and accompanied the political demonstrations they performed. Another important visit took place in April 1985, when Nobel Peace Prize winner Adolfo Pérez Esquivel arrived in Peru. He chaired the International Commission for the Investigation of Human Rights in Peru, who prepared a document on the situation in Ayacucho; that report was delivered to the President of the Republic. This visit also strengthened ANFASEP, because the struggle of the associates was internationally recognised. Under the leadership of Angélica and with the support of Pérez Esquivel, the members of ANFASEP marched for the first time in the Plaza Mayor of Huamanga,[10] Ayacucho, demanding justice for the disappeared persons.

The role of Mamá Angélica was vital not only for the women relatives of the victims of enforced disappearances but also for the survival of displaced orphans. Angélica organised fundraising events in the different markets of the city to collect food for these children. Word of their work spread, and at one point the resources became insufficient to feed all the children. For this reason, on 7 November 1985, the 'Adolfo Pérez Esquivel' Children's Dining Hall was created in honour of the Nobel Peace Prize winner who had visited the place some months before and supported the cause. The Dining Hall was able to house approximately 400 children victims of violence.

Angélica Mendoza's efforts as leader of ANFASEP transcended the borders of the city of Ayacucho and were emulated in various places to demand justice, truth, and reparation for all the disappeared and their families from the Peruvian State.

---

[10] ANFASEP (n 3).

The work of Mamá Angélica enabled information to be gathered about the victims from different places, which made it possible to expose these cases and provide greater visibility of the situation, especially the state of affairs for the most vulnerable groups, such as women and children.

In 1986, the members of the association held the first major march to the capital to denounce the serious human rights violations that had occurred in the south of the country. Mamá Angélica appeared before the Palace of Justice, the Office of the Prosecutor and the Ministry of Justice, among other institutions, demanding the respect and guarantee of the human rights of the victims of enforced disappearances. This march lasted three days and had the support of different Peruvian human rights organisations, such as the Peace and Justice Service (SERPAJ), the Commission of Human Rights (COMISEDH), the Human Rights Association (APRODEH) and the Episcopal Commission for Social Action (CEAS).

In this context, Mamá Angélica faced different forms of political harassment by Alberto Fujimori's regime. She was even accused of the crime of apology for terrorism due to her prominent role as a human rights advocate. This situation forced her to mitigate her public work for two years, until 1994, when the judiciary ruled that the accusation had no grounds.

Mamá Angélica and the members of ANFASEP also had to deal with racial discrimination and the indifference of the population in a context of widespread anxiety. At that time, the mere act of denouncing a violation of human rights already represented an act of courage. This period was not only marked by violence at disproportionate levels, but also by a context of corruption and impunity that did not allow people to trust in the authorities. In 1997, Angélica Mendoza did not report only one case: she gave the Ombudsman's Office lists with the names of more than 2,000 people who were disappeared during the period of violence.

In 1999, Mamá Angélica received the 'Angel Escobar Jurado' National Human Rights Award, from the National Board of Human Rights Organisations in recognition of her work as leader and founder of ANFASEP. Her tireless search for the truth and the promotion of human rights and justice for the victims of enforced disappearances gave hope to many families of victims.

In 2001, after the fall of the authoritarian government of Alberto Fujimori, the transitional government established the Truth and Reconciliation Commission to investigate the human rights abuses committed during the internal armed conflict (1980–2000). The TRC was a response to the legitimate social demands of truth and justice. The creation of the TRC was one of the most critical tasks in defence of human rights promoted by Mamá Angélica. To this end, a group of leaders of ANFASEP travelled to Lima to demand the creation of this commission that was to investigate, among other issues, the enforced disappearances in Peru.

During the operation of the TRC, it was possible to count on the support of all the members of ANFASEP for the search of the truth. In fact, the first testimony in the first public hearing of the TRC, held in Ayacucho on 8 April 2002, was given by Angélica Mendoza herself, who recounted the enforced disappearance of her son, Archimedes, in 1983.

The Final Report of the TRC of 2003 showcases the work of Quechua-speaking and low-income women who formed ANFASEP. It describes how, even in the most challenging moments during the armed violence, these women maintained a tenacious and courageous struggle in search of their loved ones and pursued the application of justice to those responsible for their disappearances.[11]

Without prejudice to the work done by the TRC and the positive repercussions it had in the search for missing persons, Mamá Angélica did not give up her struggle for justice relating to the disappeared. On the contrary, she reaffirmed her work in favour of human rights and the recognition of justice for the victims of the conflict. As a result, in 2003, when she was 74 years old, Angélica Mendoza received the John Humphrey Prize, awarded in Montreal by the Canadian NGO Rights and Democracy. Likewise, in 2004, the Peruvian Government, through the Ministry of Women and Social Development, awarded Mamá Angélica the 'Order of Merit of Women 2004'. Several years later, in 2012, she received the 'Ombudsman's Medal' in honour of her valuable career representing a tenacious struggle for human rights. The following year, in 2013, on the occasion of the tenth anniversary of the Final Report of the TRC, Mamá Angélica was awarded the Medal of Honor of Merit by the Metropolitan Municipality of Lima. Also in 2014, the Citizen Movement for Human Rights of Ayacucho recognised her work promoting human rights.[12]

Finally, on 18 August 2017, after more than 12 years of trial, two high officials of the Peruvian Army were convicted during the procedures for the kidnappings, torture and enforced disappearances that took place in the barracks of *Los Cabitos* in 1983. The National Criminal Chamber condemned two high-ranking army officers for the murders that took place in the *Los Cabitos* in the 1980s, a case considered one of the most emblematic of human rights violations in Peru. The relatives of the victims attended the hearing, after 34 years waiting for justice. The court ruling establishing the criminal responsibility of the army officials, and allowed the families of the victims of enforced disappearances to achieve some justice.

III. Mamá Angélica Gave Visibility and Legitimacy to the Struggle for the Search for Missing Persons in Peru

The internal armed conflict in Peru was one of the most violent and disastrous episodes in the country's history, especially for those who lived in situations of extreme vulnerability and whose life was interrupted in an instant by the kidnapping or arbitrary detention of one of their loved ones. It is vital that there is joint action by the state and society to prevent such acts from happening again.

Mamá Angélica's greatest legacy is as the embodiment of a woman who fought tirelessly for decades to find her son Archimedes and who, through her own personal experience, sought justice and truth for the victims of enforced disappearance. The creation of ANFASEP institutionalised this struggle. Mamá Angélica became an

---

[11] CVR, 'Conclusiones Generales', *Final Report*, vol VIII, third s (Lima, 2003) 37.
[12] ANFASEP (n 3) 71.

advocate for the rural women who trusted her with the search for their loved ones, when the state failed them by inaction.

Angélica Mendoza is a symbol of strength for all the families of the victims of arbitrary detention, extrajudicial execution, torture and enforced disappearance. Her work as the founder of ANFASEP enabled Peruvians to learn about the hundreds of other cases of people disappeared during this tumultuous period in Peru, which would later be corroborated by the Report of the Truth and Reconciliation Commission. The combined work of ANFASEP and the TRC made possible the opening of judicial cases and the prosecution of those responsible for the enforced disappearances. She showed that justice depends not only on the existence of laws or state bodies, but also on the brave deeds of those who suffer the most, the victims. Angélica Mendoza symbolises the struggle for justice in Peru and throughout the world, especially for those countries that have experienced extended periods of violence and terror. She represents women who continue to fight to transform their societies by denouncing abuses, exposing situations of vulnerability and demanding justice.

Mamá Angélica died on 28 August 2017, just ten days after hearing the judgment that found two state officials guilty for the disappearance and death of hundreds of young people in the barracks of *Los Cabitos*. Her legacy in defence of the human rights of the victims of enforced disappearance continues today, and her image as a woman who gave Peru the strength and hope to demand justice in favour of those who were invisible continues, as a reminder that each victim represents a face and a story to be told.

18

Rigoberta Menchú Tum
Daughter of Corn

FELIPE GÓMEZ ISA

The Norwegian Nobel Committee has decided to award the Nobel Peace Prize for 1992 to Rigoberta Menchú from Guatemala, in recognition of her work for social justice and ethno-cultural reconciliation based on respect for the rights of indigenous peoples. Like many other countries in South and Central America, Guatemala has experienced great tension between the descendants of European immigrants and the native Indian population. In the 1970s and 1980s, that tension came to a head in the large-scale repression of Indian peoples. Menchú has come to play an increasingly prominent part as an advocate of native rights. Rigoberta Menchú grew up in poverty, in a family which has undergone the most brutal suppression and persecution. In her social and political work, she has always borne in mind that the long-term objective of the struggle is peace. Today, Rigoberta Menchú stands out as a vivid symbol of peace and reconciliation across ethnic, cultural and social dividing lines, in her own country, on the American continent, and in the world.[1]

I. From Uspantán to Oslo

Rigoberta Menchú is a Mayan woman born in Uspantán, Department of El Quiché, Guatemala, on 9 January 1959. She was raised in a very poor rural family composed of Vicente Menchú, Juana Tum, and nine brothers and sisters. Although they lived on their *milpa* (small piece of land) in the highlands, where they cultivated corn and beans (*frijoles*), the whole family were forced to work in large coffee and cotton plantations (*fincas*) in the Southern Pacific coast of Guatemala for several months every

---

[1] The Norwegian Nobel Committee, Oslo, 16 October 1992, available at www.nobelprize.org/prizes/peace/1992/summary/.

year. During their time there they experienced not only systematic labour exploitation, but also racial discrimination due to their indigenous status.[2] The working conditions were so deplorable that two of her younger brothers died in a plantation, one of them from inhaling chemicals used in the fumigation of coffee leaves, and the other one from severe malnutrition. This greatly affected Rigoberta, who began to reflect on the injustices suffered by poor Guatemalans such as her family.

When she was six years old, Menchú was taken to a boarding school run by the Belgian Order of the Sacred Family so that she could learn Spanish and receive primary and secondary education. The years she spent with the nuns at the school played a highly significant part in her ideological development, since their order was strongly committed to the education of indigenous girls from poor backgrounds as a means of social transformation.

After leaving school at the age of 12, Menchú started her role as a catechist and began to help organise the community into the *Comité de Unidad Campesina* (CUC) (Committee for Peasant Unity), following her father's example. As she stated in her testimonial biography,[3] she became strongly committed to her community and her people, largely relying on her solid indigenous culture,[4] on the Bible, and on the social doctrine of the Catholic Church. Corn and respect for nature are essential pillars of the Mayan culture. According to their ancestors, the Mayan people are made of maize, and the sun is their grandfather. It is important to note that most indigenous peoples integrated their worldviews into the teachings of the Catholic Church after the colonisation period. According to Menchú's testimony, 'we feel strongly catholic, but at the same time we feel very indigenous, proud of our ancestors'.[5]

Although she is openly critical of the role played by the Catholic Church in justifying poverty, oppression and discrimination in Guatemala, religion has been highly influential in Menchú's personal and ideological development. She has referred to the 'ambivalent'[6] role played by the Church. While the Catholic hierarchy and some priests preached Christian resignation in the face of injustice, other priests and nuns, influenced by liberation theology and new forms of pedagogy to fight social inequality,[7] were very active in supporting peasants. They helped peasants to become organised and create cooperatives, raised awareness of the discrimination against the indigenous people,

---

[2] M Silverstone, *Rigoberta Menchú. Defending Human Rights in Guatemala* (New York, The Feminist Press at the City University of New York, 1999) 32.

[3] E Burgos-Debray, *Me llamo Rigoberta Menchú y así me nació la conciencia* (Barcelona, Seix Barral, 1992). There is an English translation in E Burgos-Debray, *I, Rigoberta Menchú: An Indian Woman in Guatemala* (London, Verso, 2010). The Spanish title (which can be translated as *My name is Rigoberta Menchú, and this is how my Awareness was Born*) is much more illustrative of Rigoberta Menchú's journey in life and experiences, and how they significantly influenced the development of her awareness.

[4] *Popol Vuh* (in Quiché language 'book of the community' or 'book of the people'), also known as the Mayan Bible, is a cultural narration of the mythology and history of Mayan Quiché people. Although initially it was orally transmitted from generation to generation, it was written down in the fifteenth century.

[5] Burgos-Debray (n 3) 108.

[6] ibid, 157.

[7] See especially the seminal work by Portuguese scholar P Freire, *Pedagogy of the Oppressed* (New York, Continuum, 2000). The original book was published in Portuguese in 1968, and had a very strong influence on the new pedagogical ideas that conceived education as an essential means for social transformation.

and worked to change the conditions in which they lived. Menchú's commitment to the revolutionary struggle was such that she decided not to get married, to ensure that she would have sufficient time and undivided energy to devote to it.[8]

Rigoberta Menchú's family suffered brutal repression at the hands of the Guatemalan regime. After her father's death at the siege of the Spanish Embassy in January 1980,[9] both her mother and one of her brothers were kidnapped and tortured to death. These tragic events had a decisive impact on Menchú's commitment to the revolutionary cause.

After some years of intense social and political militancy, Menchú went into exile to Chiapas, Mexico, where for more than ten years she was a guest of the Catholic Bishop, Samuel Ruiz. He was one of the leading liberation theologians who applied this new ideology to the oppression and injustice suffered by indigenous peoples in the Americas. Her stay with Samuel Ruiz was a very important step forward in Menchú's process of religious and political education.

Once in Mexico, where most commanders of the Guatemalan guerrillas were exiled and had a logistical platform, Menchú began her international career by denouncing the increasing repression in Guatemala at the hands of the army and the plight of the indigenous peoples. While on a European tour in January 1982 as a representative of the Guatemalan revolutionary movement, she met Elizabeth Burgos-Debray in Paris. Burgos-Debray is a Marxist Venezuelan anthropologist who had very close ties with the major revolutionary movements in Central America, particularly in Guatemala. She thought that Menchú's story might be of interest to the academic community, the international left, solidarity networks, as well as to human rights activists supporting revolutionary groups in the Americas. She suggested that Menchú could tape-record the description of her experiences and turn it into a book. After one week's recording at Burgos-Debray's flat, and several months of editing by the anthropologist,[10] Menchú's autobiography was published in 1983, and achieved international recognition. The book was translated into 11 languages, which considerably extended its international reach. Paradoxically, it was prohibited in Guatemala. The Guatemalan regime was aware of the effect it could have on its worldwide reputation. But the banning of the book was counterproductive; it turned Rigoberta Menchú into a legend in Guatemala, and also (particularly) at international level. Menchú's story became a symbol of the injustices suffered by indigenous peoples in the Americas and elsewhere, and she became a human rights icon.

---

[8] Once her revolutionary fervour passed, in 1995 Rigoberta Menchú married Ángel Canil, who was also Mayan Quiché, and had a son, Mash Nahual J'a (*Spirit of Water*): R Benatar, *Rigoberta Menchú. Libertad sin Ira* (Beverly Hills, Renaissance House, 2004) 30.

[9] See further details below.

[10] Some scholars suspect that anthropologist Elizabeth Burgos-Debray 'interfered too much', in an attempt to construct a narrative that could meet the strategic needs of the insurgency in Guatemala, as argued in D Stoll, *Rigoberta Menchú and the Story of All Poor Guatemalans* (Boulder, Westview Press, 1999) 181. The truth is that Rigoberta was not very satisfied with the final outcome; she did not feel that it was her book, but Elizabeth's. That is why Rigoberta Menchú herself published an autobiography in 1998: R Menchú (with D Liano and G Miná), *Rigoberta: La nieta de los Mayas* (Madrid, Aguilar, 1998). The English translation can be found in R Menchú, *Crossing Borders* (London, Verso, 1999).

She continued to denounce the brutality of the Guatemalan army and advocate indigenous peoples' rights globally. Her candidacy for the Nobel Peace Prize gained momentum as some Nobel laureates such as Adolfo Pérez Esquivel and Desmond Tutu, solidarity groups and human rights organisations became aware of the symbolic meaning of the year 1992. It was the fifth centenary of the colonisation of the Americas and the subsequent subjugation of their native inhabitants. Menchú was the right person for the award at that time. She was very active in the contestation movement that emerged against the attempt to *celebrate* the 500th anniversary of the conquest, orchestrated by the former colonial powers and some Latin American countries. Menchú was proposed as a candidate for the Nobel Peace Prize at the Second Continental Meeting 'Five Hundred Years of Indigenous and Popular Resistance' (Quito, Ecuador, 1990).[11] The Nobel Committee then decided to award the prestigious Prize to Rigoberta Menchú in 1992, 'in recognition of her work for social justice and ... as an advocate for native rights'.[12] Somehow, the Nobel Prize was intended to pay the historical debt owed to indigenous peoples[13] and to encourage a negotiated peace to end Guatemala's bloody internal conflict.

The reactions to the award in Guatemala were far from uniform. As Michael Silverstone has underlined, 'the Guatemalan government did not share the joy of the majority of the Guatemalan people'.[14] Some sectors of the elites and the government accused Menchú of being the Trojan horse that provided legitimacy to the guerrillas in their fight against the state. A representative of the army went even further, saying that she had 'defamed her fatherland'.[15]

She decided to use the proceeds from the Nobel Prize to create the *Rigoberta Menchú Tum Foundation*, in order to continue with her fight for peace, social justice, women's rights and indigenous peoples' rights, both in Guatemala and internationally. She was appointed UNESCO Goodwill Ambassador in June 1996, in recognition of her worldwide activism. In this capacity, she promoted the proclamation of the First International Decade of the World's Indigenous People (1995–2004) by the United Nations (UN).[16] Menchú was also awarded the Prince of Asturias Prize of International Cooperation in 1998; the Order of the Aztec Eagle in 2010 (the highest Mexican order awarded to foreigners); and the Legion of Honour in France, among many other prizes and recognitions. She has also been awarded multiple honorary doctorates,

---

[11] K Lucas, 'Eduardo Galeano y el lenguaje de Rigoberta Menchú' (1991) 40 *Chasqui* 79.
[12] The Norwegian Nobel Committee (n 1).
[13] On the controversial issue of the right to reparation of indigenous peoples for historical injustices, see F Gómez Isa, 'Repairing Historical Injustices: Indigenous Peoples in Post-Conflict Scenarios' in G Oré Aguilar and F Gómez Isa (eds), *Rethinking Transitions. Equality and Social Justice in Societies Emerging From Conflict* (Antwerp, Intersentia, 2011) 265–300. Some people in Norway also interpreted the Nobel award to an indigenous person for the first time ever as a sort of expiation of guilt over the historical treatment of the Sami. According to journalist Henrik Hovland, it was 'a way of making amends ... I believe it was felt collectively by a great number of Norwegians', quoted in Stoll (n 10) 213.
[14] Silverstone (n 2) 90.
[15] ibid.
[16] The International Decade was proclaimed by the UN General Assembly in its Resolution 48/163 of 21 December 1993, with the main objective of strengthening international cooperation for the solution of problems faced by indigenous people in the areas of human rights, the environment, development, education and health.

a remarkable achievement for a person that never had the opportunity to go to university and only received some basic primary and secondary education.

Menchú has also been politically active in Guatemala. Her dream was to become the first woman and the first indigenous person to be elected President of Guatemala. She founded an indigenous political party, WINAQ (meaning 'people' in the Quiché language), and ran for president for the first time in 2007 in coalition with the left-wing political party *Encuentro por Guatemala* (Coming Together for Guatemala). She was not successful, as she only obtained 3.09 per cent of the votes. It is worth mentioning that the Third Indigenous World Summit held in Guatemala in March 2007 did not support Menchú's political aspirations, since some indigenous people did not feel represented by her project. The same occurred in 2011, when the political coalition led by Menchú as a presidential candidate only obtained 3.27 per cent of the votes. Ultimately, her case illustrates that there is some truth in the saying 'nobody is a prophet in their own land'.

II. From Poverty, Discrimination and Repression to Revolutionary Awareness

Guatemala is a multi-ethnic state that was engaged in a brutal internal armed conflict for 36 years. The late 1970s and early 1980s were years of rampant repression in the rural areas of Guatemala. Revolutionary movements were very active in Central America, where the triumph of the Sandinista revolution in Nicaragua in 1979 heightened the revolutionary struggle in the whole region, including Guatemala. The reaction by Guatemalan elites and the army was a dramatic escalation of the fight against insurgency. Menchú and her family were subjected to extreme repression that included summary executions, forced disappearances, blatant use of torture, forced displacement and exile. The Commission for the historical clarification of human rights violations and acts of violence against the Guatemalan people was created on 23 June 1994 in Oslo as part of the peace negotiations between the government and the guerrilla *Unidad Revolucionaria Nacional de Guatemala* (URNG) (Revolutionary National Unity of Guatemala). It concluded that acts of genocide, crimes against humanity, and other gross and systematic violations of both International Human Rights Law and International Humanitarian Law had taken place during the internal armed conflict in Guatemala.[17]

Within this context of widespread violence Vicente Menchú, Rigoberta's father, began his work as a catechist and helped organise plantation workers. He was also a very active leader in the defence of their community's land. He participated in the setting up of the first trade union for the defence of the rights of plantation workers.

---

[17] Commission for Historical Clarification, *Guatemala. Memory of Silence. Tz'Inil Na'Tab'Al*, 1999, available at www.aaas.org/sites/default/files/migrate/uploads/mos_en.pdf. On the issue of genocide of Mayan peoples, see also F Gómez Isa (coord), *Racismo y Genocidio en Guatemala* (San Sebastián, Tercera Prensa, 1999).

The Committee for Peasant Unity (CUC) was the first inter-ethnic platform to defend the rights of both indigenous people and *ladinos* (non-indigenous people) working in plantations. He was severely beaten for his work in defence of the land and the rights of plantation workers, subjected to repression and tireless persecution and sent to prison twice, after which he had to work in hiding. The CUC would eventually join the Guerrilla Army of the Poor (*Ejército Guerrillero de los Pobres*, EGP), one of the many armed groups within the revolutionary movement in Guatemala. Repression intensified against Vicente Menchú and his comrades and collaborators, including his daughter Rigoberta, for whom he had always been a source of inspiration.

During the occupation of the Spanish Embassy on 31 January 1980 to protest against the army's increasing repression of El Quiché region and attract international attention, 37 people were killed, including her father. The security forces assaulted the Embassy, a violation of the basic principles of diplomatic law, and the fire that this started killed both the protesters and most of the hostages taken.[18] This tragic episode affected Menchú deeply. International opinion was outraged, and the assault of the Spanish Embassy became a highly powerful symbol of the brutality of the Guatemalan regime.[19]

After her father's death, Juana Tum, Rigoberta's mother, was offered the opportunity to go into exile, which she refused. She decided to continue with her role as community leader and midwife. As revenge for the political and social activities of the Menchú family, Juana Tum was kidnapped, raped and tortured to death. Petrocinio, one of Rigoberta's brothers, was also kidnapped, brutally tortured and murdered, an event that was turned into a horrific public spectacle perpetrated in front of their community. All these tragic events marked Rigoberta's life and profoundly contributed to raising her political awareness. As she explains in her oral autobiography,

> My cause radicalises with the misery of my people, the malnutrition that I have witnessed and suffered as indigenous, the exploitation and discrimination that I have felt in my own flesh, the killing of my beloved ones and neighbours.[20]

This violence was the context in which Menchú began to organise her community. They started to defend themselves against the army. Using some passages of the Bible as a justification, she advocated *just violence*, invoking the episode of David and Goliath.[21] Violence should be used only as a last resort against injustice and discrimination. This is one of the most controversial dimensions of Menchú's work, since her

---

[18] For decades, the responsibility for the burning of the Spanish Embassy was a controversial issue in Guatemala. Finally, on 19 January 2015, a Guatemalan Court sentenced Pedro García Arredondo, former Chief of the riot police that assaulted the Embassy, to 40 years in prison for crimes against humanity, homicide and for orchestrating the massacre. The Rigoberta Menchú Foundation joined the lawsuit representing the victims.

[19] The Spanish Ambassador, one of only two survivors to the assault, wrote about his tragic experience in M Cajal, *¡Saber quién puso fuego ahí!: Masacre en la Embajada de España* (Madrid, Ediciones Siddharth Mehta, 2000). The other survivor was demonstrator Gregorio Xujá, who was kidnapped from hospital and tortured to death. His body was found the next day on the campus of the University of San Carlos with a message on a piece of paper: 'The Ambassador runs the same risk': Stoll (n 10) 75.

[20] Burgos-Debray (n 3) 271.

[21] ibid, 157–60.

justification of violence gave legitimacy to Guatemalan guerrillas and led Menchú herself to join the Guerrilla Army of the Poor.

This core issue ignited a controversy about the full veracity of the oral testimony that Menchú gave to Burgos-Debray in 1982, which turned her into an international icon of the global struggle for indigenous peoples' rights. According to North American anthropologist David Stoll, although the repression suffered by Mayan peoples and Menchú's family is unquestionable, her oral autobiography includes some inaccuracies, exaggerations and omissions that open the door to questioning the underlying aims of her constructive exercise of selective memory.[22] In his opinion, her testimony in the book *I, Rigoberta Menchú* 'was a version of events with specific political objectives'.[23] According to him, by mythologising and dramatising some of the events in which she and her family had participated, Menchú painted a picture that became 'a deeply influential portrait of violence in Guatemala',[24] especially outside the country. This picture has served Menchú's foreign supporters to continue 'using her story to prove that the guerrilla movement had deep popular roots and was an inevitable response to oppression'.[25] However, there are significant doubts about the extent of the support by indigenous peoples in Guatemala of the revolutionary movement. In Stoll's view,

> Many Mayas also blamed the guerrillas for the violence and did not feel represented by them. Yet Rigoberta's version was so attractive to so many foreigners that Mayas who repudiated violence were often ignored or discounted. This bolstered the claim that the guerrillas represented the mass of Mayan peasants, long after there was good reason to doubt this.[26]

As is the case with many other internal armed conflicts, while some indigenous people opted for the revolutionary cause due to their circumstances, the majority of them were simply forced to cooperate with one armed actor or the other.[27]

In light of the doubt cast on her story,[28] some people even asked for her Nobel Peace Prize to be revoked.[29] The Nobel Committee dismissed these calls. In the words

---

[22] For a questioning of Stoll's methodology and of some of his sources, see especially V Sanford, 'Between Rigoberta Menchú and La Violencia. Deconstructing David Stoll's History of Guatemala' (1999) 26 *Latin American Perspectives* 6, 38–46. See also G Grandin, 'It Was Heaven That They Burned. Who is Rigoberta Menchú?' *The Nation* (8 September 2010), available at www.thenation.com/article/it-was-heaven-they-burned/.

[23] Stoll (n 10) 11.

[24] ibid, xii.

[25] ibid, 276.

[26] ibid, xiv.

[27] D Stoll, *Between Two Armies in the Ixil Towns of Guatemala* (New York, Columbia University Press, 1994).

[28] Although it was not Stoll's intention, his research has been appropriated by some right-wing writers to openly question Rigoberta Menchú as a credible human rights activist and the responsibility of the Guatemalan army in the atrocities perpetrated against Mayan peoples in the context of the internal armed conflict, in H Cohen, 'The Unmaking of Rigoberta Menchú' in DE Lorey and WH Beezley (eds), *Genocide, Collective Violence, and Popular Memory: The Politics of Remembrance in the Twentieth Century* (Wilmington, Scholarly Resources Inc, 2002) 54.

[29] David Horowitz, Director of the right-wing Center for the Study of Popular Culture based in Los Angeles, called Rigoberta Menchú a 'Marxist terrorist' manipulated by the Guatemalan guerrillas and the international left, and asked for her Nobel Prize to be revoked, in V Montejo, *Maya Intellectual Renaissance. Identity, Representation and Leadership* (Austin, University of Texas Press, 2005) ch 5.

of Geir Lundestad, secretary of the Committee, her prize 'was not based exclusively or primarily on the autobiography ... Stoll approves of her Nobel Prize and has no question about the picture of army atrocities which she presents'.[30]

III. Rigoberta Menchú's Legacy

It can be said that Rigoberta Menchú's major achievement is to have empowered the silenced voice of all indigenous peoples to claim their rights. Her story is part and parcel of the so-called *indigenous emergence*[31] in Latin America in the 1980s, a process in which indigenous peoples began to assert their rights both domestically and internationally, and were gradually transformed from victims to actors, and from objects of protection to subjects of rights.[32]

Her second achievement has been her contribution to the peace process in Guatemala. Not only did the award of the Nobel Peace Prize serve as a catalyst for the negotiations, but she was an active participant in them. In order to become a credible voice in the peace process, Menchú progressively distanced herself from the revolutionary movement and adopted a neutral position based on her long-standing commitment to the cause of indigenous peoples.

From the early days of the peace negotiations the indigenous organisations conceived the process as a window of opportunity to reverse the poverty, historical exclusion and marginalisation they experienced.[33] The pressure from these organisations and other social and political movements led to the signing of two key agreements for the process of clarifying past abuses and of reparation for the victims, particularly indigenous peoples. The first was the Agreement on the establishment of the Commission for the historical clarification of the past human rights violations and acts of violence against the Guatemalan people, signed in Oslo in 1994. Menchú, her foundation and many other indigenous organisations were also highly proactive in the adoption of the second agreement, the Agreement on the Identity and Rights of Indigenous Peoples, signed in Mexico on 31 March 1995.[34] The preamble of this Agreement established that the question of identity and rights of indigenous peoples is 'a vital issue of historic importance for the present and future of Guatemala'. The Agreement was firmly based on the recognition of the historical discrimination and oppression inflicted on the indigenous peoples of Guatemala. Accordingly, an ambitious programme based on truth, justice, reparation and guarantees of non-repetition

---

[30] Quoted in L Rother, 'Tarnished Laureate' in A Arias (ed), *The Rigoberta Menchú controversy* (Minneapolis: The University of Minnesota Press, 2001) 61.

[31] J Bengoa, *La emergencia indígena en América Latina* (Santiago de Chile, Fondo de Cultura Económica, 2000).

[32] I have detailed this stimulating process in F Gómez Isa, 'Indigenous Peoples: From Objects of Protection to Subjects of Rights' in A Brysk and M Stohl (eds), *Expanding Human Rights. 21st Century Norms and Governance* (Cheltenham, Edward Elgar, 2017) 55.

[33] Gómez Isa (n 13) 294.

[34] The text of the Agreement can be found at www.usip.org/sites/default/files/file/resources/collections/peace_agreements/guat_950331.pdf.

was established in 2003 as the basis for peace and reconciliation. Menchú and her foundation have made determined efforts to bring this to fruition. Although some achievements have been made, there is still much room for improvement. If adequately implemented, the reparations programme could eventually lay the foundations for social transformation and genuine reconciliation, but the lack of political will on the part of the government has been an insurmountable obstacle so far.[35]

Rigoberta Menchú's main tangible legacy is the creation of the Rigoberta Menchú Tum Foundation.[36] According to its mission, the Foundation aims at 'recuperating and enriching human values to create world peace taking as its base the ethnic, political and cultural diversity of the world'. At the same time, it works 'to create justice and democracy, especially for indigenous peoples and natives'.[37] Through her Foundation, Rigoberta has focused on initiatives to foster peace, inter-cultural education, indigenous peoples' rights and justice. One of the areas in which the Foundation has been particularly active is the fight against impunity in Guatemala. The Foundation has filed a number of complaints against those who perpetrated gross and systematic violations of human rights during the internal armed conflict.

Based on her own experience as a witness of the systematic use of sexual violence by the army in its fight against insurgency,[38] Menchú has also dedicated herself to the global struggle for women's rights. In 2006 she was one of the six women peace laureates[39] to create the *Nobel Women's Initiative* to 'magnify the power and visibility of women working in countries around the world for peace, justice and equality'. Their vision is to transform the world 'through a rejection of war, violence and militarism where global security is built around human rights, justice and equality for people and communities – human security – rather than the security of the nation state'.[40]

In the same way that corn is an essential pillar of Mayan culture, the *daughter of corn* has become a powerful symbol of the fight for justice and for indigenous peoples' rights around the globe.

[35] F Gómez Isa, 'National Reparations Commission/Comisión Nacional de Resarcimiento (Guatemala)' in L Stan and N Nedelsky (eds), *Encyclopedia of Transitional Justice*, 2nd edn (Cambridge, Cambridge University Press, forthcoming).

[36] The initial name of the foundation was Vicente Menchú Foundation to honour her father's memory, but in 1995 Rigoberta decided to change the name to Rigoberta Menchú Tum Foundation.

[37] At rigobertamenchutum.weebly.com/enduring-foundations.html.

[38] One of the most harrowing episodes of her oral autobiography is the narration of the rape of two of her friends by soldiers, as a result of which they became pregnant. One of them told Rigoberta: 'I hate this son. He is not my son' in Burgos-Debray (n 3) 168–69.

[39] Rigoberta Menchú, Mairead Maguire, Jody Williams, Shirin Ebadi, Tawakkol Karman, and Leymah Gbowee.

[40] See nobelwomensinitiative.org.

19

Victoria Lucia Tauli-Corpuz

A Life Spent Peacefully Advocating for Indigenous Peoples' Rights

DAVINIA GÓMEZ-SÁNCHEZ

Only by facilitating constructive and peaceful engagements between governments and indigenous peoples will we have a chance at achieving global peace and security.[1]

I. An Indigenous Activist from the Beginning

Victoria Tauli-Corpuz is an indigenous person from the Kankana-ey, one of the five ethnolinguistic groups within the Igorot people of the Cordillera administrative region in the Northern Philippines. The daughter of an Anglican priest and a nurse who were among the first educated generation of their indigenous community, she graduated with a nursing degree at the UP College of Nursing in Manila in 1976. It was during those days as a student that her activism awoke: 'I was shocked to realize that mainstream society looked down on us. This was when I started to educate myself about the discrimination faced by Indigenous peoples in the Philippines and around the world'.[2] She furthered her education with a Masters of Humanities (major in Women's Studies) at Scholastica's College in Manila.[3] She bore six children and is grandmother to eight grandchildren.

---

[1] V Tauli-Corpuz, 'How a Filipina Activist Fights for Human Rights at the UN' *Human Nature: Conservation International Blog*, 19 November 2014, available at blog.conservation.org/2014/11/how-a-filipina-activist-fights-for-human-rights-at-the-u-n/.

[2] T Hansen, 'Victoria Tauli-Corpuz, Kankanaey Igorot – Conversation' *Earth Island Journal* (September 2015), available at www.earthisland.org/journal/index.php/magazine/entry/victoria_tauli-corpuz_kankanaey_igorot/.

[3] Biographical information provided by UN at www.un.org/esa/socdev/unpfii/documents/members/member-corpuz.pdf.

As a young activist in the 1970s she was involved in defending the rights of indigenous peoples during the martial law period imposed on the Philippines by President Ferdinand Marcos (Head of State from 1966 to 1986). She opposed several infrastructure projects which threatened the displacement of indigenous communities and implied violations of their cultural rights, their rights to their ancestral lands and traditional usage of resources. During those early years of activism she worked successfully in mobilising indigenous communities in resisting mega development projects and defending their collective rights. It was at that time when she realised that underpinning the challenges and struggles of indigenous people and communities was their compound lack of recognition and of self-determined development. These early experiences guided her career and led her to pursue the recognition of indigenous peoples in the Philippines as well as their involvement in policy and decision-making processes at international level. She summarised how this backdrop directed her career as follows:

> In order to fight back, I needed to understand what our human rights as indigenous peoples are and where we could bring our grievances for redress... After attending a number of training courses, I established several institutions that provided trainings on human rights to indigenous communities, lawyers and paralegal workers.[4]

Since the late 1970s she has worked to fill the gap in understanding and in the process founded several community-based organisations addressing different issues related to health, education and women's rights in the context of indigenous peoples.

In February 2018, her name was included in a list of 600 alleged communist guerrillas as she was identified by the Government of the Philippines as a senior member of the Maoist rebel group[5] (a leftist group banned in the country). Those names in the list were tagged as terrorists for their links with the New People's Army, the armed wing of the Communist Party. The list was filed by the Ministry of Justice at a Manila court for the purpose of having the court declare the individuals on the list terrorists. Among the 600 names are several human rights activists like Tauli-Corpuz. Many human rights organisations, UN human rights experts as well as the European Parliament, among others, have condemned the Philippines Government act of decrying human rights activists as 'terrorists', and have called upon the authorities of the Philippines to remove her name from the list and drop the charges against her. Tauli-Corpuz has declared in several interviews that she sees her inclusion in the list as retaliation by the government for her support and advocacy work for the rights of indigenous peoples in her country. According to her statements in different media channels denying the terrorism accusations and allegations of NPA's membership, she further believes that the list aims to silence critical voices and distract public attention from the ongoing abuses, attacks by members of the armed forces and displacement that indigenous peoples are suffering in the Philippines. In December 2017, a few months before her name appeared on the government list, she published a joint statement with the Special Rapporteur on internally displaced people regarding the ongoing militarisation of the

---

[4] ibid.

[5] M Mogato, 'Philippines seeks 'terrorist' tag for 600 alleged communist guerrillas' *Reuters* (Manila, 8 March 2018), available at uk.reuters.com/article/uk-philippines-rebels/philippines-seeks-terrorist-tag-for-600-alleged-communist-guerrillas-idUKKCN1GK0DS.

second largest island of the Philippines.[6] In that communiqué, they described and condemned the militarisation, abuses and alleged violations of Lumads indigenous communities in Mindanao who are being affected by logging and mining activities on their ancestral lands. Furthermore, they urged the government to protect the human rights of indigenous peoples in compliance with its obligations under international law (ancestral lands are also protected by the Indigenous People's Rights Act 1997 which recognises, protects and promotes the rights of indigenous cultural communities/indigenous peoples in the Philippines). She has declared a deep concern about her situation (despite the fact that she enjoys legal immunity based on her role as UN Special Rapporteur to exercise her functions[7] and can rely on the protection of the organisation) as well as those of the other human rights and environmental activists included there. The escalation of threats, attacks and criminalisation of indigenous peoples (as well as their disproportionate impact on indigenous women) has become one of her major concerns,[8] together with the negative effects of climate change adaptation and mitigation measures on indigenous peoples' ways of life and survival. Her name was cleared from the government petition later in August 2018.

II. 'Create a Vision of Where We Would Like to be Ten Years from Now and Identify Steps on How to Reach that Vision'[9]

Commended for her human rights activism advocating for indigenous peoples' and women's rights, Tauli-Corpuz has held numerous positions, which illustrate her vast, rich and valuable experience. During the 1970s she opposed several infrastructure projects which threatened the displacement of indigenous communities in the Philippines and which implied violations of their cultural rights, their rights to their ancestral lands and traditional usage of resources. When she joined a movement opposing the government's infrastructure plans for constructing the Chico River Hydroelectric Dam, which was financed by the World Bank, she came to the realisation that 'in order to secure our rights, we would have to deal with the international system'.[10] She saw that a first step needed to be taken through the adoption of the UN declaration on indigenous peoples.

---

[6] UN Office of the High Commissioner for Human Rights, 'Philippines warned over "massive" impact of military operations on Mindanao indigenous peoples' 27 December 2017, available at www.ohchr.org/EN/NewsEvents/Pages/DisplayNews.aspx?NewsID=22567&LangID=E.

[7] Art 105(2) of the UN Charter and the protection conferred by the Convention on the Privileges and Immunities of the United Nations of 1946 ratified by the Philippine Government.

[8] Tauli-Corpuz expressed her concerns during her last address to the Human Rights Council in September 2018 while calling for accountability for those attacks and emphasising the importance of developing protection measures at national level and at a community-led one.

[9] V Tauli-Corpuz, 'Statement at the 4th session of the Permanent Forum on Indigenous Issues' 16–27 May 2005.

[10] ibid.

That realisation led her to undertake numerous professional challenges and responsibilities in the field of development, indigenous peoples, environmental issues and biodiversity. Tauli-Corpuz has worked for diverse organisations at national and international level, NGOs, INGOs, different forums, commissions and delegations, UN bodies, university and training centres, multi-stakeholder groups, etcetera. She served on numerous boards, committees and organisations, for example, Cultural Survival, UN Development Programme Civil Society Organizations and the International Forum on Globalization. She sat on advisory panels including the second Millennium Development Goals Report of the UN Economic and Social Council of Asia-Pacific and the UN Development Programme Human Development Report on Cultural Liberty and Diversity. Through various appointments to different organisations, such as the vice-president of the International Training Centre of Indigenous Peoples, chairperson of the UN Voluntary Fund for Indigenous Populations 1994–2005, the co-chairperson of the Indigenous Caucus of the UN Commission of Sustainable Development NGO Steering Committee, among many others, she worked to ensure a holistic approach to the protection of indigenous rights, which bear strong links to the environment. To further entrench continued activism in these areas, Tauli-Corpuz also founded several organisations (Tebtebba Foundation, Cordillera Women's Education and Resource Centre, Services and Training in the Cordillera Region, Community-Based Health Program among Indigenous Peoples, Indigenous Initiative for Peace) and has co-edited and authored dozens of publications. Furthermore, she has played a role in the organisation of multiple conferences such as the International Conference on Conflict Resolution, Peace Building, Sustainable Development and Indigenous Peoples 2000 and the Second Asian Indigenous Women's Conference 2004. And this represents only a few of her accomplishments.[11] As these roles reflect, her work covers a broad range of issues revolving around indigenous peoples' rights and development: nutrition, women's rights, gender issues, sustainable development, education, training and advocacy, civil society, environmental issues, bio-diversity, biosafety, genetic engineering and bio-piracy and peace, crosscutting and interrelated issues for the protection of indigenous peoples' rights and that respond to their holistic understanding of self-development.

Tauli-Corpuz' commitment to the defence of indigenous peoples brought her to the international scene. Her clear vision about the necessity for dealing with the international system achieved reality through her involvement with the existing UN bodies and mechanisms for the protection and advancement of indigenous peoples' rights. She served as a member and chairperson of the board of trustees of the UN Voluntary Fund for Indigenous Populations from 1994 to 2005. In this role she assisted representatives of indigenous organisations and communities in participating in the deliberations of the Working Group on indigenous peoples (attending as observers) as well as in the sessions of the Permanent Forum on Indigenous Issues (high-level advisory body to the Economic and Social Council) of which she was the chair some years later.[12] She became the Chair of the Permanent Forum on Indigenous

---

[11] For further details see n 3.

[12] After her time at the UN Voluntary Fund, the mandate of the Fund was expanded in order to include among its functions assisting representatives of indigenous communities and organisations to participate in the Expert Mechanism on the Rights of Indigenous Peoples, UNGA A/RES/63/161 of 18 December 2008.

Issues (UNPFII) from 2005 to 2010. Her appointment was backed by indigenous organisations in Asia which supported her to become the Asian representative to the Permanent Forum.[13] In that position, Tauli-Corpuz and the other 15 members of the Forum were mandated to provide advice and recommendations to ECOSOC and other UN agencies, programs and funds, to raise awareness within the UN system promoting coherence and coordination of activities within the UN on issues related to indigenous peoples, namely economic and social development, culture, environment, education, health and human rights. It was during the period that the UN Declaration on the Rights of Indigenous Peoples (UNDRIP) was adopted, on 13 September 2007, with 144 votes in favour, 4 against it and 11 abstentions.

Tauli-Corpuz was highly engaged in the negotiations and work which led to the drafting and adoption of the UNDRIP, which set the international minimum standards for indigenous peoples' rights. She proudly commends the fact that the UNDRIP was crafted together with the rights-holders themselves. In a statement during the sixteenth session of the UNPFII in May 2017 she acknowledged that '[she has] a strong attachment and sense of ownership of this historic human rights instrument'.[14]

The process leading to the adoption of the UNDRIP began in 1982 with the creation of the Working Group on Indigenous Populations (UNWGIP) mandated to develop a set of minimum standards for the protection and promotion of indigenous peoples' rights globally. The draft was concluded in 1993 and an inter-sessional working group on the draft declaration of the rights of indigenous peoples (WGDD) was established in 1995 as an expert body in order to elaborate further on the draft declaration submitted by the UNWGIP and to start negotiations which would lead to the adoption of the UNDRIP in 2007. In her description of the process leading to the adoption of the UNDRIP, Tauli-Corpuz noted that when the WGDD first met in 1995, states refused to give a voice to indigenous representatives.[15] As a result, indigenous representatives threatened to stay out of the negotiation process unless their voices were considered on equal terms with the governments. Members of indigenous communities argued that their absence from the process would deprive the document of the required legitimacy.

Further controversy arose around the term 'indigenous peoples' and with regard to collective rights such as self-determination. Indigenous representatives defended their position by referring to existing international human rights law while simultaneously demonstrating a degree of flexibility to allow for the process to continue. Throughout the process, there were dissenting views within the different indigenous caucuses. In her capacity as member of the Global Indigenous Peoples' Caucus, Tauli-Copuz presented improvements on the wording of territorial integrity aimed at reaching agreement between the African Group and Co-sponsors of the Declaration on the amendments presented by the African Group and Canada/Russia/New Zealand/Colombia Proposals (seeking approval of the Declaration adopted by the HRC). These negotiations were

---

[13] R de Chavez and V Tauli-Corpuz, 'Key Accomplishments of Tebtebba in 2007' (2007) 10 *Tebtebba* 29.

[14] V Tauli-Corpuz, 'Statement by Victoria Tauli-Corpuz, Special Rapporteur on the Rights of Indigenous Peoples' 16th Session of the United Nations Permanent Forum on Indigenous Issues, 1 May 2017, available at unsr.vtaulicorpuz.org/site/index.php/statements/186-unpfii-2017.

[15] V Tauli-Corpuz, 'How the UN Declaration on the Rights of Indigenous Peoples Got Adopted' (1999) 2 *Tebtebba*.

key for the indigenous peoples to accept the changes and to ultimately achieve the endorsement of the agreed Declaration by the UNGA. Tauli-Corpuz, in her position of chair of the UNPFII,

> ... actively participated in several strategy sessions with key indigenous organizations and with friendly governments, such as Mexico, since January 2007. The strategy sessions were aimed at, among others, identifying steps in convincing governments, specifically the African block, which had earlier called for the deferment of the Declaration's adoption in 2006, to finally vote for its passage. She was also instrumental in explaining and convincing Asian governments to vote for its adoption.[16]

She closely monitored the informal negotiations among the hesitant states and those trying to undermine the process. She got several NGOs involved in a demonstration in New York to put pressure on those governments. In spite of these difficulties, mobilisation among indigenous representatives, triggered by their common aspiration to get the draft adopted, bore fruit. They actively and strongly lobbied the delegations of the 47 HRC Member States, aiming at gaining their support for the HRC and the UNGA to adopt the consolidation position of the revised version of the Declaration. These efforts led to a successful outcome 12 years after the establishment of the WGDD: the adoption of the UNDRIP on 13 December 2007, a historic day for Tauli-Corpuz and the rest of the world. She was recognised by the Philippine government's National Commission on Indigenous Peoples for the significant role she played in the UNDRIP adoption process.[17]

Despite the success of the adoption of the Declaration, during her statement at the sixty-first Session of the General Assembly on the occasion of the adoption of UNDRIP, Tauli-Corpuz highlighted the need for its effective implementation which would give meaning to the formal commitment expressed by signatory states when they voted for its adoption. In spite of the UNDRIP not being a legally binding instrument, states that voted in favour showed their willingness and commitment to uphold the rights, obligations and principles contained therein.[18] Ten years later, during the fourth annual report to the HRC session, she highlighted as significant, that the Declaration had become a source of law in national courts and regional human rights mechanisms. She continued to emphasise the importance of 'identify[ing] and confront[ing] the obstacles faced for its effective implementation'.[19] During the tenth anniversary speech Tauli-Corpuz declared her main concern to be closing the gap between recognition of indigenous peoples' rights and de facto implementation.

---

[16] Tauli-Corpuz (n 14) 26.

[17] ibid.

[18] With regard to the legal standing of the UNDRIP, Tauli-Corpuz builds on the opinion of her predecessor, SR J Anaya: it 'is a standard-setting resolution of profound significance, as it reflects a wide consensus at the global level on the minimum content of the rights of indigenous peoples. Many of its articles are an extension of binding standards found in various human rights treaties that have been widely ratified and certain provisions, such as those relating to the protection against racial discrimination, reflect customary international law': V Tauli-Corpuz, 'Statement at the 17th Session of the UNPFII', 18 April 2018.

[19] V Tauli-Corpuz, 'Statement of Ms. Victoria Tauli-Corpuz Special Rapporteur on the Rights of Indigenous Peoples' Human Rights Council, 36th Session Geneva, 20 September 2017, 5, available at www.ohchr.org/Documents/Issues/IPeoples/SR/StatementHRC36_20Sept2017.pdf.

In 2009, while holding the position of Chair of the UNPFII, she was awarded the first Gabriela Silang Award which acclaims the 'living heroines who continue to passionately fight for the recognition of the right of indigenous peoples to their ancestral lands and the right to self-determination'.[20]

In June 2014 Tauli-Corpuz was appointed by the HRC as the third mandate holder of the position of UN Special Rapporteur on the Rights of Indigenous Peoples. She applied for this position because 'there is still a long way to go before indigenous peoples' rights are effectively respected, protected and fulfilled'.[21] At the beginning of her mandate she declared that 'through my role as Special Rapporteur, I think I can help governments better understand how the development visions and aspirations of indigenous peoples are consistent with sustainable development objectives'.[22] She continued, saying

> I believe I can bring a unique perspective and experience to the role, which could spur new thinking and innovative initiatives. I am proud to be the first woman – and first person from a developing country – to hold this position.[23]

During this three-year appointment her aim was 'to help build the confidence and abilities of indigenous peoples to assert their rights, as well as help countries more effectively uphold human rights'.[24]

In the fulfilment of her mandate, the Special Rapporteur annually presented the activities carried out during the year to the HRC. Her reports have covered the following topics: obstacles to the realisation of indigenous peoples' rights (2014); right of indigenous women and girls (2015); international investment agreements (2016); and impacts of climate change and climate finance on indigenous peoples' rights (2017). In her reporting to the UN General Assembly she has addressed the following issues: economic, social and cultural rights of indigenous peoples in the post-2015 development framework (2014); impact of international investment and free trade on the human rights of indigenous peoples (2015); conservation measures and their impact on indigenous peoples' rights (2016); and an assessment of the implementation of UNDRIP on its tenth anniversary (2017). Additionally, as Special Rapporteur she reported on the situation of indigenous peoples in specific countries, including: Paraguay/Sampi region (Norway, Sweden and Finland) (2015); Honduras and Brazil (2016); Australia and USA (2017); and Guatemala (2018). In 2018 she also presented a special report with conclusions and recommendations on international human rights law and indigenous peoples in voluntary isolation and in initial contact in the Amazonia and Gran Chaco. In all of these documents she identified challenges and difficulties as well as highlighted good practices. During these three years as Special Rapporteur she received and sent around 150 communications to governments and others (urgent appeals and letters of allegation addressing specific cases of alleged violations of indigenous peoples' rights).

---

[20] KT Okubo, 'IP int'l activist gets 1st Gabriela Silang award' *Northern Dispatch Weekly* (29 March 2009), available at www.nordis.net/2009/03/ip-int%E2%80%99l-activitist-gets-1st-gabriela-silang-award/.
[21] Tauli-Corpuz (n 1).
[22] ibid.
[23] ibid.
[24] ibid.

During her mandate as Special Rapporteur she has emphasised the importance of designing public policies affecting indigenous peoples in consultation with them as well as the relevance of adequate data and indicators to measure progress.[25] She also regrets the lack of recognition of indigenous peoples by some governments (especially in Africa and Asia) which implies no access to those countries as Rapporteur and has shown deep concern for the continuous and increasing criminalisation of indigenous rights defenders. Proof of her concern is the topic covered in her next thematic report: it will address the criminalisation and attacks against indigenous peoples, indigenous leaders defending their rights under human rights treaties and the UNDRIP.

III. Community for Indigenous Peoples is Not Just the Present Community[26]

As explained above, Ms Tauli-Corpuz was closely involved in the negotiations which led to the successful adoption of the UNDRIP. In addition, she actively engaged with the Convention on Biological Diversity and the UN Framework Convention on Climate Change to ensure recognition of the UNDRIP. As a result, during her address on the occasion of the tenth anniversary of the UNDRIP, she recalled that several decisions were adopted during the Conferences of Parties of the above environmental agreements, which referred to standards set out in the Declaration:

> During the negotiations of the Paris Agreement in December 2015, I, together with the Special Rapporteur on human rights and the environment and the Office of the United Nations High Commissioner for Human Rights successfully advocated for the inclusion of provisions on indigenous peoples and human rights'.[27]

Article 7.5 refers to indigenous peoples' knowledge as one of the bases and guidelines for climate change adaptation. Paragraph 11 of the Preamble also refers to the obligations of the States Parties with regards to the rights of indigenous peoples when taking action to address climate change. Despite that, Tauli-Corpuz regretted the exclusion of the reference to the rights of indigenous peoples as one of the base on which the agreement should be implemented which appeared in an earlier draft of the Agreement. Other references to the rights of indigenous peoples were dropped out in the final text such as in relation to the principles and guidelines of the decisions to give effect to

---

[25] The next expected appointment for Special Rapporteur on the Rights of Indigenous Peoples will take place in March 2020.

[26] During a conversation around IPs and SDGs at the 2018 High-Level Political Forum, she explained that 'Community for Indigenous Peoples is not just the present community, is the community of the past and the community of the future. And it's also a community in which you have relationships not just amongst yourselves but between you and the living and non-living things', available at webtv.un.org/search/indigenous-rights-and-agenda-2030-sdg-media-zone-at-the-2018-high-level-political-forum-2018-hlpf/5810371214001/?term=tauli%20corpuz&sort=date, at 14:55.

[27] V Tauli-Corpuz, 'Address to the Expert Mechanism on the tenth anniversary of UNDRIP' 12 July 2017, available at www.ohchr.org/EN/NewsEvents/Pages/DisplayNews.aspx?NewsID=21889&LangID=E.

the Agreement, and the involvement of indigenous peoples as relevant stakeholders.[28] Tauli-Corpuz has always stressed the relationship between preservation of biodiversity and ecosystems, and indigenous peoples. She has underlined the importance of implementation of conservation measures and of strengthening indigenous communities for themselves to continue protecting their territories.[29] Furthermore, several resolutions were included in line with her recommendations to the World Conservation Congress 2016 of the International Union for Conservation of Nature (IUCN).[30] At the WCC she stated that despite improvements in recognising the rights of indigenous peoples, implementation of those rights was still a concern and she urged

> conservation organisations and government agencies to move beyond commitments on paper and ensure that indigenous peoples are actively involved in the management of protected areas and that all conservation measures include continuous monitoring of compliance with indigenous peoples' rights.[31]

She made the connection between the creation and protection of conservation areas, their overlap with indigenous territories and the consequent displacement of indigenous peoples, ancestral guardianships of those lands and of the biodiversity they contain and violations of their rights.

Tauli-Corpuz pushed for the creation of a UNDP Policy of Engagement with Indigenous Peoples. Moreover, together with her organisation Tebtebba, Tauli-Corpuz was very active in achieving the integration of IPs' issues within the post-2015 development agenda, including with regard to self-identification and the terminology it would employ: indigenous peoples instead of indigenous and local communities. She has contributed greatly to the consolidation and recognition of the interrelation between human rights and sustainable development by devoting 'particular attention to clarify issues related to the operationalization of the right to development and economic-social-cultural and environmental rights',[32] as well as to the concept of 'indigenous peoples' sustainable self-determined development' (development with identity and culture).[33]

---

[28] V Tauli-Corpuz, 'Removing Rights for Indigenous Peoples places Forests, Climate Plan at Risk. Statemnet from Paris, COP21' 7 December 2015, available at unsr.vtaulicorpuz.org/site/index.php/statements/106-statement-cop21.

[29] References made at the World Parks Congress 2014 in Sydney and the World Conservation Congress 2016 in Honolulu.

[30] For example, WCC-2016-Res-004 'Including indigenous peoples' organisations in the structure of the Union'; WCC-2016-Res-025 'Recognising, understanding and enhancing the role of indigenous peoples and local communities in tackling the illegal wildlife trade crisis'; WCC-2016-Res-030 'Recognizing and respecting the territories and areas conserved by indigenous peoples and local communities overlapped by protected areas'.

[31] UN Office of the High Commissioner for Human Rights, 'IUCN World Conservation Congress – Honolulu (1–10 September)', available at www.ohchr.org/EN/NewsEvents/Pages/DisplayNews.aspx?NewsID=20423&LangID=E.

[32] Intervention during the High-Level event on the 10th anniversary of the adoption of UNDRIP 25 April 2017, available at www.un.org/development/desa/indigenouspeoples/news/2017/04/high-level-event-to-mark-the-10th-anniversary-of-the-adoption-of-the-undrip/.

[33] V Tauli-Corpuz, L Enkiwe-Abayao and R de Chavez (eds), *Towards An Alternative Development Paradigm: Indigenous Peoples' Self-Determined Development* (Manila, Tebtebba Foundation, 2010).

In an interview granted to the UN-non-governmental Liaison Service (NGLS)[34] immediately after her appointment as Special Rapporteur she indicated her main priorities to tackle during her mandate as: economic, social and cultural rights of indigenous peoples, and economic empowerment. Addressing these urgent matters implies understanding the causes and difficulties hampering their enjoyment and fulfilment, in order to make recommendations for action to both governments and corporations. Ever since the adoption of the UNDRIP, Tauli-Corpuz has continued to highlight her concerns regarding the challenges in the implementation of indigenous peoples' rights in her reports and communications. She acknowledges that determining the gaps and obstacles indigenous peoples are facing is an important and a necessary step. However, beyond that identification, governments need to address those difficulties by harmonising domestic legislation in accordance to international standards and by recognising IPs' rights, enforcing human rights bodies' recommendations, as well as adopting public policies tackling the root causes behind the situation of IPs.

During her address to the Expert Mechanism on the tenth anniversary of UNDRIP in July 2017, she also mentioned the lack of coherence within the UN system, stating that its agencies, programs, funds, etc fail to speak as one.[35] In addition, climate change and criminalisation are also among the many pressing issues of concern and challenges affecting indigenous peoples' members and human rights defenders which call for holistic responses addressing root causes.

Nevertheless, despite indigenous peoples' struggles being many, the challenges urgent and complex, and the obstacles difficult to overcome, Tauli-Corpuz has claimed that she is 'not ready to give up now'.[36] Her firm commitment, ongoing efforts and determined goals epitomise the seven-generation principle she often refers to: that the decisions we make today should result in a sustainable world for the next seven generations. Her legacy will reach the communities of the future including the non-living things.

---

[34] UN-NGLS, 'Interview with Victoria Tauli-Corpuz, Special Rapporteur on the Rights of Indigenous Peoples' Rights', available at unsr.vtaulicorpuz.org/site/index.php/en/interviews/16-interview-ngls.

[35] Minute 1:18 of Victoria Tauli-Corpuz's intervention during the high-level event on the 10th anniversary of the adoption of UNDRIP (25 April 2017) (n 34).

[36] V Tauli-Corpuz, 'A silent war is being waged on Philippine indigenous communities' *The Financial Times* (London, 29 March 2018), available at www.ft.com/content/4561c904-2dfb-11e8-97ec-4bd3494d5f14.

20

Asma Jahangir
A Saviour of Democracy and Human Rights[1]

MIKEL MANCISIDOR

However flawed democracy is, it is still the only answer.[2]

On 11 February 2018 we received unexpected news: Asma Jahangir, the great human rights defender, died at the age of 66, of a cardiac arrest after being rushed to hospital. Her death was a harsh blow for all who had the honour to meet her in person and for all those who value her impressive work. Her country reacted with many signs of grief and respect. That response was echoed in the international media with reports and obituaries that recalled the figure and legacy of this unique woman.

I remembered the last time we met, in Bilbao, in the Basque Country (Spain). She had come to collect the UNESCO Bilbao Prize for the Promotion of a Culture of Human Rights from the Director General of UNESCO, at that time the recently appointed Irina Bukova, and the Mayor of Bilbao, the very popular Iñaki Azkuna, who would himself pass away shortly thereafter. We spent a few days in Bilbao, where she discovered the gastronomy, the charm of the old Bilbao and the surprising architecture of the new Bilbao. She enjoyed a short stay, but her mind was constantly on her work, her cases, and the people that she felt a debt to – the victims.

On hearing the news of her death, the UN High Commissioner for Human Rights, Zeid Ra'ad Al Hussein, said 'Asma was a giant within the global human rights movement, a legendary human rights defender: pioneering, determined, calm

---

[1] As described by M Yousafzai, at twitter.com/malala/status/962644186364301312?lang=en, Tweet, 11 February 2018.

[2] W Dalrymple, 'Days of Rage: Challenges for the Nation's Future' *The New Yorker* (New York, 23 July 2007), available at www.newyorker.com/magazine/2007/07/23/days-of-rage.

and courageous'. But who was Asma Jahangir? What did she do to receive this prize and so many other prestigious awards?

I. The First Steps of a Human Rights Lawyer

Asma Jiliani Jahangir was born in 1952 in Lahore, in Pakistani Punjab. Her family and social environment was liberal, cosmopolitan and open. Her father, Malik Gulam Jiliani, fought relentlessly for democracy and human rights. Because of his position against the military dictatorship and against the genocide that was being carried out at that time in what was still East Pakistan and is now Bangladesh, he was imprisoned and subject to periods of house arrest. Asma's father may well have served as a model and a point of reference who set the path for Asma, an idealistic and socially and politically active young woman. Her mother was another important reference point in her life, as she was a woman who was able to receive a good education and was an entrepreneur running her own textile business. Having such a strong female influence surely had a profound impact on Asma. As she herself recalled not long before her death, 'I have lived in politics, I was born in a political house, it runs in my blood'.[3]

She studied at the Convent of Jesus and Mary, got a BA at Kinnaird College for Women, and then her LLB law degree from Punjab University, all in Lahore. Asma was little more than an adolescent when she fought for the release of her father, filing a petition for his release in the Lahore High Court: *Asma Jilani v the Government of the Punjab*. The Lahore High Court, however, dismissed her petition, so Jahangir appealed to the Supreme Court. And there Asma Jilani won her first case (Criminal Appeal No 19 of 1972). In the early 1980s Asma, along with her sister Hina Jilani and two friends, established Pakistan's first all-female law firm, specialising in family law, divorces, maintenance payments and custody cases. Her cases also included gender or domestic violence against women.

In 1983, Asma was arrested for participating in the movement for the restoration of democracy against the country's military dictatorship. In 1987 she was one of the founders of the Human Rights Commission of Pakistan, and served as its Secretary General until 1993, when she was promoted to the Commission Chairperson. None of this kept her unscathed from repression or from being subjected to house arrest due to her unwavering defence of democracy in her country. She was the first woman to chair the Supreme Court Bar Association, focusing on promoting professional development, exchange of information and networking with other bar associations all over the world. In the 1990s she stood out by defending the poorest and most defenceless workers, as well as for cases where she defended Christians accused of blasphemy.

---

[3] AFP, 'Condemnation of Christian Couple's Killing by Religious Parties Good Omen: Asma' *Dawn* (Karachi, 21 November 2014), available at www.dawn.com/news/1145980.

These cases earned Asma enemies, insults, threats and attacks, which forced her to remove her children from the country to guarantee their safety.

Asma was equally sensitive to the human rights situations outside her country. She worked on numerous occasions with the UN human rights system, for example serving as expert in the investigation on Sri Lanka, a member of the International Fact-Finding Mission on Israeli Settlements in the Occupied Palestinian Territory, and as a trustee of the UN Voluntary Trust Fund on Contemporary Forms of Slavery. In addition, she was appointed three times for a special mandate as an independent expert or special rapporteur, and was one of the most experienced and prestigious collaborators in the UN human rights system.

First, in what was then the Human Rights Commission, she was appointed Special Rapporteur on Extrajudicial, Summary or Arbitrary Executions in 1998–2004. Under this mandate she visited and prepared reports on countries like the Yugoslav Republic of Macedonia, Albania, Mexico, East Timor, Nepal, Turkey, Honduras, the Democratic Republic of Congo, Afghanistan, Jamaica, Brazil and Sudan. She was appointed as Special Rapporteur on freedom of religion or belief from 2004 to 2010, where she did outstanding work which will be discussed below in more detail, including missions to Nigeria, Sri Lanka, France, Azerbaijan, the Maldives, Tajikistan, UK, Angola, Israel and the Occupied Palestinian Territories, India, Turkmenistan, the former Yugoslav Republic of Macedonia, Republic of Serbia (including a visit to Kosovo) and the Lao People's Democratic Republic. Finally, on 30 September 2016, the President of the Human Rights Council appointed Asma Jahangir as the new Special Rapporteur on the situation of human rights in the Islamic Republic of Iran. She submitted her first report in March 2017. At the time of writing, this mandate is still vacant following her death, pending the appointment of the new independent expert.

Asma was married with three children. She received much high-profile recognition, such as the Martin Ennals Award for Human Rights Defenders (1995); Ramon Magsaysay Award (1995); Honorary Doctorate from University of St Gallen, Switzerland (1998); King Baudouin International Development Prize as HRCP Chair (1999); Liberal International Prize for Freedom (2000); Millennium Peace Prize by UNIFEM (the United Nations Development Fund for Women) (2001); Lisl and Leo Eitinger Prize (The University of Oslo's Human Rights Award) (2002); Nomination for the Nobel Peace Prize for the 1000 Women for Peace Project (2005); Freedom of Worship Medal at the Four Freedoms Award (2010); Hilal-i-Imtiaz Award (2010); UNESCO/Bilbao Prize for the Promotion of a Culture of Human Rights (2010); North-South Prize of the Council of Europe (2012); Pro Dignitate Humana bestowed by the Polish Ministry of Foreign Affairs (2014); Stefanus Prize, Norway (2014); Officier de la Légion d'Honneur, France (2014); Alternative Nobel – The Right Livelihood Award, Sweden (2014).

For the 60th anniversary of *Time Magazine*'s Asian edition, Asma was included among the Asian Heroes along with names ranging from Gandhi to Salman Rushdie. Thousands of people, from authorities to victims and simple citizens, went to the streets to accompany Asma Jahangir's body at her final farewell in a sign of popular respect and affection.

II. A Human Rights Lawyer's Life

Having dedicated her entire life to democracy and human rights, Asma Jahangir's contribution is very wide. She started, as noted above, while she was still a young law student when she dared to take on the system and went all the way to the Supreme Court to defend her father, who was facing reprisals for his struggle for democracy and human rights. Asma's work had a local and a global focus, from the specific cases concerning the humblest victims and reaching the general issues in the most important multilateral forums, such as the Human Rights Council and the General Assembly of the UN.

From her long career as a lawyer, several cases highlight the many facets in her career: the struggle for women's freedom, dignity and rights; the fight against torture and arbitrary detention; opposing the rules that discriminate against religious minorities and traditions that limit women's rights. For example, in 1983 Safia Bibi was a 13-year-old blind girl who was raped by her employer and his son. She left the job due to this traumatic event, but she didn't report the crime at the time. She soon showed signs of pregnancy and was unmarried; it, therefore, was assumed that she had had premarital sex. Her failure to prove that she was raped, which was mainly due to the fact that her blindness limited her ability to identify her attackers, led the judge to sentence her to three years' imprisonment and 15 lashes. Her rapists were not convicted. Asma, however, managed to ensure that the court admitted that Safi Bibi should not be punished, pleading that the pregnancy was the result of rape. This case was an early sign of the issues that would concern Asma over her life: defending women's rights and preventing the traditional or religious norms from being an excuse to subjugate women and limit their rights.

Another well-known case, which even had a major international impact, was the case for Saima Waheed, a female university student in Lahore, who got married freely when she was 22 years old. Her father challenged the marriage because it had been entered into without his consent, contrary to the local custom. Two of the three members of the Lahore High Court found in favour of Saima, while the third dissented, stating: 'We are national judges and as such custodians of the morals of the citizens'.[4] Asma's legal victory in this case had a great impact on Pakistani society as a whole.[5] In this case, Asma was also accused of abducting the young woman because she had provided Saima with shelter after she left her father's home, although Asma was ultimately cleared of the allegations. Neither the legal victory for Saima nor herself made Asma lose touch with reality. She knew that the struggle for women's

---

[4] Pakistan Legal Decisions: 1997: 341.
[5] S Toor, 'The Political Economy of Moral Regulation in Pakistan: Religion, Gender and Class in a Postcolonial Context' in L Fernandes (ed), *Routledge Handbook of Gender in South Asia* (Abingdon, Routledge, 2014) 129–42.

rights would require concrete measures and a long-term vision: 'Women may have won the battle', she said, 'but the war is not yet won'.[6]

Abuse of the offence of blasphemy is another issue that concerned Asma until her final day, and which she ceaselessly campaigned against. In recent years, as an independent expert of the UN she was involved in the international campaign for the release of Asia Bibi.[7] In 2009, Asia Bibi, a Christian, was working collecting fruit with other women and during a break she took a metal vessel to drink water with. Some colleagues protested, claiming that she, as a Christian, would contaminate the vessel and make it impure. An argument followed in which there were verbal exchanges which some considered offensive to the prophet. Bibi was ultimately arrested and subsequently sentenced to death on 8 November 2009 by the Sheikhupura District Court. It is a fitting tribute to Asma's work to note that just prior to this volume going to press, Bibi's sentence was overturned by the Supreme Court of Pakistan because the prosecution 'categorically failed to prove its case beyond reasonable doubt'.[8]

Other similar cases previously received attention from Asma, who claims that the offence of blasphemy is sometimes used to settle personal problems, family disputes or conflicts over property. She previously handled blasphemy cases as a lawyer. In 1993, three Christian men, including 11-year-old Salamat Masih and his two uncles, Manzoor Masih and Rehmat Masih, were charged with blasphemy. In one of the hearings at the Gujranwala Court, they were attacked, resulting in Manzoor Masih's death due to the serious injuries. The surviving uncle and nephew were ultimately convicted of blasphemy. However, Asma pleaded the case of Salamat Masih and Rehmat Masih in the Lahore High Court, in 1995, and after a hard battle in and out of the courtroom, Asma won the case, leading to their acquittal.

It would be impossible to sum up here her general or thematic or geographical reports throughout her UN mandates, but the following highlights the impressive impact of her work. In her first report as Special Rapporteur on Extrajudicial, Summary or Arbitrary Executions, Asma, stressed that:

> ... ending violations of the right to life is ultimately a question of Governments' genuine will and readiness to honour their obligation to protect and promote the rights of the people living under their jurisdictions. Without basic respect for the rule of law, all declarations and commitments made by Governments lose their meaning, and the texts of the international instruments become empty words.[9]

The idea that political declarations must become effective and controllable policies permeated all her reports, as well as the need for states to be governed by the rule of

---

[6] B Sarwar, 'Pakistan: Saima Wins Case; But Judgement Threatens Women's Rights' *Inter Press Service* (Lahore, 17 March 1997), available at www.ipsnews.net/1997/03/pakistan-saima-wins-case-but-judgement-threatens-womens-rights/.

[7] Human Rights Watch, 'Pakistan: Allow Pardon for Blasphemy Victim' 2 December 2010, available at www.refworld.org/docid/4cfde6121e.html.

[8] 'Asia Bibi: Pakistan acquits Christian Woman on Death Row' *BBC News*, 31 October 2018, available at www.bbc.co.uk/news/world-asia-46040515.

[9] A Jahangir, 'Report of the Special Rapporteur on Extrajudicial, Summary or Arbitrary Executions: Civil and Political Rights, Including Questions of Disappearances and Summary Executions' 6 January 1999, UN Doc E/CN.4/1999/39, para 79.

law and capable of enforcing the laws. A similar idea is reflected in her 2000 report, in which she expressed the hope that:

> the present report will serve to illustrate the scope and seriousness of the problem of extra-judicial, summary or arbitrary executions worldwide and inspire States to take joint and separate action to combat these atrocities, which continue to bring anguish and tragedy to innocent victims and their families. Declarations of commitment to the protection of human rights are only effective, and indeed meaningful, if they are translated into concrete decisions and policies at the national level.[10]

In this report, the Special Rapporteur particularly drew attention to the question of 'honours killings', emphasising that she 'further feels a personal commitment and responsibility to address the unacceptable practice of so-called "honour killings"', which she concludes 'constitute violations of the right to life when condoned or ignored by the authorities'.[11]

In 2002, furthering her influence as Special Rapporteur, Asma highlighted the impact of conflicts on her mandate and the importance of early warning to prevent conflicts leading to violence, killings, genocide or child conscription.

> The situation regarding extrajudicial, summary or arbitrary executions remains grim in areas of armed conflict. The majority of such conflicts occur as a result of ethnic and religious tensions, which remain either unaddressed or suppressed until they erupt in violence. Governments and key international bodies must as a matter of urgency explore ways of addressing situations of emerging conflict and violence at an early stage, so that the lives and security of innocent civilians can be protected. Violation of the right to life is perpetuated in countries where the democratic system does not exist or where it is in its infancy. Poor governance makes Governments dependent on security forces to control the crime rate or other forms of violence, or even dissent through violent means, which invariably raises the risk of extrajudicial executions. A culture of impunity in many countries remains a breeding ground for abuse by the security forces, including extrajudicial killings.[12]

Again, she reinforces the idea that states governed by the rule of law are an essential requirement for respecting human rights.

In 2003 Asma expanded her focus to the situation of journalists and human rights defenders, a subject which has increasing presence on the UN agenda. Here again, Asma had a vision and was able to move ahead of her time:

> There are growing reports of threats and extrajudicial killings of journalists. These must be taken notice of and specifically condemned. It is also an issue of great concern that human rights defenders, lawyers, students, trade union officials and judges are apparently being increasingly targeted.[13]

[10] A Jahangir, 'Interim Report on Extrajudicial, Summary or Arbitrary Executions' 11 August 2000, UN Doc A/55/288, para 52.

[11] ibid, para 40.

[12] A Jahangir, Report of the Special Rapporteur on Extrajudicial, Summary or Arbitrary Executions: Civil and Political Rights, Including Questions of Disappearances and Summary Executions, 9 January 2002, UN Doc E/CN.4/2002/74, para 136.

[13] A Jahangir, Report of the Special Rapporteur on Extrajudicial, Summary or Arbitrary Executions: Civil and Political Rights, Including the Questions of Disappearances and Summary Executions, 13 January 2003, UN Doc E/CN.4/2003/3, para 85.

In a global assessment of her mandate in 2004, the struggles of her mandate were acknowledged:

> Her two terms in the discharge of her mandate have been rewarding but sometimes also trying. There were occasions when timely action by her saved lives and she finds that there is a growing awareness in civil society of the work of the Special Rapporteurs.[14]

If there was indeed such 'growing awareness', the personality, credibility and work of Asma Jahangir was an important contribution toward achieving this.

But in her assessment there is a bitter aftertaste, stating 'during the last 12 months the world has generally not witnessed an improvement in the situation with regard to extrajudicial, summary or arbitrary executions'.[15] And in her final report Asma had to insist that she 'nevertheless remains concerned as the overall situation relating to her mandate has by no means improved'.[16]

In her new mandate as Special Rapporteur on freedom of religion or belief, Asma Jahangir marked a milestone and did a job that many continue to learn from and which is still a source of inspiration to us. In her first report the Special Rapporteur showed her belief 'that Governments have a delicate role in respecting the freedom of religion or belief of all individuals and groups without compromising other aspects of the human rights of its citizens'.[17] Of course, 'the situation regarding the mandate indicates growing tensions between and within religious communities in a number of countries which could break out in various forms of confrontations, including the use of violence'[18] but the responsibility is still the state's: 'This poses the challenge for Governments to resist interference through legislation and actions that could ultimately restrict the right to freedom of religion or belief, further aggravating the situation'.[19]

The following year the independent expert gave us two important ideas:

> The right to adopt a religion of one's choice, to change or to religion is a core element of the right to freedom of religion or belief and may not be limited in any way by the State. When it is challenged by non-State actors, States have a positive obligation to ensure the enjoyment of this right;[20]

on the other hand:

> Missionary activities and other forms of propagation of religion are part of the right to manifest one's religion or belief. They may be limited only under restrictive conditions, and the Special Rapporteur disapproves of the criminalization of certain acts specific to the propagation of one's religion.[21]

---

[14] A Jahangir, Report of the Special Rapporteur on Extrajudicial, Summary or Arbitrary Executions: Civil and Political Rights, Including the Questions of Disappearances and Summary Executions, 22 December 2003, UN Doc E/CN.4/2004/7, para 88.

[15] Jahangir (n 12) para 82.

[16] Jahangir (n 13) para 89.

[17] A Jahangir, Interim Report by the Special Rapporteur of the Commission on Human Rights on Freedom of Religion or Belief, 16 September 2004, UN Doc A/59/366, para 94.

[18] ibid, para 95.

[19] ibid.

[20] A Jahangir, Interim Report of the Special Rapporteur of the Comission on Human Rights on Freedom of Religion or Belief, 30 September 2005, UN Doc A/60/399, para 96.

[21] ibid, para 97.

Finally, she was obliged to draw attention to the lack of cooperation of certain states:

> The Special Rapporteur is not satisfied at the level of cooperation from States in terms of in situ visits, which are an essential aspect of the mandate. She is particularly concerned at the consequences that the lack of such cooperation may have on the system of special procedures as a whole.[22]

And she did not stop there, but went on to make an important suggestion that is still today as relevant as when it was made: 'She encourages the creation of a mechanism that would deal more systematically with countries that do not cooperate with special procedures in terms of in situ visits'.[23] In the following year Asma continued to call for greater involvement of states not only in the reaction but also in the prevention of the limitations or violations of this right: 'Instead of waiting until acts of intolerance and discrimination based on religion or belief have been perpetrated, States should devise proactive strategies in order to prevent such violations'.[24]

In 2008, Asma Jahangir dedicated the report on freedom of religion and belief conclusions to the thorny issue of the legitimate limitations on the exercise of the right where 'legitimate interests of the State have to be balanced on a case-by-case basis with the individual's freedom of religion or belief'.[25] In short: 'all limitations should be interpreted in the light and context of the particular right concerned'.[26]

The following year, she 'emphasize[d] the importance of detecting early signs of intolerance that may not be human rights violations themselves, but that may ultimately lead to discrimination based on religion or belief'.[27] In 2010, Asma completed her mandate by taking stock of the work and the conclusions drawn during her time as Special Rapporteur where she recalled an important lesson that should never be forgotten:

> [R]eligious intolerance is not a natural outcome of diverse societies. Rather, intolerance is often the product of manipulation by a few groups, political forces or individuals for various reasons. History, both contemporary and much earlier, has proven that issues of religion or belief are highly emotive. As the germs of religious intolerance spread, it is hard to contain them. The structure of the State, its method of governance and its educational policies may, depending on their design and implementation, either help in creating religious harmony or contribute to religious tension. Preventive activities by States and by non-State actors, including religious leaders, and commitment to fundamental human rights are therefore key to creating an atmosphere of religious tolerance.[28]

---

[22] ibid, para 95.

[23] ibid.

[24] A Jahangir, Report of the Special Rapporteur on Freedom of Religion or Belief, 20 July 2007, UN Doc A/HRC/6/5, para 51.

[25] A Jahangir, Interim Report of the Special Rapporteur on Freedom of Religion or Belief, 22 July 2008, UN Doc A/63/161, para 68.

[26] ibid, para 69.

[27] A Jahangir, Interim Report of the Special Rapporteur on Freedom of Religion or Belief, 17 July 2009, UN Doc A/64/159, summary, 2.

[28] A Jahangir, Interim Report of the Special Rapporteur on Freedom of Religion or Belief: Elimination of All Forms of Religious Intolerance, 29 July 2010, UN Doc A/65/207, para 68.

III. What She Has Left Behind for Us

Asma Jahangir was one of the greats. She worked for human rights as a lawyer, as an activist and as an independent expert, in the courts of justice, at demonstrations, before the microphones and at the stand of the Human Rights Council. She was also an advocate for democracy and the rule of law, defending freedoms and fighting against violence. She fought for transparency and against corruption. She picked up enemies along the way due to her work, which clearly bothered those who exercised power for their own interests or political or religious fanatics who wanted to impose their ideas or morals above the freedoms and rights of other citizens, especially women.

Her death was the moment when many people realised the importance of her legacy, both in Pakistan and globally through the UN. It was also the time when many of us realised the enormous respect and affection that she had earned over 50 years of work for democracy, the rule of law and human rights. Nowadays we cannot talk about religious freedom and human rights without bearing in mind the example, the courage and wisdom of Asma Jahangir, who taught us so much.

Part IV

Navigating the Politics of International Activism

21

Seán MacBride

A Life at the Frontline

DIMITRIOS KAGIAROS*

... it is only in a world where peace prevails, and where reasonable economic and social standards have been realized, that man's fundamental rights and freedoms can be secured and can achieve full significance. These aims will be most readily achieved by the development of international law and by the acceptance of its precepts by governments...[1]

I. Early Childhood and Rise to Prominence

Seán MacBride was born in Paris in 1904, the only child of Irish parents John MacBride and Maud Gonne. MacBride and Gonne, both prominent Irish nationalists, separated a few months after Seán's birth and for many years were involved in bitter legal battles that defined Seán's early childhood. After the separation, John MacBride returned to Ireland, while Seán remained with his mother in Paris. An ardent Irish nationalist, Gonne published a newspaper in French, *'L'Irlande Libre'*, and devoted her time to promoting the cause of Irish independence abroad. Maud Gonne's household in Paris served as a hub for political activists and the leading cultural figures of her time. The Irish poet and future Nobel laureate William Butler Yeats[2] was a frequent guest, along with many prominent nationalist exiles involved in independence movements across the world. According to one of MacBride's biographers, it was not uncommon

---

* This chapter heavily relies on the seminal work of CN Dháibhéid, W Schabas and A O'Sullivan, who are cited below. Any errors are my own.

[1] S MacBride, 'Suffolk University Law School graduation exercises: commencement address delivered by Sean MacBride of the Senior Bar of Ireland (transcript)' (1980) 4 *Suffolk Transnational Law Journal* 243, 245.

[2] Maud Gonne is considered to be one of Yeats' muses, and many of his poems and plays are considered to include thinly-veiled references to her.

for 'the writer Rabindranath Tagore and a young student en route for Oxford, called Jawaharlal Nehru',[3] to visit the household, exposing Seán to a unique intellectual environment from a very early age.

MacBride's father was a military man who had fought in South Africa in the Boer War with the Irish Transvaal Brigade. After ending his marriage to Gonne he returned to Ireland, where he joined the Irish Republican Brotherhood (IRB), a secret organisation dedicated to overthrowing British rule and establishing an Irish Republic.[4] On Easter Monday 1916, John MacBride, along with other members of the IRB and multiple other Irish nationalist organisations took over central locations in Dublin and declared Ireland's independence. This armed insurrection, that went down in history as the 'Easter Uprising' lasted for a week and culminated in the release of the 'Proclamation of the Republic', claiming 'the right of the people of Ireland to the ownership of Ireland'.[5] The response of the British forces was swift and the uprising was short-lived. John MacBride was summarily arrested for his involvement in the rebellion, court-martialled, and sentenced to death. He was executed in May 1916 by firing squad in Kilmainham Gaol.

By this time Seán MacBride had reached school age. Gonne sent him to a Jesuit boarding school outside Paris and, apart from the occasional exchange of letters, it seems that he was rarely in touch with his father.[6] Nonetheless, Seán was deeply traumatised by his father's death at the hands of British forces. As his biographer notes, after these tragic events, John MacBride was no longer a distant father figure in young Seán's mind, but became instead a hero, a role model and a martyr to the cause of Irish independence.

John MacBride's death prompted Maud Gonne to return with her son to the United Kingdom. After some time in London, they resettled in Dublin. Maud remained engaged and outspoken in the cause of Irish nationalism and, rather unsurprisingly, her activism made her a target of the British authorities. She was eventually arrested for her activities in 1918, or more accurately as Gonne described in her own words, she was 'kidnapped in the streets of Dublin [...] by five suspicious-looking ruffians who had no warrant'.[7] Rather than being detained in Dublin, Maud was sent to Holloway Prison in London, away from Seán who at the age of 14 was left without a guardian.

The young MacBride now had to face the world without any parental support. He was eventually taken in by Yeats and his wife Georgie Hyde Lees. Yeats took on the responsibility for Seán's further education and sent him away from Dublin to Mount St Benedict in Gorey, a school which had developed the reputation at the time as being 'the ideal place to receive an Irish nationalist education'.[8] His mother was released from prison soon after.

---

[3] J Byrne, 'The Extraordinary Life and Times of Sean McBride: Part 1' (1982), available at magill.ie/archive/extraordinary-life-and-times-sean-mcbride-part-1.

[4] For more see on this O McGee, *The IRB: the Irish Republican Brotherhood, from the Land League to Sinn Féin* (Dublin, Four Courts Press, 2005).

[5] Declaration of Independence 1916, available at www.failteromhat.com/declare.htm.

[6] They seemed to have corresponded intermittently according to CN Dháibhéid, *Seán MacBride: A Republican Life 1904–1946* (Liverpool, Liverpool University Press, 2011).

[7] ibid, 22, citing NAL, HO 144/1465/321387, Maud Gonne MacBride to Edward Shortt, 26 June 1918.

[8] ibid, 29.

Upon his return to Dublin in 1920 at the age of 16, MacBride immediately joined the Irish Republican Army (IRA). At the same time, he began a degree in Law and Agriculture at University College Dublin. By his own admission later in his life, MacBride was not a particularly hard-working or engaged student.[9] He did, however, manage to stand out in the University's debating society,[10] for his passionate and fiery speeches.

MacBride's involvement with the IRA in this period led to many brushes with the British authorities, which in turn raised his profile to that of a prominent member of the organisation. MacBride was exposed to, and worked closely with, key figures of the IRA at the time. He was briefly a secretary to future head of the Irish State Éamon de Valera, and accompanied Michael Collins to London for the Anglo-Irish treaty negotiation that brought an end to the Irish War on Independence. Therefore, before he was an adult, MacBride witnessed key moments in Irish history. At the same time, he participated in guerrilla warfare at a particularly turbulent time for the region. As William Schabas notes, with reference to MacBride's recruitment to the IRA and his participation in the violent struggle for independence:

> today MacBride would be stigmatized as a child soldier [...] His recruiters would be guilty of war crimes under customary international law, and be subject to prosecution before the International Criminal Court in the event that Ireland itself failed to do so.[11]

MacBride remained involved with the IRA until 1937. The driving force behind his decision to abandon the organisation was the enactment of the *Bunreacht na hÉireann*, the Irish Constitution, which effectively removed the British Monarch from his role as Head of the Irish state. MacBride believed firmly that once this was accomplished, all the remaining aims and objectives of Irish nationalism and unification could be achieved through peaceful means, relying on the political process.[12] This marked a shift in MacBride's approach. He summarily abandoned the politics of violence and mass agitation he had espoused thus far, to embrace the rule of law and peaceful means to achieve change.

In the same year, MacBride became a barrister and began taking on significant human rights cases in Ireland.[13] Notably, MacBride was involved in multiple high-profile cases challenging the deprivation of liberty without trial.[14] This was MacBride's first attempt to use the law to protect the rights of those in detainment. This would soon become the key focus of his career as a human rights defender.

In the years that followed, MacBride also became increasingly engaged in politics. He was the co-founder of a political party, Clann na Poblachta in 1946 and was elected to Parliament. Shortly thereafter, he was appointed Minister for External Affairs of Ireland in the Inter-Party Government from 1948–1951. It was during this period that

---

[9] ibid, 35.
[10] ibid.
[11] W Schabas, 'Ireland, The European Convention on Human Rights, and the Personal Contribution of Seán MacBride' in J Morison, K McEvoy and G Anthony (eds), *Judges, Transition, and Human Rights* (Oxford, Oxford University Press, 2007) 253.
[12] ibid, 254.
[13] ibid.
[14] ibid. This was provided for under the Offences against the State Act 1939.

MacBride was exposed to the burgeoning international human rights law regime, and played a key role in shaping international human rights law as we know it today.

II. 'From Gunman to Barrister'[15]

MacBride's position in the Irish government coincided with a seminal moment in European history. In the aftermath of the Second World War, states seemed more willing to accept that peace could only be sustained if they undertook to respect, protect and fulfil individual rights and if they created international mechanisms that would provide effective redress for violations. Echoing the Universal Declaration of Human Rights, which had been adopted only a few years before, there was significant movement in Europe towards the creation of a regional human rights treaty that would ensure that the atrocities committed during the war and that had decimated the continent would not be repeated. Founded in 1949, the Council of Europe, then comprised of ten founding Member States including Ireland, sought to achieve this goal by fostering 'a greater unity between its members for the purpose of safeguarding and realising the ideals and principles which are their common heritage and facilitating their economic and social progress'.[16]

MacBride, by virtue of his position in the Irish government, served as the representative of the Irish State at the foundational conference of the Council of Europe, where the European Convention on Human Rights was drafted. In 1950, he became the President of the Committee of Ministers of the Council of Europe, a body made up of government representatives of the ten founding Member States. This gave MacBride the opportunity to participate in shaping the Convention and to facilitate the design of the machinery through which it would be enforced. MacBride participated actively in the proceedings and stood out for his vehement support for establishing a right to individual petition, a right which would allow individuals to bring their grievances against unlawful treatment by their state to an international judicial body. The availability of an individual petition to an international court was a significant departure from the international framework at the time and is viewed as one of the crowning achievements of the European human rights framework.[17]

Once the Convention came into force in 1953, and after MacBride was no longer a member of the Irish government, he returned to legal practice, focusing once again on human rights. The loss of his seat in Parliament and his move from politician to human rights lawyer was a source of concern for British authorities. As John Chadwick who worked at the British Embassy in Dublin at the time noted, 'no one quite knows what Mr MacBride, who is a brilliant and dangerous person is up to'.[18]

---

[15] ibid, 272.
[16] Statute of the Council of Europe London, 5.V.1949, Chapter 1, Art 1a, available at rm.coe.int/1680306052.
[17] Famously MacBride argued that 'a Convention on human rights which did not grant any right of redress to individuals was not worth the paper it was written on': cited by Schabas (n 11) 259.
[18] H O'Shea, *Ireland and the End of the British Empire: The Republic and its Role in the Cyprus Emergency* (London, IB Tauris, 2014) 168.

For MacBride, however, the European Convention system which he helped build would become a valuable mechanism to fight for the causes close to his heart, a mechanism that did not require resort to violent means. MacBride, according to Schabas and O'Sullivan, 'hoped to use the [Convention machinery] as a forum to advance the central theme in Irish foreign policy, the campaign against partition of the island'.[19] The first few cases he was involved with illustrated that passion.

MacBride was involved in the first case to ever reach the European Court of Human Rights, the landmark case of *Lawless v Ireland*.[20] The case marked the first time a private citizen relying on a right to individual petition had brought a case against a state to be heard before an international human rights tribunal. The applicant was Gerald Lawless, a former member of the IRA. He petitioned the European Commission on Human Rights at first instance, arguing that his detainment in a military detention camp under emergency legislation in Ireland constituted a violation of his Convention rights. MacBride, always sensitive to issues facing prisoners, represented the applicant during the proceedings before the European Commission on Human Rights, arguing that Lawless' detainment violated his rights under Articles 5, 6 and 7 of the European Convention of Human Rights.[21] The petition was ultimately unsuccessful when it reached the European Court of Human Rights, but it was the first step in MacBride's reliance on the Strasbourg system to shed light on injustices, particularly those committed against prisoners. MacBride was also involved in the seminal *Greek* case,[22] an inter-state case brought by the Greek government against the United Kingdom for human rights violations committed in Cyprus, which was at the time a British colony. MacBride notably built a close relationship with Archbishop Makarios,[23] the leading figure in the struggle for Cypriot independence, and advised the Greek government in its case against the United Kingdom.

The possibility of inter-state petitions provided for under Article 26 of the European Convention was appealing to MacBride, who was also involved in another landmark inter-state case before the Strasbourg Court, that of *Ireland v United Kingdom*.[24] After information about abuse of prisoners within Northern Irish prisons came to light, MacBride, in private letters and public appearances, sought to bring to the attention of the Irish government the possibility of making such an inter-state claim before the Strasbourg machinery. This

> provoked a wave of correspondence from private citizens, non-governmental organisations and relatives of victims of ill-treatment to the Department of the Taoiseach calling for the government to bring proceedings before the European Commission of Human Rights in Strasbourg.[25]

---

[19] W Schabas and A O'Sullivan, 'Politics and Poor Weather: How Ireland Sued the United Kingdom under the European Convention on Human Rights' (2007), available at papers.ssrn.com/sol3/papers.cfm?abstract_id=2483226, 2.

[20] *Lawless v Ireland* App No 332/57 (ECtHR, 1 July 1961).

[21] Protecting the right to liberty and security of the person, the right to a fair trial and the right to no punishment without law respectively.

[22] *Greece v United Kingdom* App No 176/56 (ECtHR, 2 June 1956).

[23] Their relationship is tracked in O'Shea (n 18).

[24] *Ireland v United Kingdom* App No 5310/71 (ECtHR, 18 January 1978).

[25] Schabas and O'Sullivan (n 19) 10.

MacBride, however, quickly became aware of the limitations of such international bodies in delivering the social justice for the issues he was passionate about. It soon became apparent that for pressing global issues, further advocacy and grassroots pressure was required to change the positions of obstinate governments and to inform the broader public of violations that were all too commonly swept under the carpet. As MacBride argued:

> In my view the role of voluntary organizations is becoming more and more essential. They are the only bodies that will have the necessary independence and initiative to restore some faith and idealism in our world. They deserve a great deal more support and encouragement.[26]

MacBride's faith in civil society and voluntary organisations that could complement the work carried out by the existing international and regional human rights bodies made him shift his focus to this sector in the next few decades. From 1963 to 1971, he served as the Secretary General of the International Commission of Jurists. He also fought passionately through his advocacy for global nuclear disarmament as president of the International Peace Bureau in Geneva.

In MacBride's human rights legal career, the welfare of those in detention was at the forefront of his advocacy. At an early age he had witnessed the plight of political prisoners in Ireland after the arrest of his mother. Therefore, it is not surprising that in building a grassroots voluntary movement, MacBride was particularly inspired by the human rights abuses to which prisoners of conscience around the world were exposed. Along with Peter Benenson, MacBride helped establish Amnesty International, an organisation that was originally conceived as a means to monitor and provide assistance to anyone imprisoned because of their race, religion or political views. In 1961, MacBride became chairman of the organisation's executive, a role he served in for almost 15 years.

MacBride was keen to develop further aspects of Amnesty International's advocacy, focusing on the right to a fair trial and the torture of prisoners. Eventually, under his chairmanship in the 1970s, Amnesty International began to engage with human rights violations and injustices outside the prison walls, carrying out groundbreaking work on enforced disappearances, protection for refugees and many other global challenges. Under MacBride's influence and guidance, Amnesty International grew to become the most well-known human rights non-governmental organisation, going far beyond its original remit, to engage globally in all aspects of human rights protection.

His efforts to advance the cause of human rights and to achieve global peace were rewarded with the Nobel Prize for Peace in 1974. For his Nobel lecture, MacBride delivered an impassioned critique of nuclear weapons,[27] while signalling his support for peace through human rights and lamenting the lack of female representation in

---

[26] S MacBride, 'MacBride – Nobel Lecture' (1974), available at www.nobelprize.org/nobel_prizes/peace/laureates/1974/macbride-lecture.html.

[27] ibid.

the discussion on nuclear disarmament.[28] A year later he was awarded the Lenin Peace Prize, the only person to hold both honours. Two years after he stepped down from his role as chairman of the Amnesty International Executive, the organisation itself was awarded the Nobel Prize for Peace for its contribution to human rights.

By this stage, MacBride had made a name for himself on the international plane. Being a globally recognised and respected human rights figure allowed him to use his influence to offer support and expertise to global causes. It seems that MacBride felt a kinship between his own experience in Ireland under British rule and those of other states seeking their independence. MacBride was particularly passionate in his support for Namibia in its struggle for independence from South Africa. In 1973 he was elected by the General Assembly of the United Nations to the post of UN Commissioner for Namibia with rank of Assistant Secretary-General of the United Nations. He established the UN Institute for Namibia (UNIN), an educational body with the aim of educating Namibians for roles in a future independent 'Republic of Namibia'. Under MacBride's insistence, the entire staff of UNIN was African.[29] The fact that MacBride's father had famously participated in the Boer War also gave him access to government officials of South Africa. MacBride used this influence to advocate for bringing an end to apartheid up until the end of his life.

MacBride passed away in Ireland in 1988 after a short illness. This brought an end to 'a 70-year career that took him from street battles with the British in Dublin to the international award-ceremony podium in Oslo'.[30] In those 70 years of activism, MacBride's accomplishments left a lasting mark on international human rights law and human rights activism.

III. Tracing the Legacy of Seán MacBride

Such a short note cannot but fail to do justice to the lasting legacy of a human rights pioneer such as Seán MacBride. Especially when one considers that MacBride's career was inextricably linked to key movements of his time, the struggle for Irish independence, European integration through democracy and human rights, nuclear disarmament and decolonisation, encapsulating his contribution in a few words will inevitably leave out key achievements and controversies. It is safe to say, however, that MacBride took advantage of historical opportunities following the Second World War and fought to construct a post-war international legal order that would provide

---

[28] ibid, 'These questions are also usually regarded as the exclusive prerogative of men. Women [...] are excluded from disarmament negotiations, indeed, as they generally are from important government posts. [...] They should be given a real decisive role in all disarmament negotiations and conferences. War and peace is surely the concern of women as much as it is that of men – and perhaps much more so'.

[29] The organisation eventually became the University of Namibia after the state gained its independence. See K Wallis, 'Seán MacBride and Namibia' (2006), available at www.historyireland.com/20th-century-contemporary-history/sean-macbride-and-namibia.

[30] WG Blair, 'Sean MacBride of Ireland Is Dead at 83' *The New York Times* (16 January 1988), available at www.nytimes.com/1988/01/16/obituaries/sean-macbride-of-ireland-is-dead-at-83.html.

a forum for the individual to seek redress for violations of her rights. He set the foundations of the denuclearisation movement and remained a leading figure fighting for nuclear disarmament throughout his life. Finally, in recognition of how much more can be accomplished at the ground level, MacBride was instrumental in building what has arguably become the leading human rights organisation in the world, Amnesty International.

As a final point, it would be important to highlight Seán MacBride's faith in the power of individuals working together, rather than governments, to bring about social change. For MacBride, such change could best be achieved through the efforts of concerned citizens fighting at grassroots level for causes they believed in. During his Nobel lecture, MacBride emphasised that the unprecedented, at the time, public access to information could become the impetus for more meaningful political engagement. As he eloquently argued:

> The advent of the mass media of communication (radio and TV) coupled with higher standards of literacy and education are giving a much greater degree of influence to public opinion in the world than it has ever had in the past. The public can now be informed as to current events and policies. Governments can no longer keep their actions and policies secret from their public. [...] Once informed and alerted to the issues involved, in turn, public opinion can be formed and can make itself heard. [...] Greater vigilance than ever will have to be exercised to ensure that the press and the mass media do not become controlled by governments or financial interests.[31]

MacBride could not have predicted the evolution of mass media and the (sometimes controversial) influence of social media, but his faith in well-educated, well-informed and engaged citizens holding their governments to account for human rights violations is compelling. For MacBride, such engagement was a duty. In this regard, Seán MacBride led by example, remaining at the frontlines, both literal and figurative, of the key human rights battles of his day.

---

[31] MacBride (n 26).

22

Peter Benenson

Pioneer of Contemporary Human Rights Activism

STEFAAN SMIS

Open your newspaper any day of the week and you will find a report from somewhere in the world of someone being imprisoned, tortured or executed because his opinions or religion are unacceptable to his government. There are several million such people in prison – by no means all of them behind the Iron and Bamboo Curtains – and their numbers are growing. ... In [1948] the founder members of the United Nations approved the Universal Declaration of Human Rights. Article 18: Everyone has the right to freedom of thought, conscience and religion; this right includes freedom to change his religion or belief, and freedom, either alone or in company with others and in public or private, to manifest his religion or belief in teaching, practice, worship and observance. Article 19: Everyone has the right to freedom of opinion and expression; this right includes freedom to hold opinions without interference and to seek, receive and impart information and ideas through any media and regardless of frontiers.

There is at present no sure way of finding out how many countries permit their citizens to enjoy these two fundamental freedoms. What matters is not the rights that exist on paper in the Constitution, but whether they can be exercised and enforced in practice. There is a growing tendency all over the world to disguise the real grounds upon which 'nonconformists' are imprisoned.

Yet governments are by no means insensitive to the pressure of outside opinion. And when world opinion is concentrated on one weak spot, it can sometimes succeed in making a government relent. The important thing is to mobilise public opinion quickly and widely, before a government is caught up in the vicious spiral caused by its own repression and is faced with impending civil war. By then the situation will have become too desperate for the government to make concessions. The force of opinion, to be effective, should be broadly based, international, nonsectarian and all-party.[1]

---

[1] P Benenson, 'The Forgotten Prisoners' *The Observer* (London, 28 May 1961).

I. A Young Idealist Groomed into the Nascent Human Rights Movement

Born in London as Peter James Henry Solomon on 28 July 1921, Benenson died in Oxford at the age of 83 on 25 February 2005. From his early childhood it was clear that he was destined to be at the vanguard of the twentieth century human rights movement. He grew up in a wealthy and privileged family, which was beneficial to his activism later in life as he could easily approach and petition the very elite of British society as a result of his membership in that group. His mother, Flora Benenson, was the daughter of Giorgi Benenson, a Jewish-Russian immigrant who had made his fortune in the Russian mining and banking sectors but fled the country just before the revolution broke out, eventually establishing himself in Britain and the US. As a tribute to his grandfather Peter Benenson took his mother's maiden name. His father, Harold Solomon, made a career in the army and the colonial administration and also tried his luck with politics, unsuccessfully running for the 1929 parliamentary elections as a Tory candidate. As a child of the British elite, the young Benenson was tutored by the English-American poet WH Auden. Despite these solid beginnings Benenson's youth was nevertheless far from untroubled: after losing his father at the age of nine, he was then confronted with the difficulties of an economic recession that hit his prosperous family hard. Moreover, while a pupil at Eton he witnessed the prelude to Second World War, which turned the old continent upside down.

It was during his time at Eton that Benenson's idealism began to take shape. There, his awakening interest in politics eventually pushed him into human rights activism, all while being groomed to be one of the nation's elites. For an adolescent with his background the 1930s gave ample space to sharpen his political conscience: there was the banking crisis with the nationalistic-protectionist responses by most states; the Spanish civil war that resonated across Europe and divided societies; and, of course, the emergence of Fascism and Nazism not only in Italy and Germany but elsewhere. At the age of 15 he and his classmates participated in actions to collect and send funds to a relief committee in Spain and supported orphan children victims of the Spanish civil war. Shortly thereafter, Benenson was active in a London-based refugee children's group helping German Jewish children emigrate to safer places. For his higher education Benenson attended Balliol College at Oxford University to read history, but with the onset of the Second World War he joined the army, serving as an intelligence officer at Bletchley Park, where his unit worked on German secret codes. It is there that he met Margaret Anderson, whom he married during the war and eventually had two daughters. He later divorced and remarried Susan Booth in 1973, having another daughter and a son.

Following the war he returned to study at Oxford and after obtaining a law degree he became a barrister, despite never relinquishing his passion for politics and fighting for a common cause. In reality he was more interested in politics than law. As an active member of the Labour Party he unsuccessfully ran for parliament three times during the 1950s, but it was his activities linked to trade unions and the civil liberties movement that paved the way to his later role as a tireless defender of prisoners of conscience. The Trade Union Congress invited him to observe political trials in Franco's Spain in the postwar period and to similar trials in South Africa under the growing system of apartheid. As Cyprus struggled for independence from Britain, and Hungary tried to free itself from Soviet communist domination in the mid-1950s, Benenson was also involved as a trial observer. The networks that grew from these activities brought him close to the civil liberties movement in the US. When the American Civil Liberties Union (ACLU) took the initiative to create a Society of Labour Lawyers in the UK, Benenson joined the executive committee. In 1956 he was instrumental in forming 'JUSTICE' a platform that would become the British branch of the International Commission of Jurists (ICJ), an international non-governmental organisation created in 1953 to ensure respect for international human rights standards through the rule of law. This mainly jurist organisation now has sections all over the world and members representing all possible legal traditions. Being deeply involved in these initiatives and organisations gave him the inspiration, expertise, and necessary network to launch a more personal initiative appealing to the sense of humanity of the broader public. The call for amnesty he would later launch was therefore not an initiative that emerged in a vacuum: on the contrary, it was deeply rooted in the idealism and political activism of a person who had been at the centre of human rights activism for numerous years.

After becoming seriously ill in 1959, he retired early from the bar and travelled to Sicily to recover. While convalescing, and having recently converted to Catholicism, he had ample time to reflect and evaluate his prior involvement with initiatives such as JUSTICE. The latter being essentially a lawyers' organisation he came to conclude that it would always be 'excessively cautious and would never catch the public imagination'.[2] Lawyers are 'not able sufficiently to influence the course of justice in undemocratic countries' he said.[3] The answer had to be 'an all-embracing organization to fight for Civil Liberties' open to the general public 'anxious to see a wider respect for human rights'.[4]

Energised, and with an idea crystallising, he returned to London in October 1960 ready to start a new chapter in his advocacy for human rights. It was only a matter of time before that opportunity would present itself.

II. The Making of Amnesty International

The story goes that on a morning in late 1960, while travelling on the London tube, Benenson came across an article in the *Daily Telegraph* telling the story of two unfortunate students in Salazar's Portugal who had been sentenced to seven years'

---

[2] T Buchanan, '"The Truth Will Set You Free": The Making of Amnesty International' (2002) 37 *Journal of Contemporary History* 583.
[3] ibid.
[4] ibid.

imprisonment for having toasted for liberty in a café in the university city of Coimbra. The article produced such a strong effect on him that he felt an urgent desire and need to act. The drama of the moment is remembered in a passage where Benenson personally recalls that life-changing event:

> This news item produced a righteous indignation in me that transcended normal bounds. At Trafalgar Square Station I got out of the train and went straight into the Church of St. Martin's in the Field. There I sat and pondered on the situation. I felt like marching down to the Portuguese Embassy to make an immediate protest, but what would have been the use? Walking up the Strand towards the Temple my mind dwelt on World Refugee Year, the first of those years dedicated to international action. What a success it had been! The DP (displaced person) camps in Europe had been finally emptied. Could not the same thing be done for the inmates of concentration camps? I speculated. What about a World Year against political imprisonment?[5]

The months that followed served to develop a strategy to launch that initiative. Together with an inner circle of activists, whom Benenson had developed strong bonds of friendship and trust with through his previous years of human rights activism (among them Louis Blom-Cooper, Eric Baker and Peter Archer), they set headquarters in the White Swan, a pub in North Kensington where their weekly lunch meeting served for debating and preparing the 'Appeal for Amnesty 1961' campaign to be launched in May 1961. This idea eventually matured into a publication that told the story of a number of political prisoners while Benenson and his colleagues also convinced a popular London newspaper to publish an opinion on the same topic, announcing the start and objectives of the campaign. Back in Italy in the spring of 1961 Benenson prepared the newspaper article and finalised the manuscript of *Persecution 61*, a book published by Penguin Books in October 1961, which told the story of nine persons (Maurice Audin, Ashton Jones, Agostinho Neto, Patrick Duncan, Olga Ivinskaya, Luis Taruc, Constantin Noica, Antonio Amat and Hu Feng) who had been, or were being, imprisoned for their ideals. Nine persons representing the whole spectrum of political ideologies of the early Cold War and coming from all parts of the world to show that anyone, anywhere could be confronted with similar situations. On Sunday 28 May 1961 the two-page article, *The Forgotten Prisoners*, appeared in *The Observer*'s Sunday supplement. It was accompanied by six photographs of political prisoners or prisoners of conscience (Constantin Noica, Reverend Ashton Jones, Agostinho Neto, Archbishop Josef Beran, Toni Ambatiel and Cardinal József Mindszenty) some of whom would have their story told in *The Persecution 61*. In the opinion piece, reference was made to the relevant standards of Articles 18 and 19 of the Universal Declaration of Human Rights and then described the faith of some of those who had been imprisoned by their governments for having expressed their opinions. The article's main aim was nevertheless to explain the campaign *Appeal for Amnesty 1961* and its objectives while trying to convince the broadest possible audience that action needed to be taken immediately. Quoting the main passage of the plea:

> The campaign, which opens to-day, is the result of an initiative by a group of lawyers, writers, and publishers in London. We have set up an office in London to collect information

---

[5] Quoted in L Rabben, 'Amnesty International: Myth and Reality' (2001) 54 *Agni* (Amnesty International Fortieth Anniversary Issue) 9.

about the names, numbers, and conditions of what we have decided to call 'Prisoners of Conscience', and we define them thus: 'Any person who is physically restrained (by imprisonment or otherwise) from expressing (in any form of words or symbols) any opinion which he honestly holds and which does not advocate or condone personal violence'. We also exclude those who have conspired with a foreign government to overthrow their own. Our office will from time to time hold press conferences to focus attention on Prisoners of Conscience selected impartially from different parts of the world. And it will provide factual information to any group, existing or new, in any part of the world, which decides to join in a special effort in favour of freedom of opinion or religion.

According to the article the campaign served four objectives:

1   to work impartially for the release of those imprisoned for their opinions;
2   to seek for them a fair and public trial;
3   to enlarge the right of asylum and help political refugees to find work;
4   to urge effective international machinery to guarantee freedom of opinion.

Some of these objectives built upon activities Benenson and other initiators had worked on in the past but this time, and contrary to prior initiatives, the campaign had to bring the activists and volunteers from the periphery to the centre of human rights advocacy and activism. Their involvement had to directly affect the beneficiaries. Inspiration partly came from the 1958 International Refugee Year, a very successful year-long campaign set up by the United Nations to bring attention to the refugee problems in Europe that were a direct result of Second World War. The 1951 International Convention on the Status of Refugees, which entered into force in 1954, had a geographical focus limiting it to Europe but increasingly louder voices were demanding that other non-European refugees should also benefit from the same protection, a move that was later confirmed with the 1967 protocol to the Refugee Convention. The UN refugee campaign served as a model for *Appeal for Amnesty 1961* for yet another reason: it was originally conceived as a one-year campaign. *Appeal for Amnesty 1961* was led by a policy committee composed of the old friend-activists of Benenson but quickly joined by new names unfamiliar to the initiators who shared their expertise and network in support of the campaign (a good example is Seán MacBride). Many had a religious background and that clearly influenced the movement and the functioning of Amnesty International in its early years.[6]

Moreover, because the campaign was not meant only for the British public the *Appeal* was published in many other newspapers, was relayed in radio programs, and discussed in numerous other fora. Against all expectations the strategy took off and the public response was overwhelming: thousands supported the cause and letters from the most remote parts of the world were received in London praising and encouraging the initiators, informing them about new cases and proposing to volunteer for the campaign. Confronted with this unexpected success the initiators had to improvise and make quick decisions. By July 1961 it was agreed that the Appeal would serve to lay the foundations of a permanent organisation and that it would drive a politically inclusive path by seeking the support of all three major British political formations. Members

[6] S Hopgood, *Keepers of the Flame: Understanding Amnesty International* (Ithaca, Cornell University Press, 2006) 18–20, 62–65.

of Parliament from the Labour, Conservative and the Liberal Parties were approached to offer their support to the movement.

The organisation gave itself a web-type structure, with its headquarters in London and local Amnesty groups spread all over the country and later the world. Local Amnesty groups are semi-autonomous cells mainly composed of volunteers and doing advocacy work according to what was called the three principles, meaning that Headquarters would send them guidelines and information about prisoners and they would then work on three cases simultaneously to keep a certain ideological neutrality, something that the initiators cherished. One prisoner of conscience from each of the three ideological 'courants' of international politics of the time (one from the capitalist world, one from the communist world and one from the developing world) would be 'adopted' and become the focus of their activities. The typical work of the local group would consist of writing letters to state officials and trying to get these prisoners free while at the same time organising support and relief for the prisoners and their families. Fundraising for the organisation and mobilising people for the cause also belonged to local groups' activities.

The founders wanted Amnesty also to have a strong international presence, and Benenson travelled to many European capitals to rally support during the campaign. Even though he initially had more success in the northern European Protestant countries such as Sweden, Germany, Norway, the Netherlands and Denmark, Austria, Belgium and France quickly joined together with Anglo-Saxon countries including Australia, New Zealand, the US and Canada. Today support from countries outside the West is much more difficult to receive. On 30 September 1962 the organisation was named Amnesty International after it was agreed at an international conference in Belgium. An International Secretariat and International Executive Committee was established in London to manage the growing network of Amnesty International's national organisations, which, in the jargon of the organisation, are called sections. Interestingly two types of profiles could be distinguished at the heart of the organisation: the founding fathers and early supporters (see above), who were often male lawyers, academics, and activists and who led and advised the organisation but for all sorts of reasons were unable to devote much time to the organisation; and a predominantly female group who did most of the work as volunteers (including Peggy Crane, Christel Marsh, Marlys Deeds, Dorothy Warner, Diana Redhouse).[7] By the end of the decade Amnesty International had grown into a strong organisation with local groups and sections in many parts of the world. It was awarded consultative status by the UN, the Council of Europe and UNESCO. By then, however, Benenson had already resigned from the organisation officially due to a quarrel over whether the British secret services had infiltrated Amnesty International. In reality, however, the relationship between Benenson and the organisation had turned sour because though Benenson was a charismatic and energetic person full of ideas, when it came to implementation he lacked the management capacity to steer an increasingly professional organisation.[8]

---

[7] ibid, 65–68.
[8] ibid, 68–70.

In the 1980s he reconciled with the organisation he initiated but by that time Amnesty International had already become a well-established and respected player on the human rights scene.

III. Amnesty International: A Pillar of the Human Rights Movement

After more than 50 years of action at the centre of human rights activism, Amnesty International is not only one of the oldest human rights NGOs but certainly one of the leading organisations with a brand name known in all corners of the world. Its symbol, the candle wrapped in barbed wire, refers to the Chinese proverb 'better to light a candle than curse the darkness'. With its light it also brings hope to all those who are oppressed and want to break free. Since its inception as an international organisation, it has grown to include over seven million members and sympathisers, has at least 70 sections (country offices), international structures (aspiring sections) and 10 regional offices spread over Africa, Asia, the Americas, and Europe. The organisation mainly depends on volunteers and a small number of paid professional staff. Sections and international structures are represented in the International Council that meets every two years to determine the overall direction of the movement and to appoint international governing bodies including the International Board, which meets at least twice a year to take decisions on behalf of the organisation, implement the strategies developed by the International Council, and to ensure compliance with the organisation's statutes. The daily affairs, however, are implemented by the International Secretariat in London led by the Secretary General of the organisation. Several hundred paid staff members work at the Secretariat.

Starting as an organisation that wanted to be on the frontlines of human rights action with a focus on the freedoms of thought, conscience, and religion and that of opinion and expression (Articles 18 and 19 of the Universal Declaration of Human Rights), Amnesty International has evolved into an organisation with a general human rights scope, addressing issues from fighting impunity, to supporting the rights of indigenous peoples, to supporting the right to live in dignity, and to corporate social responsibility. The focus of activities revolve around three complementary issues: (i) research to document and accurately report on human rights violations; (ii) advocacy and lobbying to influence and press governments, organisations, companies, and decision-makers to act in accordance with human rights standards or support their action; and (iii) campaign and action via petitions, letters, protest to involve human rights activists worldwide to put the weight of the numbers into the balance. This formula delivers a very effective organisation whose support for human rights victims is felt on the ground. Julio de Pena Valdez, a trade union leader of the Dominican Republic, explains:

> When the 200 letters came, the guards gave me back my clothes. Then the next 200 letters came and the prison director came to see me. When the next pile of letters arrived, the director got in touch with his superior. The letters kept coming and coming – 3,000 of them.

The president was informed. The letters still kept arriving and the president called the prison and told them to let me go.[9]

The number of prisoners of conscience who witnessed their plight taken to heart by unknown volunteers who literally wrote them free is immeasurable. For its achievement Amnesty International was awarded the 1977 Nobel Peace Prize 'for protecting the human rights of prisoners of conscience' and the 1978 UN Prize in the Field of Human Rights, which was instituted by the UN General Assembly in 1966 to honour and commend individuals and organisations who have made an outstanding contribution to the promotion and protection of human rights as embodied in UN human rights instruments. Other prizes awarded to Amnesty International include: the Erasmus Prize (1976), the Council of Europe Human Rights Prize (1983), the Four Freedoms Award for the freedom of expression (1984), and the Olof Palme Price (1991).

Of course the organisation has had its share of critics and at numerous times weathered a variety of storms not only because governments attacked by Amnesty tried to discredit the organisation. Criticism was also uttered for the excessive salaries and severance pay paid or awarded to its management, for not always sufficiently protecting staff on the field who sometimes work under very strenuous and life-threatening conditions, for a certain western bias in its campaigns and policy options, and its pro-choice position in the abortion debate.

What we learn from the organisation and its founders is that – as with many other human rights initiatives – they were established by men and women who had the courage to refuse injustices and to stand up, not for themselves but for those whose life is threatened by authorities who cannot accept that all human beings equally enjoy human rights. These men and women believed that it was their responsibility to resist and act against abuses. For Benenson and his peers who stood at the origin of Amnesty International it was important to have broad based support from all over the world and from all layers of society because together they could make a difference. And a difference they have unquestionably made. However, after more than half a century of relentless effort the fight is not yet won because, as Benenson said, 'Only when the last prisoner of conscience has been freed, when the last torture chamber has been closed, when the United Nations Universal Declaration of Human Rights is a reality for the world's people, will our work be done'.

---

[9] Quoted by A Barnett, 'The Man who Fought for the Forgotten: Peter Benenson Obituary' *The Guardian* (London, 27 February 2005).

23

Max van der Stoel

The Indefatigable Traveller for Human Rights

ANTOINE BUYSE

> If we devote our attention only to the wars of today, we will have reasons to mourn again tomorrow.[1]

I. A Doctor's Son Goes into Politics

A doctor's visit. Or rather, a visit with a doctor – that is how, in his own view, the social conscience of Max van der Stoel was awakened. Indeed, the younger years of Van der Stoel, as for many human rights defenders, were formative for his later commitment to human rights. Born in Voorschoten, a small suburb of the Dutch city of Leiden on 3 August 1924, he was the son of a general practitioner. His father took him along on visits to his patients. The social and economic differences between the families of visited patients struck young Max and made him feel embarrassed, as he later recounted, looking back at the roots of his political commitment to social democracy.[2] That commitment started at a really young age, as he recounted simulating parliament with his friends at the age of ten and joined the social democrat party the day after it was created.

---

[1] M van der Stoel, 'The Role of the OSCE High Commissioner on National Minorities in Conflict Prevention', Address at *An Agenda for Preventive Diplomacy*, Skopje, Republic of Macedonia, 18 October 1996, available at www.osce.org/hcnm/36485?download=true.

[2] D Martin, 'Max van der Stoel, Diplomat Who Uncovered Hussein's Abuses, Dies at 86', *New York Times* (New York, 27 April 2011).

But Van der Stoel was also greatly influenced by unwanted encounters with the two ideologies that caused so much destruction and human suffering in the twentieth century: Nazism and Communism. His teenage years were marked by the Second World War. He experienced the effects of state terror early on, as the Nazis killed both the director of his primary school and the vice-principal of his secondary school, the Stedelijk Gymnasium Leiden. Van der Stoel went on to study law and later sociology at Leiden University. During his student days, he visited Czechoslovakia several times, both before and after the 1948 communist takeover, making him even more aware of how free societies can succumb to dictatorship.

It was in this Cold War context that Van der Stoel started his career. Although it was a political career from the outset, it was not immediately a career in active politics. He started to work for the research institute of the Partij van de Arbeid (PvdA), the main social democrat party of the time, under its later leader Joop den Uyl. In the Dutch political system each party in Parliament has its own state-subsided research institute tasked with supporting its party by way of in-depth policy-oriented research. Van der Stoel's interest in international affairs continued to grow and led to his appointment as 'international secretary' within the party in 1958, the key person entrusted with the social democrats' international cooperation efforts – a position he occupied until 1965. He combined this with his first function in the Dutch parliamentary system when elected as senator in 1960, a part-time function, and subsequently as Member of Parliament in 1963. For a short stint of just over a year, 1965–66, Van der Stoel was Secretary of State for Foreign Affairs – a function directly under the Minister of Foreign Affairs, in the short-lived government of Prime Minister Cals. Later, after another term as Member of Parliament, Van der Stoel became the first social-democrat Minister of Foreign Affairs in the government of Joop den Uyl (1973–77), known as the most left-wing government the Netherlands have ever had. Ironically, the resistance against his appointment was most fierce in his own party, both before and during his term as Minister. He was considered to be insufficiently leftist and too moderate – the latter would be a trait of character that would be crucial in his later human rights career. 'In that government, it might have been easier for me if I would have delivered indignant speeches every now and then', he said later, when looking back at the 1970s, a time of left-right polarisation in Dutch politics.[3] Also, in appearance and posture Van der Stoel was far from the barricade-building street-fighter that quite a few of his fellow party members would have liked him to be. Always spotlessly dressed, courteous and loyal, the tall Dutchman was in appearance and demeanour almost the archetype of an old-fashioned diplomat. It was only because of the continuing support of party leader and Prime Minster Den Uyl that Van der Stoel retained his post. It was telling of his constant diplomatic approach that when campaigning in election time in the north of the Netherlands, he tried to convince people of the importance of 'non-proliferation', while his fellow campaigners had to clarify to voters that he meant, in plain language: beware of nuclear weapons.

[3] P van der Ploeg, 'Oud-minister Max van der Stoel overleden', *NRC* (23 April 2011).

II. Speaking Out in Public and Behind Closed Doors

The self-professed lack of indignant speeches did not mean that Van der Stoel was not speaking out. Rather, he did so in ever-factual, unemotional wording. Indeed, these early political years also marked Van der Stoel's entry on the international stage as a staunch advocate of human rights. During his term as a parliamentarian, the Council of Europe appointed him, in 1968, as rapporteur on the situation in Greece, where a military junta had seized power a year earlier. In his reports on the situation, he relayed the human rights violations committed by the so-called Regime of the Colonels. In his first year as Minister of Foreign Affairs in 1973, he also explicitly welcomed Greek political refugees to the Netherlands. It earned him the ire of the Greek military, but a hero's welcome in Athens after 1974 when democracy had been restored – crowds were chanting his name when he arrived at the airport. He awarded an honorary doctorate, by the University of Athens in 1977, and a street in the Greek capital was also named after him.

It did not matter to Van der Stoel whether dictatorships were left-wing or right-wing: his earlier years had shown him that freedom can be threatened from both sides. Thus, when he went back to Czechoslovakia in 1977, this time no longer a student but his country's highest diplomat, he defied the communist government. After his talks to the official authorities, he also met up with Jan Patočka, one of the leaders of Charta 77, the later famous civil society movement that criticised the authorities. In the Cold War context, Van der Stoel's initiative was a courageous and visible act of support. He could have easily confined himself to just meeting government officials on his visits, but in order to reflect his own and his government's commitment to human rights, he was the first to openly support the human rights-based Charta movement. Since 2017, a monument in a Prague park serves as a memorial to this exceptional Cold War meeting. These are only a few examples in which Max van der Stoel took a principled stance on human rights, with such diplomatic adeptness that it did not result in major foreign policy backlashes.

By the 1980s, the seasoned veteran of international politics – after another short stint as Minister of Foreign Affairs (1981–1982, in one of the shortest-lived governments in recent Dutch history, an uneasy marriage between socialists, liberals and Christian-democrats) – was appointed as the Dutch ambassador to the United Nations. In Dutch politics he became less visible, being appointed to the Council of State – the country's highest advisory body to the government, and later, in 1991, being awarded the prestigious honorary title of Minister of State, a purely honorary advisory function granted to respected politicians on a very exceptional basis. On the international stage, by contrast, Van der Stoel unabatedly continued to criticise human rights abuses, just as he had in the 1970s. Most markedly so in his position as UN Special Rapporteur on the human rights situation in Iraq from 1991 to 1999. Such were the atrocities by the regime of Saddam Hussein that he reported on that he labelled them as amongst the worst since the Second World War. To give just one example, Van der Stoel remarked on the Iraqi decrees which prescribed disfigurement and amputation that 'a Government which is capable of publicly declaring and publicizing such clear violations of human rights is no doubt capable of even worse conduct behind closed doors'.[4] It may not come as a surprise that as soon as he first started reporting on the dismal human rights record of Iraq in the 1990s, the government barred him from entering the country. To collect facts, Van der Stoel and his staff based their work on written evidence and interviews with refugees from Iraq. The publicly available, meticulously researched and precisely phrased reports made an important contribution to discrediting the Hussein regime. Years later, US President George W Bush even cited these older reports when he was making his very contested case to invade Iraq in 2003.

Most of Van der Stoel's time during the 1990s, and maybe his most important professional activity in his career, was based on confidentiality rather than publicity. In 1993, he was appointed as the first High Commissioner on National Minorities for the Organization for Security and Co-operation in Europe (OSCE). The new function was a product of the end of the Cold War and reflected the concerns in Europe about tensions around national minorities spiralling into full-fledged war, such as the one raging in the former Yugoslavia. The mandate of the Commissioner described the function as providing 'early warning and, as appropriate, early action at the earliest possible stage in regard to tensions involving national minority issues that have the potential to develop into a conflict'.[5] Thus the function was one of prevention – ongoing armed conflicts fell outside the mandate. *The Economist* tellingly described the work as

> ... an odd sort of job, a bit like being head prefect in a run-down boys' school where there is no headmaster, the board of governors is far too big, and none of the teachers really knows who is doing what. The prefect's main job is to stop big boys bullying little ones, and to stop boys of all sizes from fighting among themselves. He is not allowed to use his own fists.[6]

Indeed, the position is an extremely tough one, with the only clout being the persuasiveness and moral standing of the person doing the job. It is also unglamorous work, as its success can only be measured by conflict that did not erupt.

Van der Stoel went about the arduous task with characteristic perseverance and a strong work ethic. More than ever, it turned him into a travelling diplomat, going to Europe's most remote corners and sleeping in 'hotels with cockroaches', in order to negotiate between governments and representatives of national minorities. For his staff, his dedication to the job was both an inspiration as well as an occasional source of stress. A typical visit started with a working breakfast at 6:30 am and ended with a late working dinner at 9:00 pm.[7] In the Baltic region he helped to mediate between the governments of the newly-independent states and the ethnic Russian minorities. He also worked to protect the rights of Hungarian minorities in Hungary's

---

[4] M van der Stoel, Special Rapporteur of the Commission on Human Rights, 'Report on the Situation of Human Rights in Iraq' 15 February 1995, UN Doc E/CN.4/1995/56, para 57.

[5] See more at www.osce.org/hcnm.

[6] 'Max van der Stoel, Minority Man', *The Economist* (London, 9 September 1999).

[7] S Troebst, 'A Tribute to Max van der Stoel: Speech on the Occasion of the Conference "HCNM 20 Years On"' 6 July 2012, available at www.ecmi.de/about/about-ecmi/a-tribute-to-max-von-der-stoel.

neighbouring states. He intervened many times on behalf of Roma in order to make governments take their rights more seriously. In Macedonia, often seen as one of his greatest successes as one of the very few former Yugoslav states to avoid armed conflict, he managed to help create the trilingual South East European University in Tetovo, for which he raised millions of dollars in funds. He did so by personally convincing big donors such as the United States, the European Commission, and several European countries and foundations to contribute to the educational cause. He saw the university as serving the goal of preventing conflict by investing in education. Locally, the university was lovingly called 'stuloviot univerzitet' or 'Van der Stoel University'. In another looming conflict, he persuaded ethnic Russians in Crimea to accept autonomy rather than to seek independence from Ukraine. He did so through a round-table conference that he organised in the Netherlands and by carrying out intensive diplomatic efforts to make Ukraine accept autonomy for the Crimea. The latter example shows that even the work of Van der Stoel does not always last, as the annexation of Crimea by Russia in 2014 reflects.

His constant negotiating had the prevention of conflict escalation as the main aim. To him, the situation in Europe was part of a shifting bigger picture, in which large-scale military confrontation between the opposing Cold War blocs had been replaced by smaller conflicts. He remarked that 'we have also learned that questions relating to national minorities can trigger off such conflicts'.[8] The wording reflects the diplomat he was. He did not say that ethnic tensions cause conflicts and he left open the possibility that both governments and minority groups could instrumentalise ethnic and national identities in order to get their way. This is why it was so important to him to emphasise time and again that he was Commissioner *on* and not *for* national minorities. Even if his work in practice helped to protect their interests, to Van der Stoel this was a by-product of his conflict prevention aims. He was not there to promote secession or nationalism, but democracy, the rule of law and human rights, crucial and shared values in his view. In fact, he understood that no matter how diplomatically he behaved he would always make enemies in his work. As he said:

> These enemies are almost invariably extreme nationalists. I think this is inevitable. I would even feel that I would not perform my task properly if they would not object to my activities and views. These nationalists are not interested in promoting inter-ethnic harmony – they prefer to stir up inter-ethnic hatred.[9]

To Van der Stoel, history had shown that in situations of discontent, it was all too easy to look for easy answers, blaming scapegoats for problems, and portraying others as the enemy. To him this type of ethno-nationalism was not an answer, but one of the symptoms of underlying problems and injustice.

His approach, firmly based on very principled foundations, was at the same time very practical and hands-on. He did not hesitate to focus on small practicalities which might make all the difference in diffusing a potential conflict. In doing so, he applied

---

[8] M van der Stoel 'The OSCE and Conflict Prevention: The Role of the High Commissioner on National Minorities', Kompagnietor Lecture 1, 10 April 1997, available at www.ecmi.de/about/about-ecmi/first-ecmi-lecture.
[9] ibid.

three key principles: impartiality, confidentiality and cooperation. The impartiality was reflected in not taking sides, but always listening to and trying to understand both the viewpoint of a government and of a national minority. Confidentiality entailed countless talks behind closed doors and a lot of shuttle diplomacy. Rather than seeking publicity, this job involved avoiding making newspaper headlines, as such publicity might make concessions on either side more difficult. Finally, cooperation was key. Not only because he carried very few carrots and sticks in his diplomatic luggage, but also because cooperation rather than coercion produced much more durable results.

The effectiveness and even-handedness of his work as High Commissioner was certainly appreciated by others. This did not only show in formal or informal naming of streets or universities. OSCE governments showed their trust in him by prolonging his mandate and in 1999 the Dutch government even nominated him for the Nobel Peace Prize.

III. An Enduring Diplomat

In 2001, at a rather advanced age, the grand old man of preventive diplomacy was called upon for one last, but most delicate task by the Dutch government. The Dutch crown prince Willem-Alexander had announced he would marry Máxima Zorreguieta. The cheerfulness of the impending marriage was overcast when heated public and parliamentary debate ensued about the father-in-law, who had been a cabinet Minister in Jorge Videla's military dictatorship in Argentina in the 1970s. Van der Stoel was tasked with convincing the father not to attend the wedding and, after three trips across the Atlantic, succeeded in doing so. The irony of the whole operation must not have been lost on Van der Stoel, even if he was known for never making jokes. Or, as one commentator put it 'Dull he may be. But he has helped to make the continent a safer place'.[10] He passed away in 2011, at the age of 86, lauded by the Prime Minister of the Netherlands, Mark Rutte, as an icon for human rights.

In his memory and as a testimony to his tireless work for human rights, two prizes have been created in his name. The first is the award of the High Commissioner on National Minorities and the Government of the Netherlands. It has been handed out every other year since 2003 to persons, groups or institutions 'for extraordinary and outstanding achievements in improving the position of national minorities in the OSCE participating States' – among the winners are the Russian NGO Memorial and the European Roma Rights Centre. The second award is an academic one, awarded since 2002 for 'academic publications in the area of human rights, with a view to draw more attention to this field of study in academic education and research'.[11]

The life and work of Max van der Stoel carry a few key messages. The first is that speaking out against human rights violations, no matter by whom they are

---

[10] See n 5.
[11] The author of this chapter was its grateful recipient in 2008.

committed, is crucial. This can be done in public, through words and visits, in order to morally and practically support the oppressed, but also behind closed doors, steadily nagging on about the importance of shared values and fundamental principles of humanity. Second, the way in which one works should be adjusted to the task. Positions as Foreign Minister, Special Rapporteur or High Commissioner provide a platform, but the tone used and the stature and principledness of the person occupying such positions matter greatly. Here the medium is not the only the message: one's personality matters too. As to tone, a dry factual description of facts may often work better than rhetorical fireworks or emotional, angry tweets. Finally, Van der Stoel would argue that it is important to tackle problems at a very early stage, in order to avoid armed conflict, violations of rights and human suffering. To him, prevention efforts were one of the best investments in peace and stability one could make. And prevention could be achieved not just through diplomacy, but even more importantly by addressing the root causes of conflict and injustice: by taking the application of human rights seriously, everywhere, for everyone. Or, as he phrased it himself: 'If we devote our attention only to the wars of today, we will have reasons to mourn again tomorrow'.[12]

---

[12] Van der Stoel (n 7).

24

Tadeusz Mazowiecki

The Human Rights Envoy of the Former Yugoslavia

ROMAN WIERUSZEWSKI

The entire human history could be considered as a history of the struggle for human rights. The issue of human rights in the contemporary world, and today's understanding of them, is by no means an ephemeral, seasonal interest. And although there certainly are and will be changes in its configuration, it expresses deeply established aspirations. They do not vegetate on the periphery of human dreams of a conflict-free world, but indicate the direction to achieve a certain universal minimum, and determine the threshold for the realization of a sense of freedom, security and participation.[1]

I. A Life of Navigating the Past, Politics and People

Tadeusz Mazowiecki assured his place in the history of Poland as the first democratic prime minister after the overthrow of communism. In a word, as a social activist, thinker and publicist, he was an 'authority'. As a teenager, Mazowiecki survived the trauma of the Second World War. On the day the war ended, he was 18 years old and carried behind him the baggage of difficult experiences from the war: he saw death and terror and he found poverty. He also had a difficult familial life. His father died early and an older brother was arrested by the Germans for conspiracy activities, sent to a concentration camp and his fate remained unknown. He was twice widowed and raised three sons alone.

Mazowiecki was associated with the Catholic social movement tolerated by the communist authorities of Poland. He was, for a couple of years at the beginning

[1] T Mazowiecki, *Druga twarz Europy* (*The Second Face of Europe*) (Warsaw, Biblioteka Więzi, 1990) 77; the book contains selections of his earlier writings.

of the 1960s, a Member of Parliament of the Polish People's Republic. He served as editor-in-chief of the influential Catholic periodical *Więź*, and was a propagator of the Church's social teaching, with an emphasis on the imperative of protecting human rights.

When writing and expressing himself on the issue of human rights, which he did often, especially in the context of the discussion on the role of human rights in Christianity, Mazowiecki placed particular emphasis on the social dimension of human rights. He pointed out that human rights are a common inheritance and, citing international documents, including the International Covenants on Human Rights, he stressed that recognition of the inherent human dignity and equal and inalienable rights of all people is the foundation of freedom, justice, and world peace.

Mazowiecki's texts devoted to the Christian vision of human rights prompt interesting reflections and enable a better understanding of the principles he followed when fulfilling his mission during the conflicts in the Balkans. In this regard, two aspects demand attention. The first is the imperative of action, expressed as:

> ... a Christian can fight for and serve human rights in various ways, but he cannot do one thing: when freedom and human dignity are oppressed and where there is a fight for human rights, he cannot allow oneself to adopt Pilate's gesture.[2]

The second theme is the emphasis on the construction of social infrastructure, that is, the consolidation in society of the habit of active participation in strengthening human rights and fundamental values. Interestingly, at the end of the 1970s he claimed that 'the threat today is not so much ideological indoctrination, but depoliticization, passivity, what we call social retreat. [...] In this situation, creating a social infrastructure that awakens and develops our identity is essential'.[3] One can ask whether today, 40 years later and in the context of different political and international conditions, these remarks still remain relevant and applicable. A rhetorical question indeed.

Individual rights, emphasising the importance of human dignity as a source of such rights and freedoms, while at the same time indicating the individual's duty towards the community – these pillars shaped Mazowiecki's way of thinking and acting.

II. The Uphill Battle for a More Efficient Role of Special Rapporteur

The conflict in the Balkans, which broke out with ferocious force at the beginning of the 1990s, was a great surprise for Europe. At the time, it was celebrating the end of the Cold War, the triumph of Solidarity and the fall of the Berlin Wall. These events were considered evidence of the victory of the universal concept of human rights, and it was assumed that human rights would further develop and strengthen throughout the world.

---

[2] Mazowiecki (n 1) 83.
[3] ibid, 78.

Meanwhile, the Balkans witnessed the outbreak of a brutal war marked by mass and serious violations of fundamental human rights. At the same time, the mechanisms that were designed to prevent such atrocities, whether within the framework of the UN, the Council of Europe, or the OSCE, among others, failed to fulfil their functions. There was also a lack of ideas about how to break the growing spiral of crime and hatred in the Balkans. Though negotiation processes were launched in an effort to stem the downward spiral, prolonged talks and diplomatic consultations did not bring about any results. The media continued to report further massacres of civilians, mass displacements and the creation of concentration camps. A new term, reminiscent of the worst times in the history of the European continent, was created – 'ethnic cleansing'. It quickly became evident that without external intervention, this conflict would not end. However, public opinion, especially in Europe, was both opposed to armed intervention and also reluctant to bring the United States into the conflict resolution process in Europe. The conviction was that Europe should be able to cope with internal 'European' problems on its own.

The UN also remained passive in the face of the conflict in the Balkans for a long period. It was not until August 1992, more than a year after the outbreak of fighting in Croatia and a few months after the start of the siege of Sarajevo that the UN Commission on Human Rights met in Geneva at an extraordinary session and decided to appoint a Special Rapporteur to investigate human rights violations in the former Yugoslavia. People who did not know the UN system well could have had the impression that, as the UN Special Rapporteur for Human Rights in the Former Yugoslavia, Mazowiecki was supposed to be a kind of 'envoy of peace'. This was the hope that he himself nourished.

Mazowiecki was never someone who was referred to as a 'human rights defender'. Of course, in his actions as a leading member of the democratic opposition during the communist rule in the People's Republic of Poland, he was always claiming these rights. This, however, was only part of the overall struggle to change the system. So when he agreed to take over the function of the Special Rapporteur, he did not fully realise what role he was expected to play. He was also sceptical of the UN bureaucracy and determined not to become its hostage. However, he sincerely hoped that his mission would have a positive impact in interrupting of the bloody conflicts raging in the former Yugoslavia. It was with this intention that Mazowiecki started his mission.

It is worthwhile pondering why Mazowiecki was entrusted with this unanticipated role. In order to provide an answer to this question, one should begin with a brief recapitulation of his views and stances on human rights. As he himself admitted, when he accepted this appointment, he had never been particularly interested in the institutional dimension of the system of protection of human rights. However, the very idea of human rights was always very close to him and accompanied him from the beginning of his public activities. This is evident in the maxim he put forth in 1990 and to which he always remained faithful: 'By putting emphasis on basic values, hope is created; a hope without which it is difficult to live, not only for the individual but also for the community'.[4]

---

[4] Mazowiecki (n 1) 7.

But what role was the Special Rapporteur intended to play in the early 1990s in the Balkans and what difference could he make? At that time, the UN Commission on Human Rights, although the principal UN body in the field of human rights, occupied a relatively low level in the hierarchy of UN bodies. It did not have the power to make final decisions and its resolutions had to be approved by the Economic and Social Council (ECOSOC). It is characteristic that although the war in the Balkans had already been ongoing for almost two years, the Commission had taken that long to proactively address rising human rights concerns. The fact that serious violations of human rights occurred during the conflict was well known and widely reported in the world media. International organisations operating there, such as the UN High Commissioner for Refugees (UNHCR) and the International Committee of the Red Cross, were constantly receiving dramatic reports about the fate of civilians in the areas affected by the fighting. In the summer of 1992 poignant pictures of people behind barbed wire appeared in the press. The term 'ethnic cleansing' also became the term *de jour* to encapsulate the forced exodus of people from areas dominated by opponent forces.

In 1992, two experienced diplomats were delegated to conduct peace negotiations – Britain's Lord David Owen and America's Cyrus Vance. The task of the Special Rapporteur was to document and present the scale of the crimes committed and to give recommendations on what should be done to put an end to them. Usually, special rapporteurs are diplomats or experts. For the first time it was decided to appoint a so-called politician, who was well known from the front pages of newspapers. As the first democratic prime minister in post-communist Eastern Europe, Mazowiecki was a widely respected figure in Europe and he enjoyed substantial popularity. The idea was to distribute his reports as widely as possible in order to gain public support for and acceptance of engagement, including potential military intervention, in the Balkans. Mazowiecki was perfect for such a role.

In addition to his reputation as a politician, he was also, in a sense, a 'media man'. He understood and appreciated the role of the media and he was able to generate interest in the international media. The importance of objective international media information was all the greater because, unfortunately, the local media falsified the situation in the field and even fuelled the moods of hostility and hatred.[5] In his first report as Special Rapporteur, Mazowiecki raised the alarm that one of the main methods of fuelling hatred and willingness to retaliate is by spreading rumours and misinformation. With a few exceptions, national media presented the conflict and human rights violations in a distorted way.[6] During his meetings with representatives of the local media, he called for the cessation of these practices. Usually however, his efforts were met with retorts such as, 'You should not blame us, we are only tools in the hands of politicians'. Mazowiecki disagreed with this philosophy, but in the atmosphere that prevailed at that time in the Balkans, he had no chance of convincing

---

[5] T Mazowiecki, *Fifth periodic report on the situation of human rights in the territory of the former Yugoslavia*, UN Doc E/CN.4/1994/47, 17 November 1993, paras 133–35.

[6] T Mazowiecki, *Second periodic report on the situation of human rights in the territory of the former Yugoslavia*, UN Doc E/CN.4/1994/4, 19 May 1993, para 12.

local journalists to change their attitude. However, he did find allies in the international media. Speaking at the forum of the Commission on Human Rights in Geneva in November 1992, Mazowiecki stated: 'The international press deserves our great gratitude. In fact, for many months, and often risking their lives, journalists from around the world have revealed the truth about the events taking place in former Yugoslavia'.[7]

The first mission, in August 1992, illustrated the scale of the difficulties and revealed the limited tools available to the Special Rapporteur. He was meant to collect reliable, confirmed information about human rights violations, an exceptionally difficult task. The parties to the conflict were competing with each other in giving out exaggerated data about their victims, about destruction, etc. Verification of data was often impossible due to the lack of access to the regions in which the battles took place. Therefore, Mazowiecki found it necessary to set up field offices in the conflict countries, especially in Bosnia and Herzegovina, Croatia, Serbia and Macedonia. While these offices were created gradually, they significantly streamlined the process of gathering information and improved its quality. This information was to be the basis for formulating evidence-based proposals aimed at ending the grave violations of human rights. It is precisely with regard to the nature of these recommendations that serious differences of opinion between the UN bureaucracy – sometimes supported by diplomats, especially peace negotiators – and Mazowiecki were revealed. A good example is the ongoing artillery and sniper fire in Sarajevo, as a result of which people died almost daily and all inhabitants lived in an atmosphere of fear and terror.[8] It seemed obvious that demanding an end to this situation was a basic condition for improvement with respect to the human rights situation, and therefore fell entirely within the remit of the Special Rapporteur. However, diplomats felt that demanding that the heavy weapons located in the area of Sarajevo be placed under international control was not a human rights issue under the purview of the rapporteur. Mazowiecki consistently disagreed with such a narrow interpretation of his role and the failure of diplomats to link control of weaponry to human suffering on such a grand scale, exhorting 'without applying sufficient pressure to force an end to human rights violations any attempts to find a just and lasting political solution will be doomed to fail'.[9]

A very controversial issue from the very beginning of his mandate was the problem of punishing the perpetrators of serious violations of human rights. During the mission many documents, photos, and testimonies describing the crimes and identifying the perpetrators were passed to the Special Rapporteur and his team. It was not entirely clear what he was to do with this evidence. His mission did not have the opportunity to analyse everything scrupulously or even properly store the documents. From the outset, some diplomats, especially the Americans, insisted on the need to create mechanisms for punishing criminals. The local judiciary could not be counted on because it was difficult, under war conditions, to secure their independence and objectivity.

---

[7] Mazowiecki (n 1) 55.

[8] T Mazowiecki, *Third periodic report on the situation of human rights in the territory of the former Yugoslavia*, UN Doc E/CN.4/1994/8, 6 September 1993, paras 25–29, 35.

[9] Mazowiecki (n 6) para 44.

Initially, Mazowiecki was quite sceptical about these ideas. He believed his duty was to help the victims, not deal with prosecuting the perpetrators. Gradually, however, he changed his mind. The breakthrough was a visit to Gornij Vakuf in central Bosnia and Herzegovina. Before the war the area was multi-ethnic – Muslim and Serbian. In a conversation with residents in a part controlled by government forces, he asked whether they would agree to the return of their Serbian neighbours. Their answers were unequivocal: yes, but on condition that the killers and rapists be punished. He then understood that there could be no talk of reconciliation without punishing the guilty. At the request of Mazowiecki, along with others, an International Commission of Experts was appointed to collect evidence of war crimes.[10] Mazowiecki also endorsed the idea of the establishment of an international criminal tribunal for perpetrators of war crimes and crimes against humanity.[11] Ultimately, the International Criminal Tribunal for the Former Yugoslavia was established in May 1993 and benefited from very good cooperation from the Special Rapporteur.[12] In his reports to the UN Commission on Human Rights, he unequivocally reiterated the importance of the international tribunal to try war crimes and the necessity for cooperation from the international community.[13]

Contact with peace negotiators also posed serious problems. The negotiators decided that their role was completely separate from Mazowiecki's mandate, and they were very reluctant to respond to his proposals for meetings.[14] This stand-off presents the crux of the problem. Mazowiecki, bearing witness to human sufferings and dramas, believed that the negotiators should demand an end to practices of ethnic cleaning, the use of concentration camps, attacks on civilians, among others. According to his suggestions, the continuation of peace talks should have depended on the termination of these practices, as the credibility of the human rights commitments of the parties to the conflict was a great concern. In addition, he believed that the international community should be ready to intercede to protect against further human rights abuses with the use of force. He argued that the threat of armed intervention should be real, not just apparent. He often quoted the Latin proverb, *Si vis pacem, para bellum*.[15] The negotiators had a different opinion. They were reluctant to point out violations of human rights because that created the need to punish the perpetrators. They were of the opinion that in order to secure a peace agreement it would be necessary to promise impunity for human rights violators.

A separate but, in the context of this mission, key issue involved the disputes between religious leaders. In the case of the former Yugoslavia it was difficult to speak of national conflicts. This applies in particular to the situation in Croatia, Bosnia and

---

[10] T Mazowiecki, *Report on the situation of human rights in the territory of the former Yugoslavia*, UN Doc E/CN.4/1992/S-1/9 28 August 1992, para 70.

[11] T Mazowiecki, *Report on the situation of human rights in the territory of the former Yugoslavia*, UN Doc, E/CN.4/1993/50, 10 February 1993, para 72.

[12] The Court was established by Resolution 827 of the United Nations Security Council, which was passed on 25 May 1993.

[13] Mazowiecki (n 5) para 230.

[14] D Owen, *Balkan Odyssey* (London, Indigo, 1995) 329.

[15] 'If you want peace, prepare for war'.

Herzegovina and Serbia. Ethnic and linguistic separations, usually 'forcibly', began to accelerate after the collapse of the federal state. This was a result of decades of largely secularised communist indoctrination. Traditionally however, the Croats were mostly Catholics, Serbs Orthodox, and Bosnians[16] were followers of Islam. It was the religious differences that made it possible to emphasise their ethnic separateness.[17] Hence the protagonists – interestingly, this concerned all parties to the conflict – very strongly emphasised that in the Balkans it was a religious war. Mazowiecki rejected this argument with absolute vigour. Although temples and other objects of worship were often attacked and destroyed, it was not about religion but about identity symbols of the enemies. Therefore, Mazowiecki constantly tried to point out that religious leaders should play the role of peacemakers and promote reconciliation. Meetings with clerics of all religions were a regular item on the agenda of his field mission programme. Unfortunately, they did not bring about the desired results. The bishops and the Imams inscribed themselves as in the atmosphere of a religious war and claimed that their followers were victims of this war and, therefore, they must be defended.

Following his first two missions and after presenting reports to the UN Commission on Human Rights, Mazowiecki realised that the effects of his actions were negligible. The armed struggle continued, people died and the policy of ethnic cleansing continued to bring about tragic results. The lack of political will at the international level to use all necessary means to end the drama became evident. Mazowiecki became dejected and determined to resign to avoid being no more than the accountant who in subsequent reports gives new numbers of killed, raped, displaced persons and adds geographic locations of places where these crimes take place despite his recommendations which he felt were either ignored or only partially implemented. He felt he could not help.[18]

Driving this idea out of his head would not have been possible if not for one circumstance. Whenever he mentioned his resignation in conversations with the victims of the conflict, explaining the reasons for them, he was met with unequivocal reactions imploring him not to resign as he was the one voice that gave the plight of the Balkans international attention. In one interview, in response to the question whether he had the feeling that he really helped, he answered:

> Yes and no, because help in individual cases was not enough. But my reports were important for people on the spot. Also, the reaction after these reports, both positive and negative, showed that they were not without significance. And that for many people it was the voice of truth. Their voice.[19]

Mazowiecki fulfilled his mission for almost three years. However, his mandate and the problems he highlighted throughout his reports seemed to have been in vain when in July 1995 the Serbian forces captured the city of Srebrenica, a Muslim enclave in Bosnia and Herzegovina. It was in one of the so-called security zones,

---

[16] The identification as 'Bosnian' began to be used only in the mid-1990s, earlier in their official documents they were referred to as Muslims.
[17] All of Mazowiecki's reports as Special Rapporteur spoke to this issue.
[18] Personal observations of the author.
[19] T Mazowiecki, *Rok 1989 i lata następne* (Warszawa, Pruszyński and Co, 2012) 289.

or areas supervised by UN troops. The creation of these zones had been one of his recommendations as Special Rapporteur. The Serbs not only took Srebrenica, but committed horrific crimes on the civilian population. Immediately after the news about Srebrenica broke, Mazowiecki came to Tuzla, the city in Bosnia where the escapees who had managed to avoid death were gathering. He spent many hours in conversations with them. It is estimated that about 7,000–8,000 people were murdered. The War Crimes Tribunal for the former Yugoslavia has recognised these acts in Srebrenica as the crime of genocide.[20]

It should be emphasised that although the survivors of the Srebrenica massacre had understandable rage and hostility towards the UN for its failure to act and protect them, Mazowiecki himself was warmly welcomed. After Srebrenica, he decided to resign. With this decision, he became a unique figure in the history of the UN. He was the first ever UN Special Rapporteur who took such a step. He managed to resist the strong pressure from the UN Secretary General Boutros Boutros Ghali who urged him not to resign but to no avail. The resignation of the Special Rapporteur received extremely wide coverage in the media around the world. Photos of Mazowiecki appeared on the front pages of the most widely read newspapers. He gave dozens of interviews, firmly demanding immediate action against the aggressors. Today we know in hindsight that his decision was the first stone that launched an avalanche, as a result of which a few months later a peace agreement in Dayton was concluded.

III. Principles Over Pretence

The letter in which Mazowiecki informed the UN Secretary General and the Chairman of the Commission on Human Rights of his resignation was both a cry of despair and at the same time a clear testimony to the unwavering principles that guided the author. The following brief excerpt of this extraordinary document summarises the determination of its author:

> The present critical moment forces us to realize the true character of those crimes and the responsibility of Europe and the international community for their own helplessness in addressing them. We have been fighting in Poland against a totalitarian system with a vision for the Europe of tomorrow. How can we believe in a Europe of tomorrow created by children of people who are abandoned today? I would like to believe that the present moment will be a turning point in the relationship between Europe and the world towards Bosnia. The very stability of the international order and the principle of civilization is at stake over the question of Bosnia. However, I am not convinced that the turning point hoped for will happen and therefore cannot continue to participate in the pretence of the protection of human rights.[21]

---

[20] See ICTY, *Prosecutor v Ratko Mladić*, judgment of 22 November 2017, IT-09-92-T.
[21] T Mazowiecki, *Genocide in Srebrenica, Report of the special rapporteur*, UN Doc E/CN.4/1996, 22 August 1995, Annex I, Letter dated 27 July 1995 addressed by Mr Tadeusz Mazowiecki to the Chairman of the Commission on Human Rights.

Tadeusz Mazowiecki, in exercising his difficult mandate in the former Yugoslavia, was guided both by his vision of human dignity as a supreme value and the need to defend human rights at all costs. His mission constituted a remarkable testimony to fundamental values and non-acceptance of false compromises. For this reason, in the former Yugoslavia he became the symbol of 'human rights envoy' in the deep human-istic sense of the word – a person who is ready to fight uncompromisingly for the rights of victims, for their dignity, for the restoration of the observance of elementary human rights. This attitude has gained wide recognition both among the people affected by the conflict and in the circles of human rights defenders and symbolised by honorary doctorates at the University of Tuzla and the University of Warsaw. In the course of fulfilling the three-year mandate as the UN Special Rapporteur on Human Rights in the former Yugoslavia, Tadeusz Mazowiecki revealed a great sensitivity to human tragedy, human rights violations and an aversion to falsely-understood diplomacy or political correctness. In many ways, he became less a politician and more a human rights defender than even he could have anticipated.

25

James Earl 'Jimmy' Carter Jr

'But ye brethren, be not weary in well doing':[1] A Continuing Faith and Persistence in the Cause of Human Rights

MICHAEL STOHL

> Our commitment to human rights must be absolute, our laws fair, our national beauty preserved; the powerful must not persecute the weak, and human dignity must be enhanced.[2]

I. Early Life and Career

James Earl 'Jimmy' Carter Jr was born in the segregated American south on 1 October 1924. His parents, Earl and Lillian Carter, were owners of a peanut farm, a warehouse and a store near the small town of Plains, Georgia. While the family became relatively prosperous later in his childhood, the house in which he first lived as a child lacked electricity and indoor plumbing and was in a very modest neighbourhood. The Carter family had arrived in the American colonies in the 1630s and resided in Georgia since shortly after the American Revolution. Jimmy's mother, Lillian Carter, who trained as a nurse, was not only intellectually curious, but also a woman of strong convictions, as evidenced by her choice to ignore the segregation customs of 1920s

---

[1] King James Bible, 2 Thessalonians 03:13.
[2] J Carter, Presidential Inaugural Address, 20 January 1977, available at www.presidency.ucsb.edu/ws/index.php?pid=6575.

Georgia to care for black women and to invite them into her home.[3] Surprisingly, his father, James Earl Carter, by all accounts a more typical rural southern white of the era and thus a segregationist, did not, according to Lillian Carter, stop her 'from doing what I wanted to do'.[4] James, Sr was clearly, however, a good businessman and his son learned from his entrepreneurial attitudes. By the age of 13, having saved money from hauling goods from the family farm to town and selling them, Jimmy bought five houses in the Plains area (the depression had caused many foreclosures and very low prices) and then rented them.

Jimmy was also a good and ambitious student and set his sights on admission to the US Naval Academy. After he graduated from high school he spent two years in further preparation at Georgia Southwestern College and the Georgia Institute of Technology before entering the Naval Academy in 1943, graduating in the top 10 per cent, with a BS degree in 1946. He married Rosalynn Smith, also from Plains and three years his junior, just prior to graduation and they recently celebrated their seventy-second wedding anniversary. They have four children, three sons and a daughter.

Carter was initially commissioned as a Lieutenant in the Navy and assigned to a training program in Norfolk, Virginia. He then was posted to Pearl Harbor, Hawaii, and assigned as an electronics officer on the *USS Pomfret*. Further postings followed in Groton, Connecticut; San Diego, California and Washington, DC. Carter requested assignment in the submarine service and soon after was sent for graduate studies in Nuclear Physics at Union College in Schenectady, New York. He was subsequently selected by Admiral Hyman Rickover for appointment as an engineering officer of the second US nuclear submarine, the Sea Wolf. An incident occurred during this period which illustrates Carter's commitment to civil rights: 'While his submarine was moored in Bermuda, British officials there extended a party invitation to white crewmembers only. Partly at Carter's urgings, everyone on the submarine refused to attend'.[5]

After seven years in the Navy, Carter resigned his position when his father died of cancer and out of duty to his family, returned to Plains to try and save the family business, which had suffered in the last few years of James, Sr's life. It was not until 1959 that he was able to make it fully successful again. In this difficult period of his personal life, which coincided with the landmark Supreme Court decision in *Brown v Board of Education*, a White Citizens' Council was formed to fight against the changing civil rights landscape. Jimmy Carter was the only white male in Plains to refuse to join and his business was boycotted as a result.[6] A few years later he and wife Rosalynn were two of the three dissenting votes when their church voted against

---

[3] C Evans, 'Lillian Carter Is Dead At 85; Mother of the 39th President,' *The New York Times* (New York, 31 October, 1983), available at www.nytimes.com/1983/10/31/obituaries/lillian-carter-is-deat-at-85-mother-of-the-39th-president.html.
[4] ibid.
[5] RA Strong, 'Jimmy Carter: Life Before the Presidency' (UVA Miller Center, nd), available at miller-center.org/president/carter/life-before-the-presidency.
[6] J Carter, *A Full Life* (New York, Simon and Schuster, 2015).

desegregating itself.[7] As his business improved Carter became more involved in local community affairs. In addition to his role as a Deacon and Sunday School Teacher at the Plains Baptist Church and service on the local hospital board, he was elected to the local County Board of Education in 1955 and then in 1962 was elected to the Georgia State Senate. He unsuccessfully ran for the Democratic nomination for governor in 1966 but was successful in winning the governorship in 1970. In his inaugural address he surprised the state (and the nation) two years after the divisive race-charged presidential campaign of 1968 (when the segregationist candidate George Wallace won more than 43 per cent of the vote in Georgia as an independent against the two major party candidates in a three-way race) when he declared 'I say to you quite frankly that the time for racial discrimination is over'.[8] During his time as governor he was known for appointing a large increase in African Americans to state agencies and for reforming Georgia's governing bureaucracy, promoting environmental protection and improving funding for education. He also began preparing for a run for the presidency. Benefiting from the backlash from Watergate, Carter eked out a victory in the presidential election of 1976, defeating the incumbent Gerald Ford by winning just over 50 per cent of the vote while winning the Electoral College. Most Americans perceived the Carter presidency as a failure and he was swept from office by a landslide victory for Ronald Reagan.

However, while his policies were often unpopular at the time, it is clear that there were major long-term positive effects of his presidency and policies which were deemed unpopular are now seen as visionary, such as his support for energy reform and the environment. In addition to his human rights achievements, discussed below, he notably negotiated the Panama Canal treaties that returned control of the canal to Panama and guaranteed the canal's neutrality. He also secured the agreement of Egyptian President Anwar Sadat and Israeli Prime Minister Menachem Begin to the Camp David accords, ending the 30-year state of war between the two countries.

II. Career and Contribution to Human Rights: Continuing Faith and Persistence in the Cause of Human Rights

Jimmy Carter came to the Presidency following the decades of the American civil rights movement, the backlash against American involvement in Vietnam and the disenchantment with the amoral realpolitik character of the Nixon-Kissinger-Ford foreign policy. These events had shaken the entrenched national myth that the

---

[7] I Jones, 'Thanks, Jimmy Carter, for Stating What Should Be Obvious: Trump's Campaign Is Racist,' *The Nation* (New York, 26 May 2016), available at www.thenation.com/article/thanks-jimmy-carter-for-stating-what-should-be-obvious-trumps-campaign-is-racist/.

[8] J Nordheimer, 'New Governor of Georgia Urges End of Racial Bias' *The New York Times* (New York, 13 January 1971), available at www.nytimes.com/1971/01/13/archives/new-governor-of-georgia-urges-end-of-racial-bias-georgia-governor.html.

United States had a unique heritage of morality and respect for human rights worldwide, and in the later years of the Nixon and Ford presidency a democratic party-controlled Congress passed the first legislation to tie foreign aid to human rights. They enacted a series of Bills that recommended that the President 'deny any economic or military assistance to the government of any foreign country which practices the internment or imprisonment of that country's citizens for political purposes', and to 'substantially reduce or terminate security assistance to any government which engages in a consistent pattern of gross violations of internationally recognized human rights'.[9]

Not only was Carter supportive of the legislation that Congress had passed in the previous few years, but he demonstrated a commitment to create the framework and machinery to better achieve the intent. From the first day of his administration Carter spoke frequently with passion and force in support of human rights and their central role in the formation of US foreign policy. In his inaugural address the President emphasised his commitment to human rights, saying:

> Our commitment to human rights must be absolute ... Because we are free, we can never be indifferent to the fate of freedom elsewhere. Our moral sense dictates a clear-cut preference for those societies which share with us an abiding respect for individual human rights.[10]

Jimmy Carter's signal achievement while president was to elevate human rights to a central position and to reaffirm 'America's commitment to human rights as a fundamental tenet of our foreign policy'.[11] The commitment was not simply a matter of rhetoric, as he also created new bureaucratic machinery to solidify the consideration of human rights in the development and execution of foreign policy initiatives and policies. And while that commitment has clearly wavered (and at times, unfortunately, been completely ignored) by the succeeding presidents in the years following, Carter's impact has been such that all subsequent presidents (with the current exception of Donald Trump) either have had to pay tribute to the commitment, at least in rhetoric, or explain why they were deviating from the now fundamental expectation underlying US foreign engagement.

Carter began immediately to explore how to reshape the organisation of human rights policy making within the government. By the end of his first year as president, Carter had directed the Secretary of State to establish the Bureau of Human Rights and Humanitarian Affairs within the Department, and named Patricia Derian as Assistant Secretary for Human Rights and Humanitarian Affairs in charge of the Bureau. To comply with section 502B of the Foreign Assistance Act, Carter directed the Department of State to produce country reports on human rights practices of all recipient countries and, unlike President Ford, he directed that these reports be

---

[9] D Carleton and M Stohl, 'The Foreign Policy of Human Rights: Rhetoric and Reality from Jimmy Carter to Ronald Reagan' (1985) 7(2) *Human Rights Quarterly* 205.

[10] J Carter, 'Inaugural Address of President Jimmy Carter' 20 January 1977 in *Public Papers of the Presidents of the United States 1977* Book I (Washington, DC, US Government Printing Office, 1977).

[11] J Carter, 'Address at Commencement Exercises at the University of Notre Dame' 22 May 1977, available at klau.nd.edu/events/2011/09/27/president-carters-1977-notre-dame-commencement-address-in-the-history-of-human-rights.

made public. The consequence was a great improvement in the quality of the reporting process. Foreign service officers, who initially sought to avoid service in the new department of humanitarian affairs, did not appreciate the criticisms that were publicly levelled at them by activists and NGOs. They were also being judged by their immediate superiors as to the quality of their reports. Thus, they demanded that the US embassies turn over better information and analyses. Best practices were shared across embassy posts and the reports became of greater and greater utility and importance.[12] These reports continue to provide important human rights information not only for government officials (including providing important information for adjudicating asylum claims) but also for human rights activists and organisations around the world. The Department of State website continues to introduce the reports by indicating 'We are a nation founded on the belief that every person is endowed with inalienable rights. Promoting and defending these rights is central to who we are as a country'.[13]

Another important initiative was the issuance of Presidential Review Memorandum/NSC 28, which directed a review of US human rights policy in order to define policy objectives, evaluate actions designed to improve rights, review national security considerations, and propose implementing actions in May 1977. In February 1978, President Carter introduced Presidential Directive 30 based on the memorandum's study findings. The directive included 30 specific guidelines for policy and indicated that

> It shall be the objective of the U.S. human rights policy to reduce worldwide governmental violations of the integrity of the person (e.g., torture: cruel, inhuman or degrading treatment; arbitrary arrest or· imprisonment; lengthy detention without trial, and assassination and, to enhance civil and political liberties (e.g., freedom of speech, of religion, of assembly, of movement and of the press; and the right to basic judicial protections). It will also be a continuing U.S. objective to promote basic economic and social rights. (e.g., adequate food, education, shelter and health).[14]

The President also directed changes within the Department of State to better coordinate human rights considerations across all the bureaus through the Human Rights Coordinating Group (HRCG), consisting of Department of State officials at the deputy assistant secretary level; Assistant to the President for National Security Affairs, Zbigniew Brzezinski, established the National Security Council (NSC) Global Issues Cluster which was charged with overseeing issues such as human rights and arms control. Under Carter's direction, Secretary of State Vance and Secretary of the Treasury W Michael Blumenthal also established the Interagency Working Group on Human Rights and Foreign Assistance to further coordinate and incorporate human rights into economic considerations with respect to the allocation of foreign assistance in all forms. In addition, he also directed the Agency for International Development

[12] M Stohl and C Stohl, 'Human Rights, Nation States, and NGOs: Structural Holes and the Emergence of Global Regimes' (2005) 72(4) *Communication Monographs* 442.
[13] J Sullivan, 'Country Reports on Human Rights Practices for 2017' Bureau of Democracy, Human Rights and Labor, available at www.state.gov/j/drl/rls/hrrpt/humanrightsreport/#wrapper.
[14] Presidential Directive/NSC-30, 17 February 1978, available at fas.org/irp/offdocs/pd/pd30.pdf.

and the United States Information Agency to make human rights a priority in every project.

Having criticised the amoral realpolitik policy of his immediate predecessors during his presidential campaign, upon assuming office Carter also took advantage of the opening that the Helsinki accords provided. While the accords were seen as a realpolitik betrayal by many observers in the immediate aftermath of their signing in 1975, Carter perceived an opportunity.[15] Building on the visionary work of Representative Millicent Fenwick prior to his election, Carter instructed the US Helsinki Mission to the Committee on Cooperation and Security in Europe (CCSE), to engage as much as possible with the various dissident groups whose existence was made possible by the accords, ie Czechoslovakia's Charter 77, Poland's Solidarity, and the Helsinki Watch groups in East Germany and the Soviet Union. He corresponded with dissidents such as Russian physics Nobel laureate Andrei Sakharov, indicating 'You may rest assured that the American people and our government will continue our firm commitment to promote respect for human rights not only in our country, but also abroad'. Brinkley recounts that

> Czech Republic president Vaclav Havel went so far as to claim that Carter's human rights agenda so undermined the legitimacy and self-confidence of the Warsaw Pacts chieftains that dissidents across Eastern Europe regained the hope that carried them on to democracy.[16]

This is further supported by former CIA Director and Secretary of Defense Robert Gates, who noted, 'Whether isolated and little-known Soviet dissident or world-famous Soviet scientist, Carter's policy encouraged them to press on'.[17]

Jimmy Carter had a one-term presidency. At the time of his leaving the presidency, many observers characterised his term of office as a failure. The Soviet invasion of Afghanistan and the response to it shifted media attention away from the focus on human rights, while the prolonged Iran hostage crisis and stagnant US economy led directly to his electoral defeat by Ronald Reagan in 1980. But with the hindsight of almost 40 years, we can see the lasting impact of the Carter initiatives in human rights. But, as important as these initiatives were for shaping US human rights policy and machinery, Carter's legacy as a fundamental figure in the development of human rights norms, standards and practice, are largely attributed to his work since leaving office. This legacy is not limited to the field of human rights, but also to peace processes and economic and social development.

Upon leaving the presidency, Carter established the Carter Center at Emory University in Atlanta, Georgia in 1982. Consistent with his lifelong ideals, Carter transformed the expectations and purposes of the Presidential Libraries and Museums that had begun after the presidency of Herbert Hoover in 1932. Those institutions

---

[15] L Charlton, 'The Helsinki Accord: Advance or Retreat?' *The New York Times* (New York, 31 July 1975) 2.

[16] D Brinkley, 'Rave on, Jimmy Carter,' *CNN* (Atlanta, 13 August 2015), available at www.cnn.com/2015/08/13/opinions/brinkley-jimmy-carter/index.html.

[17] RM Gates, *From the Shadows* (New York, Simon and Schuster, 1996).

were primarily vast archives, the repositories of documents and historical materials of the presidents, ie artifacts, interesting educational and public programmes, and informative websites. However, the Carter Center, which is attached to the Jimmy Carter Presidential Library, befits the human rights, peace and development activist that characterises Carter post-presidency. Unencumbered by the duties and responsibility of the office or the national and party politics that often constrain even that most powerful of actors, Carter devoted the centre to the pursuit of human rights, democracy and social and economic development. The centre's activities are clear from its mission statement:

> The Carter Center, in partnership with Emory University, is guided by a fundamental commitment to human rights and the alleviation of human suffering. It seeks to prevent and resolve conflicts, enhance freedom and democracy, and improve health.[18]

The mission is backed by an extraordinary set of successful activities which include: official observation of 104 elections in 39 countries to help establish and strengthen democracies; participating in peace missions in Ethiopia, Eritrea, Liberia, Sudan, South Sudan, Uganda, the Korean Peninsula, Haiti, Bosnia and Herzegovina, and the Middle East; creation and leadership of a coalition that has reduced the incidence of guinea-worm disease from an estimated 3.5 million cases in 1986 to 25 at present, making it likely to be the first human disease since smallpox to be eradicated; helping to establish a village-based health care delivery system in thousands of communities in Africa; working with national ministries of health in Latin America and Africa to eliminate river blindness, with success declared in Colombia (2013), Ecuador (2014), Mexico (2015) and Guatemala (2016).

III. A Continuing Faith and Persistence in the Cause of Human Rights

In 2002, after the first 21 years on the global stage post-presidency Jimmy Carter was awarded the Nobel Peace Prize. It is useful to reflect upon what the committee had to say in their presentation:

> The Norwegian Nobel Committee has decided to award the Nobel Peace Prize for 2002 to Jimmy Carter, for his decades of untiring effort to find peaceful solutions to international conflicts, to advance democracy and human rights, and to promote economic and social development. That long sentence reflects the fact that this year's Laureate has contributed in practically all the areas that have figured most prominently through the one hundred and one years of Peace Prize history. He was the politician who during his presidency attempted to bring about a more peaceful world. He was, and continues to be, the mediator who seeks peaceful solutions to international conflicts. He was, and is, engaged in disarmament and arms control. He has shown, and still shows, an outstanding commitment to

---

[18] The Carter Center, 'Our Mission', available at www.cartercenter.org/about/mission.html.

democracy and human rights. His humanitarian and social activities have been, and are still, far-reaching.[19]

Sixteen years later, he continues his work, and while age and illness have slowed his pace in very recent years, he remains actively engaged in the Carter Center's voluminous activities. He also continues as perhaps the globe's most well-known and persistent human rights voice and activist with the ability to gain access to the leadership of both states and oppositions.

The lessons we can draw from Jimmy Carter are based in his persistence of commitment, unwillingness to accept failure, the belief that we each need to play a role in the fight for human rights and an unyielding faith in the ability of human beings to take responsibility for themselves and each other.[20] As Douglas Brinkley, his foremost biographer, wrote on his 90th birthday with reference to his persistence 'Rave on Jimmy Carter'.[21]

While he was formed by, and remains firmly based in, the American political culture in which he was raised, Carter's vision has always also been global. These ideas and ideals are captured in his farewell address upon leaving the American presidency. He argued:

> The battle for human rights – at home and abroad – is far from over. We should never be surprised nor discouraged because the impact of our efforts has had, and will always have, varied results. Rather, we should take pride that the ideals which gave birth to our nation still inspire the hopes of oppressed people around the world. We have no cause for self-righteousness or complacency. But we have every reason to persevere, both within our own country and beyond our borders.[22]

Thirty-six years later, in April 2017, delivering the Bederman Lecture at Emory University and in responses to audience questions he was still 'preaching' the gospel of human rights and bringing the message to all citizens in terms of what anyone and everyone could do to improve human rights conditions for others. Throughout, he invited his audience to think about 'how human rights applies to people who are different from us and how it affects us indirectly'. In responses to audience questions he urged that each person read the Universal Declaration of Human Rights and then

> ... take two or three of those commitments that you know are being violated and do what you personally can to end the violation ... If you run for office, being a champion of human rights may not be the most popular thing to do ... let human rights guide you.[23]

[19] The Norwegian Nobel Committee, 'The Nobel Peace Prize for 2002', available at www.nobelprize.org/prizes/peace/2002/press-release.

[20] A Banks, 'I Still Have Faith in the Ability of Human Beings. At 93 Jimmy Carter Talks About His New and Possibly Last Book' *Salt Lake Tribune* (Salt Lake City, 10 April 2018), available at www.sltrib.com/news/politics/2018/04/16/i-still-have-faith-in-the-ability-of-human-beings-at-93-jimmy-carter-talks-about-his-new-and-possibly-last-book.

[21] D Brinkley (n 14).

[22] J Carter, 'Farewell Address to the Nation' 14 January 1981, available at www.presidency.ucsb.edu/ws/index.php?pid=44516.

[23] K Williams, 'President Carter Discusses Human Rights in Bederman Lecture' *Emory Report* (Atlanta, 10 April 2017), available at news.emory.edu/stories/2017/04/er_carter_bederman_lecture_human_rights/campus.html.

The impact of Jimmy Carter's life and example is perhaps best expressed by one of the victims whose survival was directly affected by the changes that he championed and effected in US human rights policy and all that he did following his presidency. Upon emerging from the depths of the repressive machinery of the former Argentine regime, Jacobo Timerman publicly expressed his gratitude for Carter and his human rights policy, saying, 'Those of us who were imprisoned, those who are in prison still, will never forget President Carter and his contribution to the battle for human rights'.[24]

[24] Reuters, 'Timerman Criticizes Reagan on Human Rights Policy,' *New York Times* (New York, 15 June 1981), available at www.nytimes.com/1981/06/15/world/around-the-world-timerman-criticizes-reagan-on-human-rights-policy.html.

26

Peter Leuprecht
Human Dignity as a Lifetime Compass

WOLFGANG BENEDEK

> Democracy, rule of law, and human rights must show their strength at times of crisis and stress, when the going is rough. Never should a democratic state based on the rule of law and respect for human rights use the same methods as the terrorists ... Combatting terrorism requires the reaffirmation of human rights values, not their rejection.[1]

20 years ago, on the occasion of the 50th anniversary of the Universal Declaration of Human Rights, Peter Leuprecht published an article, the title of which still sounds very topical for the 70th anniversary, ie 'Macht und Ohnmacht der Menschenrechte' (Power and Impotence of Human Rights),[2] in which he drew attention to the growing role of irrationality and nationalism. Today, in times of a backlash against human rights and of international law in general, combined with a shrinking space for civil society, the challenge is even greater. In such difficult times there is a particular need for role models, for personalities who show the way forward by their life, and from whom others can learn and gain confidence in their own beliefs. Such a person is Peter Leuprecht.

I. An Optimistic Servant of Human Rights

Peter Leuprecht was born in 1937, the year before the 'Anschluss', in Salzburg, Austria. Since his parents were in trouble under the Nazi regime, Leuprecht spent the early

---

[1] P Leuprecht, 'An International Perspective on Anti-Terrorism Laws and Academic Freedom' in JL Turk and A Manson (eds), *Free Speech in Fearful Times: After 9/11 in Canada, the US, Australia & Europe* (Toronto, James Lorimer & Company Ltd, 2007) 115.

[2] P Leuprecht, *Macht und Ohnmacht der Menschenrechte: Überlegungen zum 50-jährigen Jubiläum der Allgemeinen Erklärung der Menschenrechte* (Vaduz, Verlag der Liechtensteinischen Akademischen Gesellschaft, 1998).

years of his childhood in the area of 'Ausserfern', also known as the district of Reutte in the countryside of Tyrol. There he experienced solidarity among the people, which shaped his commitment to European values. He studied law at the University of Innsbruck, where from 1958 to 1961 he worked as assistant to Professor Felix Ermacora, the first Austrian member of the European Commission of Human Rights. His father was a lawyer and after his studies Leuprecht worked for some time in his office.

In 1961 Leuprecht joined the General Secretariat of the Council of Europe. From 1961 to 1976 he worked in the Office the Parliamentary Assembly, then moved on to the Committee of Ministers and from 1980 to 1993 he served as Director of Human Rights. In 1993 he was elected Deputy Secretary General but ultimately resigned from his post in 1997 because of his concern about the dilution of Council of Europe standards in the enlargement of the organisation.

Leuprecht was actively involved in bringing Portugal and Spain and later post-communist countries from central and eastern Europe into the Council of Europe. However, he had serious misgivings about the lowering of standards with regard to some admissions, in particular Croatia (under Tudjman) and Russia, which, in his view, did not as yet meet the requirements for membership.

In 1997 Leuprecht moved to Canada. From 1997 to 1999 he was visiting professor at the Faculty of Law of McGill University and at the Department of Juridical Sciences of the Université du Québec à Montréal (UQAM), while working – as adviser to the Federal Department of Justice of Canada – to promote the domestic implementation of international human rights law in Canada. From 1999 to 2003 he served as Dean of the Faculty of Law of McGill University.

From 2000 to 2005 he acted a Special Representative of the UN Secretary General for human rights in Cambodia. From 2003 to 2008 he was the Director of the Montreal Institute of International Studies and professor of public international law at the Department of Juridical Sciences of UQAM. He also taught at several other universities, such as the Universities of Strasbourg and Nancy (France) and at the European Academy of Law in Florence (Italy). For his engagement he received several prizes such as the 'Prix du Civisme Européen' in 1991 and the Human Rights Award of the Lord Reading Law Society in 2001.

His personality is characterised by modesty and integrity, with a strong sense of humour. He also has a love for music and sports. He is a fine lawyer, not dogmatic, but open to new ideas, committed to the cause. As a human rights advocate he always preserves his high ethical standards. As an optimistic servant of human rights, he can be quite outspoken, when there is a need for something to be said, following a moral compass in good and turbulent times. He also is a realist with no concession on substance, a critical mind, showing patience and perseverance in his work. As a man of principle he is living the European and universal values of human rights, rule of law and pluralist democracy, strongly believing in the equal dignity of all human beings, including migrants.

II. Shaping the History of Human Rights

In the course of his career, Leuprecht was confronted with major human rights challenges such as the three dictatorships in western Europe, including those in Greece, Portugal and Spain. From 1967 he played a prominent role in the fight of Europe against the Greek military dictatorship, as the staff member working with Max van der Stoel, rapporteur of the Parliamentary Assembly, who later became the first High Commissioner on National Minorities of the OSCE.[3] For the first time he was directly confronted with the practice of torture. In 1969, van der Stoel and Leuprecht were both declared persona non grata by the regime. In December 1969 it came to the de facto suspension of Greece from the Council of Europe. After the fall of the dictatorship in 1974, Leuprecht was sent to Greece to prepare the readmission of the country to the Council of Europe. He was also actively involved in bringing Portugal and Spain into the organisation, after the collapse of the dictatorships in the two countries.

As Director of Human Rights Leuprecht played a key role in the negotiation and conclusion of Protocol 6 to the ECHR concerning the abolition of the death penalty. He also was among those who early on saw a need to protect the human rights of asylum seekers and migrants. Leuprecht was quoted as saying 'The efficacy of a human rights protection system can be best evaluated by its treatment of prisoners and foreigners'.[4] In 1984 he denounced the threats against the right to asylum in *Le Monde Diplomatique*.[5]

He had a crucial role in the elaboration and conclusion of the European Convention for the Prevention of Torture and Inhuman and Degrading Treatment, adopted in 1987. The original idea of providing an international body with free access to all places of detention in order to prevent torture and inhuman treatment came from the former Swiss banker Jean-Jacques Gautier, with whom Leuprecht kept close relations.

As Director of Human Rights, Leuprecht pushed for the streamlining of human rights activities within the Council of Europe. He persuaded the Secretary General to transfer the secretariats of the European Social Charter and of the European Committee for Equality between Women and Men to the Directorate on Human Rights.[6] He then actively promoted the reform of the European Social Charter in order to make it more efficient.

---

[3] P Leuprecht, 'Max van der Stoel: A Tireless Defender of Greek Democracy' (2011) 22(3) *Security and Human Rights* 183.

[4] O Delas, 'Le Renvoi des Étrangers vers un Risque de Mauvais Traitment: L'Arrêt N. c. Royaume Uni ou la Cour Européene des Droits de L'Homme en Terrain Glissant?' in O Delas and M Leuprecht (eds), *Liber Amicorum Peter Leuprecht* (Brussels, Éditions Bruylant 2012) 323.

[5] P Leuprecht, 'Menaces sur le Droits d'Asile, Inquiétude dans l'Europe de droits de l'homme' *Le Monde Diplomatique* (August 1984), 16.

[6] A Drzemczewski, 'Reflections on a Remarkable Period of Eleven Years: 1986–1997', in Delas and Leuprecht (n 4) 105, 106.

Leuprecht played an important role in the preparation and work of the Vienna Summit of Heads of State and Government of the Council of Europe in October 1993, which produced a number of very important decisions to respond to the new challenges emanating from the end of the Cold War and the enlargement of the Council of Europe. One of the decisions of the Conference supported the struggle against racism, antisemitism, xenophobia and intolerance, an old concern of Leuprecht, and with his assistance led to the Summit decision of the creation of the European Commission on Racism and Intolerance (ECRI). Another concerned the protection of minorities, which was also a concern of Leuprecht, and resulted in the adoption of the Framework Convention on National Minorities in 1994.

According to the former President of the European Court of Human Rights, Rolv Ryssdal, Leuprecht was one of the fathers of the reform of the European Court of Human Rights by Protocol 11 to the ECHR.[7] He chaired the working party set up on his advice to prepare the transition. Thus, he helped transform the dualist institutional mechanism to a permanent single court, which turned out to be indispensable in the light of the number of applications coming from new Member States.

Leuprecht spoke out against major human rights violations such as the ones occurring in the wars in the successor states of former Yugoslavia in the early 1990s. He used his speeches at various occasions to highlight 'the relapse to barbarism in the very heart of Europe'. And he personally contributed to establishing a centre for human rights at the University of Sarajevo after the war.[8]

Leuprecht was and is highly critical of market fundamentalism and its negative impact on human rights, especially economic, social and cultural rights. In his view the pan-economic ideology threatened human rights. In this way he also commented on the impact of globalisation on human rights against which he put the concept of the common good.[9]

As Deputy Secretary General from 1993 to 1997 Leuprecht had responsibility for the whole operational work of the Council of Europe, with a staff of 1,600, but also the major task of dealing with the historic situation after the end of the Cold War and the fall of the Berlin wall in 1989. Before and after 1993 he was closely involved in the accession negotiations of central and eastern European countries to the Council of Europe, insisting that they respect the European human rights standards.[10] In response to the problem of maintaining the standards of the Council of Europe in view of the accession of new countries, which were often not ready for their new obligations, he supported the establishment of a confidential general mechanism to monitor compliance, which was introduced in 1995. It reviewed the performance of all Member States regarding certain priorities, such as freedom of expression. In his work of opening the Council of Europe to the east, he insisted on firm standards

---

[7] ibid, 105, 110.

[8] P Leuprecht, 'Human Rights: The Foundation of Justice and Peace' in W Benedek (ed), *Bosnia-Herzegovina after Dayton: From Theory to Practice* (The Hague, Martinus Nijhoff, 1999) 15.

[9] P Leuprecht, 'Idéologie pan-économique et bien commun' in O Delas and C Deblock (eds), *Le bien commun comme réponse à la mondialisation* (Bruxelles, Èditions Bruyllant 2003) 1.

[10] P Leuprecht, *General Course on Human Rights in the New Europe, Academy of European Law, Collected Courses 1996* (The Hague, 1997).

versus 'realpolitik' and remained committed to preserving the 'soul' of the European system.[11]

He used to argue caution when compromising principles in order to partner with power. This concern can be seen in his position that the 'margin of appreciation' should be handled with extreme care so as not to risk a dilution of the substance of human rights.[12] He always had an open ear for civil society and human rights defenders and promoted the establishment of the Office of the European Commissioner for Human Rights, realised in 1999. This office has the mandate to deal also with new human rights challenges not as yet adequately covered by the other instruments of the Council of Europe.

The promotion and protection of the rights of minorities and their languages was another concern of Leuprecht, who participated in conferences on the Slovene minority in Carinthia and opened the Council of Europe Centre on Modern Languages in Graz in 1995. In Canada he continued work in this field, focusing on indigenous people.

His strong commitment to the principles of the Council of Europe made him resign after 36 years with the Council in 1997, before the end of his mandate, because he could not accept the watering down of the principles and values of the Council by the admission of the Russian Federation, which at that time was engaged in a bloody war in Chechnya. He also had misgivings about the – in his view premature – accessions of Romania and Croatia.[13] Because his concerns were not sufficiently supported by the European governments, Leuprecht decided that he could not stay in government as a dissident.[14]

It is also important to highlight the role of Peter Leuprecht, together with Catherine Lalumière, Antonio Cassese and Mary Robinson in the 'Comité des sages', entrusted with elaborating a human rights agenda for the European Union during the Austrian chairmanship of the EU in 1998.[15] The Committee advocated accession of the European Union to the ECHR (an idea debated for many years) and to the European Social Charter.

Moving to Canada in 1997, Leuprecht quickly impressed his academic colleagues as an exemplary intellectual who fascinated his audiences. In his work as a professor and Dean of Law at McGill University, and later as Director of the newly-created Montreal Institute of International Studies and Professor of Public International Law at the Département des Sciences Juridiques de l'UQAM, but also in his work for the Department of Justice in Ottawa, he showed particular concern for the danger of a decline or neglect of international law, coming under pressure in particular after the events of 9/11.[16] At the Department of Justice and thereafter he tried to help

---

[11] C Lalumière, 'Un Grand Serviteur des Droits de L'Homme' in Delas and Leuprecht (n 4) 215.

[12] P Leuprecht, 'Introduction: Special Section on European Integration' (2001) 46(4) *McGill Law Journal* 845.

[13] Drzemczewski (n 6) 115.

[14] See 'Interview with Peter Leuprecht' *Neue Zürcher Zeitung* (Zurich, 30–31 August 1997).

[15] A Cassese et al, 'Leading by Example: A Human Rights Agenda for the European Union for the Year 2000: Agenda of the Comité des Sages and Final Project Report' (Florence, Academy of European Law, European University Institute, 1998).

[16] P Leuprecht, *Déclin du droit international?* (Québec, PIL, 2009).

Canadian judges to overcome their anxieties about international law.[17] He was also concerned with internal Canadian human rights issues, such as the rights of aboriginal peoples.

As Special Representative of the UN Secretary General for human rights in Cambodia from 2000 to 2005 he undertook his mission in a spirit of compassion and solidarity with the Cambodian people. He had a stormy relationship with Cambodia's strongman, Hun Sen. He denounced the irresponsible management of land and natural resources and the lack of independence of the judiciary, while supporting the emergence of a Cambodian civil society. Leuprecht did not fear the confrontation with the Cambodian government, which wanted to silence him. He detected four basic evils affecting the country: ie poverty, violence, corruption and lawlessness. In front of the UN General Assembly he said that the country had been left alone by the international community in the most difficult moments of its troubled history, and criticised 'deals' in the UN to the disadvantage of the people of Cambodia. In his passionate last speech before the General Assembly he pleaded to keep Cambodia on its agenda, but in vain. Nonetheless, he provided regular and thematic reports to the Human Rights Commission, ending his mandate with 'disillusioned frankness' in his final report.[18] After his resignation the Cambodian King Sihanouk sent him a letter expressing his sincere appreciation.[19]

Leuprecht also involved himself in the work of NGOs he found worth supporting. He has been a member of Amnesty International for some 40 years. He sat on the board of the francophone section of Amnesty International in Canada, which made him an honorary member. He was also involved in the People's Movement for Human Rights Education, which promoted the UN Decade on Human Rights Education and human rights at the local level through human rights cities.[20] He drew early attention to the relevance of human rights education also in the context of the new Europe.[21] He also argued in favour of the abolition of study fees in Quebec in order to ensure the right to education.[22]

Furthermore, Leuprecht contributed to the debate on the inclusion of human rights in the information society by playing a key role in a seminar on Information Society, Human Dignity and Human Rights in Geneva during the World Summit on the Information. Society in 2003 and in Montreal in 2004.[23] This issue has since become very important.

---

[17] M Rivet and M Montpetit, 'La Réception du Droit International dans le Droit Interne Canadien: Une Ouverture Dynamique des Systèmes Juridiques' in Delas and Leuprecht (n 4) 367, 388.

[18] P Leprecht, *Situation of Human Rights in Cambodia, Report of the Special Representative of the Secretary-General for Human Rights in Cambodia*, 20 December 2004, UN Doc E/CN.4/2005/116.

[19] M Picken, 'The Special Representative of the UN Secretary-General for Human Rights in Cambodia (2000–2005)' in Delas and Leuprecht (n 4) 265 ff.

[20] W Lichem, 'The Growing Societal Dimension of our Human Rights Agenda' in Delas and Leuprecht (n 4) 16 ff.

[21] P Leuprecht, 'L'éducation aux droits de l'homme: nouveau défis dans une Europe nouvelle' (1992) 92(2) *Inter-Dialogos* 11.

[22] P Leuprecht, 'Une ambition pour le Quebéc: une éducation accessible à tous' *Le Devoir* (Montreal, 16 June 2012).

[23] See P Leuprecht, 'Der Weltgipfel zur Informationsgesellschaft aus der Sicht der Menschenrechte (The World Summit on the Informations Society from the Perspective of Human Rights)' in W Benedek

Leuprecht co-signed an amicus curiae brief to the Supreme Court of the United States on the case of a young Canadian, Omar Khadr, held in detention in Guantánamo since 2002. In his writings and on Canadian television he strongly criticised the 'anti-terrorist' measures taken by President George W Bush and the US administration after 9/11, in particular in Guantánamo, the Military Commissions and the practice of torture by the US.[24]

III. The Legacy of Peter Leuprecht

According to the former Secretary General of the Council of Europe, Catherine Lalumière, 'Peter Leuprecht was one of the persons who had the largest influence on the action of the Council of Europe in the period before and after the fall of the Berlin wall'.[25] She pointed out that Leuprecht personally represented the social and human dimension of the European construction. His strategy was to build an alliance of like-minded progressive countries and to isolate those who resisted. Being a rigorous lawyer, his authority was respected also in other international organisations.[26] The former President of the European Court of Human Rights, Jean-Paul Costa, emphasised Leuprecht's contribution to the system of human rights protection in Europe, in particular in the establishment of the permanent European Court of Human Rights by the 11th Protocol.[27] The number of complaints addressed to the European Court on Human Rights has increased significantly.

Others pointed to the mark he left in Canada: he encouraged new ways of thinking and new approaches to the domestic implementation of international obligations, critical that Canada was not receptive enough to international law, and making practical proposals that had a lasting effect on Canadian practice, which has since opened up to international law.[28]

He was an inspiring teacher who provided a moral compass to generations of students by his personal example. As a Dean he was highly engaged with students, relating to them directly and authentically. He usually would not give them the answers, but let them develop their own minds in relation to the problems discussed. He raised

and C Pekari (eds), *Menschenrechte in der Informationsgesellschaft (Human Rights in the Informations Society)* (Stuttgart, Richard Boorberg, 2007) 23; M Lavoie, P Leuprecht 'Beyond WSIS: Incorporating Human Rights Perspectives into the Information Society Debate' (2005) 18(1) *Revue Québécoise de Droit Internationale* 1.

[24] P Leuprecht, 'Torture made in USA' (2008) 729 *Relations*, available at cjf.qc.ca/revue-relations/publication/article/torture-made-in-usa/; P Leuprecht, 'Résurgence de la bête immonde: retour et banalisation de la torture' in *Les droits de l'homme en évolution, mélanges en l'honneur du Professeur Petros J Pararas* (Athens, Bruylant, 2009) 349; P Leuprecht, 'La torture banalisée' (2006) 712 *Relations*.

[25] Lalumière (n 11) 211.

[26] ibid, 212.

[27] JP Costa, 'Peter Leuprecht et la Convention Européene des Droits de L'Homme' in Delas and Leuprecht (n 4) 425, 429.

[28] J Scratch, 'Peter Leuprecht and Canada's Ratification and Implementation of International Human Rights' in Delas and Leuprecht (n 4) 389, 395.

their awareness of the corruptive force of power. Generous with his time, he helped students advance their careers in law and human rights.[29]

He always remained a critical observer of threats to human rights. Though a convinced European, he felt and feels that the EU is going the wrong way by being at the same time a promoter and a victim of market fundamentalism, by abandoning the European social model and by building Europe as a fortress. Against this trend he emphasises the idea of the '*bonum commune*' and of solidarity, hoping that European citizens will take ownership of the European construct in a bottom-up approach.[30]

Leuprecht has written widely on issues of human rights and international law with a focus on Europe and Canada, but also examining the universality of human rights and intercultural and interreligious dialogue. His book *Reason, Justice and Dignity, A Journey to Some Unexplored Sources of Human Rights*, published in 2012, is a contribution to this dialogue.[31] He begins with quotes from the preamble and Article 1 of the Universal Declaration of Human Rights and addresses three stages of a journey presented in individual chapters. In the first chapter on 'Harmony Through Humaneness', he analyses ancient Chinese sources focusing on Confucius and Mencius; in the second on 'Faith and Reason' he explores medieval Islamic sources based on Avicenna, Averroes and Ibn Khaldun; and in the third on 'Equal Dignity of Others' he investigates the sixteenth century writings of Bartolomé de Las Casas and Francisco de Vitoria. Leuprecht shows us in this book that there is a larger basis for the universality of human rights than commonly assumed when human rights are presented as a western concept, but that there also is a need to accept diversity, though this might not be easy.[32] Interreligious and intercultural dialogues can benefit from the ideas behind human rights, which can be found in all major civilisations, as demonstrated in the book's examination of insufficiently-explored sources of human rights. Leuprecht submits that comprehension of the 'other' and 'otherness' is the way to identifying commonalities and the unity of humankind.[33] As he wrote on another occasion: 'Peace and harmony must be built on respect for the other and for otherness, difference and diversity, on the basis of a shared ethic of humanity – that of the equal dignity of every human being'.[34]

He followed this publication with articles such as 'Islam – enemy of human rights?' in which he showed that, contrary to what is often claimed, Islam as such is not opposed to human rights, but that an enlightened Islam as represented by the great thinkers of

---

[29] N Weisbord, 'The Dean's Compass' in Delas and Leuprecht (n 4) 411 ff.

[30] P Leuprecht, 'L'Europe fait-elle fausse route ?' in J-P Jacqué et al (eds), *On the International Community: Legal, Political, Diplomatic Issues* (Athens, I Sideris Publishing, 2017) 223.

[31] P Leuprecht, *Reason, Justice and Dignity: A Journey to Some Unexplored Sources of Human Rights* (Leiden/Boston, Martinus Nijhoff Publishers, 2012).

[32] P Leuprecht, 'The Difficult Acceptance of Diversity, in Accommodating Differences: The Present and the Future of the Law of Diversity' (2006) 30(3) *Vermont Law Review* 551.

[33] Leuprecht (n 31) 5, 103.

[34] Leuprecht (n 32) 564.

the golden age of Islam can make an important contribution to the worldwide efforts in favour of human rights.[35]

In the best ways he has devoted his life to human rights, professionally and personally.[36] A presentation of him by the Austrian Radio and TV in 2009 was appropriately entitled 'For a Europe of law and humanity'.[37] But it should be added that his concern has always been humanity as a whole.

[35] P Leuprecht, 'L'Islam: ennemi des droits de l'homme ?' in L Panella and E Spatafora (eds), *Studi in onore di Claudio Zanghi* vol II (Turin, Giappichelli Editore, 2012) 435.

[36] GW Li-Jing, 'An Interview with Dr Peter Leuprecht: A Life devoted to Human Rights' (2003) 23 *Singapore Law Review* 22.

[37] J Kneihs, 'Menschenbilder: Peter Leuprecht: Für ein Europa des Rechts und der Humanität' (2009) 1 ORF (1 May 2009).

27

Juan E Méndez

A Figurehead of the Fight Against Impunity for Grave Rights Violations

ELAINE WEBSTER

> Victories are hard fought and often won, but new challenges appear, and Sisyphus-like human rights activists must start again to push the rock upward.[1]

I. Responding to State Repression in Argentina

Juan E Méndez has a power of relaying his extraordinary life events whilst still allowing one to identify strongly with him and his experiences. This is because he has spoken and written so honestly about his personal experiences and exile from his native Argentina in the 1970s. He has been open about pain, loneliness, relief, family separation and reunification, gratitude, hope, and frustration. This willingness to share alongside his commitment to solidarity and constant advocacy over the past four decades have made Méndez a symbol of human rights movements. As Mark S Ellis has written: 'In the field of human rights, there is no greater advocate than Juan Méndez'.[2] Méndez' work shows that he is at his core an advocate for social justice.

Méndez was born on 11 December 1944 and spent much of his youth, with his parents and siblings, in the town of Mar del Plata. Méndez' early years, the mid-1940s to mid-1950s, were marked by the presidency of military officer General Juan D Perón, brought to power through widespread popular electoral support and deposed by military coup in 1955. This period followed, and was itself followed by,

---

[1] JE Méndez with M Wentworth, *Taking a Stand: The Evolution of Human Rights* (New York, Palgrave MacMillan, 2011) 74.
[2] Méndez (n 1) front matter.

economic depression and decades of precarious civilian governments and military rule. The political landscape of Méndez' young adult years, including his years as a law student in the 1960s, was characterised by political division, political violence and repression of political opposition in the context of large-scale labour movements, social uprisings and student occupations. Méndez has himself described the early 1970s, in which the military government was forced to concede to elections and which saw the return of Perón to the presidency, as a time of political turmoil and factionism. Perón aligned with the right wing of the Peronist movement, and Méndez has written, '[b]y 1974, there were early signs that these right-wing groups were beginning to enjoy support from the police and the military, as they had during the military dictatorship'.[3] After graduating in 1970, Méndez had become a teacher at the Universidad Católica Stella Maris where he had himself studied. He also practised law, including acting on behalf of student activists and political prisoners. This work, alongside his own political engagement in this context of increasingly repressive governance, ultimately led to torture, detention and exile. He has written that previous threats he had suffered as a result of his political views and legal work began to pale in comparison to his experience of police actions in the early 1970s. In 1974, he was arrested and detained for the first time. Federal Police officers concocted criminal charges and manipulated evidence in support of his detention. The political climate in Argentina had shifted for the worse.

During a state of emergency under the government of Isabel Perón, who had become President after her husband's death, Méndez was again arrested in August 1975 after having moved to Buenos Aires. He was transferred to the Intelligence Service of the Police of the Province of Buenos Aires. Méndez has written openly about his experience of being held in secret detention where interrogators inflicted electric shocks and severe beatings; he was neither permitted to eat nor drink and was subjected to psychological torture, including mock execution. When transferred to another region in the country, a judge heard and dismissed fabricated car theft and weapon possession charges, but Méndez was transferred to administrative detention without charge under the rules of the state of emergency. He has described this period of detention 'as a time of utter desolation'[4] on account of the uncertainty, poor conditions, periods of solitary confinement, severe physical ill-treatment of other prisoners, repressive measures of control, violent searches, and humiliations. He remained there for 18 months. In 1977, he was escorted to the airport and left Argentina in exile.

After some months in France, he moved with his young family to the United States. He later qualified to practise law there, attending the American University in Washington part-time. He focused on the fate of other political prisoners at home and the urgent need to respond to the practice of forced disappearance, which had become systemic in Argentina between the mid-1970s and early 1980s. He remained propelled by an unshakeable sense of solidarity and an urgency to provide support for accountability in Latin America.

---

[3] ibid, 2.
[4] ibid, 13.

II. Giving Substance to Human Rights through Solidarity and Accountability

After arriving in the US, Méndez lived in Illinois and Chicago with his family before moving to Washington, DC. In his first jobs he worked in community-based legal advice (1977–78) and undertook paralegal work for a public interest law firm (1978–81). He concurrently tried to support relatives of the Argentinian disappeared and supported advocacy efforts to move towards justice. In 1982, he was responsible for opening the Washington DC office of Human Rights Watch, his first job after having studied to be admitted to the US Bar. This was the emergence of the global human rights NGO movement. Over a period of almost 15 years (1982–96), he made a decisive contribution in this role: to practices of monitoring, reporting, strengthening due process and evidential rules, and aggressively pursuing prosecution, truth and accountability. He played important roles campaigning on human rights violations in Central America and acting on behalf of the relatives of disappeared persons, including in the landmark judgment in *Velásquez Rodríguez v Honduras* of the Inter-American Court of Human Rights in 1988,[5] recognised as a defining moment in Inter-American *and* international human rights litigation. Méndez later served as General Counsel of Human Rights Watch. In 1991, Méndez was also one of the founding members of the Centre for Justice and International Law, focused on supporting human rights protections in the Americas, which recently marked its 25th anniversary.[6]

Following Méndez' pivotal impact during this time at Human Rights Watch, he undertook other regional human rights leadership roles, including within the Inter-American human rights regime. He served as Executive Director of the Inter-American Institute of Human Rights (1996–99), in which a key focus was electoral monitoring and reform in the region, and during his time as Professor of Law and Director of the Center for Civil and Human Rights at the University of Notre Dame (1999–2004), he was elected by the Organization of American States as a member of the Inter-American Commission on Human Rights. He served as Special Rapporteur on the Rights of Migrant Workers and Their Families, as Vice-President and later President of the Commission.

After a four-year term at the Inter-American Commission, Méndez was invited to become President of the International Center for Transitional Justice (ICTJ) (2004–2009) and remains its President Emeritus. The ICTJ was established in 2001 to support justice and accountability for victims and the rebuilding of the rule of law in societies after gross human rights violations. In 2017, the ICTJ nominated Méndez to sit on the Colombian Selection Committee, established by the Colombian Peace agreement to select those who would play a key role in the institutions of the peace process.

---

[5] *Velásquez Rodríguez Case*, Inter-AmCtHR (Ser C) No 4 (1988).
[6] See www.cejil.org/en.

Méndez' contribution to human rights is also recognised at the international level. He was the first UN Special Adviser to the Secretary General on the Prevention of Genocide (2004–2007) and Special Advisor to the Prosecutor of the International Criminal Court on Crime Prevention (2009–10). In 2010, Méndez became the fifth UN Special Rapporteur on Torture and Other Cruel, Inhuman and Degrading Treatment or Punishment (2010–16). The Special Rapporteurship on Torture and Other Cruel, Inhuman or Degrading Treatment or Punishment is one of the most well-established of the United Nations Special Procedures. In interviews, he has expressed frustration about the limitations of this role (and other roles he has undertaken) – non-responsive governments and lack of financial resources[7] – but he achieved results. A key example of this is on solitary confinement. In a 2011 report, Méndez considered evidence of the impact of solitary confinement on individuals, concluding that solitary confinement of more than 15 days and solitary confinement of minors and persons with disabilities could amount to cruel, inhuman and degrading treatment and in some cases torture, and that shorter periods could also constitute prohibited treatment.[8] He was clear that this assessment applied to various contexts of detention, beyond prisons. The 2011 report has been described as 'groundbreaking and historic'.[9] It lent support to the efforts of those advocating for stricter standards,[10] influencing the drafting of the 2015 Nelson Mandela Rules. These rules were adopted by Resolution of the UN General Assembly in 2015 as an amendment of the UN's Standard Minimum Rules for the Treatment of Prisoners;[11] the key standard of reference for prison governance and monitoring.[12] The Nelson Mandela Rules include for the first time international limits for solitary confinement. Méndez' other thematic reports during this mandate included addressing practices of investigating patterns of torture and other ill-treatment,[13] the conceptualisation of torture and other ill-treatment in healthcare contexts,[14] and the prohibition as applied to children deprived of liberty.[15] In fulfilling this mandate over two terms, Méndez took

---

[7] Amnesty International, 'Juan Mendez: The Torturers' Worst Nightmare', 10 December 2014, available at www.amnesty.org/en/latest/news/2014/12/juan-mendez-torturers-worst-nightmare.

[8] UN General Assembly, 'Interim Report of the Special Rapporteur of the Human Rights Council on Torture and other Cruel, Inhuman or Degrading Treatment or Punishment' 5 August 2011, A/66/268.

[9] JE Méndez, *Seeing into Solitary: A Review of the Laws and Policies of Certain Nations Regarding Solitary Confinement Detainees* (Weil, Gotshal and Manges LLP, Cyrus R Vance Center for International Justice, Anti-Torture Initiative, Center for Human Rights and Humanitarian Law at American University Washington College of Law, October 2016).

[10] ibid, 12.

[11] UN General Assembly, United Nations Standard Minimum Rules for the Treatment of Prisoners (The Nelson Mandela Rules) (8 January 2016) UN Doc A/RES/70/175.

[12] OSCE Office for Democratic Institutions and Human Rights and Penal Reform International, *Guidance Document on the Nelson Mandela Rules: Implementing the United Nations Revised Standard Minimum Rules for the Treatment of Prisoners*, 2018, 2, available at s16889.pcdn.co/wp-content/uploads/2018/07/MR_Guidance_Doc.pdf.

[13] UN Human Rights Council, 'Report of the Special Rapporteur on Torture and Other Cruel, Inhuman or Degrading Treatment or Punishment, Juan E Méndez' (18 January 2012) UN Doc A/HRC/19/61.

[14] UN Human Rights Council, 'Report of the Special Rapporteur on Torture and Other Cruel, Inhuman or Degrading Treatment or Punishment, Juan E Méndez (1 February 2013) UN Doc A/HRC/22/53.

[15] UN Human Rights Council, 'Report of the Special Rapporteur on Torture and Other Cruel, Inhuman or Degrading Treatment or Punishment, Juan E Méndez' (5 March 2015) A/HRC/28/68.

a characteristic subtle-yet-radical approach: a pragmatic perspective whilst neverthe-less pushing the boundaries of current understandings.

Méndez' work has been recognised through several awards: the Monsignor Oscar A. Romero Award for Leadership in Service to Human Rights,[16] the Jeanne and Joseph Sullivan Award,[17] the Louis B Sohn Award,[18] the Letelier-Moffitt Human Rights Award,[19] the Rafael Lemkin Award,[20] the Goler T. Butcher Medal,[21] the Adlai Stevenson Award,[22] and the Eclipse Award.[23] In 2017, Duke University and the Washington Office on Latin America renamed their collaborative non-fiction book award to become the 'Juan E Méndez Book Award for Human Rights in Latin America', in honour of Méndez' distinguished contributions.

Méndez is currently Professor of Human Rights Law in Residence at Washington College of Law, American University – which he himself attended in those early years after arriving in the US – and Director of the College's Anti-Torture Initiative. In 2011, Méndez' book was published: *Taking a Stand: The Evolution of Human Rights*.[24] It is an invaluable and accessible record of Méndez' experience and contribution to contemporary human rights history. It reads as part memoir and part masterclass. Méndez takes the reader on his journey, as he encountered major challenges and achievements of international human rights in contexts from arbitrary detention and torture to accountability for atrocity and the role of civil society.

Méndez' range of professional experience has allowed him to encounter a wide spectrum of human rights issues. He has made contributions that have positively impacted individuals and their families. He has been instrumental in the development of human rights advocacy methods and the development of regional and interna-tional human rights litigation, including procedural dimensions within litigation and interpretation of legal standards. He has contributed in both small and monumen-tal ways to addressing arbitrary detention, forced disappearances, torture and cruel, inhuman and degrading treatment and punishment, genocide, electoral reform, politi-cal corruption and censorship, and transitional justice. Underpinning all of Méndez' contributions across these fields is evidence of his commitment to solidarity and accountability.

This commitment manifests in two key threads evident across Méndez' work, writings and interviews over the years: recognition of the contributions and sacri-fices of individuals and faith in the rule of law. The first is a recognition of the complex roles and impacts of individuals, whether perpetrators, enablers, victims, or resisters. He has acknowledged how those inflicting torture in the name of the state are themselves forced to betray their profession. He has observed the role of medical experts who have facilitated torture, but others who have prevented it.

---

[16] University of Dayton, 2000.
[17] Heartland Alliance, 2003.
[18] United Nations Association of the National Capital Area, 2014.
[19] Institute for Policy Studies, 2014.
[20] Auschwitz Institute on Peace and Reconciliation, 2010.
[21] American Society of International Law, 2010.
[22] United Nations Associations of the United States, Princeton-Trenton Chapter, 2015.
[23] Center for Victims of Torture, 2016.
[24] Méndez (n 1).

He has acknowledged the individuals who were murdered and disappeared, always describing those that he knew by name and highlighting their contributions. He has acknowledged the role of individual judges in his own experiences when the rule of law was under threat, who did what they could to hold police to legal process. He has recognised the anguish faced by victims' relatives and their trying but impactful role in pressing for accountability. He has been marked by individuals who have shown resistance (a lone prison guard who refused to inflict ill-treatment on political prisoners) and the friends who stood up for him, from near and far, including the lawyers who supported his family and others to use the law for protection despite the inherent dangers of doing so. It is perhaps Méndez' experience of grave human rights violations that has led him to always recognise the individuals behind the wrongs and behind the legal texts. Drawing attention to the voices and faces of those individuals, which might otherwise seem abstract, far away and unrealistic, was a natural part of Méndez' own influential civil society activism, including, it seems, his decision to speak openly about the reality of his experience as a victim. Méndez also experienced first-hand the persistence and power of civil society advocates, having himself been adopted as an Amnesty International Prisoner of Conscience in 1976. He has recognised the crucial contribution that this and other international efforts made in his own case. He has demonstrated and promoted the power of civil society advocates as pivotal actors in making the stories of individuals known to the wider community and has stressed the impact of such stories on the opinions of ordinary people within that wider community; stories that are able to foster individual resistance and dilute tolerance of rights violations. His writings are perceptive of what philosopher Jonathan Glover has called 'the human responses';[25] ordinary people's natural inclination to solidarity which, when strong, can sustain resistance, but when weakened by a combination of fear and 'muted or diplomatic language' about the need for 'extraordinary measures in extraordinary times'[26] can be an enabling force for atrocity.

The second thread that runs throughout Méndez' contribution is a faith in and respect for the institution of law. He has explicitly expressed his long-standing desire to test the law's capacity to address injustice. The roots of this are evident in Méndez' writings about his own experience in the 1970s: of giving legal advice to friends through the bars of a police detention cell and of efforts amongst his peers to rely upon provisions of the Argentinian Constitution in response to administrative detention.[27] He shows a pragmatic belief in the capacity of the law and lawyers to act as a 'counterweight' to politics,[28] including in the pursuit of accountability. In relation to his own experience of being subjected to arbitrary State power, he has written that the 'real terror' came from understanding that state officials could do whatever they

---

[25] J Glover, *Humanity: A Moral History of the Twentieth Century* (London, Yale University Press, 1999) 406.

[26] JE Méndez, 'Torture in Latin America' in K Roth, M Warden and AD Bernstein (eds), *Torture: Does it Make Us Safer? Is it Ever OK? A Human Rights Perspective* (New York, New Press, 2005) 63.

[27] Méndez (n 1) ch 1.

[28] ibid, 63.

wanted without political or legal censure.[29] Alongside other sources of pressure, the law must play a key role. In *Taking a Stand*, Méndez wrote:

> Even with progressive legislation, the law is insufficient to protect all victims of all human rights violations; that is why I am convinced that the struggle for human rights requires multidisciplinary approaches and the coordinated efforts of many people with different talents and skills. But I am also persuaded that the law and lawyers must continue to play a decisive role at the center of that struggle.[30]

III. The Why and How of Human Rights

Méndez embodies the values and practices of the modern human rights regime: humanity above politics, and pragmatic persistence. Sharing his experiences helps others to understand the value of protecting human dignity. He has openly shared vulnerability and struggle but also grit and leadership. From his example we learn the need for vigilance. Of the grave rights violations in Argentina, he has written: '... the tragedy of torture, arbitrary arrest and disappearances could only happen because of a total and deliberate breakdown of the rule of law'.[31] He has reminded us that the breakdown of the rule of law within a state is a gradual process. He has also taught us the importance of public perceptions. He has talked about the insipid influence of 'entertainment' in popular culture on public opinion. He reminds us that there are no shortcuts; it is necessary to work ceaselessly to keep 'hearts and minds'[32] on board and to change them when damaging narratives take hold in response to security fears. We learn also about the need to innovate. This comes across in Méndez's early career experience of developing methods of documenting atrocities, and more recently in writings about his experience as adviser on genocide prevention: there is a need to continuously strive to increase the effectiveness of legal and advocacy tools and approaches. In his experience of human rights practice, Méndez has pointed out positives and possibilities even in bleak landscapes. He has highlighted limitations of the international human rights regime but at the same time its adaptability and achievements. In short, he has shown pragmatism but never scepticism. He has maintained a quiet hope that grave rights violations, like torture, can be eradicated. His manner has not been a loud and impassioned defence of human rights, but instead an ingrained commitment to act upon a very deeply-rooted sense of social justice. Even this is not explicit in Méndez' writings or interviews but rather seems so entrenched that it becomes almost unremarkable. In an interview in 2017 about his work on solitary confinement, he was described as

---

[29] ibid, 11.
[30] ibid, 115.
[31] ibid, 62.
[32] Sur International Journal of Human Rights, 'Juan E. Méndez: "We have lost a sense of purpose about eliminating torture', 25 July 2017, available at www.sur.conectas.org/en/juan-e-mendez-lost-sense-purpose-eliminating-torture.

possessing 'a natural air of dignity and conviction'.[33] This captures the personal qualities of Méndez as well as the nature of his responses and actions over the last four decades.

Méndez then, has been a constant advocate and leader, and has inspired others to defend human rights through sharing his experiences and demonstrating solidarity in his actions. The core of what lawyers, activists and others gain from Méndez is a clarity of purpose. As noted above, Méndez has a power of relaying his extraordinary life whilst still allowing one to identify with his experiences. Through vivid truthfulness he has made his own and others' experiences accessible. His approach nurtures an understanding of the purpose of human rights and the values that they seek to uphold. If the point and purpose of rights are not at the forefront, those rights will be static and – worse – undermined. He has contributed to many battles in his work, which, like the fight against torture and other cruel, inhuman and degrading treatment or punishment, are not battles that will be won in a lifetime and so to inspire younger generations to take up that task is an important legacy, one which is assured for Méndez. From the earliest days of his career until the present, educating others has been a key feature whilst also acknowledging his own inspirations and mentors. At the end of the day, human rights defenders will always be motivated by a clear and unshakeable purpose. There is nothing else as certain; it is the only thing that can be steadfast, even more so than the legal instruments. That purpose is a determination to pursue justice based on recognition of individuals, their families and their communities. It must be nourished in the face of oppression, challenge and lost struggles, and Méndez' work as an advocate, educator and leader will nourish this purpose for generations of human rights defenders within and beyond Latin America. This is perhaps the core of Méndez' heritage for human rights.

As Méndez was born on 11 December 1944 it is a fitting coincidence that when we acknowledge the Universal Declaration of Human Rights on 10 December 1948, we can also celebrate the work of a literal child of the human rights era who has become one of its inspiring guardians.

---

[33] Solitary Watch, 'Looking Back on Six Years of Leadership Against Solitary Confinement With UN Torture Expert Juan Méndez', 30 January 2017, available at www.solitarywatch.com/2017/01/30/looking-back-on-six-years-of-leadership-against-solitary-confinement-with-un-torture-expert-juan-mendez/.

28

Mary Robinson
A Woman of Meitheal

REBECCA SMYTH

My own direct experience of witnessing violations of human rights and listening to the accounts of victims has left me with a series of vivid images just below the surface of my active consciousness, easily recalled if I discuss a situation, or some passing reference acts as a trigger. At one level it is a burden of troubling memories seared in my mind. At another it has given me an enduring empathy with courageous victims who are often agents of change in their very tough situations.[1]

I. Tomboy, Thinker, Voice for Change: Early Life and Career

Mary Bourke was born in May 1944 in Ballina, County Mayo, to doctors Aubrey de Vere Bourke and Tessa O'Donnell. Brought up in an environment of comfort and privilege, where many evenings were spent in a drawing room playing the piano or listening to her father reading them children's classics, Mary and her four brothers were given 'the best of everything ... always well turned out and looked after'.[2]

A tomboy, bookworm and dreamer, from a young age Mary was aware and critical of distinctions and discrimination on the basis of class and gender.[3] Her father's dedication to his patients, letters from her aunt Ivy (a nun in the missions in India), her paternal grandfather Henry Charles' stories of practising law in the name of justice, fairness and rights, and her mother's and maternal grandmother Nellie's running of

---

[1] M Robinson, *Everybody Matters: A Memoir* (London, Hodder & Staughton, 2012) 245.
[2] Robinson (n 1) 4, 5, 6.
[3] ibid 7, 8, 9, 11, 13. See also O O'Leary and H Burke, *Mary Robinson: The Authorised Biography* (London, Hodder & Staughton, 1998) 5–16.

numerous local charitable efforts further fuelled her desire to effect real-world change.[4] Another important role model and source of support throughout her life was Annie 'Nanny' Coyne, the family housekeeper, 'a rock of common sense' who helped raise Mary and her brothers, kept house for them when they attended university in Dublin, and also helped raise Mary's own children.[5]

At the age of ten, Mary was sent to the private school Mount Anville in Dublin, where she was placed in the secondary school on account of being tall and having a strong academic record.[6] The nuns directed their charges' attention to poverty in the developing world, and access to a vast library with works on Eleanor Roosevelt, Martin Luther King, Jr and Gandhi fuelled Mary's desire to do something worthwhile with her life.[7] She considered becoming a nun, but first spent a year in Paris at Mademoiselle Anita Pojninska's finishing school; her time in the city opened her eyes to feminism, secularism, and anti-racist/colonial struggles.[8] She began to question the hierarchy and dogma of the Catholic Church, and decided to study law rather than take the veil. Upon her return to Ballina, she informed her parents of this decision, as well as her desire to no longer attend Mass. This caused not inconsiderable tension, as the issue of religion often did in an otherwise very loving relationship between Mary and her parents.[9]

She won a scholarship to Trinity College Dublin in 1963 but, as a Catholic, she required the permission of the Archbishop of Dublin to attend the Protestant university. Permission acquired and the risk of mortal sin thus averted, she moved in with her brothers and Nanny Coyne and began her studies. Nanny cooked, cleaned, mothered and 'put up with a great deal of partying and sheer student exuberance' on the part of the Bourke siblings.[10] Mary resolved to become a barrister, but recognised that as a woman she 'would have to be that bit better' and 'work that bit harder so as to argue with utter confidence'.[11] Becoming a Trinity Scholar, a skilled debater, and the first woman auditor (president) of the Law Society helped hone the requisite skills. She considered the law to be an instrument for realising desperately needed social change in Ireland: in her first speech as auditor, she set out key issues that would inform her work in the coming years, namely 'the constitutional prohibition on divorce, the ban on the use of contraceptives, the criminalisation of homosexuality and suicide'.[12] The exclusion and discrimination faced by the Travelling community were also areas she focused on during her studies and career.[13] It was during her time at Trinity that she met her future husband, Nick Robinson. Fellow classmate and talented political cartoonist, he 'pursued her gently' but she insisted on maintaining a platonic relationship so that she could focus on her studies and professional ambitions.[14]

[4] Robinson (n 1) 15, 16, 18.
[5] ibid, 15.
[6] ibid, 20. Children normally begin secondary school around the age of 12 or 13 in Ireland.
[7] ibid, 21.
[8] Robinson (n 1) 24, 27, 29; O'Leary and Burke (n 4) 17–21.
[9] Robinson (n 1) 30, 65, 72.
[10] ibid, 34.
[11] ibid, 39.
[12] ibid, 45.
[13] ibid, 44, 96.
[14] ibid, 47.

Having obtained an impressive hat trick of first-class honours in her LLB in Law, BA in Legal Science – both from Trinity – and her BL (the Barrister-at-Law degree, the professional stage of training for the Bar of Ireland) from King's Inns, she began her LLM at Harvard in 1967. One of only a handful of female students on the programme, she learned a great deal in and out of class on matters ranging from constitutional law to the civil rights movement.[15] In her memoir, she recalls the spontaneous celebration that greeted the news of Johnson's announcement to not seek re-election due to the unpopularity of the Vietnam War, as well as the 'devastation' she felt when she heard the news Martin Luther King, Jr and Robert Kennedy's assassinations.[16] Returning to Ireland shortly after the latter's murder, by the age of just 25 she had been called to the Bar, appointed the youngest ever Reid Professor of Law in Trinity College Dublin, and elected to *Seanad Éireann* (the senate, or upper house of the bicameral Irish parliament).

It was around this time that her relationship with Nick Robinson blossomed into something more. The two had corresponded while she was in Harvard studying and he was in London working as a freelance cartoonist, and by 1969 they were both back in Dublin.[17] A political cartoonist with *The Irish Times*, Nick was supportive of Mary's professional and political ambitions. So too were his family, who warmly approved the match. The same could not be said for hers, however: they wanted 'a professional, a doctor or lawyer, well-established, moving in the 'right social circles, and a paid-up Catholic – and Nick, budding cartoonist and Protestant did not fit these criteria!'[18] For the second, but not the last, time in her life, religion became a source of tension in her relationship with her parents. They were 'furious' when the two decided to get married and neither her parents nor her brothers attended her wedding in December 1970. She took her husband's name as, ironically, an act of defiance. She and her parents reconciled some months later and eventually Mary's mother even referred to Nick as 'her favourite son-in-law'.[19]

From her first days in the *Seanad*, Robinson put pressure on the Government to liberalise the country's restrictive legislation on contraception, with mixed results.[20] The first attempt in 1971 prompted intense debate in the country, with the Catholic Church hierarchy coming out in vocal opposition to the proposed changes. For example, the Bishop of Ballina Cathedral denounced her and the Bill from the pulpit, causing considerable distress to her parents.[21] She was also an active member of the Anti-Amendment Campaign, which opposed the insertion of the Eighth Amendment into the Irish Constitution, an amendment which was an integral part of the country's near-total ban on abortion until its repeal in May 2018.[22]

[15] Robinson (n 1) 50–56; O'Leary, Burke (n 4) 34–39.
[16] Robinson (n 1) 55.
[17] ibid, 58, 63, 66.
[18] ibid, 65.
[19] ibid, 71.
[20] ibid, 64, 71.
[21] ibid, 72.
[22] 1982 leaflet from the anti-amendment campaign, available at irishelectionliterature.com/2018/05/07/1982-leaflet-from-the-anti-amendment-campaign; O'Leary and Burke (n 4) 97–103.

As a senator and barrister, Robinson fought a number of emblematic campaigns and cases in Ireland's often recalcitrant – and still unfinished – transition to a more progressive and equitable society. Among many others, she successfully argued the case that resulted in the effective prohibition on women sitting on juries being lifted,[23] as well as three European Court of Human Rights cases that were vital in paving the way for legal separation and divorce, the recognition and legal protection of children born to unmarried parents, and the decriminalisation of consensual same-sex activity.[24] An active member of European Movement Ireland, she served as Ireland's representative on the Vedel Committee on the enlargement of the EEC (now EU), with Ireland gaining membership in 1973.[25] The 1970s were eventful on a personal as well as a professional level, with the births of her daughter Tessa and son William bookending the sudden death of her mother in 1973.

Robinson joined the Labour Party in 1976 and sought the party's nomination as a candidate to the *Dáil* (lower house of parliament) elections; while she won the nomination, the party lost the Rathmines West seat to *Fianna Fáil*. She served as a city councillor for three years and in 1981, with her newly-arrived third child Aubrey in tow, she again attempted to win a seat in the *Dáil* without success. She then decided to focus her energies on the *Seanad* and her role as a senior counsel.[26] The loss of Nanny, a vital source of love and practical support on the domestic front,[27] and her younger brother Aubrey to cancer in the early 1980s were deeply felt but did not slow her professional progress: as an active senator and barrister, in 1988 she also established the Irish Centre for European Law along with her husband. Having decided to step back from her role as a senator after 20 successful years, and having resigned from Labour so that she could freely express her concerns about the limits of the Anglo-Irish Agreement, her intention was to focus on her work as a barrister in the Irish, British and European courts. Others had a different opportunity in mind for her, however.

II. President and High Commissioner

In February 1990, Robinson was approached by former attorney general John Rogers on behalf of the Labour Party and asked to consider running in the upcoming presidential election:

> I looked at him in absolute astonishment, my jaw dropped, my eyes widened, and I immediately said to myself, no way! ... As far as I was then concerned, the president was very much the ceremonial head of state: style and little substance, receiving ambassadors, red carpet events and all that, but no role that I could envisage for myself.[28]

---

[23] *Mairin de Burca and Mary Anderson v AG* [1976] IR 38 at 57.
[24] ECtHR, *Airey v Ireland* (Application no 6289/73) 9 October 1979; *Johnston and Others v Ireland* (Application no 9697/82) 18 December 1986; *Norris v Ireland* (Application no 10581/83) 26 October 1988.
[25] Robinson (n 1) 78.
[26] ibid, 104, 114–15.
[27] ibid, 94.
[28] ibid, 128–29.

After a weekend of reflection and conversation with close confidantes such as her husband, however, she decided to enter the race and so 'contribute to a new idea of the Irish presidency, an office of head of state with little real executive power, but with scope of influence, moral influence, and the potential to define the modern Ireland'.[29] She ran as an independent candidate nominated by Labour and with the support of the Workers' Party, Democratic Left and some 'like-minded' independents. Her campaign slogan, 'a president with a purpose' was intended to indicate her desire for 'a proactive presidency founded on inclusivity, the idea of a president for *all* the people'.[30] A key theme of the campaign was the concept of *meitheal*, 'a traditional, rural practice of people coming together to work ... It expresses the idea of community spirit and self-reliance ... an idea of human interconnectedness and solidarity'.[31] Against the energising backdrop of a tumbling Iron Curtain and Ireland's first time qualifying for the World Cup finals, Robinson and her campaigns team sensed the appetite for change and the growing support for her candidacy.[32] Notwithstanding some political scandal *à l'irlandaise* paradoxically giving a boost to rival *Fianna Fáil* candidate Brian Lenihan and some vicious, sexist attacks on Robinson and her marriage from politicians and clergy,[33] the campaign was a resounding success. On 3 December 1990, Mary Robinson became the first Irish president that was neither a man nor a member of the dominant *Fianna Fáil* party.[34] As if this was not sufficient, in the same year she also represented the applicants in *Cotter and McDermott v Ireland* at the European Court of Justice, winning the case that resulted in £200 million back pay to married Irish women who had been discriminated against under the social welfare code vis-à-vis state child benefit payments.[35] In her acceptance speech, she again asserted her vision for the presidency and recognised the historic nature of her election:

> I *want* to be a president for all the people. Because I was elected by men and women of all parties and none, by many with great courage who stepped out from the faded flags of the Civil War and voted for a new Ireland, and above all by the women of Ireland, *mná na hÉireann*, who instead of rocking the cradle, rocked the system, and who came out massively to make their mark on the ballot paper and on a new Ireland.[36]

As President, Mary Robinson immediately set about 'freshening up the *Áras*' (the official presidential residence) both literally and figuratively with new staff, a new visitor centre and a new focus on local, participatory democracy and those often excluded and forgotten by the country, such as the LGBT community, the Traveller community, people with disabilities, the unemployed, women, and the Irish abroad.[37]

---

[29] ibid, 131.
[30] ibid, 140.
[31] ibid, 136.
[32] ibid, 137, 139.
[33] ibid, 141–42.
[34] ibid, 131, 144.
[35] *McDermott and Cotter v Minister for Social Welfare and Attorney-General*, Case C-377/89, European Court Reports 1991 I-01155, 13 March 1991.
[36] President Robinson's Acceptance Speech, 9 November 1990, available at www.president.ie/en/media-library/speeches/president-robinsons-acceptance-speech.
[37] Robinson (n 1) 192–93.

The only European head of state to meet the Dalai Lama on his visit to the continent in 1991, the first head of state to visit Rwanda post-genocide, the first Irish President to meet a British monarch, and the first Irish President to make a working visit to Northern Ireland, Mary Robinson was acutely aware of the symbolic importance of these gestures. They represented Ireland's commitment to human rights abroad, to a good relationship with its closest neighbour, and to an equitable Northern Irish peace process that responded to the needs and concerns of all those involved.[38] In 1992, following a visit to Somalia to promote the work of Irish NGOs and to bear witness to the ravages of the conflict, drought and famine there, she made an impassioned and emotional speech about the need to respond to the situation.[39] While she was 'furious' with herself for struggling to hold back the tears and keep her voice steady,[40] for many this spontaneous demonstration of her heartfelt commitment to justice and dignity made her an even more admirable human rights champion. She became a vocal campaigner on the need for an urgent, coordinated response to the famine, raising the issue in her visits as Head of State, and also sending a letter to the Heads of State of the United Nations Security Council, European Community and Council of Europe calling for action.[41]

This visible commitment to the protection and promotion of human rights won her praise at home and abroad, and speculation mounted during the mid-1990s as to whether Robinson would be put forward as a candidate for Secretary General of the UN. Circumstances dictated otherwise, however, with the unexpected resignation of the first UN High Commissioner for Human Rights, José Ayala-Lasso, in the middle of his first term in March 1997. Deciding not to run for a second term as President, Mary Robinson set her sights on the High Commissioner position; UN Secretary General Kofi Annan supported her candidacy, and she became the second UN High Commissioner for Human Rights in September 1997.[42]

A job that is 'not for the faint of heart', Mary Robinson had to be 'equal parts lawyer and teacher, prosecutor and witness, hard talk and soft shoulder'[43] in the face of not just resistance to and outright violation of human rights by states worldwide, but also internal disorganisation and bureaucracy, low morale and a lack of funding.[44] While she found the job 'hectic and gruelling', she was motivated by her responsibility 'to bear witness to violations of human rights; to shine a light on problems the world wanted to forget; and to demand accountability – from states, in particular but also from the UN itself, and, where appropriate from corporations'.[45] In the space of five years she made 115 trips, visiting over 70 countries including Kosovo, Sierra Leone,

---

[38] ibid, 162–64, 168, 171–72.

[39] ibid, 179, 182.

[40] ibid, 182.

[41] Letter from President Robinson to Heads of State in M Robinson, *A Voice for Somalia* (Dublin, The O'Brien Press, 1992) 84–85.

[42] UN Human Rights Office of the High Commissioner, 'Mary Robinson', available at www.ohchr.org/EN/ABOUTUS/Pages/Robinson.aspx.

[43] K Annan, 'Foreword' in K Boyle (ed), *A Voice for Human Rights* (Philadelphia, University of Pennsylvania Press, 2006) i.

[44] Robinson (n 1) 200–201, 216.

[45] ibid, 215, 213.

East Timor, Chechnya, Israel and the Occupied Palestinian Territories.[46] Towards the end of her mandate, she was tasked with being Secretary General of the World Conference against Racism, Racial Discrimination, Xenophobia and Related Intolerance to be held in Durban in September 2001. By many accounts she managed the running of the Conference well, but it was marred by a number of high-profile controversies, including the US and Israel withdrawing entirely from proceedings.[47] In many respects, these difficulties foreshadowed the major geopolitical shift ushered in by the neoconservative turn in US politics and its response to the terrorist attacks of 11 September 2001.

III. An 'Uncomfortable Voice' for Human Rights and Climate Justice

Towards the end of her time as UN High Commissioner, Mary Robinson became 'the UN's "uncomfortable voice"' on the erosion of human rights that was taking place in the name of counter-terrorism and the 'War on Terror'.[48] Following the end of her mandate in 2002, she accepted an invitation to become the honorary president of Oxfam International.[49] Her numerous speaking engagements focused on the relationship between human rights, counter-terrorism, poverty and, increasingly, climate change.[50] In the same year, she founded Realizing Rights: the Ethical Globalization Initiative in collaboration with The Aspen Institute, Columbia University and the International Council on Human Rights Policy.[51] It came to a planned end in 2010: its aim was to develop projects that would have long-term impact outlasting the involvement of the initiative, and to approach issues such as labour rights, health rights, migration, women's rights and good governance from both a bottom-up and top-down perspective.[52]

In 2007, Nelson Mandela invited Robinson to be one of the first Elders, 'an independent group of global leaders working together for peace and human rights'.[53] She has been particularly active with the Elders' mission to encourage peace efforts in the Middle East, visiting Israel and the West Bank, Jordan and Syria in 2009, 2010 and 2012.[54] Ending child marriage and tackling climate change have been two other main areas on which she has worked in this capacity.[55]

---

[46] ibid, 228, 230–36, 241.
[47] See Robinson (n 1) ch 15.
[48] ibid, 268.
[49] Robinson (n 1) 274.
[50] Boyle (n 43) chs 19 and 20.
[51] Realizing Rights – The Ethical Globalization Initiative, available at www.who.int/workforcealliance/members_partners/member_list/realizingrights/en.
[52] Robinson (n 1) 281.
[53] The Elders: see theelders.org/about.
[54] The Elders – Mary Robinson, see theelders.org/mary-robinson.
[55] ibid.

As a member of the International Commission of Jurists, she was asked to preside over the Eminent Jurists' Panel on Terrorism, Counter-Terrorism and Human Rights, which published a report in 2009 documenting the negative human rights impact of counterterrorism measures globally since 11 September 2001. This report condemned the 'serious violations of international human rights and international humanitarian law' carried out in the name of counter-terrorism, and made nine recommendations concerning international, regional and domestic actors.[56] These recommendations emphasise the centrality of human rights and reject the use of the war paradigm in responding to terrorism.

During this time, Robinson became increasingly aware of the 'constant negative factor impeding the development of poor countries': whether health rights, labour and trade issues, women's rights or peace and security, the path always led back to 'the negative impact of climate change'.[57] Becoming a grandmother also led her to think more about future generations and the world they will inherit.[58] In response to this, she founded the Mary Robinson Foundation – Climate Justice in Dublin in 2010.[59] The Foundation brings together grassroots actors, policy makers and world leaders to develop solutions to international climate change that are informed by a commitment to sustainable development and human rights.[60] Focusing on three areas – human rights and climate change, women's leadership on gender and climate change, and future generations[61] – the work of the Foundation continues to represent the principles of leadership, bearing witness, and giving voice to the voiceless that have informed every chapter of Mary Robinson's career.

Perhaps abiding by her father's adage that it is 'better to wear out than to rust out',[62] Mary Robinson shows little sign of relenting in her tireless campaigning for social and climate justice. This should perhaps come as little surprise, given her character and the fact that so many challenges remain. While Ireland has had two female Presidents, it has yet to see a woman serve as *Taoiseach* (Prime Minister). Women make up only 22 per cent of TDs (Members of Parliament) in the *Dáil* and only 30 per cent of Senators in the *Seanad*.[63] Social and economic rights in Ireland are under considerable strain since the 2008 global recession, with the beleaguered healthcare system, the treatment of asylum seekers and refugees, and a lack of access to decent, affordable housing serving as constant reminders of this.[64] Women, the LGBTQ community and

---

[56] International Commission of Jurists, *Assessing Damage, Urging Action: Report of the Eminent Jurists Panel on Terrorism, Counter-Terrorism and Human Rights* (Geneva, ICJ, 2009).

[57] Robinson (n 1) 317.

[58] M Robinson, *Climate Justice: Hope, Resilience, and the Fight for a Sustainable Future* (London, Bloomsbury, 2018) 6–7.

[59] Mary Robinson Foundation – Climate Justice, at www.mrfcj.org.

[60] Mary Robinson Foundation – Climate Justice, 'How We Work', see www.mrfcj.org/our-work/how-we-work.

[61] Mary Robinson Foundation – Climate Justice, 'Areas of Work', see www.mrfcj.org/our-work/areas-of-work.

[62] Robinson (n 1) 6.

[63] I Bacik, 'Women in Politics', available at www.ivanabacik.com/womeninpolitics.

[64] See for example Committee on Economic, Social and Cultural Rights, 'Concluding Observations on the Third Periodic Report of Ireland' 8 July 2015, UN Doc E/C.12/IRL/CO/3.

the Travelling community have won some hard-fought victories in recent years, but structural inequality and resistance to social change persist.[65]

On the international level, the concerns Robinsons voiced as UN High Commissioner for Human Rights regarding the negative impact on human rights wrought by religious intolerance, racism and xenophobia, far-right politics, and securitisation continue to resonate in new and worrying forms in the latter half of the 2010s.[66] The urgency of remedying the deleterious impact of climate change on human rights, and indeed human survival, has been brought home once more by the UN Intergovernmental Panel on Climate Change's most recent report.[67] The need for people of *meitheal* like Mary Robinson, people with a sense of justice, solidarity and our common humanity, remains as vital as ever.

[65] See for example CEDAW Committee, 'Concluding Observations on the Combined Sixth and Seventh Periodic Reports of Ireland' 9 March 2017, UN Doc CEDAW/C/IRL/CO/6-7; Human Rights Committee, 'Concluding Observations on the Fourth Periodic Report of Ireland' 19 August 2014, UN Doc CCPR/C/IRL/CO/4; Committee on the Elimination of Racial Discrimination, 'Concluding Observations on the Third and Fourth Periodic Reports of Ireland' 9 March 2011, CERD/C/IRL/CO/3-4. Marriage Act 2015 (legalising marriage equality in Ireland); M O'Halloran and M O'Regan, 'Travellers formally recognised as an ethnic minority' *The Irish Times* (Dublin, 1 March 2017); 'Abortion referendum: Yes secures landslide victory' *The Irish Times* (Dublin, 26 May 2018).

[66] See collected speeches in Boyle (n 43).

[67] Intergovernmental Panel on Climate Change, *Global Warming of 1.5o: An IPCC Special Report on the Impacts of Global Warming of 1.5°C above Pre-Industrial Levels and Related Global Greenhouse Gas Emission Pathways, in the Context of Strengthening the Global Response to the Threat of Climate Change, Sustainable Development, and Efforts to Eradicate Poverty* (8 October 2018).

Part V

Human Rights and their Defenders: Moving Forward

29

Radhika Coomaraswamy

Standing Up for the Oppressed and Neglected

INGRID WESTENDORP

> We must let the world know children's stories and we must take effective protective, legal and political actions to ensure that as many children as possible are spared the brutalities of war. Our joint action has, and will, make a difference, if only we make the effort.[1]

I. Living in a Country Torn by Civil Strife

Radhika Coomaraswamy was born in Colombo, Sri Lanka, on 17 September 1953, into one of the most respected Tamil families as the daughter of Rajendra and Wijeyamani Coomaraswamy. Her father, who was known for his flamboyant personality, started his career as a civil servant at the Sri Lankan Ministry of Finance, but after 23 years, in 1961, he left Sri Lanka when he was appointed Director of UN Development Program's Regional Bureau for Asia and the Far East. Consequently, the family, including Radhika and her older brother Indrajit, moved to New York. Radhika was an excellent student, and after graduating from the United Nations International School, she went to Yale University, where she obtained her bachelor's degree with a major in political science and a minor in economics. Subsequently she went to Columbia University for her law degree (Doctorate of Jurisprudence or JD), and finally to Harvard University where she obtained a Master of Laws.[2]

---

[1] Statement by R Coomaraswamy, Special Representative of the Secretary-General for Children and Armed Conflict at the Symposium on Children and Young People Affected by War: Learn, Understand, Act, Rome, 23 June 2009.

[2] The personal data were gleaned from different interviews with Radhika Coomaraswamy. More specifically R Bhagat, "'Sri Lankan women are better off but…", Radhika Coomaraswamy, UN Special

Radhika was born in a country where ethnic conflicts flared up after the country gained its independence from Great Britain in 1948. The majority of the population (75 per cent) are Sinhalese, who are mostly Buddhist. The largest minority is formed by the Tamils, whose main religion is Hinduism and who predominantly populate the North (where they are the majority), the East, and the capital Colombo. The Tamils are not a homogenous group; they can be distinguished into Sri Lankan and Indian Tamils. The first Sri Lankan Government after decolonisation took several measures that were discriminatory against the Tamils. Examples include the adoption of Sinhala as the only official language, which resulted in Tamil-speaking public servants being forced to resign; introducing the policy of standardisation, thus making it more difficult for Tamil students to enter university; evicting Tamils from ancestral lands in favour of Sinhalese peasants; and making Buddhism the most prominent religion in the Constitution. The Indian Tamils were hit hardest because their citizenship was withdrawn and consequently they became stateless. After long negotiations between India and Sri Lanka the issue was settled by the Sirima-Shastri Pact of 1964 and the Indira-Sirimavo agreement of 1974. This made it possible for 600,000 Tamils of Indian origin to settle in India, while another 375,000 Indian Tamils were accepted as citizens of Sri Lanka.

In this climate of harassment and oppression, several groups of mainly young Tamils formed militant organisations and the call for an independent Tamil State became ever louder. Of these militant groups, the Liberation Tigers of Tamil Eelam (LTTE or Tamil Tigers) emerged as the strongest, ultimately eliminating the other groups. Numerous violent attacks and riots between 1977 and 1983 escalated into a civil war that lasted for 26 years. India got involved in 1987, but withdrew in 1990, and Indian sympathy and support for the Tamil Tigers rapidly dwindled after the assassination of Rajiv Gandhi by an LTTE suicide bomber in 1991. The violence culminated in a bloodbath in May 2009, killing more than 100,000 civilians and more than 50,000 fighters, displacing tens of thousands of people, and inducing about one third of the Tamil population to flee the country.

Both the Sri Lankan army and the LTTE have been accused of war crimes, torture, attacks on civilians, execution of combatants and prisoners.[3] LTTE is furthermore accused of recruiting children as combatants, while the Sri Lankan authorities allegedly committed genocide in 2009 according to Human Rights Watch.[4]

Rapporteur' *Hindu Business Line* (Colombo, 4 January 2002), available at www.thehindubusinessline.com/2002/01/04/stories/2002010400191300.htm; R Dain, 'Interview with Radhika Coomaraswamy, Special Representative of the Secretary-General for Children and Armed Conflict (CACC)' 10(2) *Network: the UN Women's Newsletter* (April–June 2006) 1–5; N Wijedasa 'Interview with Dr. Coomaraswamy' *Lanka Monthly Digest* (Colombo, July 2006), available at www.sangam.org/taraki/articles/2006/07-13_Radhika_interview.php?print=sangam.

[3] See, for example, Report of The Secretary General's Panel of Experts on Accountability in Sri Lanka, 31 March 2011, available at www.un.org/News/dh/infocus/Sri_Lanka/POE_Report_Full.pdf.

[4] The data concerning the civil war in Sri Lanka and the position of the Tamils as an ethnic minority have predominantly been gathered from reports published by Human Rights Watch and Amnesty International, most importantly, the Human Rights Watch Asia report on Sri Lanka of 1990 available at www.hrw.org/reports/1990/WR90/ASIA.BOU-11.htm#P718_161127, and the Amnesty International report, 'Sri Lanka; When Will Justice Be Done?' ASA 37/15/94, July 1994, available at www.amnesty.org/download/Documents/ASA370151994ENGLISH.pdf.

The climate of discrimination, oppression and violence undoubtedly had an impact on Radhika's thinking. In addition, her father's appointment with the UN Development Program and his work concerning development in Asia and the Far East sparked her interest in human rights. In the USA, she was greatly influenced by the feminist movements in the 1960s. She became a woman with strong convictions and a sense of justice. A feminist who believes in the empowerment of women, but who also wants to preserve the values of family, community, and society. When her father retired from the United Nations in 1977 and went home, Radhika also returned to Sri Lanka. There she was inspired by Kumari Jayawardene, a Sinhalese woman, who is a leading feminist and academic and whose research focused on third-world feminism. Together with Kumari Jayawardene, Radhika used to meet with Muslim women to discuss peace and racism.

Although the war officially ended nine years ago, the atmosphere in Sri Lanka is still one of distrust, hatred and emotion between the different groups of the population. The North of the country is in economic chaos, with unemployment, alcohol abuse, and high rates of violence against women. Being a Tamil herself, Radhika was, and still is sometimes expected to side with the militant Tamil movements. However, she always tries to be the voice of reason, and she openly criticised the violence that was used by the LTTE. She is convinced that the Tamils as an ethnic minority would have been better off today if they had used non-violent protests, and had instead tried to gain influence through political participation.[5] This point of view has led to heavy criticism by some in the Tamil community, who even tried to prevent her from being appointed as a UN official. While she clearly thinks that accountability for the human rights violations that have happened is important, at the same time she urges her fellow countrymen to leave the past behind and to stop accusing each other of atrocities. Her approach is to find political solutions through discussions and dialogue and to improve the human rights situation for all in a united Sri Lanka.

II. Human Rights Work at Home and Abroad

Radhika Coomaraswamy's career is characterised by great diversity: a mixture of academic work; activism; and performing official functions both in Sri Lanka and for the UN. That is why, for clarity's sake, the information below is not chronological, but has been categorised into her work in Sri Lanka, her work for the UN, and her academic achievements.

A. Sri Lanka

When Radhika returned to Sri Lanka in 1977, she started working for the Marga Institute, a centre for development studies, where she remained until 1982, when the

---

[5] R Coomaraswamy, 'Mahatma Gandhi Memorial Oration. Non-Violence: An Article of Faith' Speech given at the International Centre for Ethnic Studies (ICES), Colombo, 2 October 2004.

International Centre of Ethnic Studies was founded and she was invited to become its Director. In this function she took the lead in research projects on issues that were – and are – of the utmost importance for her country, such as ethnicity, multiculturalism, women's human rights, federalism and constitutional reform.

In 2003, she was appointed Chairperson for the Sri Lanka Human Rights Commission, a function she fulfilled until 2006. As a national human rights institution, the Commission is an independent organ established to promote and protect human rights in the country by developing a better human rights climate. It is the Commission's mission to safeguard the fundamental rights that are contained in the human rights treaties to which Sri Lanka is a party. Chairing the Commission during this timeframe was particularly tough, since the country was in the middle of a civil war. Under her leadership, the Commission introduced a zero-tolerance policy on torture, and started with surprise visits to custodial institutions. A database on disappearances was set up as well as a committee for the protection of migrant workers. Furthermore, under her chairwomanship a national conference was organised concerning the rights of people with disabilities. After the Tsunami of 26 December 2004, the Human Rights Commission created a Disaster Relief Monitoring Unit to assist the tens of thousands who had lost their homes and their possessions and to monitor the reconstruction work.[6] Latterly, Radhika was nominated as the independent civil representative of the Sri Lankan Constitutional Council in 2015. It is the aim of the Council to depoliticise the public service. Radhika's term ended in September 2018.

B. Special Rapporteur on Violence Against Women

Radhika became the first UN Special Rapporteur on Violence Against Women in 1994. She held this position until she stepped down in 2003. Her appointment was extremely topical since at the World Conference on Human Rights in Vienna in 1993, the world community had become acutely aware that gender-based violence, ie violence exclusively or predominantly targeting women and aimed at women because they are women, was an issue that needed international attention. Scores of women's non-governmental organisations (NGOs) had travelled to Vienna to put the issue of Violence Against Women (VAW) on the world's agenda and to demand action. Two of the most important consequences were the adoption of the Declaration on the Elimination of Violence Against Women by the UN General Assembly (1993),[7] and the creation of the mandate of a Special Rapporteur on Violence Against Women, its causes and consequences, as one of the Special Procedures of the then Commission of Human Rights (1994).[8]

---

[6] Human Rights Commission of Sri Lanka, '2004-2005 Annual Report of the Human Rights Commission of Sri Lanka' (Colombo, 2005).

[7] The Declaration on the Elimination of Violence Against Women was adopted without vote by the United Nations General Assembly in its resolution 48/104 of 20 December 1993.

[8] The Commission of Human Rights was a sub-organ of the Economic and Social Council until June 2006. In its Resolution 1994/45 it decided to appoint – initially for a period of three years – a Special Rapporteur on Violence Against Women. The Commission was replaced in 2006 by the Human Rights Council, a sub-organ of the General Assembly. The Human Rights Council decided to continue the mandate of the Special Rapporteur on Violence Against Women.

The Commission could not have found a more suitable expert for this mandate. In her Preliminary Report she laid the groundwork by mapping the types of violence and the different kinds of actors that perpetrate acts of VAW. This was an extremely useful exercise to create awareness of the seriousness of the situation and to display the pervasiveness of this kind of violence in society. She showed that women and girls may be victims of different kinds of gender-based violence in the community and in society at large, but first of all, within their own families where they may be beaten, raped, or killed, or suffer because of traditional practices, all at the hands of their nearest and dearest. In Radhika's own words:

> Throughout a woman's life cycle, there exist various forms of gender-based violence that manifest themselves at different stages. Most of this violence is domestic, occurring within the home, perpetrated by those to whom the woman is closest.[9]

With regard to the causes of this violence, Radhika made it clear that while poverty or alcohol abuse may exacerbate the violence or the incidence of violent acts, the violence perpetrated by men against women fundamentally originates from unequal power positions and the lack of independence of women in comparison to men. The consequences of VAW are that women's human rights are undermined and annihilated.[10]

In respect of sexual violence against women, she clearly analysed and explained the role that honour plays in conflict situations. In many states, honour is attached to women's bodies. A good woman remains pure and only has a sexual relationship with her husband. In this way, women guarantee the purity of their ethnic group. This emphasis on ethnic purity makes women particularly vulnerable in times of war. Sexual attacks on women are not incidents, committed by individual enemy soldiers, but a structural and deliberate war strategy, because raping and sexually humiliating women is considered as an attack on the whole community. Women can be defiled and as such they can bring down the integrity of the ethnic community in which they live. Women suffer not only at the hand of the enemies in conflict situations, but also at the hands of their own families, since in order to protect the community's honour, men may decide that it is better to kill their women before they fall into the enemy's hands. The same perception also drives women to kill themselves, since it may be considered dishonourable to let themselves be raped rather than taking their own lives. As a solution to break this connection between women's bodies and communities' honour, Radhika advocates getting rid of the barriers between communities and individuals, and instead striving for plural societies where sexual violence is regarded as a perpetration against the physical integrity of the woman herself, but no longer as an assault on the honour of her specific community.[11]

In the course of her mandate, Radhika travelled to Japan, South Korea and North Korea to address the plight of the 'comfort' women who were kept as sex slaves for the

---

[9] R Coomaraswamy, 'Report by the Special Rapporteur on Violence Against Women, its causes and consequences', 5 February 1996, UN Doc E/CN.4/1996/53, para 54.

[10] R Coomaraswamy, 'Preliminary report by the Special Rapporteur on Violence Against Women, its causes and consequences', 22 November 1994, UN Doc E/CN.4/1995/42.

[11] R Coomaraswamy, 'A Question of Honour: Women, Ethnicity and Armed Conflict', delivered at the Third Minority Rights Lecture, 25 May 1999, available at www.sacw.net/Wmov/RCoomaraswamyOnHonour.html.

Japanese army during World War II. She went to Brazil and Liechtenstein to expose the extent and seriousness of domestic violence. Her visits to Poland, India, Nepal and Bangladesh were focused on trafficking in women and girls. In South Africa she looked into rape in the community, and in the USA she investigated the situation of women in prisons. The situation of VAW during armed conflict was the topic of her reports on Rwanda, Colombia, Indonesia and East Timor, and Sierra Leone, while her visits to Cuba and Haiti concerned gender-based violence in general and those to Afghanistan addressed religious extremism. In addition to these country visits, Radhika sent scores of interventions (communications) to governments on behalf of numerous women who were the victims of gender-based violence. The wealth of information included in her reports clearly shows her dedication and perseverance.[12]

C. Special Representative for Children and Armed Conflict

UN Secretary General Kofi Annan appointed Radhika Coomaraswamy as Special Representative for Children and Armed Conflict (CAAC) in 2006, a function she performed until 2012. Her mandate comprised raising awareness of the situation of children caught in the middle of conflict situations and exploring how to best protect their rights. The prime concern of the mandate was the recruitment of children as soldiers, but attention was also given to other serious violations that children may suffer in conflict situations, such as killings, maiming, sexual violence, denying them access to humanitarian aid, and attacks on schools and hospitals.

In her reports, Radhika emphasised the importance of education in emergency situations. It is her conviction that if more efforts are made to provide children in refugee and IDP camps with the opportunity to get an education, the better equipped the children will be for the future and the more difficult it will be for recruiters to conscript them as child soldiers. She was adamant that schools should be respected as no-go zones by all parties, where children can find safety and routine:

> We are very concerned about attacks on schools by aerial bombardment, the direct targeting of schools, teachers and students, or the use of schools for military activities. These attacks represent a violation of international humanitarian law and perpetrators must be held accountable for such actions.[13]

In the context of her mandate, Radhika visited conflict areas throughout the world such as Afghanistan, Burundi, Cote d'Ivoire, Democratic Republic of Congo, Somalia, Myanmar, Israel, Palestine and Southern Thailand, where she met state and non-state actors, with the aim of protecting children from grave violations.

During her term as Special Representative, Radhika paid specific attention to the situation of girls, since their circumstances may differ significantly from those of boys

---

[12] All the reports she published in her function of Special Rapporteur can be found at www.ohchr.org/EN/Issues/Women/SRWomen/Pages/AnnualReports.aspx.

[13] UNESCO Media Services, 'Interview with Radhika Coomaraswamy, Special Representative of the Secretary-General for Children and Armed Conflict' 25 May 2009, available at www.unesco.org/new/en/media-services/single-view/news/interview_with_radhika_coomaraswamy_special_representative/.

who are recruited as child soldiers. Girls are often abducted or given away to armed forces and they may become combatants, but in addition, they may be used as sex slaves, and/or be enslaved in order to cook and clean in the camps:

> Increasingly, women and girls are also becoming combatants in these new wars. In some cases like Sierra Leone, women and girls were abducted, made into sex slaves and used as soldiers. In other wars, women and girls appear to join voluntarily, supporting a cause or escaping poverty. Sadly, it is these women and especially girls who are put on the front lines. They are rarely in the command structure and are often the first to be placed in battle and, as a consequence, the first to die.[14]

The girls' situation is therefore much more complex than that of boys. Furthermore, the re-integration of girls into society when the fighting is over may be problematic, because families may not want to take them back if they have been raped, had children, or have taken up arms:[15]

> Reintegrating women and girl combatants after war into society is often difficult. I spent some time in Colombia with former women combatants. They told me of their very difficult circumstances. Men were frightened to go out with them because they had been combatants so none of them had formed lasting relationships. The skills they had learned as combatants were not valued by women in peaceful society so they were having trouble finding a livelihood. Some of the women I met had become sex workers just to survive.[16]

Radhika does not think that the children themselves should be prosecuted for war crimes, since generally they have just obeyed adults who often left them no choice – coercing and threatening them, or giving them drugs:

> I believe that the Sierra Leone formula is the best formula: they tried the adult leaders; those who are most responsible and bear the greatest responsibility for war crimes. With regard to the children we need to think of truth and reconciliation and other processes to try to make them acknowledge that what they did was wrong and allow the community to reaccept them.[17]

D. Women, Peace, and Security

In 2014, UN Secretary General Ban Ki-Moon appointed Radhika as the lead author of a global study on the implementation of Security Council Resolution 1325 (2000) on women, peace, and security. The study was designed to assess developments in the 15 years since the Resolution was adopted. The study, including guidelines and general recommendations, was published in 2015 under the title: 'Preventing Conflict,

---

[14] R Coomaraswamy, 'Reflections on Women, Girls and Armed Conflict' *Huffington Post* (New York, 8 March 2011, updated 6 December 2017), available at www.huffingtonpost.com/radhika-coomaraswamy/women-girls-armed-conflict_b_832559.html.

[15] All the reports of the Special Representative on Children and Armed Conflict can be found online at childrenandarmedconflict.un.org/virtual-library/.

[16] Coomaraswamy (n 14).

[17] Dain (n 2).

Transforming Justice, Securing the Peace'.[18] It highlights the disappointing lack of progress made in terms of the attention paid to women's involvement in conflict situations, both with regard to attention to female victims and the involvement of women in peace-making processes. Despite growing awareness, still very few perpetrators have been prosecuted for sexual violence during conflict situations, and only nine per cent of peace negotiators were female. The UN itself involved only a negligible number of women – a mere three per cent – in its peacekeeping and peace-building missions.

The most important conclusions of the study entail not only more that perpetrators of grave violent acts against women have to be held accountable, but also that attention has to be paid, and action has to be taken, to remove the underlying unequal positions of men and women in society that render girls and women particularly vulnerable in conflict situations. In addition, the UN is advised to appoint more women as senior gender advisers throughout the UN, and to set up an International Tribunal for Sexual Exploitation and Abuse by UN peacekeepers and UN staff, since sexual violence perpetrated by UN representatives greatly undermines the respect for and the effectivity of the UN as an organisation.

E. Academic Work

When Radhika returned to her country in 1977 she had enjoyed an excellent education in the US. She put her academic skills to good use and in spite of the manifold other tasks that she took upon herself, she published several books and scholarly articles on constitutional law, ethnic studies, and women's human rights.[19] As an academic, she taught a yearly summer course on women's human rights between 1996 and 2006 at New College, Oxford University and she was a member of the Global Faculty of New York University School of Law between 2010 and 2014, where she taught Women's International Human Rights law and Children and Armed Conflict courses. Her life and career experiences and research clearly shaped her academic pursuits.

III. Major Achievements

Looking at all the human rights work that Radhika Coomaraswamy has done so far, it can only be concluded that she is tireless and completely devoted to protecting the vulnerable and advocating their rights. It is no wonder that universities and human rights institutions around the world wish to honour her. She has received several

---

[18] The study is available at www.peacewomen.org/sites/default/files/UNW-GLOBAL-STUDY-1325-2015%20(1).pdf.

[19] Some of the books she has published are R Coomaraswamy, *Sri Lanka: The Crisis of the Anglo-American Constitutional Tradition in a Developing Society* (New Delhi, Vikas, 1984); R Coomaraswamy, *Ideology and the Constitution: Essays on Constitutional Jurisprudence* (Colombo, International Centre for Ethnic Studies, 1997); and R Coomaraswamy and D Fonseka (eds), *Peace Work: Women, Armed Conflict and Negotiation* (New Delhi, Women Unlimited, 2004).

honourary PhDs,[20] and many prestigious international awards.[21] In her own country, in 2005 she was awarded the title Deshamanya, the second-highest national honour, by the then President for her 'service to the country and the world'.

Radhika Coomarswamy's particular contribution to the development of human rights, concerns the position of women in society and the vulnerability of children in conflict situations. She changed the view on violence against women. Time and again she demonstrated in her work that power dynamics put women in a vulnerable and subordinate position, whether gender-based violence was perpetrated by or on behalf of the state, the community, or the family, and that this is not only happening in poor developing countries, but in every state of the world and in every layer of society.

In this author's opinion, Radhika's greatest achievement in respect of VAW has been the developments concerning domestic violence. In 1994, domestic violence was still regarded as an intimate crime happening in the private sphere. The authorities did not undertake much action to prevent it and perpetrators were hardly ever prosecuted because states did not feel in any way responsible. Of course she was not the only one who raised the issue, but she made an important impact by calling states' attention to domestic violence in her preliminary report as Special Rapporteur on VAW:

> Wife murderers receive greatly reduced sentences, domestic battery is rarely investigated and rape frequently goes unpunished. These examples stand in direct contrast to the treatment of violent crimes against male victims.[22]

She pointed out that:

> The problem of violence against women brings into sharp focus an issue that has been troubling the international community – State responsibility for the actions of private citizens.[23]

The issue of states' accountability for domestic violence received particular attention in her special report on violence in the family: 'Violence against women in the family raises the jurisprudential issue of State responsibility for private, non-State actors'.[24]

That these efforts paid off became clear in her final report, in 2003, when she came to the conclusion that:

> Since 1994, a great deal has occurred at the standard-setting level with regard to domestic violence. In order to protect women's human rights Governments are expected to actively intervene even if the rights are violated by a private individual. By failing to intervene, in

---

[20] She received honourary PhDs from Amherst College, the University of Edinburgh, the University of Essex, Katholieke Universiteit Leuven, and City University New York School of Law.

[21] The international awards that she has received include the International Law Award of the American Bar Association, The Human Rights Award of the International Human Rights Law Group, the Bruno Kreisky Award, the Leo Ettinger Human Rights Prize of the University of Oslo, the Oscar Romero Award of the University of Dayton, The William J Butler Award from the University of Cincinnati, and the Robert S Litvack Award from McGill University.

[22] Commission on Human Rights, 'Preliminary report submitted by the Special Rapporteur on violence against women, its causes and consequences, Ms Radhika Coomaraswamy, in accordance with Commission on Human Rights resolution 1994/45' 22 November 1994, UN Doc E/CN.4/1995/42, para 105.

[23] ibid, para 99.

[24] R Coomaraswamy, 'Integration of the Human Rights of Women and the Gender Perspective: Violence against Women in the Family' 10 March 1999, UN Doc E/CN.4/1999/68, para 22.

particular if this failure is systematic, the Government itself violates the human rights of women, too.[25]

While there is still much to be done, as domestic violence remains a prevalent crime against women all over the world, more and more states have adopted specific legislation and some have accepted obligations in respect of preventing, investigating, and punishing domestic violence, such as the states that have ratified the Istanbul Convention.[26]

As regards her take on child soldiers, one of her biggest achievements is that she managed to show their humanity. No matter the atrocities they have committed, they remain children who are confused, damaged, and repentant:

> When I talk to the children many of them have been induced to do this through drugs. In addition, they do it because children generally obey adults; they have no capacity to refuse adults especially in a war context. When you speak to them they seem to be haunted by their experiences and express remorse.[27]

Coerced by adults to do unspeakable things, they need a chance to be re-integrated in society and to return to the bosom of their families and communities. It is particularly meaningful that Radhika emphasised the special circumstances of girl combatants and has shown that they have different problems and needs in comparison to boy combatants. Some societies regard girl child soldiers that have been raped as spoiled goods, no longer fit to live among them, and that is why their re-integration requires special attention and delicate handling to bring about a change of mentality.

Radhika's indefatigable fight for human rights makes it unthinkable that she will cease to play a prominent role as a human rights activist and academic any time soon. The world needs people like Radhika. Her inspiring example can serve as a model for us all.

[25] Commission on Human Rights, 'Integration of the Human Rights of Women and the Gender Perspective: Violence against Women' 6 January 2003, UN Doc E/CN.4/2003/75, para 27.
[26] Council of Europe, Convention on preventing and combating violence against women and domestic violence (The Istanbul Convention) 12 April 2011. See especially Art 5 on state obligations and due diligence.
[27] Dain (n 2).

30

Gerard Quinn

A Powerhouse for Disability Human Rights

ANNA BRUCE AND ANNA LAWSON

> In essence, the human rights perspective on disability means viewing people with disabilities as subjects and not as objects. It entails moving away from viewing people with disabilities as problems towards viewing them as holders of rights. Importantly, it means locating problems outside the disabled person and addressing the manner in which various economic and social processes accommodate the difference of disability – or not, as the case may be. [This debate] is therefore connected to a larger debate about the place of difference in society.[1]

I. The Makings of a Champion of Justice

The personal experience of grave injustice and abuse of power can fuel a person with pain and hatred and send them down the road of sectarianism and retaliation. Or, as in the case of Gerard Quinn, it can spark a passion for justice and lead to a life devoted to bridge-building and the practical realisation of human rights and the rule of law for one and all.

In the autumn of 1920, Gerard Quinn's father Alfred was four years old. While resting peacefully with his mother on the stone wall of their garden on the Gort-Galway road, Alfred Quinn witnessed his mother being gunned down and killed. The murder took place in the turmoil of Irish struggles for independence and was at the hands of police officers, angered by local nationalist upsurges, whose convoy of

---

[1] G Quinn and T Degener, 'Executive Summary' in G Quinn and T Degener (eds), *Human Rights and Disability: The Current Use and Future Potential of United Nations Human Rights Instruments in the Context of Disability* (New York, United Nations, 2002) 1.

trucks happened to be passing the Quinn household as Alfred and his mother were enjoying the sunshine. The police kept on driving, leaving Eileen Quinn to bleed to her death later that day. The harm caused by the callousness of the passing police officers was intensified by the reluctance of the law enforcement authorities to investigate the crime.

Gerard Quinn, born on 25 August 1958 in Galway, grew up in the shadow of the quiet devastation of his father brought about by this early experience. This gave him first-hand experience of how conflict (such as the one for Irish independence) breeds pain, anger and deep-seated sadness, which all too often travel down through generations. But Gerard also knows that painful experiences can engender empathy and a conviction that there are no winners in the game of violence. Gerard has been known to refer to Aeschylus' poem:

> He who learns must suffer
>
> Even in our sleep, pain which cannot forget
>
> Falls drop by drop upon the heart
>
> Until in our own despair, against our will
>
> Comes wisdom through the awful grace of God.

Family history, and how one makes sense of it, is inextricably intertwined with life choices and endeavours. Gerard's decision to study political philosophy and law is no accident. These disciplines promise to guide both the search for answers to questions about the meaning of justice and the search for tools through which justice can be achieved.

The fact that Gerard has devoted so much of his energy, drive and intellectual creativity to realising the human rights of disabled people is another demonstration of how lived experience can be a powerful engine for harnessing professional skills to achieve change. Navigating the world alongside a daughter who uses a wheelchair and has complex health conditions has undoubtedly demonstrated to Gerard how much of it remains closed off to people with disabilities. This lived experience grounds Gerard's tireless commitment to using the law to narrow the yawning gap between the promise of human rights and the daily reality faced by disabled people. Compelled by the knowledge that meaningful change requires more than change in the circumstances of a single person, family or community, his work has influenced change at national, European and global levels.

Gerard's human rights work is shaped by his drive to identify and engage every actor with the potential to contribute to processes of change. No doubt steeped in the knowledge that one's perspective is dependent on where one is standing, he acknowledges the constraints (including the investment in the status quo) relevant to each of them. Through speaking their language with sincerity and understanding, Gerard succeeds in harnessing the potential of different stakeholders to contribute to processes of law and policy reform in the quest for truly universal human rights. In this quest, he is mindful of the fact that the mere existence of a treaty or a law will not bring about the change that is needed unless its principles and norms are used by different stakeholders, including at the grass-roots level. Thus, soon after the entry into force of the long-awaited UN Convention on the Rights of Persons with Disabilities (CRPD) in 2008, he wrote:

> ... [T]he true test of the Convention will not be whether it generates nice, but essentially self-referencing jurisprudence within the pure ether of international law. Instead the true test will be whether it can help reshape 'normal' politics to the point that a consideration of the just claims and the rights of persons will become a natural reflex rather than an after-thought – a question of justice rather than a question of welfare. If it can be used to leverage a new politics of disability – a new natural reflex of justice and rights and a new kind of partnership between Government and civil society – then we may be able to say that it is a success.[2]

So, underpinning his academic ingenuity and political skill, is Gerard's hard-earned personal knowledge that human rights are only as real as they are lived and given effect in our day-to-day lives. This resonates with Eleanor Roosevelt's famous words:

> Where, after all, do universal human rights begin? In small places, close to home – so close and so small that they cannot be seen on any map of the world.

A stone wall outside a family home is one such 'small place'. An inaccessible primary school is another.

II. Closing the Gap between Disability Injustice and Human Rights

Gerard Quinn's career in human rights and his talent for problem-solving is founded on an extensive period of interdisciplinary and multinational study. He graduated with first class honours in two separate degree programmes (one in legal and political science and one in law) from University College, Galway. He then obtained a Bachelor of Laws at the Kings Inns, Dublin, where he was called to the Irish Bar, prior to spending two years studying in Harvard funded by a Harvard University Fellowship. In 1987 Gerard took up his first lectureship, at University College Cork. Five years later he moved to the National University of Ireland, Galway, where he worked for 25 years. After serving as Head of the Law School from 2001–2005, he founded Galway's pioneering Centre for Disability Law and Policy in 2006 and served as its director until 2018. Since then, Gerard has taken on two concurrent chair positions: one at the Raoul Wallenberg Institute of Human Rights, University of Lund, Sweden; and one at the School of Law, University of Leeds, UK, where he is part of the Disability Law Hub and the Centre for Disability Studies. These two chairs provide him with a powerful base from which to continue his important work.

---

[2] G Quinn, 'Resisting the "Temptation of Elegance": Can the Convention on the Rights of Persons with Disabilities Socialise States to Right Behaviour?' in O Arnardóttir and G Quinn (eds), *The UN Convention on the Rights of Persons with Disabilities: European and Scandinavian Perspectives* (Leiden, Martinus Nijhoff, 2009) 218.

Gerard's scholarship has played a foundational role in the field of international and comparative disability law. One of his early publications, *Disability Discrimination Law in the United States, Australia and Canada*, published in 1993,[3] was the first extensive comparative analysis of disability equality law. It was described as 'breaking new ground' and as 'not only fill[ing] a gap with respect to our factual knowledge about disability legislation, but also provid[ing] ... a wealth of inspiration concerning the contribution the law can make to break down prejudice against people with disabilities.'[4]

In a number of edited collections, Gerard has continued to play a key role in stimulating and disseminating thinking at the cutting-edge of law and policy on disability and human rights. These include a book on disability in the UN human rights system co-edited with Theresia Degener and from which the opening quotation of this chapter is drawn.[5] The importance of this work was recognised by Mary Robinson, the then UN High Commissioner for Human Rights, who commended it to 'all concerned with human rights and disability', saying:

> On behalf of the Office of the High Commissioner for Human Rights I thank the authors and researchers who have worked together to provide us with an indispensable and practical resource for the use of international and national human rights mechanisms to defend the human rights of those with disabilities.[6]

This volume proved instrumental in the politics leading up to, as well as in the negotiation of, the CRPD. Later books explore the implications of the CRPD[7] and other related issues such as genetic discrimination.[8]

Alongside such publications, Gerard contributed to shaping and growing the discipline through initiatives such as the annual Galway Disability Law Summer Schools for students, civil society and governments around the world; and the EU Framework Marie Curie Initial Training Network project (Disability Rights Expanding Accessible Markets), which brought together five European academic institutions from different countries and trained 14 early-career researchers to become disability policy entrepreneurs.

Strong engagement with law and policy reform is evident throughout Gerard's career. As early as 1993 he worked closely with the UN Committee on Economic Social and Cultural Rights, along with Theresia Degener and Philip Alston, to draft what became General Comment No 5, entitled 'Persons with Disabilities'. This provided ground-breaking articulations of the implications of granting economic, social and cultural rights to disabled people and was, in many respects, a vital stepping stone to the more comprehensive CRPD adopted some 12 years later.

---

[3] G Quinn, M McDonagh and K Kimber, *Disability Discrimination Law in the United States, Australia and Canada* (Luton, Oak Tree Press, 1993).

[4] A Hendricks, 'Book Review: Disability Discrimination Law in the United States, Australia and Canada' (1994) 12(1) *Netherlands Quarterly of Human Rights* 99–103.

[5] Quinn and Degener (n 1).

[6] ibid, 'Foreword' ix.

[7] Arnardóttir and Quinn (n 2); G Quinn and C O'Mahony, *Disability Law & Policy: An Analysis of the UN Convention* (Dublin, Clarus Press, 2017).

[8] G Quinn, P Blanck and A de Paor (eds), *Genetic Discrimination: Transatlantic Perspectives on the Case for a European-Level Response* (Abingdon, Routledge, 2014).

Collaboration has been a hallmark of Gerard's career, but his collaboration with Theresia Degener is particularly noteworthy. Degener, who at the time of General Comment No 5 was an intern with the UN Committee on Economic Social and Cultural Rights, quickly rose to become a leading disability law scholar and has also served as Chair of the UN Committee on the Rights of Persons with Disabilities. Degener introduced Gerard to the idea of a UN disability treaty, and the study they co-edited for the UN and published in 2002 played a key role in exposing how disability issues often fell through the cracks in the UN human rights monitoring system and demonstrating the need for a new disability-specific treaty. In the conclusion to this book, they wrote that:

> To consign six hundred million people to the episodic consideration of six different treaty monitoring mechanisms does not do full justice to them. A specific convention would at least signal to the world that this section of the population exists and has equal rights, hopes, dreams and aspirations.[9]

The CRPD of course carries far more than symbolic value. Gerard was heavily involved in negotiating its terms, representing both the International Coordinating Committee of National Human Rights Institutions and Rehabilitation International. Gerard's contributions were particularly significant on two issues: reasonable accommodation; and monitoring.

First, the duty to provide reasonable accommodations requires a positive response to difference. It is a legal tool designed to ensure that adjustments are made to environments, policies and practices, which are too often organised only for non-disabled people. Duties to make reasonable accommodations or 'reasonable adjustments' for disabled people have appeared in the equality legislation of various jurisdictions since they first appeared in the US Americans with Disabilities Act 1990. They require employers, service-providers and others to take reasonable steps to change their standard policies, practices, physical infrastructure and other ways of operating in order to remove disadvantages which a particular disabled person (eg employee, customer or applicant) would otherwise experience. Prior to the CRPD, it was not always made clear whether a failure to provide such reasonable accommodations would constitute actionable disability discrimination. Gerard deserves credit for the fact that the CRPD does unequivocally categorise denial of reasonable accommodation as a form of discrimination, making it a much stronger obligation than it would otherwise have been.

Second, on monitoring, Gerard used his influence to include in the CRPD what he often refers to as the 'transmission belt' between international law and lived reality – mechanisms for effectuating change within States Parties. These mechanisms (not found in previous UN human rights treaties) require the designation of a governmental focal point and co-ordination mechanism for disability-related matters; and the establishment of a national framework for monitoring CRPD implementation, which must include an independent body such as a National Human Rights Institution. The CRPD also requires that disabled people's organisations be involved in these mechanisms.

---

[9] G Quinn and T Degener, 'Expanding the System: The Debate about a Disability-Specific Convention' in Quinn and Degener (n 1) 295.

As well as contributing intellectual and political ingenuity to the CRPD negotiations, Gerard also contributed humour. For example, after expressing frustration that
the old promise of human rights for all had so long remained unfulfilled for disabled
people, Gerard joked that the CRPD should be called the Nike Convention because of
Nike's then famous advertising slogan – 'Just Do it!'.

Alongside his global work, Gerard has been instrumental to change closer to home,
on the European level. Together with Lisa Waddington, he established the 'European
Yearbook on Disability Law'. This initiative contributed greatly to the development
and quality of disability human rights scholarship in Europe and beyond. In 1996
Gerard spent some time working for the European Commission as an *agent auxiliaire*
(temporary civil servant) and drafted the document which marked a decisive change
in European Community disability policy – the Commission Communication on
'Equality of Opportunity for People with Disabilities: A New European Community
Disability Strategy'.[10] As Professor Lisa Waddington has noted,[11] this represented 'the
first comprehensive European Community strategy produced by the Commission' and
marked a move away from the 'medical model of disability' which arguably underpinned the Community's previous approach. In her words:

> This medical model, or charity model as it is sometimes called, dominated the formulation
> of disability policy within European countries for years, if not centuries. It provided a theo-
> retical justification for practices such as the institutionalisation and segregation of disabled
> people. In the sphere of employment, the model led to an almost exclusive focus on rehabili-
> tation and vocational training, and income maintenance for people who were classified as
> unable to work.[12]

The 1996 Communication, by contrast, drew upon the UN Standard Rules on the
Equalization of Opportunities for Persons with Disabilities and aimed to give 'a renewed
impetus towards the rights-based equal opportunities approach to disability',[13] away
from institutionalisation and segregation of disabled people and towards an emphasis
on dialogue with disabled people's organisations, mainstreaming of disability in all
policies, and social inclusion.

Gerard was particularly active within the Council of Europe system in the first
decade of the 21st century, being elected onto the European Committee of Social
Rights in 2001 and becoming its First Vice President before leaving in 2007. He took
responsibility for the Committee's case law on equality, non-discrimination, and the
rights of older and disabled people. It was during his time on the Committee that
the landmark ruling in the case of *Autism-Europe v France* was decided – a ruling
which significantly strengthened the right to inclusive education for disabled children.
During the same period, between 2001 and 2005, he also co-directed the network of
experts on non-discrimination law funded by the European Commission.

---

[10] COM (96) 406 final.
[11] L Waddington, *From Rome to Nice in a Wheelchair: The Development of a European Disability Policy*
(Groningen, Europa Publishing, 2006) 13–14.
[12] ibid, 13.
[13] COM (96) 406 final, para 7.

In relation to community living in Europe, Gerard has made a significant contribution to directing EU funding away from supporting large residential institutions, such as social care homes, orphanages and psychiatric hospitals, and toward the support which disabled individuals need in order to live and participate in their communities. His report, co-authored with Suzanne Doyle and published by the OHCHR in 2012,[14] was a major intervention in the field. It helped ensure that the documents regulating how Member States can spend EU Structural Funds specify that these must be used towards community living and in a way which is compatible with the CRPD, ie not on large, segregated residential institutions where people have little influence over their own life choices, big or small. In order to gather data on the disability-related impact of these funds, Gerard was instrumental in establishing (in collaboration with Lumos, an organisation established by JK Rowling) the Structural Funds Watch project.

Alongside these contributions to disability rights in academia and policy, Gerard has worked tirelessly to embed disability concerns firmly within the strategies and practices of influential human rights bodies and programmes. He was, for instance, a member of the Scientific Committee of the EU's Agency for Fundamental Rights from 2013 to 2018. In this capacity, he assumed responsibility for broad equality issues, including antisemitism and the rights of older people as well as the rights of disabled people. He was also a member of the Human Rights Advisory Board of the Open Society Foundation, from 2012 to 2016.

Since the adoption of the CRPD, Gerard is particularly known for his work in two substantive areas: community living (as evident from the account of his work above); and legal capacity. The focus on legal capacity flows from his conviction that the voice of every person matters on both a policy and an individual level. His talks and writings on the decisive move the CRPD makes from substituted decision-making (where the power to make one's own life choices is handed over to a substitute) to supported decision making (where one has support to navigate one's own way through life) have helped raise the profile of this critical issue on the global stage. Whilst not attempting to provide simplistic solutions to the policy challenges involved, Gerard's work has helped draw attention to the link between the right to exercise legal capacity and the fact that we all have the right to take risks and to make mistakes.

Given his considerable contributions to the particular field of disability law and policy and to the field of human rights more generally, it is unsurprising that Gerard has already been awarded three international lifetime achievement awards. These were issued by Rehabilitation International 2008; the United States International Council on Disability (USICD) in 2014; and the European Association of Service Providers in 2016.

---

[14] G Quinn with S Doyle, *Getting A Life: Living Independently and Being Included in the Community: A Legal Study of the Current Use and Future Potential of the EU Structural Funds to Contribute to the Achievement of Article 19 of the United Nations Convention on the Rights of Persons with Disabilities* (Geneva, Office of the United Nations High Commissioner for Human Rights, Europe Region, United Nations, 2012).

III. An Architect of Lasting Change

Gerard's heritage is varied, extensive and still growing. It reaches into the worlds of academia, law and policy, and practical politics. And while wholly distinct, it is in many respects a heritage based on collaboration and partnership and is therefore entwined with the heritage of other key figures – notably, as mentioned above, Theresia Degener.

Gerard's academic heritage is a body of literature which is set to remain core reading for disability law and human rights scholars of the future. Combining careful attention to detail with insightful political imagination, it draws on a deep understanding of current law and policy to envisage positive directions for future travel. The appeal of his scholarship lies partly in its practical good sense and partly in its compelling prose and vision. It is unsurprising that Gerard Quinn has long been, and is set to remain, one of the most frequently quoted of scholars in this field.

Heritage in the form of influence on law and policy cannot be identified by searching databases or author names. It requires more nuanced probing into the roles of people behind initiatives taken in the name of governments and regional or international institutions. As is clear from the brief account of Gerard's career above, he played key roles behind a number of landmark multinational disability-related initiatives. These include General Comment No 5 of the UN Committee on Economic Social and Cultural Rights, the European Commission's Disability Strategy of 1996 and the UN Convention on the Rights of Persons with Disabilities. It is no exaggeration to say that Gerard, together with his partners and collaborators, has played a pivotal role in shifting disability law and policy around the world, and in persuading states to accept (at least in theory) that law and policy have a critical role to play in ensuring that societies are shaped in ways that do not condemn disabled people to lives of degradation, disadvantage and exclusion in which their preferences and talents go unnoticed and unfulfilled.

In terms of practical politics, Gerard's heritage is a commitment to dialogue and collaboration – between disabled people's organisations, national human rights institutions, academia and government. The 'new politics' he calls for depends on grass-roots leadership, where people affected by particular policies are themselves involved in the policy process. As well as conversations across stakeholder boundaries, conversations across national borders are also continually fostered by Gerard and harnessed to facilitate mutual learning and shared approaches to problem-solving. State monitoring and reporting, as well as litigation, have important roles in these conversations. Indeed, they provide fora in which conversations can be mediated and mechanisms through which governments can be nudged to take part in conversations they might otherwise avoid.

While Gerard is perhaps best known for his international and regional work, his heritage includes sustained work and collaboration-building within particular countries. In his native Ireland, he has contributed to law reform on issues of equality, inclusion and legal capacity through his roles as member of the Law Reform Commission, the Irish Government Commission for the Status of Persons with Disabilities and the Irish Human Rights Commission. He has also been a long-standing adviser to the President on constitutional matters. He has collaborated on work concerning issues including legal capacity and independent living in Israel and in China; on issues such as inclusive and supported employment and inclusive education in China; and in establishing inclusive disability approaches more generally in Eastern Europe and the Middle East.

The ripple effects of the influence of a person such as Gerard Quinn are impossible to measure. All those who have been influenced by his knowledge and drive continue their work. Scholars whom he has inspired with the belief that making a difference to the lives of people is what matters continue to achieve change through their own work. Civil society, governments and national human rights institutions continue to use and build upon ideas, practices and partnerships rooted in Gerard's earlier contributions. Gerard continues to provide those contributions – especially on issues or in circumstances where rights are particularly at risk or where engagement and collaboration across stakeholder or national boundaries has hitherto been neglected.

In October 2018, he addressed an East Asian Disability Studies Forum Conference in Taipei on the role of academia in change, saying:

> Finally, a personal plea. .... We are all part of an eco-system for change now in the 'new politics of disability' created by the UN CRPD. This fits with a philosophy of the university as a temporary custodian of knowledge that comes from the people and has to be given back in service to the people. It comes from a philosophy of seeing universities as good citizens – ready and willing to play their part in the process of change.[15]

Finally, we fear that Gerard would not look forgivingly on this chapter if it failed to mention that he was once the Irish National Champion Accordion player. Despite all the accomplishments above, it is often by reference to this achievement alone that he introduces himself in high level meetings. It is clearly an achievement of which he is immensely, and rightly, proud.

---

[15] Delivered paper on file with the authors.

31

David Kato

A Life Spent Defending the Human Rights of LGBTI People in Uganda

AIMAR RUBIO LLONA

If I run away, who is going to defend the others?[1]

I. The LGTBI Fight in the South beyond Stonewall

He did not even have a peaceful funeral. On 28 January 2011, many activists, friends, supporters and diplomatic representatives attended the burial of the Ugandan activist David Kato to say their final goodbyes. He was murdered in cold blood at his home just two days earlier on the fateful 26 January 2011. His funeral was held in Namataba, a town close to Kampala, the capital of Uganda. This was the ancestral land of Kato, the place where he developed as a person, activist and defender of the human rights of lesbian, gay, bisexual, transgender and intersex people (LGBTI). Namataba was also the place chosen to pay tribute to him on a sunny day marked by the most profound pain and sadness at the loss of a historic figure for the community, who put human rights violations of Ugandan LGBTI people on the map.

During the burial, the homophobe Anglican Pastor Thomas Musoke appeared with the aim of making the torment of the day worse, giving a warning to all those in attendance: 'Gays will repent or be punished by God'.[2] Nobody expected those words. None of those in attendance were able to pay silent homage to their friend David Kato. There was no time to say goodbye, or for silence. Once again, known activists

---

[1] D Kato.

[2] X Rice, 'Ugandan gay activist David Kato's funeral marred by angry scenes' *The Guardian* (Nairobi, 28 January 2011), available at www.theguardian.com/world/2011/jan/28/gay-activist-david-kato-funeral.

and anonymous people had to take on the absurdity of homophobia and transphobia in a country where the issue of sexual orientation has been visibly present in the political and religious agenda and in numerous media outlets. These parties have always articulated a message of hate, contempt, denial of diversity, ignorance of identities, control of desire and condemnation of pleasure.

However, Kato will forever be remembered for his tireless struggle. This young Ugandan activist, a victim of a hate crime motivated by his sexual orientation and his actions defending LGBTI rights, epitomises an argument for resistance, firm commitment and courage. Despite the enormous hostility in the social and regulatory environment in which he was involved on a daily basis, characterised by discrimination and violence, Kato worked both for his community and his own dignity. His is the victory of having fought, with scarce resources but plenty of energy, institutional state-sponsored homophobia, the draconian laws that sought to void sexual diversity, hate speech from religious fundamentalists prominent in the country, as well as incendiary media outlets that publicly identified LGBTI people and called for the population to hang them.

David Kato was born in 1964, two years after Uganda gained independence from the United Kingdom. In those days, as in other British colonies, Uganda criminalised sodomy and so-called crimes against nature. In fact, the wake left behind by British colonisation in terms of sexual diversity was characterised by its historical precedent of confinement and condemnation. When Henry VIII criminalised sexual intercourse between men through the Buggery Act in 1533, the United Kingdom introduced a law intended to distinguish between legitimate and illegitimate desires and pleasures. Centuries later, during the vibrant Victorian period, the metropolis imposed on all its colonies the rules that governed a civilised and virtuous British society, exporting the condemnation of sexual diversity to all its domains, including Uganda. More specifically, this was one of Kato's first battles: to combat colonial heritage and its consequences in which yielded homophobic laws imprisoning pleasure, desire and affection.

Undoubtedly a turning point for the young activist, who pursued his university studies while living both with the legacy of the colonial laws and the consequences of the bloody regime of Idi Amin, was his time in South Africa. In the early 1990s, Kato lived in Johannesburg at a crucial time for the LGBTI movement in the rainbow nation. During the transition away from the practice of apartheid, Nelson Mandela's South Africa wanted to be everything apartheid was not, including more open toward sexual diversity. In the southern country, the first democratic elections in its history were held on 27 April 1994 with the victory of the African National Congress. In 1996, it ratified its first constitution, which explicitly prohibited discrimination on grounds of sexual orientation. Mandela's government moved swiftly to abolish the criminal laws that had criminalised homosexuality during the violent, segregated and racist apartheid regime.

In this respect, Kato experienced one of the historic moments in the collective memory of African LGBTI people. The establishment of inclusive laws with sexual orientation and gender identity were possible thanks to LGBTI movements and notable figures such as Simon Nkoli, an iconic gay rights and anti-apartheid South African activist. In the 1990s experience by Kato, the streets of Johannesburg brimmed with a vibrant activism that included a multitude of elements and demands from an intersectional perspective. In South Africa, LGBTI movements not only fought for sexual liberation but also for the end of racial oppression, social injustice and HIV/AIDS. In addition, in the city of Johannesburg, the most populous in the rainbow nation, from the 1990s onwards, a homosexual and black subculture flourished. This was reflected in the opening of meeting and leisure spaces such as pubs, cafés, dance halls, inclusive churches and LGBTI associative areas.

Kato returned to Uganda in 1998 with this South African uprising in his pocket. In Uganda, where the homosexuality was not widely accepted, the activist broke the silence by coming out publicly, established a close relationship with organisations fighting for the world's sexual liberation, and made himself known within the ILGA (the International Lesbian, Gay, Bisexual, Trans and Intersex Association). However, this decision changed his life and forever made him a visible target for harassment, discrimination, extortion, blackmail and homophobic violence.

II. The Kuchus at War Against State-Sponsored Homophobia

In the late 1990s, David Kato became a visible and powerful activist at a time when an unprecedented wave of homophobia began to sweep across Africa in general and Uganda specifically. While the issue of sexual orientation and gender identity had certainly gone unnoticed by the emerging African political leaders since the start of colonial emancipation, by the end of the century hate speech, criminalisation of sexual diversity and the condemnation of non-heteronormative identities extended across the continent. Many nationalisms took on a new meaning with an identity that described the new black man freed from the Western stranglehold. The true African was supposed to be a person representative of a claimed idiosyncrasy where sexual diversity does not exist since it is contrary to African traditions, spirituality and world view.

Some laws, discourse and violations of human rights towards LGBTI people were grouped under a perverse dogma stating that 'homosexuality does not exist in Africa'. To find the beginning of the wave of homophobia, there is a fairly generalised consensus among activists and scholars that it was the 1995 condemnation of the Gay and Lesbians of Zimbabwe (GALZ) organisation during the International Book Fair held in Harare by the then President of Zimbabwe, Robert Mugabe, who, after banning the participation of GALZ in the event, proudly stated 'If dogs and pigs don't do it, why must human beings?'[3]

The echo of these words rang out in many African states, including Uganda. To understand the articulation of state-sponsored homophobia in the country that

---

[3] Quoted in N Hoad, *African Intimacies: Race, Homosexuality and Globalization* (Minneapolis, University of Minnesota Press, 2007).

Winston Churchill christened 'The Pearl of Africa', we need to look at the vibrant evangelist and fundamentalist churches whose claims gradually entered the government's political agenda. Specifically, in 1999, the country's President, Yoweri Museveni, began to bring in an openly-homophobic political agenda. At that time, which coincided with the start of Kato's activism, the government began to make explicit the detention of numerous homosexuals as well as hate speeches, condemning sexual diversity. There was an increase in homophobic rhetoric from religious actors, political leaders and media outlets; this would subsequently become exponential.

At the same time as the harassment and institutional criminalisation of the desires and breakaway groups from heteronormativity, religious fundamentalists were gaining ground and organising to make their most urgent moral demands more scalable. In this respect, Museveni, with his aim to remain in power, lost a lot of support both within and outside the country. In 2005, he planned a constitutional reform which sought principally to increase the number of presidential terms, allowing the president to renew his mandate as well as to introduce a multi-party system as a counterpart. Badly weakened by the constitutional reform bill launched in 2005 to stand for a third elected term, and by the internal opposition within his party, Museveni approached religious sectors, specifically the evangelical church, with the intention of gaining new support.

In effect, the President exchanged some of his power with religious fundamentalists in order to gain the necessary support to continue his term. These religious actors were very interested in using this new-found power to regulate the morality of Ugandan society. In their efforts to create a state where heteronormative sexuality and the patriarchal order were dominant, evangelical churches began to organise themselves with international support. According to Demange, March 2009 saw the organisation of the conference *The Gay Agenda: The Whole Hidden and Dark Agenda* in Kampala. This meeting was the first milestone for the religious fundamentalists who were looking to lay the foundations for the fight against homosexuality.[4] The conference was backed by US ultraconservative and homophobic organisations such as Exodus International and Family Life Network, and benefited from the participation of fundamentalist religious leaders who had already become popular thanks to their fierce and brutal homophobic speeches. In fact, it was only then that many of the protagonists who would lead the crusade against sexual diversity came to prominence, people who Kato would go on to fight on a daily basis.

Among the protagonists was the ultraconservative Ugandan Pastor Martin Ssempa, known as one of the architects in the organisation of the anti-gay religious movement in the country. As an example, he was behind the promotion of forums such as the 'Uganda National Pastors Task Force against Homosexuality', the aim of which was to introduce the death penalty for same-sex practices. At that time, Martin Ssempa also contributed to the gaining momentum of the 'National Coalition against Homosexuality and other Sexual Abuses', intended to fuel homophobia in Uganda with slogans such as 'Kick sodomy out of Uganda'. Other demands designed to

---

[4] É Demange, 'De L'abstinence á l'homophobie: La "moralisation" de la société Ougandaise, une ressource politique entre Ouganda et États-Unis' (2012) 126 *Politique Africaine* 25.

control the sexuality of the Ugandans, such as the prohibition of pornography, were also part of the agenda. Therefore, religious fundamentalists condemned not only homosexuality, but sexual diversity.

In any case, one of the great claims of the religious sectors was ultimately the introduction of a new law intended to recriminalise sexual diversity in the country, known as the Anti-Homosexual Bill. While the religious fundamentalists were organising themselves outside of government, the new draft law was presented before the Ugandan National Assembly on 14 October 2009, by a parliamentarian who would become another figure Kato would come up against: David Bahati, who went on to lead the legal reform to recriminalise homosexuality in the country.

Popularly known as the *Kill the Gay Bill*, the proposed law increased the penalties imposed on Ugandan sexual minorities, including considering life imprisonment or the death penalty depending on its different versions. The proposed law would also have a detrimental effect on other groups of the Ugandan population by expand-ing criminal punishment to those heterosexuals who knew of non-heteronormative individuals: anyone having contact with a homosexual and not reporting it would be punished. Kato, along with his allies, knew very well that the proposed legal reform was unconstitutional, legally incoherent and contrary to the international human rights treaties subscribed to by the Ugandan State. In addition, it was an instrument serving the state that sought to recriminalise sexual diversity in an attempt to divert attention from other issues, such as the urgent economic and social problems faced by Uganda at the time.[5]

In addition to religious groups and parliamentarians, media outlets also played a role as agents channeling state-sponsored homophobia. In 2010, local tabloids such as Kampala's *Rolling Stone* or *Red Pepper* published, in several editions, the personal details and photos of over one hundred men and women presumed to be homosex-uals. In addition, the tabloids called for Ugandan society to react, calling for their 'hanging'.

David Kato's fight, therefore, was on these three fronts: the state and its plan to recriminalise homosexuality; the religious fundamentalists with their continuous messages of hate; and the homophobic propaganda from the media outlets. As a tire-less activist, Kato faced them all.

In 2004, the coalition of LGBTI associations, Sexual Minorities Uganda (SMUG) was born, and David Kato was a founding member. SMUG, as well as combatting the criminalisation of homosexuality, also incorporated feminist organisations where the fight against patriarchy also includes a strong stance against homophobic and chauvinistic violence. As a SMUG activist, Kato began an exhaustive international campaign against the recriminalisation of homosexuality in the country, discrediting the statements of MP David Bahati and Pastor Martin Ssempa, and directly confront-ing those promoting the Anti-Homosexual Bill in Ugandan and international media outlets, as well as in various universities and the United Nations.

Initially, the draft law was subject to parliamentary debate on several occasions and was finally approved in December 2013. Previous to the approval, Kato managed

---

[5] A Rubio, 'Homofobia de estado y diversidad sexual en África: relato de una lucha' (2017) *Cuadernos de Trabajo, Hegoa, Instituto de Estudios sobre Desarrollo y Cooperacion Internacional* 7.

to get the international community to take a negative view of the draft law intended to recriminalise homosexuality in the country, as it proposed violation of the human rights of LGBTI people both in Uganda and in Africa more generally. Though this visibility caused him to be the victim of unprecedented harassment, his activism and effort meant that the proposed law never came to light.

That said, on the fourth anniversary of David Kato's death, and thanks to the internationalisation of the Ugandan backlash started by him, the law was declared invalid. More specifically, in August 2014 the country's Constitutional Court ruled on its invalidity due to not having the quorum required for its approval, thus returning to the criminalisation of homosexuality in accordance with the colonial Law of 1950, which is currently in force. Currently, if you are found having same-sex relations, you can expect to spend seven years in prison.

This is the undying figure of Kato who, despite all the difficulties, won enormous battles both during his lifetime and after his death against the State and the immoral demands of the religious fundamentalists. He also fought off the media outlets that contributed to the spread of state-sponsored homophobia among the population. Just a few weeks before Kato's assassination, he won a case against the weekly newspaper *Rolling Stone* which deliberately published the photos and personal details of Ugandan LGBTI people, including Kato himself. Thanks to his fight against the weekly newspaper in the courts, Kato managed to get the Ugandan courts to acknowledge that *Rolling Stone* had violated his basic rights and freedoms as well as his constitutional right to privacy.[6] The weekly newspaper was closed down as a result of the case.

In Uganda, 'Kucha' is a pejorative term used to refer to people perceived to be homosexuals. This word conceals the harassment, institutional violence and human rights violations of LGBTI people in the country. However, Kuchu is also a term for resistance, fight, activism, empowerment and strength for the Ugandan LGBTI community. David Kato is remembered as 'the grandfather of the kuchus'. And his fight continues, more alive than ever.

David Kato is one of many figures of resistance who continue the twenty-first century fight for their identities and their lives in a homophobic, chauvinistic and patriarchal context, where heteronormativity is deemed to be the only legitimate and acceptable reality. We have much to learn from our Ugandan associates as well as from other allies who fight for sexual diversity and for human rights in a vast and heterogeneous Africa. At a time when, in the West, LGBTI rights have made significant progress over the past few years, in countries like Uganda there is vindication of the discrimination suffered by lesbian women, the extreme vulnerability to violence of transgender people and the empowerment of the intersexual community. In addition, the LGBTI groups present in the 54 countries comprising Africa, 32 of which criminalise sexual diversity, continue to battle in an environment where homophobia and transphobia are deeply-rooted in society.

In Africa there is an authentic intersectional LGBTI agenda that proudly incorporates sexual liberation as well as the fight against gender violence, chauvinism,

---

[6] ibid.

socioeconomic inequalities, racism and xenophobia. They are protagonists of a revolution that embraces diversity in all its forms.

III. More Alive than Ever, in Uganda the Fight Continues

The human rights of lesbian, gay, bisexual, transgender and intersex people continue to be violated in over 70 countries around the world. People with desires, pleasure and feelings that are not heterosexual can be punished and imprisoned, sentenced to life in prison or the death penalty. In many states, manifestations of pride are repressed with violence, the right to freedom of speech of sexual minorities is silenced and the registration of their organisations is denied in a context characterised by harassment, extortion, discrimination, intimidation, persecution, torture, verbal and physical violence towards LGBTI people. Condemning sexuality and criminalising LGBTI identities are used to legitimise the violation of human rights and attack the sexual diversity and identity that characterises humanity. However, political leaders, religious fundamentalists and media outlets extend the homophobia and transphobia introduced by colonial legislation while claiming the merit of morality, integrity of tradition and divine justice. In this respect, notable advances due to a growing number of States that adopt legislations inclusive of LGBTI people contrast with those territories that actively promote state-sponsored homophobia and deny the natural existence of sexual diversity.

Alongside the institutionalisation of homophobia and transphobia, however, there are people who fight against the criminalisation of sexual diversity and identity on a daily basis. They are brave activists and anonymous heroes. Visible people who speak out against intolerance and hate on a daily basis, defending human rights. This is the case of David Kato, whose contribution to the defence of the human rights of LGBTI people was invaluable. Since his assassination in January 2011, the debate concerning the recriminalisation of homosexuality in Uganda has continued. However, the role that he played in defending LGBTI human rights has inspired his community and allies. At present, Ugandan civil organisations, including LGBTI organisations such as SMUG, are far from being passive participants in a state that promotes the condemnation of sexual diversity. They fight openly in defence of their identities and lives both within and outside the country.

In 2012, one year before the approval of the draconian Anti-Homosexual Bill, Ugandan LGBTI activists went out onto the streets of Entebbe for the first time to celebrate and show their pride. In the last decade, prominent activists such as Kasha Jacqueline Nabagesera have worked to offer safe spaces for the LGBTI community and information concerning the community can be accessed from the virtual portal *Kucha Times*. *Bombastic Magazine* also publishes resistance biographies and identities that fight off homophobic hate speech.

When Kato founded the coalition of LGBTI associations Sexual Minorities Uganda (SMUG) in 2004, it incorporated four LGBTI organisations. It has grown to include 18 organisations, each fighting for the human rights of LGBTI people and sexual diversity on a daily basis. In Uganda, new associations have been formed to play a key role in the defence of the rights of sexual minorities as well as promoting the inclusion of sexual minorities in spiritual and religious spaces. Since December 2016, Uganda has also held a LGBTI film festival, Queer Kampala International Film Festival, which promotes stories that embrace sexual diversity through art – a medium that is not free of difficulties.

Each and every one of these breakthroughs reflects the fact that the spirit of David Kato continues to be filled with obstacles. As an example, the police violently forced the closure of the Queer Kampala International Film Festival in December 2017. Pride marches are also prohibited and censorship, harassment, extortion and urgent search for safe spaces continue to be part of daily life for the LGBTI community. Likewise, LGBTI people in Uganda suffer numerous discriminations in a context characterised by intersectional logic, which diminishes the life skills and dignity of many people. Specifically, they are denied the right to life, freedom and physical integrity as well as fundamental rights such as freedom of association, freedom of expression, the rights to privacy, work, education and medical treatment. In addition, there are countless cases of the use of disproportionate force by law enforcement authorities, the practice of torture, hate crimes based on sexual orientation and gender identity, and the systematic use of violence against the community.

Against this background, David Kato's legacy is present in the resistance and struggle of the Ugandan LGBTI community. It is a visible motivation of empowerment against the state, religious fundamentalists and media outlets promoting the imprisonment of Ugandan sexuality. Thanks to Kato, Uganda has witnessed minor and major victories such as the triumph against the weekly newspaper *Rolling Stone* or the blocking of the draft law intended to recriminalise homosexuality in the country. These triumphs are proudly claimed by the LGBTI community and Kato would undoubtedly be proud of the work carried out by his friends and allies. We should not forget that in some countries with state-sponsored homophobia, figures such as David Kato will continue to inspire groups to fight and resist, and to try to deconstruct and decolonise homophobia and transphobia in all its forms and manifestations on a daily basis.

32

Malala Yousafzai
A Portrait in Courage and Conviction

GAMZE ERDEM TÜRKELLI

> My story is the story of thousands of children from around the world. I hope it inspires others to stand up for their rights.[1]

I. She is Malala: One Girl's Story of Taking a Stand, Surviving and Thriving

Malala Yousafzai was born on 12 July 1997 in Mingora in the Swat region in the northeast of Pakistan. Malala Yousafzai's father Ziauddin Yousafzai, who was an educator and ran the private girls' school in Swat which she attended, named her after Malalai of Maiwand (in today's southern Kandahar, Afghanistan), the Pashtun Joan of Arc who was a legendary warrior, inspiring victory in a battle against British colonisers in the Second Anglo-Afghan War in 1880.[2]

Encouraged by her father, Malala Yousafzai became an advocate for girls' right to education at an early age. During the same period, the Taliban took control of the Swat region of Pakistan and began instigating policies that closed and later destroyed schools, forcing men to grow beards and arranging beheadings of alleged opponents.[3] As education for girls was banned, girls were forced to quit school and

---

[1] M Yousafzai with P McCormick, *Malala: The Girl Who Stood Up for Education and Changed the World* (London, Orion Publishing, 2014).

[2] M Yousafzai with C Lamb, *I Am Malala: The Girl Who Stood Up for Education and was Shot by the Taliban* (London, Weidenfeld & Nicholson, 2013).

[3] J Boone, 'Malala Yousafzai: Pakistan Taliban Causes Revulsion by Shooting Girl who Spoke Out' *The Guardian* (London, 10 October 2012), available at www.theguardian.com/world/2012/oct/09/taliban-pakistan-shoot-girl-malala-yousafzai.

more than 400 schools for girls were burnt down. Malala Yousafzai began writing a blog about life under the Taliban as a seventh grader under the pen name Gul Makai for BBC Urdu entitled 'Swat: The Diary of a Pakistani Schoolgirl'.[4] The blog chronicled Malala Yousafzai's experience as a young schoolgirl under the Taliban regime, her fears while going to school after the Taliban edict that called for banning girls' education, her yearning to go back to school after the ban was instigated, schoolmates moving to other regions with their families in order to attend school, destruction of schools by the Taliban as well as the displacement of Swat residents during the military operations. She featured in two documentaries by *The New York Times* reporter Adam B Ellick in 2009 which were broadcast on the website of the newspaper.[5] The young Malala Yousafzai started enjoying recognition after the documentaries and met alongside other grassroots activists from Swat with the US Special Envoy to Afghanistan and Pakistan, Richard Holbrooke, to enlist his help in her campaign for girls' education in Pakistan.[6]

The Pakistani army staged a successful ground offensive in Swat in 2009 and pushed most Taliban militants out of Swat. Nonetheless, intermittent Taliban attacks in the region continued.[7] As young Malala Yousafzai's previously anonymous blog posts were recognised as her own, she became more prominent through her nomination by Archbishop Desmond Tutu for the International Children's Peace Prize in 2011 and reception of Pakistan's National Youth Peace Prize in 2012. Unfortunately, at the same time, she began receiving death threats for speaking out against the Taliban. In an interview with the English-language newspaper *Express Tribune* in Pakistan in January 2012, Malala Yousafzai said she wished to help rebuild the 400 schools in Swat that had been destroyed by the Taliban and that she did not wish to enlist security help against the threats.[8]

On 9 October 2012, Malala Yousafzai was attacked by an armed gunman who stopped her school bus on its way back from school, asked for Malala Yousafzai to be identified, then proceeded to shoot her in the head and shoot two of her schoolmates. Taliban's Pakistani offshoot, Tehreek-e-Taliban Pakistan (TTP), claimed responsibility for the attack, blaming her for speaking up against the Taliban and for 'promoting western culture in Pashtun areas'.[9] Malala Yousafzai was left unconscious and in a critical condition, and was airlifted to Peshawar to be treated by Pakistani army surgeons. She was later flown to Queen Elizabeth Hospital in Birmingham,

---

[4] BBC News, 'Diary of a Pakistani Schoolgirl' *BBC News*, 19 January 2009, available at news.bbc.co.uk/2/hi/south_asia/7834402.stm.

[5] AB Ellick and I Ashraf 'Class Dismissed: Death of Female Education' *The New York Times* (New York, 22 February 2009), available at nyti.ms/qwFqer; AB Ellick, 'A Schoolgirl's Odyssey' *The New York Times* (New York, 11 October 2009), available at nyti.ms/SM211A.

[6] N Blumberg, 'Malala Yousafzai', *Encyclopædia Britannica* (Online), available at www.britannica.com/biography/Malala-Yousafzai.

[7] Associated Press in Islamabad, 'Malala Yousafzai's book banned in Pakistani private schools' *The Guardian* (London, 10 November 2013), available at www.theguardian.com/world/2013/nov/10/malala-yousafzai-book-banned-pakistan-schools.

[8] 'Bacha Khan's Philosophy of Non-Violence and Benazir Bhutto's Charisma Inspires Malala' *The Express Tribune* (Karachi, 16 January 2012), available at tribune.com.pk/story/322054/bacha-khans-philosophy-of-non-violence-and-benazir-bhuttos-charisma-inspires-malala/.

[9] Boone (n 3).

United Kingdom, to receive further treatment for her brain and neck injuries. Many at the time correctly believed that the attack on her life would be a turning point in Pakistan in standing up for girls' right to education and against extremism. Malala Yousafzai survived the attack after a long period of treatment, during which she underwent numerous reconstructive surgeries.

Malala Yousafzai became the youngest person to receive the Nobel Peace Prize in 2014 at the age of 17, sharing it with Indian children's rights advocate Kailash Satyarthi, 'for their struggle against the suppression of children and young people and for the right of all children to education'.[10] She has also received the European Parliament's Sacharov Prize (2013) and the United Nations Human Rights Prize (2013). She was appointed as UN Messenger of Peace to promote girls' education in April 2017 by the UN Secretary General Antonio Guterres. She is currently a student at Lady Margaret Hall, University of Oxford, studying a course in philosophy, politics and economics.

Malala Yousafzai returned to Pakistan and her hometown of Mingora on 29 March 2018 for the first time since the attempt on her life. Her visit to her hometown in Swat was done under strict security protocols, as the Taliban threat to Yousafzai's life is ongoing. She continues to be active with the Malala Fund, an education fund for girls co-founded by Malala Yousafzai and her father using her Nobel Peace Prize money, which also supported the construction of a girls' school in Swat.[11]

II. A Child Standing up for Her Right to Education

Despite her young age, Malala Yousafzai has achieved recognition and influence above and beyond that of most activists by fearlessly standing up to the Taliban and demanding her right to education. She chronicled life under the Taliban as a girl child who was denied her right to education and spoke out first in local meetings, then later in international and national media. Even before the assassination attempt, her father remarked: 'I named her Malala after … a brave lady who urged her country-men to fight against intruders through her poetry … She has fulfilled my dream and played the role of Malala in the true sense'.[12] Since her recovery, Malala Yousafzai has become the foremost advocate for girls' right to education and female empowerment through education.

Article 28 of the Convention on the Rights of the Child (CRC), which enjoys almost universal ratification, enshrines the right of the child to education. Article 28.1(a) establishes an obligation to provide compulsory and free primary education to all children, while Article 28.1(b) creates an obligation to encourage secondary education

---

[10] Nobel Prize Website, 'The Nobel Peace Prize 2014', available at www.nobelprize.org/prizes/peace/2014/summary/.

[11] A Shahzad and J Ahmad, 'Nobel Winner Malala visits Hometown in Pakistan for First Time Since Shooting' (*Reuters*, 31 March 2018), available at www.reuters.com/article/us-pakistan-malala-swat/nobel-winner-malala-visits-hometown-in-pakistan-for-first-time-since-shooting-idUSKBN1H7052.

[12] The Express Tribune (n 7).

in various forms and to make secondary education 'available and accessible to every child'. In addition, Article 2 of the CRC, which is considered one of its General Principles,[13] creates an obligation of non-discrimination, stating that children shall not be discriminated against, including based on sex. Notwithstanding the clear obligations created by the CRC, current estimates based on 2014 figures reflect that 131 million of the 1.1 billion girl children in the world are out of school.[14] What is even more worrying is that out-of-school girls are likely to be completely excluded from education, while boys have a greater likelihood of entering or re-entering school. While the gender gap tended to widen at the secondary school level in 2000, 2014 data reflects that despite the progress that has been made, the gender gap persists at the primary school level. According to UNESCO Institute for Statistics, 15 million girl children versus 10 million boy children will not have the possibility to attend primary school. In Malala Yousafzai's home region of Southern Asia, estimates show that out of every five out-of-school girls, four will never have the opportunity to enter the formal education system (compared with two out of five boys). Besides the gender gap issue, the number of secondary school age out-of-school children continues to be worryingly high at over 100 million both for girls and boys.[15]

The right to education is even more severely impacted in conflict situations, with conflict-affected countries being home to 35% of out-of-school children globally.[16] In conflict-affected zones, girls find themselves at a further disadvantage with respect to access to education. Girls' education may be hampered by conflict directly where schools for girl children are targeted, damaged or used for other purposes such as hosting military, armed groups or displaced persons. In certain regions, girl children may also be targeted for recruitment into armed groups. Girls may be displaced alongside their families as a result of conflict with no access to education where they are forced to flee, but they may also be physically attacked and or sexually abused.[17] Conflict situations also create impediments to girls' education through increasing its opportunity cost and making alternatives such as child labour especially in the household or early marriages more attractive to parents or caregivers.[18] A UNESCO report found that girls were nearly 'two and a half times more likely to be out of school if they live in conflict-affected countries', which translated into adolescent girls being 90 per cent more likely to be out of secondary school.[19] The picture is even bleaker for refugee children, with 86 per cent of the world's refugees hosted in developing regions: where education opportunities are already limited for the local

---

[13] CRC Committee, 'General Comment 5 on General Measures of Implementation of the CRC' 27 November 2003, UN Doc CRC/GC/2003/5.

[14] UNESCO, *Leaving No One Behind: How Far on the Way to Universal Primary and Secondary Education?* (Paris, UNESCO, 2016). (This number does not include girl children in refugee camps or internally displaced children in conflict-affected zones, who are not reflected in the global data.).

[15] ibid, 5.

[16] ibid, 4.

[17] P Pereznieto and A Magee with N Fyles, *Evidence Review: Mitigating Threats to Girls' Education in Conflict-Affected Contexts: Current Practice* (New York, United Nations Girls' Education Intitiative, 2017) 5.

[18] ibid.

[19] UNESCO, *Education for All 2000-2015: Achievements and Challenges* (Paris, UNESCO, 2015).

population, refugee children find themselves five times more likely to be out of school.[20] Only 61 per cent of all refugee children have access to primary education, but these opportunities diminish even further as they grow older: only 23 per cent of refugee adolescents have access to education and merely 1 per cent make it to higher education. The average global ratio of refugee girls to boys in primary school is 8 to 10 and further decreases to 7 to 10 at the secondary level, but may even be much worse in some parts of the world.[21] Especially as refugee children reach the age to transition from primary to secondary education, refugee families tend to devote their limited resources to prioritise boys' education over girls' due to prevailing patriarchal attitudes and because boys' future earning potential is seen to be greater.[22]

The benefits of girls' education both for girl children themselves and for the society at large are numerous. It is estimated, for instance, that increased enrolment of girls in primary and more importantly secondary education will curb child marriage rates drastically.[23] Girls' education creates intergenerational benefits for all, by considerably increasing a woman's earnings down the road, improving child nutrition and by creating a positive environment for children, in particular girl children, to pursue further levels of education, as educated mothers are more likely to send their children to school.[24] In addition, research found a correlation between increased levels of girls education and the decreased likelihood of threat to children's lives from communicable diseases such as diarrhoea, malaria and pneumonia as educated girls have become mothers.[25]

There is a strong element of intersectionality at the cross-roads of education, gender, conflict and displacement. As a young girl child in pursuit of education, Malala Yousafzai found herself at the intersection of being a girl child, living in a conflict-affected zone, and being displaced, albeit much more briefly than most of her peers in conflict situations. What she was able to accomplish against this background of intersectionality was nothing short of formidable. Here, the role that children's parents and families play in helping children overcome intersectionality is also worth noting. Malala Yousafzai's father, Ziauddin Yousafzai, himself an advocate for girls' education, was able to provide the direction and guidance consistent with Malala Yousafzai's evolving capacities, as foreseen by CRC Article 5, which helped Malala raise her voice and ultimately thrive despite the odds.

In her Nobel Lecture, Malala Yousafzai spoke out for girl children around the globe, including in her native Pakistan as well as girls in conflict situations in Syria and Nigeria who had lost educational opportunities under the threat of violence and extremism but also because of child labour and child marriages.[26] She again called for global action to give all children, including girls, the opportunity to realise

[20] UNHCR, *Left Behind: Refugee Education in Crisis* (Geneva, UNHCR, 2017) 9.

[21] ibid, 10, 9.

[22] UNHCR, *Her Turn: It's Time to Make Refugee Girls' Education a Priority* (Geneva, UNHCR, 2018).

[23] UNESCO, *Education Transforms Lives* (Paris, UNESCO, 2013).

[24] UNESCO, *Education Counts: Towards the Millennium Development Goals* (Paris, UNESCO, 2011).

[25] E Gakidou et al, 'Increased Educational Attainment and its Effect on Child Mortality in 175 Countries between 1970 and 2009: A Systematic Analysis' (2010) 376 *The Lancet* 959.

[26] M Yousafzai, 'Malala Yousafzai – Nobel Lecture', 10 December 2014, available at www.nobelprize.org/nobel_prizes/peace/laureates/2014/yousafzai-lecture_en.html.

their potential through education. More recently, Malala Yousafzai has been focusing her efforts on mobilising funding to support girls' secondary education and for advocates of girls' rights to education through the Malala Fund. The Malala Fund, founded in 2013, works in two main areas. First, the Fund invests in providing secondary education opportunities to girls, including in conflict-affected areas. The priority countries include Malala Yousafzai's home country Pakistan, its neighbours Afghanistan and India, as well as Nigeria, where girl children are kept away from school because of extremism, and countries such as Jordan, Lebanon and Turkey that house Syrian refugees. Second, the Fund supports individual educational advocates for girls' education in developing countries through the Gulmakai Network. In addition, the Fund shares stories of activist girls from across the globe to magnify these voices on its website and through its media channels.[27]

III. The Voice of One, the Voice of Many

Malala Yousafzai has brought to the forefront the importance of both political and socioeconomic conditions in achieving the right to education for all children, especially for girls. But what is more defining about Malala Yousafzai's advocacy and activism beyond its content is the very fact of it. Article 12 of the CRC embodies the child's 'right to express his or her views freely in all matters' affecting him/her and those views 'being given due weight in accordance with the age and maturity of the child'. Yet, as analyses from different country contexts reveal, there are usually gendered differences in the way girls and boys participate in decision-making and are able to exercise their right to be heard, with girls being at a clear disadvantage.[28] The Committee on the Rights of the Child has noted in its General Comment 12 that since gender stereotypes and patriarchy impede girl children's enjoyment of their participation rights under Article 12, states need to pay special attention in facilitating the right of the girl child 'to be heard, to receive support, if needed, to voice her view and her view [to] be given due weight'.[29] What the young Malala Yousafzai claimed for herself and on behalf of her peers was squarely this right to express her views and to be heard.

Empirical evidence from developmental psychology has shown that children as young as six years of age are able to find that restrictions on freedom of speech and religion are not acceptable.[30] Furthermore, by the time children are between the ages of 8 and 11, they have usually developed complex interpretations of concepts such

[27] The Malala Fund Website, see www.malala.org.
[28] G Lansdown, *Every Child's Right to Be Heard: A Resource Guide on the UN Committee on the Rights of the Child General Comment No 12* (London, Save the Children and UNICEF, 2011).
[29] Committee on the Rights of the Child, 'General Comment 12 (2009): The Right of the Child to be Heard' 1 July 2009, UN Doc CRC/C/GC/12, para 77.
[30] CC Helwig and E Turiel, 'Children's Social and Moral Reasoning' in PK Smith and CH Hart (eds), *Blackwell Handbook of Childhood Social Development*, 2nd edn (Malden, Blackwell Publishing, 2004) 486.

as freedom and rights in their personal and sociocultural implications.[31] By speaking up, the young Malala Yousafzai, as a child and a girl, challenged not only the Taliban but also the broader relations and structures of power in the society. She became a very visible example of the fact that children are active agents in their own lives and in the pursuit of their rights, not just 'becomings' who will one day develop adult capabilities. Children's agency lies at the very essence of children's rights in fostering children's empowerment, and thus engendering societal transformation.[32] As such, Malala Yousafzai was more broadly among the many children who are or have been advocates of their own rights. Malala's trailblazing advocacy as a girl child seeking to have her voice heard is often overshadowed by her successful engagement in girls' right to education. Malala Yousafzai's activism is reminiscent of her compatriot Iqbal Masih, a child advocate against slavery, bonded labour and economic exploitation of children, especially in the carpet industry, who was unfortunately killed on 16 April 1995 at the age of 12 in an alleged assassination.[33] Kailash Satyarthi, with whom Malala Yousafzai shared her Nobel Peace Prize in 2014, referenced Iqbal Masih alongside children from his movement as martyrs for children's freedom and dignity.[34] Malala Yousafzai was distinguished by being a girl child advocate in a conflict-affected area where women were brutally repressed. It must be noted, of course, that her ability to deliver her message far beyond the confines of her country or region to reach individuals across the globe was facilitated by the *zeitgeist* and the opportunities offered by fast-circulating online media, including her blog on BBC Urdu and the documentaries from *The New York Times* in which she was featured.

Malala has remained steadfast in her message of global action to ensure education, especially for girls, to achieve equality and to promote peace. Perhaps it is again her own words, spoken on 12 July 2013, 'Malala Day', nine months after the assassination attempt and on her sixteenth birthday at the UN General Assembly, that convey this message most clearly:

> We call upon all governments to ensure free, compulsory education all over the world for every child. We call upon all the governments to fight against terrorism and violence. To protect children from brutality and harm. We call upon the developed nations to support the expansion of education opportunities for girls in the developing world. We call upon all communities to be tolerant, to reject prejudice based on caste, creed, sect, colour, religion or agenda to ensure freedom and equality for women so they can flourish. We cannot all succeed when half of us are held back. We call upon our sisters around the world to be brave, to embrace the strength within themselves and realise their full potential.[35]

[31] ibid.

[32] J Tobin, 'Understanding a Human Rights Based Approach to Matters Involving Children: Conceptual Foundations and Strategic Considerations' in A Invernizzi and J Williams (eds), *The Human Rights of Children* (Farnham, Ashgate, 2011) 82.

[33] T McGirk, 'Boy Leader of Child Labour Protest is Shot Dead' *The Independent* (London, 19 April 1995), available at www.independent.co.uk/news/world/boy-leader-of-child-labour-protest-is-shot-dead-1616194.html.

[34] K Satyarthi, 'Let Us March!' Nobel Lecture by Kailash Satyarthi' 10 December 2014, available at www.nobelprize.org/prizes/peace/2014/satyarthi/26070-kailash-satyarthi-nobel-lecture-2014/.

[35] 'The Full Text: Malala Yousafzai Delivers Defiant Riposte to Taliban Militants with Speech to the UN General Assembly' *The Independent* (London, 12 July 2013), available at www.independent.co.uk/news/world/asia/the-full-text-malala-yousafzai-delivers-defiant-riposte-to-taliban-militants-with-speech-to-the-un-8706606.html.

Her willingness to risk her life for her right to education arose from a much deeper conviction that she had the right to demand her rights. In fact, this deep conviction was reflected in the title of her first public speech in September 2008 at the age of 11 in reaction to Taliban's closing of girls' schools: 'How Dare the Taliban Take Away My Basic Right to Education?'. As Malala Yousafzai's father once remarked:

> A lot of people were speaking out about education when the Taliban were bombing schools in Swat Valley, but Malala's voice was like a crescendo. It spread all around the world. She was the smallest but her voice was the biggest, because she was speaking for herself.[36]

From now on, thanks to the legacy of Malala Yousafzai and other child advocates, when children like Malala speak up, adults will be more likely to listen.

---

[36] A Leach, 'Interview – Ziauddin Yousafzai: Learn from Malala, Use Your Own Voice to Demand Rights' *The Guardian* (London, 9 April 2014), available at www.theguardian.com/global-development-professionals-network/2014/apr/09/ziauddin-yousafzai-malala-girls-education.

33

Theo van Boven

Passing the Torch because People Matter

MANFRED NOWAK

> Peace, development and human rights are essentially inter-related, inter-dependent and indivisible.[1]

Theo van Boven is one of the true human rights champions of our time. He is a Dutch lawyer, born in the Netherlands in 1934. He received his law degrees from the University of Leiden in the Netherlands (Master of Law and Doctor of Law) and the Southern Methodist University in Dallas, USA (Master of Comparative Law). As Professor emeritus of International Law, he continues to teach human rights at the University of Maastricht and is actively engaged in various non-governmental organisations, including the Berlin-based European Centre for Constitutional and Human Rights.

In an interview with Theo van Boven on the occasion of a Liber Amicorum published for his 65th birthday, Fred Grünfeld did his best to get some information on Theo's childhood and to what extent his experiences in the 1930s and during the Second World War had influenced his later enthusiasm for human rights.[2] But Grünfeld did not receive the answer he expected. When he asked whether his childhood experience during the interbellum period had influenced Theo's interest in economic, social and cultural rights, Theo replied that he had no conscious memory of the 1930s and that he knew little about these years. Instead, he thought that his interest was rather a consequence of his witnessing the poverty in developing countries. However, one of his earliest memories was 10 May 1940 when the German invasion occurred:

> I remember the German presence on the streets, the searching of houses and suchlike. I think that the foreign occupation and its events, the lack of legal certainty, people being

---

[1] T van Boven, at www.rightlivelihoodaward.org/laureates/theo-van-boven/.
[2] F Grünfeld, 'Interview with Theo van Boven' in F Coomans et al (eds), *Rendering Justice to the Vulnerable – Liber Amicorum in Honour of Theo van Boven* (The Hague, Kluwer, 2000) 1.

arrested and taken away, the unsparing way in which reprisals were taken, the deportation of Jews, etc. were serious breaches of human rights. I do not know exactly how all of this has influenced me, but I am sure it has.

He was evacuated from the city of Voorburg (now a suburb of The Hague) to the river area of *Alblasserwaard* and *Vijfherenlanden* (near the city of Dort), where he experienced the Hunger Winter, living on a farm owned by relatives where most people were strict Calvinists. Theo van Boven's parents had remained faithful Protestants, born as members of the *Gereformeerde Bond*, a Calvinist organisation within the Netherlands Reformed Church. Religion played an important role in their lives.

When he was asked whether he was a pacifist and to what extent his thoughts were influenced by religion, van Boven replied:

> I had never been a pacifist on principle. I welcomed the decision to mobilize the armed forces for peace operations. At the time I was very much involved in the anti-nuclear movement. I also participated in the peace tribunal in the *St Laurens* church in Rotterdam against the deployment of cruise missiles. Where are my roots? Perhaps in religion, because arms are generally aimed at the destruction of life, which I find repugnant. I have a deep respect for all life, including animal life. For example, slaughtering animals was very common on the farm, but I could not bear it and I could not eat them. I have a strong aversion to the death penalty, the killing of people and of other living beings. I think my viewpoint is intuitive rather than religious.[3]

Theo van Boven had been interested in the United Nations from early on in his life. In his student years at Leiden University, he was Chairman of the Dutch UN Student Association. They campaigned for the individual right of petition to the European Court of Human Rights because for a long time the Netherlands had been state party to the European Convention of Human Rights without recognising that right. This was the time when the International Convention on the Elimination of All Forms of Racial Discrimination (CERD) and the two International Covenants were drafted within the UN, and the right to individual petition was heavily debated. Socialist countries were strongly against the right of individuals to bring a human rights complaint against their own countries before an international monitoring body. Van Boven's position on this issue is very clear:

> Some say that patterns and systems are what matter, and that individual cases are a time-consuming luxury. I disagree. The individual right to petition is an example. The problems which are brought forward as a result of this right will be more concrete. And furthermore, the interpretation of the norms in question will be better defined. In 1965 the Netherlands' delegation made a concerted effort to achieve this purpose. We were supported by the Africans, who appreciated the same right in the framework of the trusteeship system and the self-governing system. ... A year later, this precedent opened the door to the Optional Protocol to the International Covenant on Civil and Political Rights. I managed to push it through, despite the scepticism of the Netherlands Ministry of Foreign Affairs.[4]

This was in 1966, one year before van Boven received his doctorate from Leiden University and started his academic career as lecturer in human rights at Amsterdam

---

[3] ibid, 2.
[4] ibid, 4.

University. Between 1992 and 1999, he served as member of the UN Committee on the Elimination of Racial Discrimination and in this function dealt, inter alia, with individual complaints. Unfortunately, at the time only a few states had accepted the individual complaints procedure under CERD, and the Committee received few petitions. However, the UN Human Rights Committee, which monitors states' compliance with the International Covenant on Civil and Political Rights, has developed the individual complaints procedure into a fairly powerful tool and today all core UN human rights treaties allow for individual complaints. When Martin Scheinin and I started to campaign for the establishment of a World Court of Human Rights during the first decade of the twenty-first century, van Boven strongly supported our campaign, unlike other esteemed colleagues, above all Philip Alston, who called this a 'truly bad idea'.[5] I also remember another dispute we had with Alston. The three of us were members of a group of international experts invited by the Government of Taiwan in 2013 to monitor Taiwan's compliance with its 'obligations' deriving from the two UN Covenants, which Taiwan had voluntarily accepted despite not being allowed to become a state party. While Theo and I were in favour of strongly criticising the Government of Taiwan for its continued practice of sentencing persons to death and executing them, Alston maintained the position that the death penalty was still in accordance with international human rights law and that we had no right to criticise the Government of Taiwan as violating the Covenant.

But let's go back to the early years. Between 1970 and 1975, van Boven represented the Netherlands in the UN Commission on Human Rights. Although the Commission, as the highest body of the UN dealing with human rights and predecessor of the Human Rights Council, was composed of states, it was at that time not unusual that academics, rather than diplomats, were appointed to represent their states. The Austrian law professor, Felix Ermacora, a colleague of van Boven, served for many years as head of the Austrian delegation to the Commission and even as its President in 1974. This was the time when the Commission has just given up its 'No Power to take Action Doctrine'. It had also started to deal with individual complaints in the confidential '1503 Procedure' and to address gross and systematic human rights violations in the public '1235 Procedure', both procedures named after respective resolutions of the Economic and Social Council (ECOSOC), the parent body of the Commission. The first country-specific 'Special Procedure', the UN Ad Hoc Working Group of Experts on Human Rights in Southern Africa, had been established in 1967, but now the focus was more on the gross and systematic human rights violations in the emerging military dictatorships in Latin America. In September 1973, General Augusto Pinochet assumed power in a bloody military coup against the democratically elected government of Salvador Allende. Many thousands of leftist supporters of Allende were arrested, severely tortured, summarily executed or subjected to enforced disappearance. At that point, the UN Commission on Human Rights had only addressed gross and systematic human rights violations in the context of decolonisation and apartheid (in Southern Africa) and in the context of armed conflicts (in Israel). To take up the situation in Chile was still widely regarded as an interference with national

---

[5] P Alston, 'A Truly Bad Idea: A World Court for Human Rights', *Open Democracy* (13 June 2014).

sovereignty, in violation of the 'domestic jurisdiction clause' in Article 2(7) of the UN Charter. Together with Ermacora, van Boven was actively engaged and successful in putting the situation of Chile on the agenda of the Commission, and in 1975 in establishing a Working Group of Independent Experts entrusted with the investigation of gross and systematic human rights violations in Chile. This was considered as a breakthrough in the protection of human rights by the UN.

His active role in the Commission earned van Boven, who was at that time still a lecturer in human rights at the University of Amsterdam, wide recognition as a fearless and outspoken human rights defender. In 1977, he was appointed by UN Secretary General Kurt Waldheim as Director of the Division of Human Rights of the UN in Geneva. This was a top-level position in the UN hierarchy, comparable to the current UN High Commissioner for Human Rights, as the former Division and later Centre for Human Rights was subsequently transformed in 1994, after a respective decision during the 1993 Vienna World Conference on Human Rights, into the Office of the High Commissioner for Human Rights (OHCHR). I still remember vividly meeting van Boven for the first time in 1980 in his office in the Palais des Nations in Geneva. He was well-known in the then human rights community as an 'activist' Director of the Division who was fighting for a greater role of human rights in the overall architecture of the UN, for a more adequate budget and for a stronger involvement of non-governmental organisations (NGOs) in UN human rights work.

He was particularly engaged with the widespread practice of enforced disappearances and similar gross violations of human rights during the military dictatorship of Argentina. He was among those who advocated for the establishment, by the UN Commission on Human Rights, of a special working group of experts to investigate some 30,000 cases of enforced disappearances in Argentina. For various reasons, including the support of the Soviet Union for the Argentinian military junta, this attempt failed in the Commission. However, thanks to van Boven's diplomatic negotiation skills, the Commission agreed, as a compromise, to establish such a working group, but with a universal mandate rather than one restricted to Argentina. This compromise was the beginning of the so-called 'thematic special procedures' of the Commission, first only in relation to gross violations of human rights (Working Group on Enforced or Involuntary Disappearances 1980, Special Rapporteur on Extrajudicial, Summary or Arbitrary Executions 1982, Special Rapporteur on Torture and other Cruel, Inhuman or Degrading Treatment or Punishment 1985), and later established in relation to most human rights, including economic, social and cultural rights. When I served on the Working Group on Enforced Disappearances between 1993 and 2001, Argentina was still high on our agenda, and we regularly met with associations of families of the many thousands of persons, who had disappeared during the time of the military junta.

Theo van Boven's strong fight against the Argentinian military junta led to the abrupt end of his career as the most prominent UN civil servant in the field of human rights. In 1982, the Peruvian career diplomat Javier Pérez de Cuellar was appointed UN Secretary General. He did not support the activist style of the Director of the Human Rights Division, and van Boven was soon replaced by the Austrian career diplomat Kurt Herndl. However, the Argentinian military junta was replaced in December 1983 by a democratically elected government under the lead of President Raúl Alfonsín, who courageously took up the fight against impunity. When the Argentinian generals were first tried and sentenced before Argentinian criminal courts in 1985, van Boven testified against them and admitted that he

> ... derived a certain amount of satisfaction from it. Argentinian diplomats have thwarted me countless times with false arguments. They tried everything to frustrate me and they more or less succeeded in the UN. It was very important to me to do something in return.[6]

Soon afterwards he experienced, however, the early release of the generals, on the basis of a highly disputed amnesty law, as a kind of personal defeat:

> What offended me most was that when former President Videla was released, the first thing he did to justify his actions was to take Communion in a Catholic church. He showed no remorse. A person can only take Communion when he has come to terms with himself and with the community. I found his deed highly objectionable.[7]

For civil society, far beyond Latin America, van Boven's strong stand against the Argentinian generals was the foundation of his reputation as a true human rights hero. In honour of his achievements in this high UN position, in 1982 Hans Thoolen edited the book *People Matter*, which stands until today as a strong symbol of van Boven's commitment to the people who suffer from gross and systematic human rights violations.[8] Thoolen had established the Netherlands Institute of Human Rights (SIM) in 1982 as one of the first human rights research and documentation centres worldwide. I had the honour of having been appointed in 1987 as Thoolen's successor at the University of Utrecht. At that time, van Boven was Professor of International Law at Maastricht University. We jointly carried out many academic and activist human rights activities at this inspiring time towards the end of the Cold War. In 1988, we organised a big conference in Utrecht on the occasion of the 40th anniversary of the Universal Declaration of Human Rights. One of the persons who worked with me at SIM was Cecilia Medina Quiroga, a refugee from Chile who later became the first female President of the Inter-American Court of Human Rights. I write this short contribution about van Boven in July 2018 in San José, where the current President of the Court, Eduardo Ferrer, organised an impressive conference on the occasion of the 40th anniversary of the entry into force of the American Convention on Human Rights. He invited eight former Presidents of the Court, including Cecilia Medina Quiroga, to panel discussions on their experience with the Inter-American human rights system. Theo van Boven supervised Cecilia's well-known doctoral thesis on *The Battle for Human Rights in Latin America*, and we both served on her defence commission in the University of Utrecht.[9] The highly traditional and academic atmosphere of defending a PhD thesis with capes and gowns in the Netherlands was very frightening indeed for Cecilia. But Theo was a highly humane examiner, and Cecilia passed with distinction.

---

[6] Grünfeld (n 2) 8.

[7] ibid, 3.

[8] H Thoolen (ed), *People Matter – Views on International Human Rights Policy* (Amsterdam, Meulenhoff, 1982).

[9] C Medina Quiroga, *The Battle for Human Rights: Gross, Systematic Violations and the Inter-American System* (Dordrecht, Martinus Nijhoff Publishers, 1988).

The fact that Theo van Boven lost his job as Director of Human Rights at the UN does not mean that he lost his interest in the UN. On the contrary, he continued to carry out many prestigious functions as independent human rights expert for the UN. By 1975 and 1976 he had served on the Sub-Commission on the Prevention of Discrimination and Protection of Minorities, and he was appointed again in 1990 for a four-year term. The Sub-Commission of the UN Human Rights Commission was composed of 26 independent experts and served as an advisory body to the Commission. In that time, the Sub-Commission interpreted its mandate in a fairly broad manner and to some extent duplicated the country-specific work of the Commission by adopting strongly worded country-specific resolutions in which the experts condemned gross and systematic human rights violations. These votes were taken by secret ballot, and in 1991 the Peoples' Republic of China was for the first time condemned by the Sub-Commission for its human rights violations in Tibet. A similar resolution against China in the Commission proved impossible, as Chinese diplomats exercised heavy pressure on other states not to vote in favour of such a resolution. The historic Tibet resolution contributed to increased criticism by its parent body for being too politicised. During the late 1990s, the Sub-Commission was gradually deprived of its powers, and the current Advisory Committee of the Human Rights Council has a much less powerful mandate.

The most lasting impact of van Boven's membership in the Sub-Commission is provided by the UN 'Basic Principles and Guidelines on the Right to a Remedy and Reparation for Victims of Gross Violations of International Human Rights Law and Serious Violations of International Humanitarian Law', adopted by the UN General Assembly in 2005. He was the main author of these Guidelines, which provide victims of severe human rights violations not only with the right to an effective (usually judicial) procedural remedy, but also with just reparation for the harm suffered. Reparation measures include restitution, rehabilitation, satisfaction, compensation and measures of non-repetition. For many victims of gross and systematic human rights violations, such as genocide, ethnic cleansing, arbitrary executions, torture and enforced disappearances, satisfaction is only obtained when the perpetrators are brought to justice. This shows that the fight against impunity and the right of victims to reparation are closely interconnected. Both themes run like a thread through the professional life of Theo van Boven as a human rights defender. It started with his fight against impunity in Latin America during the 1970s, continued with his testimonials against the Argentinian generals before Argentinian criminal courts, his function as the first Registrar of the International Criminal Tribunal for the former Yugoslavia in 1994, his role as head of the Netherlands delegation to the UN Diplomatic Conference for the Establishment of an International Criminal Court in 1998 in Rome, and culminated with the adoption of the 'van Boven/Bassiouni Principles and Guidelines' by the General Assembly in 2005, after many years of heated discussions in the Sub-Commission and later in the Commission. By 2000, some of van Boven's closest collaborators at Maastricht University had found the most proper title for a Liber Amicorum in Honour of his 65th birthday: *Rendering Justice to the Vulnerable*. For van Boven, justice can mean criminal justice aimed at the perpetrators, but it can also mean medical and psychological rehabilitation for torture victims, clarifying the fate of the disappeared by means of exhumations, restitution of lands to indigenous peoples, financial compensation for the poor or simply establishing the truth.

Establishing truth, justice and reparation also played an important role in Theo van Boven's mandate as UN Special Rapporteur on Torture between 2001 and 2004. His two predecessors in this function were his countryman Peter Kooijmans, and Sir Nigel Rodley, who recently passed away. In October 2003, Theo van Boven carried out a fact finding mission to Spain. He carefully analysed the situation in the Basque region and concluded that 'torture or ill-treatment is not systematic in Spain, but that the system as it is practised allows torture or ill-treatment to occur, particularly with regards to persons detained incommunicado in connection with terrorist-related activities'.[10] His report was critical but fair. It stated that torture was practiced 'more than sporadically' by state security and police forces, and that safeguards and the investigation of torture allegations were 'ineffective'. Nevertheless, this report was strongly criticised by the then Spanish Government, which even did not shy away from attacking van Boven's professionalism and his reputation as one of the leading human rights lawyers of our time. In a report dated 4 March 2004, the Spanish Government categorically denied the findings of the report, which was 'full of mistakes', alleged the lack of 'an objective and well-founded analysis' and even asserted the Special Rapporteur's 'total lack of knowledge of both the reality of Spain and the bases and functioning of our legal system'.[11] This was too much for Theo. In 2003, he had told me that he wished to resign and had asked me whether I would like to become his successor. At that time I declined, as I wished to encourage him to continue with this important mandate. But when he finally resigned in 2004, I was ready to take up this challenge and to continue his legacy.

In carrying out this difficult mandate between 2004 and 2010, I often benefited from the wisdom of my predecessor. In years of negotiations with the Chinese Government, Nigel and Theo had laid the ground for the fact that the Government, shortly after my appointment, issued an invitation and enabled me to conduct a fact-finding mission to China, including the autonomous regions of Tibet and Xinjiang, in November 2005. Similarly, together with four other special procedures, Theo had started an investigation into the conditions of detention and torture practices by the US in the notorious military detention facilities at Guantánamo Bay. Our joint Guantánamo report of February 2006 was repudiated by the US Government in similarly strong terms as Theo's report by Spain. No other government, including states where I had found systematic practices of torture, ever criticised me as strongly as the Bush Administration. It is an interesting experience that democratic states seem to react even more rigorously against findings of torture than the most brutal dictatorships. With respect to Uzbekistan, where Theo had found during his fact finding mission in 2002 a systematic practice of torture, I tried several times to convince the Uzbek Government to invite me for a follow-up mission, but without success. When the then Uzbek Minister of Interior, Zokirjon Almatov, who bore primary

---

[10] UN Special Rapporteur on Torture on his visit to Spain from 5 to 10 October 2003, UN Doc E/CN.4/2004/56/Add.2, Summary.

[11] Notes verbales of the Spanish Government, contained in UN Doc E/CN.4/2004/G/19 of 4 March 2004.

responsibility for torture and for the Andijan massacre in May 2005, travelled to Germany in November 2005 to receive medical treatment, I cooperated with my predecessor and Human Rights Watch in calling on the German Government to arrest Almatov and initiate criminal proceedings against him in accordance with its obligation, under the UN Convention against Torture, to exercise universal jurisdiction. Although we had both offered to testify before the German courts, the German authorities opted not to open an investigation, thereby allowing Almatov to evade justice.[12]

The Almatov case was the first case in which Theo and I started a cooperation with Wolfgang Kaleck and the European Centre for Constitutional and Human Rights (ECCHR) in Berlin, which Wolfgang founded in 2007 together with the late Michael Ratner. We are both members of its Advisory Council, which regularly meets in Berlin. Like its role model, the US-based Centre for Constitutional Rights, the ECCHR aims at rendering justice to the vulnerable by means of strategic litigation. It defends victims of human rights violations before the European Court of Human Rights, initiates civil litigation against transnational corporations, provides evidence to the International Criminal Court and encourages national prosecutors in various European states to start criminal litigation before domestic courts against prominent perpetrators of gross human rights violations, such as Donald Rumsfeld or high Syrian officials responsible for crimes against humanity and war crimes.

We are living in times of political turmoil, in which the very idea of human rights is being attacked more than at any other time since the end of the Second World War. This is the time when human rights defenders have to stand up, raise their voices, fight for human rights and ensure that the current backlash will eventually turn into a new and even more powerful movement for a just, peaceful and prosperous world order based upon the universal values of human rights, democracy and the rule of law. For more than half a century, Theo van Boven has inspired many thousands of young people in all world regions to stand up for human rights. He is strong in his principles, leading by example, persuasive by empathy and modest in his personality. For him, people matter. That is why he has the moral authority of passing the torch to ever new generations of human rights defenders.

[12] See M Nowak and E McArthur, *The United Nations Convention against Torture – A Commentary* (Oxford, Oxford University Press, 2008) 295 ff.

Index